Hong Kong Constitutionalism

Hong Kong is widely regarded as an exemplar of authoritarian jurisdictions with a positive history of adhering to Rule of Law-shaped governance systems. British Hong Kong provides a remarkable story of the effective development and consolidation of such a system, which has continued to apply since 1997, when it became the Hong Kong Special Administrative Region (HKSAR) within the People's Republic of China (PRC).

This book adopts a fresh approach in examining the evolution of Hong Kong's political-legal experience. It establishes that these prominent governance achievements were built on particular British constitutional foundations forged over many centuries. The work shows how the analysis of the British theorist Albert Dicey and, in particular, "Diceyan Constitutionalism" was fundamental, within the pivotal context of "Chinese Familism", in shaping the development of governance institutions and operational procedures within the new British Colony.

It discusses how Hong Kong's system of Authoritarian Legality has come to pass. Exploring the essence of that system, the study probes how thoroughly it has been stress-tested, not least in 2019, and how well it may be placed to cope with tests yet to come. It also analyzes Hong Kong–Beijing relations and the long-term prospects for the HKSAR within the PRC based on a balanced contemporary assessment of China's exceptional One Party State.

Richard Cullen is a Visiting Professor in the Faculty of Law, University of Hong Kong. He first began working in Hong Kong in 1991. His research interests are in Public Law, Taxation Law, Comparative Law, Fundamentals of the Common Law, and Media Law. He has published extensively on these and related areas.

The Rule of Law in China and Comparative Perspectives

Series Editors

Yuwen Li, Erasmus University Rotterdam, The Netherlands, and
Fu Hualing, University of Hong Kong, Hong Kong

There is no doctrine more effective than the rule of law in portraying the complex transformation of Chinese society from the rule of men towards the rule of law – a process inaugurated in post–Mao China which is continuing to advance legal reforms to the present day. In other parts of the world, striving for the rule of law is also evident: countries in transition face a similar mission, while the developed democratic countries are forced to tackle new challenges in retaining the high benchmark of the rule of law that has been established.

Research on the legal system in China and in comparison with other countries in the framework of the rule of law covers broad topics of public and private law, substantive law and procedural law, citizens' rights, and law enforcement by courts. Based on this broad understanding of the rule of law, the series presents international scholarly work on modern Chinese law including: comparative perspectives, interdisciplinary, and empirical studies.

Other titles in this series

Conservation and Recreation in Protected Areas
Yun Ma

Administrative Litigation Systems in Greater China and Europe
Edited by Yuwen Li

The Judicial System and Reform in Post–Mao China
Yuwen Li

The Power of the Supreme People's Court
Reconceptualizing Judicial Power in Contemporary China
Ding Qi

China, the EU and International Investment Law
Reforming Investor-State Dispute Settlement
Edited by Yuwen Li, Tong Qi, and Cheng Bian

Hong Kong Constitutionalism
The British Legacy and the Chinese Future
Richard Cullen

Hong Kong Constitutionalism

The British Legacy and the Chinese Future

Richard Cullen

Routledge
Taylor & Francis Group
LONDON AND NEW YORK

First published 2020 by Routledge

2 Park Square, Milton Park, Abingdon, Oxon OX14 4RN
605 Third Avenue, New York, NY 10017

Routledge is an imprint of the Taylor & Francis Group, an informa business

First issued in paperback 2021

Publisher's Note

The publisher has gone to great lengths to ensure the quality of this reprint but points out that some imperfections in the original copies may be apparent.

British Library Cataloguing-in-Publication Data
A catalogue record for this book is available from the British Library

Library of Congress Cataloging-in-Publication Data
Names: Cullen, Richard, author.
Title: Hong Kong constitutionalism: the British legacy and the Chinese future/Richard Cullen.
Description: Abingdon, Oxon; New York, NY: Routledge, 2020. |
Series: The rule of law in China and comparative perspectives |
Includes bibliographical references and index.
Identifiers: LCCN 2019044884 (print) | LCCN 2019044885 (ebook) |
ISBN 9781138320130 (hardback) | ISBN 9780429453502 (ebook)
Subjects: LCSH: Constitutional law–China–Hong Kong. | Constitutional history–China–Hong Kong | Hong Kong (China)–Politics and government–1997.
Classification: LCC KNQ9341 .C86 2020 (print) | LCC KNQ9341 (ebook) | DDC 342.5125–dc23
LC record available at https://lccn.loc.gov/2019044884
LC ebook record available at https://lccn.loc.gov/2019044885

ISBN: 978-1-138-32013-0 (hbk)
ISBN: 978-1-03-217440-2 (pbk)
DOI: 10.4324/9780429453502

Typeset in Galliard
by Deanta Global Publishing Services, Chennai, India

Dedicated to my wife and to my parents

Contents

Preface

Hong Kong today faces renewed political stress testing at an elevated level. In June, 2019, I was physically restrained by a self-appointed "student security guard" at Hong Kong University who demanded to see my identification (something which in Hong Kong is usually the prerogative of a member of the Police Force). I first arrived to work in Hong Kong in late 1991. This was the first time, since 1991, that I had ever encountered such coercion.

The core of this book relies on a comparative interpretation of applied Public Law – grounded within a review of germane political, economic, and social influences. The key arguments are founded on a detailed historical account of the development of Hong Kong's political-legal experience and an overview of relevant aspects of China's history.

The support of my remarkable wife has been crucial as I have written this book. I have also been much assisted in the writing of this book by wide-ranging discussions with many generous colleagues. A number of them have read different portions of this work in draft form. To all who have assisted, my sincere thanks. I owe special thanks to Professor Fu Hualing, and Professor Harry Glasbeek. Many others I am grateful to, include Colin Bray, Oriol Caudevilla Parellada, Henry Chan, Andrew Coleman, Grenville Cross, Michael Edesess, Robin Edwards, Danny Gittings, Peter Gordon, Brian Graville, Flora Leung, Albert Lin, Colin Milton, Tor Krever, P.Y. Lo, Sonny Lo, Michael Pendleton, Qiu Dongmei, Tim Summers, Richard Simmons, Kevin Tso, Jingyi Wang, Antonietta Wong, and Xu Yan. I am fortunate to have been able to spend more than a decade at the Faculty of Law at the University of Hong Kong. Many colleagues there have been especially helpful over this period including Cora Chan, Johannes Chan, Albert Chen, Tony Carty, Wilson Chow, Evan Gibson, Chin Leng Lim, Michael Tilbury, and Simon Young. The discussion of the work of John Rawls in this book draws notably on work by Professor David Campbell (arising from our joint work) and is included with his permission. David Campbell is a Professor at the Lancaster University Law School, UK. Sincere thanks are expressed for this key contribution and for significant other input during the writing of this book and, indeed, encouragement to write this book. Another regular co-author is Christine Loh, who is now associated with both the Hong Kong University of Science and Technology and UCLA's Anderson School of Management. Previously she was a member of Hong Kong's Legislative Council (1992–1997 and 1998–2000) and an undersecretary in the Hong Kong Government (2012–2017). In 2000, she co-founded *Civic Exchange*, which swiftly grew to be a key think-tank in Hong Kong. Christine Loh has been exceptionally generous with her support generally and with respect to this project. Recent joint work includes *No Third Person* (Abbreviated Press, Hong Kong, 2018) and *Hong Kong in China*, available at https://ippreview.com/index.php/Blog/single/id/869.html. I also wish to thank my student research assistant, Natalie Ng, who prepared a distinctly helpful Timeline of the 2019 Protests and Riots. Finally, I am most grateful for the excellent assistance and support I have received from the publishers, from start to finish, during the process of publishing this book. Responsibility for the final content of this book lies solely with the author.

All online references were available at the time of writing. Hard copies of these reference materials have been retained by the author. This book discusses developments up to August 31, 2019.

Glossary of abbreviations

AFC	Asian Financial Crisis
AL	Authoritarian Legality
ALP	Australian Labor Party
BHK	British Hong Kong
BORO	Bill of Rights Ordinance
CA	Court of Appeal (HKSAR)
CFA	Court of Final Appeal (HKSAR)
CPC	Communist Party of China
DP	Democratic Party (HKSAR)
DPP	Democratic People's Party (Taiwan)
ECI	Electoral Commission of India
EIC	East India Company
ERO	Emergency Regulations Ordinance
EU	European Union
ExCo	Executive Council of the HKSAR
FC	Functional Constituency
FOO	Fugitive Offenders Ordinance
GBA	Greater Bay Area
GDP	Gross Domestic Product
GFC	Global Financial Crisis
HCA	High Court of Australia
HKBA	Hong Kong Bar Association
HKSAR	Hong Kong Special Administrative Region
HKU	Hong Kong University
HKU POP	Hong Kong University Public Opinion Programme
HOS	Home Ownership Scheme
ICAC	Independent Commission Against Corruption
ICCPR	International Covenant on Civil and Political Rights
IPCC	Independent Police Complaints Council
IRO	Inland Revenue Ordinance
JCPC	Judicial Committee of the Privy Council
KMT	Kuomintang
LAD	Legal Aid Department

LegCo	Legislative Council of the HKSAR
MTR	Mass Transit Railway
NATO	North Atlantic Treaty Organization
NPC	National People's Congress
NPCSC	National People's Congress Standing Committee (see SCNPC)
NPJ	Non-Permanent Judge (of the CFA)
OCTS	One Country – Two Systems
OECD	Organization for Economic Co-operation and Development
OPS	One-Party State
PD	Pan-Democrat
POORD	Public Order Ordinance
PRC	People's Republic of China
PRH	Public Rental Housing
RPD	Radical Pan-Democrat
RR	Revenue Regime
SARS	Severe Acute Respiratory Syndrome
SCC	Supreme Court of Canada
SCNPC	Standing Committee of the National People's Congress
SO	Societies Ordinance
SOO	Summary Offences Ordinance
TATP	Triacetone Triperoxide
UK	United Kingdom
UKSC	United Kingdom Supreme Court
UN	United Nations
US	United States
USSC	United States Supreme Court
USSR	Union of Soviet Socialist Republics
WJP	World Justice Project
WTO	World Trade Organization

1 Introduction*

For 150 years, the British ran Hong Kong with no directly elected representation within the Legislative Council (LegCo). The "all-powerful" Governor was simply appointed (and replaced, as needs be) by London from 1842 to 1997. After World War II, however, the British visibly improved on what was already a successful Authoritarian Legality (AL) governance structure, not least through increased reliance on the quality and independence of the British Hong Kong (BHK) judiciary. The basic precepts of this AL system have continued to apply since July 1, 1997, when BHK became the Hong Kong Special Administrative Region (HKSAR) within the People's Republic of China (PRC).

"Authoritarian" is a key term used in this book. Different types of authoritarianism are regularly distinguished. It is, thus, common to speak of "soft authoritarianism" and "hard authoritarianism", autocracies, and oligarchies, for example.[1] Authoritarian Legality, as it is employed in this book, refers to authoritarian government which is operationally committed to a measurable, continuing degree of

* Parts of this work repeat arguments and text from previous work by Richard Cullen

1 The literature on the typology of authoritarianism is extensive. See, for example, Howard, Marc and Roessler, Philip G., "Liberalizing Electoral Outcomes in Competitive Authoritarian Regimes" (2006) 50 *American Journal of Political Science*, 365; Levitsky, Steven and Way, Lucan A., "The Rise of Competitive Authoritarianism" (2002), 13 *Journal of Democracy*, 51; Diamond, Larry Jay, "Thinking about Hybrid Regimes" (2002) 13 *Journal of Democracy*, 21; Art, David, "Review Article – What Do We Know about Authoritarianism after Ten Years?" (2012) 45 *Journal of Comparative Politics*, 351 (reviewing: Gandhi, Jennifer, *Political Institutions under Dictatorship* (Cambridge University Press, New York, 2008); Levitsky, Steven and Way, Lucan, *Competitive Authoritarianism: Hybrid Regimes after the Cold War* (Cambridge University Press, New York, 2010); Magaloni, Beatriz, *Voting for Autocracy: Hegemonic Party Survival and Its Demise in Mexico* (Cambridge University Press, New York, 2006); Policzer, Pablo, *The Rise and Fall of Repression in Chile* (University of Notre Dame Press, Notre Dame, 2009); Riley, Dylan, *The Civic Foundations of Fascism in Europe: Italy, Spain, and Romania,1870–1945* (Johns Hopkins University Press, Baltimore, 2010); Slater, Dan, *Ordering Power: Contentious Politics and Authoritarian Leviathans in Southeast Asia* (Cambridge University Press, New York, 2010). See also *Bibliography for Authoritarianism – The University of Glasgow*, available at: http://readinglists.glasgow.ac.uk/lists/B1D31BAC-A8DC-F911-8C66-A2F637734EC9/bibliography.html, and the *Authoritarianism Bibliography – Philpapers*, available at: https://philpapers.org/browse/authoritarianism (accessed October 1, 2019).

constitutionalism.[2] The meaning of these terms is detailed more thoroughly in the Appendix.

Over many decades – before and since 1997 – predictions that the political-legal sky was about to fall in Hong Kong have been numerous. This has not happened, however, apart from the period of brutal Japanese occupation from 1941 to 1945, which can rightly be regarded as an exception which demonstrates the general rule. Hong Kong, with its long, embedded experience of Rule of Law–based governance (within a non-democratic political scheme), is, consequently, regarded as an exemplar of AL.[3] Acute, fresh tests which have been applied to this system in 2019 are discussed in the closing chapters.

There is scope for continual debate over the detail of what the Rule of Law means, however. Randall Peerenboom deals with this hazard well when he argues that:

> Debates about the meaning of the Rule of Law should not blind us ... to a broad consensus as to its core meaning and essential elements. At its most basic, Rule of Law refers to a system in which law imposes meaningful limits on the state and individual members of the ruling elite, as captured in a notion of a government of laws, supremacy of law and equality of all before the law.[4]

2 The principle that the authority of government is derived from and is limited by a body of fundamental law.

3 According to one resolute definition of the Rule of Law, *there is no Rule of Law without democracy.* If this be the case, there was no Rule of Law in Hong Kong for the entire period of British rule (1842–1997). See Dupre, Jean-Fancois, "Legality and Equality Are Not Enough – There Is No Rule of Law in Hong Kong without Democracy", *Hong Kong Free Press,* August 8, 2019, available at: https://www.hongkongfp.com/2019/08/08/legality-equality-not-enough-no-rule-law-hong-kong-without-democracy/ (accessed October 1, 2019).

4 Peerenboom, Randall, "A Government of Laws, Democracy, Rule of Law and Administrative Law Reform in the PRC" (2003) 12 *Journal of Contemporary China*, 45. See also Peerenboom, Randall, *China's Long March toward Rule of Law* (Cambridge University Press, Cambridge, 2002). Scholarly perspectives on the Rule of Law are numerous and varied with the widely agreed seminal contribution being found in Dicey, A. V, *Introduction to the Study of the Law of the Constitution* (MacMillan, London, 1885). See also, for example, Raz, Joseph, "The Rule of Law and Its Virtue" (1997) 93 *Law Quarterly Review*, 195; Carothers, Thomas, "The Rule of Law Revival" (1998) 77 *Foreign Affairs*, 95; Fuller, Lon L., *The Morality of Law* (Yale University Press, New Haven, 1969); Allan, T. R. S., *Constitutional Justice: A Liberal Theory of the Rule of Law* (Oxford University Press, Oxford, 2003); Hart, H.L.A., *The Concept of Law* (2nd ed.) (Oxford University Press, New York, 1994); Finnis, John, *Natural Law and Natural Rights* (Oxford University Press, Oxford, 2001); Rawls, John, *A Theory of Justice* (Oxford University Press, Oxford, 1999); Dworkin, Ronald, *Law's Empire* (Hart, Oxford, 1998); Radin, Margaret Jane, "Reconsidering the Rule of Law" (1989) 69 Boston University Law Review, 781; Fletcher, George P., *Basic Concepts of Legal Thought* (Oxford University Press, Oxford, 1996); de Soto, Hernando, *The Other Path: The Invisible Revolution in the Third World* (Harper & Row, New York, 1989); de Soto, Hernando, *The Mystery of Capital: Why Capitalism Triumphs in the West and Fails Everywhere Else* (Basic Books, New York, 2000); Thompson, E.P., *Whigs and Hunters: The Origin of the Black Act* (Pantheon Books,

The World Justice Project (WJP), based in Washington, D.C., and Seattle in the US, has been compiling a Rule of Law Index for over ten years. The WJP defines the Rule of Law in similar terms to those set out above with one added rider, that:

> Justice is delivered by competent, ethical, and independent representatives and neutrals who are of sufficient number, have adequate resources, and reflect the makeup of the communities they serve.[5]

Peerenboom draws a distinction between "thin" and "thick" versions of the Rule of Law. The definition above is the *thin version*. The *thick version* includes additional elements, including certain market-based economic systems, institutions of democratic governance, and conceptions of human rights.[6]

As we look closely at the BHK political-legal experience, it becomes clear that the prominent governance achievements were built, within an AL context, on particular British constitutional foundations forged over many centuries. Due to the largely unwritten nature of the evolved (far more than disruptive revolutionary) British Constitution, the way was left open for a scholar possessed of remarkable understanding, Professor Albert Venn Dicey, to analyze and describe – indeed, reveal – the essence of this historically tempered set of resilient governance principles.

Quite recently, in the midst of the intense *Brexit* debates at Westminster, a leading UK historian argued that, once again, it was being shown that "the

New York, 1975); Fallon, Richard H., "'The Rule of Law' as a Concept in Constitutional Discourse" (1997) 97, *Columbia Law Review*, 1; Tsang, Steve (ed.) *Judicial Independence and the Rule of Law in Hong Kong* (Palgrave, Basingstoke, 2001); Kleinfeld-Belton, Rachel, "Competing Definitions of the Rule of Law", *Carnegie Papers,* available at: http://www.carnegieendowment.org/files/CP55.Belton.FINAL.pdf (accessed October 1, 2019); and Li, Bo, "What Is Rule of Law?", available at: http://www.oycf.org/Perspectives/5_043000/what_is_rule_of_law.htm (accessed October 1, 2019). See further Hampton, Mark, *Hong Kong and British Culture* (Oxford University Press, Oxford, 2015); and Shklar, Judith, "Political Theory and the Rule of Law" in (Hutchinson and Monahan (eds)) *The Rule of Law: Ideal or Ideology* (Carswell, Toronto, 1987). In this volume, Judith Shklar questions whether the Rule of Law "may well have become just another of those self-congratulatory rhetorical devices that grace the public utterances of Anglo-American politicians".

5 The World Justice Project defines the Rule of Law system as one in which the following four universal principles are upheld: (1) The government and its officials and agents are accountable under the law; (2) The laws are clear, publicized, stable and fair, and protect fundamental rights, including the security of persons and property; (3) The process by which the laws are enacted, administered, and enforced is accessible, efficient, and fair; (4) Justice is delivered by competent, ethical, and independent representatives and neutrals who are of sufficient number, have adequate resources, and reflect the makeup of the communities they serve. See *World Justice Project,* available at: https://worldjusticeproject.org/ (accessed October 1, 2019).

6 See Peerenboom, *China's Long March toward Rule of Law*; and "Thin Rule of Law versus Thick Rule of Law", *Asia Law*, November 26, 2015 (where the difference is concisely discussed), available at: https://asialaw.wordpress.com/2015/11/26/thin-rule-of-law-versus-thick-rule-of-law/ (accessed October 1, 2019)).

British Constitution is more robust, flexible and capable of dealing with intensely difficult issues than excited media commentators suggest".[7]

The analysis here relies significantly on showing how "Diceyan Constitutionalism" was fundamental in shaping the development of governance institutions and operational procedures – within the pivotal socio-economic context of "Chinese Familialism" – in the new British Colony.[8] It is here that central answers lie to the question posed above: what does the Rule of Law mean in Hong Kong?

The influence of Dicey's seminal constitutional writing has, thus far, been rather narrowly explored within a Hong Kong context by other writers, with a primary focus on the customary Rule of Law aspects of that writing. A fairly recent discussion of a notable Hong Kong film from 1997 draws on a Diceyan understanding of the Rule of Law, related to Hong Kong, within an interesting review hinging on that 1997 film.[9] This book provides, I believe, the first comprehensive exploration of the influence of Diceyan thinking, generally, on the development of Hong Kong's political-legal and economic history.

Book structure

Chapter 2 explains the fundamentals of Diceyan Constitutionalism and central aspects of Chinese Familialism, which have mutually shaped modern Hong Kong since 1842.[10] Chapter 3 briefly introduces certain theoretical bases for assessing

7 Parry, Jonathan, "Educating the Nation", *London Review of Books*, April 18, 2019, available at: https://www.lrb.co.uk/v41/n08/jonathan-parry/educating-the-nation (accessed October 1, 2019).

8 The first edition of A.V. Dicey, *An Introduction to the Study of the Law of the Constitution* was published in 1885. The text was established in the seventh edition of 1907, though a long and important new introduction was added to what proved to be the last edition by the author, the eighth edition of 1914. What has served as the standard edition is the tenth edition of 1959 by E.C.S. Wade. Wade's introduction, which is itself a work of significance in constitutional law, describes Dicey's influence at a time when it had only recently but nevertheless unarguably passed its zenith and a distanced perspective could be taken. A variorum edition of two volumes by J.W.F. Allison has recently appeared as *The Oxford Edition of Dicey: Volume 1, The Law of the Constitution* (Oxford University Press, Oxford, 2013); *Volume 2, The Comparative Study of Constitutions* (Oxford University Press, Oxford, 2013). Dicey published, by modern standards, a small number of other works on British constitutional law and politics, but outstanding amongst these is his other great book: A.V. Dicey, *Lectures on the Relation between Law and Public Opinion in England during the Nineteenth Century* (Liberty Fund, Indianapolis, 2008). First published in 1905, a second edition and also last edition also appeared in 1914. Though not very extensively revised, this edition also contained a substantial and important new introduction.

9 See Wan, Marco, "Lawyer, Lawyer, Albert Venn Dicey, Joe Ma, and the Rule of Law in Hong Kong" (2014) 18 *Law Text Culture*, 82.

10 The terminology used is either *Familialism* or *Familism*. Briefly, "Familialism is part of a traditional view of society that highlights loyalty, trust, and cooperative attitudes within the family group. Familialism is found in the bourgeois class family and reflects the cultural belief that it is the family that is the foundation of society and the source of human identification

the legitimacy – or lack thereof – of authoritarian governance systems. Chapter 4 reviews, in detail, the political-legal history of BHK. Chapter 5 examines how the successful revenue system in BHK has underwritten the success of the Rule of Law. The complex political-legal experience of the HKSAR since 1997 is reviewed in Chapter 6. Chapter 7 considers how AL has been regularly "stress-tested" over the course of Hong Kong's history and especially during its more recent history. This chapter provides, inter alia, an in-depth analysis of the 2014 *Occupy Central Movement* (also known as the *Umbrella Movement*), which resulted in hugely disruptive, mass political reform protests running for almost three months. The political rioting in Hong Kong, which unfolded over the course of one evening in February 2016, together with the extended 2019 protests and riots, are also carefully examined. Chapter 8 considers the wider context of challenging aspects of democratic development, operation, and reform worldwide over the last two decades. Chapter 9 considers the way China has changed categorically since 1978 (and especially over the last 20 years) and how Hong Kong is experiencing the transition to being a unique city permanently re-established *within* a rapidly rising China. Chapter 10 provides a systematic, concluding discussion and considers how well Hong Kong Constitutionalism may be placed to cope with tests yet to come and what the prospects are for ongoing political reform in the HKSAR.

---

and moral discipline". See *Familialism (Definitions)*, available at: http://sociologyindex.com/familialism.htm (accessed October 1, 2019). Chinese Familialism was explained particularly well, in 1981, by Professor Lau Siu-kai in his seminal article, "Chinese Familism in an Urban-Industrial Setting: The Case of Hong Kong" (1981) 43 *Journal of Marriage and the Family*, 181: "In the urban-industrial setting of Hong Kong, Chinese familism has taken the form of utilitarianistic familism. This new type of Chinese familism is characterized by: primacy of familial interests, perception of the social-political context as the arena for the pursuit of familial interests, utilitarianistic considerations in the structuring of intrafamilial relationships, the non-significance of the social status of the familial group, utilitarianistic recruitment of familial members and the resultant vagueness of the boundary of the familial group, and the dilution of authority relationships between familial members".

2 Significant pathways

Path dependence theory provides a useful framework for understanding the way in which modern Hong Kong has developed in its own particular and remarkable way since 1842. One definitional statement argues that:

> Path dependence is the idea that decisions we are faced with depend on past knowledge trajectory and decisions made, and are thus limited by the current competence base. In other words, history matters for current decision-making situations and has a strong influence on strategic planning. Competences that have been built in the past define the option range for today's moves.[1]

In Hong Kong, Diceyan Constitutionalism and Chinese Familialism have jointly and acutely shaped its development since 1842. No *fixed-essence* argument is made here – to the effect that certain particular conditions in Hong Kong have mandated certain outcomes. As Oliver Wendell Holmes noted at the beginning of his book *The Common Law*:

> The Law embodies the story of a nation's development through many centuries and it cannot be dealt with as if it contained only the axioms and corollaries of a book of mathematics.[2]

1 "Definition of Path Dependence", *Financial Times Lexicon*, available at: http://lexicon.ft.com/Term?term=path-dependence (accessed October 1, 2019). As this definition notes: "A well-known example [of Path Dependence] is the QWERTY layout for typewriters. Despite the fact that different keyboard layouts in modern computer keyboards would allow faster typing, the QWERTY layout prevails." For a critical but positive review of this theory as applied to political studies, see Greener, Ian, "The Potential of Path Dependency in Political Studies" (2005) 25 *Politics*, 62. See, further, Sourgens, Frederic G., "The Virtue of Path Dependence in Law" (2016) 56 *Santa Clara Law Review*, 303.

2 Holmes, Oliver Wendell, *The Common Law* (Macmillan, London, 1882).

I have adopted a similar perspective: my main purpose is to review relevant, broad outcomes over time and to provide a measured analysis of what has organically shaped Hong Kong's social ontology[3] and its closely related political economy.

Diceyan Constitutionalism

Edmund Burke was an influential Anglo-Irish politician and political scholar. He was born in 1729, over 100 years before Dicey's birth in 1835. Burke is particularly well remembered for his eloquent (and controversial in the UK) support for the demands of the American Colonists (and the American Revolution – dating from 1776) and his equally eloquent (and also controversial) severe criticism of the French Revolution about a decade later (1789).[4]

Dicey is on record as saying that Burke was one of the writers he "read with perpetual profit and enjoyment". He also regarded Burke as an "adventurer" – though one with principles. Ultimately he felt that Burke was "not a just man". He explained that "Not a single weak point in the position of the French Revolutionists escaped his glance … but to the good or better side of the revolutionary movement [in France] he was as blind as the stupidest of Tory squires".[5]

Dicey was dismayed by the brutal Jacobin excesses which swiftly filled the space created by the French Revolution and the rapid transition to military authoritarianism under Napoleon. He, like Burke, saw the grim dangers to public order and public good which could arise so readily from "mob rule". But he was equally clear about the good done by the French Revolution in sweeping away the manifestly vast awfulness of the Ancien Regime in France with its malevolent, enduring alignment of power and religion.[6]

These views are informing. They show Dicey's powerful joint concern about abuses of power arising from unrestrained power in the hands of either rulers

3 Although the term social ontology is not in everyday use, it has been put to work for over 100 years with possibly the first recorded usage being in 1910, by the German philosopher, Edmund Husserl. Briefly, it denotes the pith and substance of advanced social existence within a particular society. With no single (or multiple) ultimate canonical text(s) setting out the essence of the British Constitution, its central principles (more than where the norm of a written Constitution applies) need to be derived and understood from the study of its State–Citizen interactive operation, above all. It is a term which is also helpful for both describing and analyzing the manner in which Diceyan Constitutionalism put down such sturdy roots within Hong Kong's specific social ontology. A more detailed explanation of the meaning of social ontology is set out in the Appendix.

4 *Edmund Burke (1729–1997),* BBC History, available at: http://www.bbc.co.uk/history/historic_figures/burke_edmund.shtml (accessed October 1, 2019). Dicey saw in Burke a man whose political vision, in this instance, was distorted by his fixation on the destructive aspects of the French Revolution.

5 Macaig, Drew, *Edmund Burke in America: The Contested Career of the Father of Modern Conservatism* (Cornell University Press, Ithaca, 2013), 112 ff.

6 Ibid.

or the mass of people (the otherwise "ruled") within any modern jurisdiction.[7] These comments also emphasize the fundamental importance which Dicey placed on the need for balanced judgement – and through this – justice.

All of this thinking, research, and writing by Dicey took place in the midst of brutal nineteenth century poverty in the UK, by then replete with countless "dark satanic mills"[8] crammed into numerous cities hugely and grimly enlarged in terms of population by the Industrial Revolution.[9] Moreover, the darkest side of the British Empire, during its peak period, included terrible famines both far away and very nearby. Shocking examples included famine in India and right within the (then) UK, in Ireland, where, collectively, millions perished from starvation. Despite (and, to a degree, because of) this reality, the concept of the modern "free and lawful" citizen was still reinforced as a central norm of the Common Law.[10] Reflections in the UK today on horrific episodes from the British Empire

7 By the time Dicey was making these observations, Napoleon had long been defeated. This was not the case when Burke was writing on the French Revolution – Napoleon presented a growing, serious threat to the UK.

8 Blake, William, "Jerusalem", *BBC Poetry*, available at: http://www.bbc.co.uk/poetryseason/poems/jerusalem.shtml (accessed October 1, 2019).

9 The documentation of this harsh and dismal reality is extensive. A good point of reference is Thompson, E. P., *Whigs and Hunters* (Penguin, Harmondsworth, 1977) (and his other work). See also *BBC History: Victorian Britain*, available at: http://www.bbc.co.uk/history/british/timeline/victorianbritain_timeline_noflash.shtml (accessed October 1, 2019). The wretchedness of the masses living in the new poverty engendered by the Industrial Revolution in the UK was a matter of international censure also. The German philosopher, Georg Hegel, wrote an essay for the *Preussiche Staatszeitung* (the Prussian Government Newspaper) in 1831 (shortly before he died that year). The essay focused on the UK Reform Bill of 1830 – which became the Reform Act (1832) . This reform measure increased the UK franchise to around 20% of the adult male population, abolished a range of "Rotten Boroughs" (tiny, controlled Parliamentary seats), and established additional seats in Parliament to represent the new large cities created as a result of the Industrial Revolution . Hegel argued that the reform of the voting system could not cure the manifest social problems in the UK . He also noted how the reform measures, above all, advantaged the rising Middle Class (which was benefitting significantly from the radical economic revolution underway) . See Hegel, Georg Wilhelm Friedrich, *The English Reform Bill*, available at: https://www.marxists.org/reference/archive/hegel/works/er/english-reform.pdf (accessed October 1 2019). Yet more fierce condemnation followed, not least in the works of Marx and Engels, of course . See, for example, Engels, Frederick, *The Condition of the Working Class in England* (1845), Marx/Engels Internet Archive, available at: https://www.marxists.org/archive/marx/works/1845/condition-working-class/index.htm (accessed October 1, 2019); and Marx, Karl and Engels, Frederick, *The Communist Manifesto* (1848), available at: http://marx.eserver.org/1848-communist.manifesto/cm1.txt (accessed October 1, 2019). For a forceful, modern catalogue of all the claimed grim legacies of the British Empire era, see "Most Hated Countries – United Kingdom [Number 8]", *Top Ten*, available at: http://www.thetoptens.com/most-hated-countries/united-kingdom-232448.asp (accessed October 1, 2019).

10 These examples of terrible, vast poverty and mass human ruination were matters of intense political debate in the UK (especially with respect to Ireland) in the nineteenth century, which saw the Government in Westminster change hands between Conservatives (led by Benjamin Disraeli) and Liberals (led by William Gladstone). These debates prompted a

era have intensified with many lists of atrocities being drawn up by the media and numerous commentators.[11] By one reckoning, there were at least a dozen major famines in India during the period of British rule (including rule under the British East India Company and under the British Crown) from 1765 to 1947, most of which involved the loss of millions of lives.[12] One recent account argues that the policies of the UK Prime Minister Churchill during World War II contributed to the last of these in 1943.[13] While the ruthlessly successful Japanese invasion of British Burma, cutting off a major source of rice imports by India, is noted in passing, British (especially Churchill's) culpability is stressed.[14]

The UK, where religious belief was still the norm for the vast majority, evolved into a functionally secular State. Although there was an established church, the Church of England, basic religious toleration was recognized as a societal requirement. Above all, it was a State where law, with all its limitations, compromises, and flaws, mattered greatly. During the prime of Dicey's life, it was a State where public institutions counted and where the free and lawful (albeit still mainly non-voting) citizens could go about their lives, defended, by the law, *from power's all-intrusive claims,* as Thompson put it.

The nineteenth century was also the time when Parliamentary (or Representative) Government was developed, consolidated, and confirmed (from the time of the coronation of Queen Victoria in 1837) within the UK. All ultimate political power (according to the doctrine of Parliamentary Sovereignty explained by Dicey) was placed within the Parliament at Westminster, where regular elections (for the House of Commons) were mandated to select new governments or to confirm sitting governments. Each Government had to be composed, according to Constitutional Convention, of members of the Westminster Parliament.

The process of profound foundation building for the modern British constitutional system began with the victory (over the Stuart King Charles 1st and his Royalist supporters) of Oliver Cromwell and Parliament in the English

---

series of statutory reforms over several decades aimed at relieving poverty, preventing famine, improving education provision, and widening the franchise. See *BBC History: Victorian Britain,* ibid.

11 See, for example, Osborne, Samuel, "5 of the Worst Atrocities Carried out by the British Empire" *The Independent,* January 19, 2016, available at: https://www.independent.co.uk/news/uk/home-news/worst-atrocities-british-empire-amritsar-boer-war-concentration-camp-mau-mau-a6821756.html (accessed October 1, 2019). A Google search of "Horrors of the British Empire" produces countless pages of such lists and related critical coverage.

12 See "Timeline of Major Famines in India during British Rule", Wikipedia, available at: https://en.wikipedia.org/wiki/Timeline_of_major_famines_in_India_during_British_rule (accessed October 1, 2019).

13 Safi, Michael, "Churchill's Policies Contributed to 1943 Bengal Famine – Study", *The Guardian*, March 29, 2019, available at: https://www.theguardian.com/world/2019/mar/29/winston-churchill-policies-contributed-to-1943-bengal-famine-study (accessed October 1, 2019).

14 Ibid.

Civil War (1642–1651). The failure of the Cromwellian government led to the restoration of the Stuart monarchy under Charles 2nd. Despite its name, the Glorious Revolution in 1688, which overthrew the Catholic Stuart Monarchy, brought further evolutionary change rather than any complete rewriting of the basic constitutional system. This era saw a transfer of a significant share of paramount power from the Monarch (with advisors) external to Parliament into the Parliament. Limited Monarchy and the emergence of Cabinet Government by the early eighteenth century had by 1837, irrevocably become Constitutional Monarchy – combined with Parliamentary Sovereignty.[15]

It was, overall, an optimistic era in the UK – at least for those who were not caught within the extensive zone of abject poverty. It was also an era of notably less complex political and social mores. There was a shared understanding about what was right and wrong. Sometimes this was self-serving but also clear-headed and constructive.

Thus, Edmund Burke could (famously) proclaim, in Bristol, in 1774, at the end of polling in an election (emphasis in the original):

> Parliament is not a *congress* of ambassadors from different and hostile interests; which interests each must maintain, as an agent and advocate, against other agents and advocates; but parliament is a *deliberative* assembly of *one* nation, with *one* interest, that of the whole; where, not local purposes, not local prejudices, ought to guide, but the general good, resulting from the general reason of the whole. You choose a member indeed; but when you have chosen him, he is not member of Bristol, but he is a member of *parliament*. If the local constituent should have an interest, or should form an hasty opinion, evidently opposite to the real good of the rest of the community, the member for that place ought to be as far, as any other, from any endeavour to give it effect. I beg pardon for saying so much on this subject. I have been unwillingly drawn into it; but I shall ever use a respectful frankness of communication with you. Your faithful friend, your devoted servant, I shall be to the end of my life: a flatterer you do not wish for.[16]

Dicey, with his deep analysis and in his writing, built on this tradition of constructive clarity by now fixed within the social ontology of the UK. The basic public policy optimism went hand in glove with a capacity to avert one's mind from considering, for too long, the extant, extensive misery and/or to retain a faith that

15 Walker, David M. *The Oxford Companion to Law* (Oxford University Press, Oxford, 1980), "Monarchy", "Parliamentary Government", "Parliament of England", "Parliament of Great Britain", and "Parliament of the United Kingdom".

16 "Edmund Burke Speech to the Electors of Bristol, November 3, 1774", available at: http://press-pubs.uchicago.edu/founders/documents/v1ch13s7.html (accessed October 1, 2019).

classical liberal progress would put most of that misery right. But it would take time and the best hope of real amelioration lay with the classical liberal project.[17]

Around 100 years after Victoria came to the Throne, George Orwell wrote his 1941 essay, "England Your England", which is the first part of the longer work, "The Lion and the Unicorn: Socialism and the English Genius".

The essay, written during the German Blitz that was unleashed on England and especially London, famously begins:

> As I write, highly civilized human beings are flying overhead trying to kill me.[18]

In the course of the essay, Orwell does not use the term *social ontology*. His insightful study of what, at that time, made England England can be aptly so characterized, however. He canvasses the powerful and complex binding forces within a highly class-based, hierarchical society. The hatred of war, militarism, and power worship all existed alongside acceptance, indeed, pride, in the then still vast British Empire. The "binding" nature of the shared experience of the weather, the continual dampness, bad teeth, bitter beer, heavy coins, gentle manners, suet puddings, red pillar boxes – and more – all helped forge the deep sense of national loyalty and bottom-up, potent (though mainly non-demonstrative) patriotism.

For our purposes, one passage may be quoted with benefit:

> Here one comes upon an all-important English trait: the respect for constitutionalism and legality, the belief in 'the law' as something above the State and above the individual, something which is cruel and stupid, of course, but at any rate incorruptible.
>
> It is not that anyone imagines the law to be just. Everyone knows that there is one law for the rich and another for the poor. But no one accepts the implications of this, everyone takes it for granted that the law, such as it

17 One established definition of Classical Liberalism is: "A political ideology that values the freedom of individuals – including the freedom of religion, speech, press, assembly, and markets – as well as limited government. It developed in 18th-century Europe and drew on the economic writings of Adam Smith and the growing notion of social progress". This definition lends significant strength to the idea that empowering the commercial classes (freedom of markets, meaning "freedom of money" as well as freedom from monopolies, etc.) is fundamental to furthering the overall public interest. Classical Liberalism is often contrasted with Progressive Liberalism (encompassing Social Democracy) and Left-Liberalism/Radical Liberalism. See, further, Kaminski, Joseph, "Four Types of Liberalism", *History, Sociology and More,* February 4, 2016, available at: https://josephkaminski.org/2016/02/04/liberalism/ (accessed October 1, 2019); Babones, Salvatore, *The New Authoritarianism* (Polity Press, Cambridge, 2018); and "Liberalism", *Stanford Encyclopedia of Philosophy*, available at: https://plato.stanford.edu/entries/liberalism/ (accessed October 1, 2019).

18 Orwell George, "England Your England", available at: http://orwell.ru/library/essays/lion/english/e_eye (accessed October 1, 2019).

> is, will be respected, and feels a sense of outrage when it is not. Remarks like 'They can't run me in; I haven't done anything wrong', or 'They can't do that; it's against the law', are part of the atmosphere of England.
>
> The professed enemies of society have this feeling as strongly as anyone else. One sees it in prison-books like Wilfred Macartney's Walls Have Mouths or Jim Phelan's Jail Journey, in the solemn idiocies that take place at the trials of conscientious objectors, in letters to the papers from eminent Marxist professors, pointing out that this or that is a 'miscarriage of British justice'. Everyone believes in his heart that the law can be, ought to be, and, on the whole, will be impartially administered. The totalitarian idea that there is no such thing as law, there is only power, has never taken root. Even the intelligentsia have only accepted it in theory.

Putting aside the contrast between Dicey's faith in "justice" (generally and within the law) and Orwell's manifest lack of a similar level of confidence, one can see a remarkable continuity in the shared understanding of the essential nature of law – and the way in which the law stands not shamelessly – beneficially hand in glove with centralized power but at a very clear distance. This central political-legal phenomenon was a product of several centuries of often fractious but continuous and evolved, shared (elite mass) interactive experience.

The system of Parliamentary Government, based on regular elections (outlined above), was incorporated into the largely white components of the British Empire, including Canada, Australia, and New Zealand from the mid-nineteenth century. The incorporation of this system of government was signified by the use of the term "British Dominions". This status was not, at the same time, conferred on many other component colonies and territories within the Empire.[19]

The new colony of Hong Kong, like many other similarly ranked jurisdictions within the Empire, took a form of Government structurally based on the established (pre-Parliamentary[20]) Government model such as applied during the reign of George III (1760–1820): a strong Executive Government, headed by the Governor created (and operating essentially) outside of the Legislature. The Legislative Council (LegCo) within BHK was, in keeping with this model, fully appointed by the Governor (this remained the case for almost 150 years). Combined with these two institutions was the independent Judiciary – with its equally independent Legal Profession.[21]

19 Walker, *The Oxford Companion to Law*, "Dominion Status".

20 The system of full, Responsible or Parliamentary Government (retaining a Constitutional Monarch) evolved in Britain, in completed form, during first decades of the nineteenth century.

21 This "George III" model provided the template for the drafting of the new US Constitution in the late eighteenth century. At that time, of course, there was no representative, ***parliamentary*** model to emulate. It is, thus, not surprising that the US Presidential system of government, with its extensive executive powers, operating outside of the legislature, significantly resembles pre-parliamentary Britain during the reign of George III. Alongside these

Incorporated within this formally authoritarian governance structure, however, were powerful governance principles derived from Diceyan Constitutionalism. These are discussed in detail below, but at this point we can note that included within this framework were the independent judicial-legal system, just noted, and commitment to a "single-track" system of regulating State–Citizen relationship. That is, the same courts applied the Common Law (and LegCo Ordinances) to the interaction between State and Citizen and in Citizen–Citizen disputation.

An argument can be made that Dicey's influence on the development of governance structures in Hong Kong (and a number of other similar, smaller jurisdictions within the British Empire) was not significant because the UK, even in Dicey's time, was gradually transforming itself into a modern pluralistic, representative democracy. This is so, but it remains the case that British colonial–constitutional thinking was fundamentally influenced by British constitutional thinking – as seminally explained by Dicey. One would hardly expect otherwise.

It is true that the British chose not to introduce any sort of elected legislatures and thus Parliamentary Government across many of the colonies within the British Empire – but this did not inhibit the application of fundamental Diceyan protocols in the framing of colonial governance institutions. The Rule of Law paradigm with its stress on judicial independence is pivotal to Dicey's constitutional standpoint, and these aspects of his thinking have been crucially relevant in Hong Kong since the inception of British Hong Kong until the present day.

The relevance of Dicey to authoritarianism is not that he supported or advocated authoritarian government as a first choice. The relevance arises from the fact that the British (a) used authoritarian forms of governing across so many of the smaller colonies; and (b) then drew on Diceyan concepts, time and again, in setting up these particularly British systems of authoritarian governance. History has shown that this Diceyan influence has been durable, distinctly significant, and, comparatively, more fair and effective than otherwise.

As it happens, Dicey's own views on extending the limited franchise (around 60% of adult males and 0% adult females) at about the time he was writing his most influential work were that it could be dangerous to good governance to do this.

Chinese Familialism

Around 95% of the population of Hong Kong is Chinese. The Chinese have created and maintained the largest, most enduring civilization on the planet. They have created a culture of immense depth and, despite its complexity, a culture which has displayed a set of clear hallmarks over many centuries. Chinese culture

institutions stood the independent judiciary (headed by the US Supreme Court). See, further, Walker, *The Oxford Companion to Law*, "Dominion Status". There is a significant resonance between the basic political frameworks in BHK (and now the HKSAR) and the US.

has been deeply influenced for over 2,000 years by the seminal writings of the venerated philosopher Confucius (551–479 BC).[22]

One noted Sinologist, Simon Leys, put it this way:

> From a western point of view, China is simply the other pole of the human mind. All the other great cultures are either dead (Egypt, pre-Columbian American and so on), or too exclusively absorbed by the problem of surviving in extreme conditions (primitive cultures), or too close to us (Islamist cultures, India) to present a contrast as total, a revelation as complete, an "otherness" as challenging, an originality as illuminating as China. It is only when we contemplate China that we can become exactly aware of our own identity and that we begin to perceive which part of our heritage truly pertains to universal humanity, and which part merely reflects Indo-European idiosyncrasies.[23]

A good way to proceed in this short review of certain Chinese cultural and social traits which have recognized advanced collective impact (Chinese social ontology) is to begin by considering children and child-rearing. There has been a significant amount of research done on the raising of Chinese children. Much effort is put into the early socialization of children so that they fit within the family structure.[24] It is almost impossible to overestimate the fundamental significance of the family within Chinese culture. Professor Allison explained that significance in this way:

> In the case of Kongzi [Confucius], filial piety and the place of the family in general receives a strong emphasis in the development of ethical values. This is re-emphasised in Mengzi [Mencius] and remains constant throughout the Chinese tradition. One has to genuinely search very hard to find any Western analogue to this emphasis upon family relations as the originating source of ethical values. When one finds any Western counterpart, such as Hegel, the emphasis on the family only occurs because of Hegel's systematic need to fit everything together in one organic whole. For the Chinese mind, the value of the family is self evident. It is not simply an ingredient in an overall proof structure such that the entire world can be seen as fitting into an overall organic whole. What makes for this difference between East and West? If my general theory of at-homeness is correct, then, for the Chinese mind, the

22 See, for a succinct discussion of Confucianism, Smith, H., *The Religions of Man* (Harper & Row, New York, 1964), Chapter 4. For discussion of the influence and impact of Confucian thinking on Chinese culture through until modern times, see Wang, Gungwu, *China and the Overseas Chinese* (Times Academic Press, Singapore, 1991); and Wang, Gungwu, *Bind Us in Time: Nation and Civilization in Asia* (Times Academic Press, Singapore, 2012) .

23 Leys, Simon, *The Burning Forest* (Paladin, London, 1988), 42.

24 Bond, Michael Harris, *Beyond the Chinese Face* (Oxford University Press), Chapter 2.

family represents a *natural* extension of oneself. There is no need to prove the priority of the family. It is accepted as a given fact.[25]

The process of socialization of Chinese children typically involves much loving care but also (a) early restrictions on movement; (b) early schooling commencement; and (c) a firm corrective regime.[26] The crucial socio-economic role of the family is as deeply embedded in Hong Kong as in other Chinese societies.[27] Another historical, abiding concern in Chinese societies is the maintenance of social order. The family rather than the State has been seen (and experienced) as the most important hedge against chaos.[28]

The central role of the family and the need to fit into one's family structure comprises an actively practised, fundamental, belief system which has evolved over more than 2,000 years. It is fair to argue that the *family* is the "religion" of China in the sense that it provides a comprehensive creed (in which adherents have faith) for living a collectively-respected life that has been handed down from generation to generation (within the family).[29] Coincidentally, at least, Chinese culture is also one which has relied to a comparatively abbreviated degree on the consumption of alcohol.[30]

Various other important values proceed from the operating structure of the Chinese family. These include a stress on self-reliance and self-help (within the family unit); the clearest understanding of the value of hard work; a powerful respect for and commitment to betterment through education; a focus on the acquisition of material wealth (within the family) as a hedge against bad fortune within the family (and outbreaks of social disorder); a clear understanding of the

25 Allison R. E. (ed.) *Understanding the Chinese Mind* (Oxford University Press, Hong Kong, 1995), 19.

26 Bond, *Beyond the Chinese Face*, Chapter 2.

27 Lau, Siu-kai, *Society and Politics in Hong Kong* (Chinese University Press, Hong Kong, 1991), Chapter 3.

28 Han, Suyin, *The Crippled Tree* (Triad/Panther, London, 1984), 71.

29 Many Chinese, especially in Hong Kong, practise more conventional religions, mainly Taoism, Buddhism and, to a lesser degree, Christianity. In all cases, however, religious practice remains secondary, as a matter of fundamental importance to living life, to the family. In the case of the Judeo-Christian and Islamic worlds, the respective religions have absorbed various doctrines related to family as part of their fundamental structure. That is, they have made the family "sacred" by incorporating it within the larger (more fundamental) system of religious belief. Within Chinese culture, the family remains, as Allison (*Understanding the Chinese Mind*) has explained, pre-eminent and without need of religious sanction or justification.

30 Alcohol consumption has been rising in China, especially over the last two decades, as the economy has grown. Consumption remains modest compared to Australia, the UK, or the US, for example, see, "List of Countries by Alcohol Consumption Per Capita – 2010", *World Health Organization*, available at: https://en.wikipedia.org/wiki/List_of_countries_by_alcohol_consumption_per_capita#2010_WHO_data (accessed October 1, 2019). Consumption levels in Hong Kong (where there is zero excise on beer or wine) and Singapore are still lower (ibid.).

value of thrift[31]; and a reverence for age and wisdom (with a predictable male-centred focus). Across the majority of Chinese families, there is a potent commitment to and respect for one's family.[32]

The very important state-craft aspects of "macro" Confucianism were, in many respects, highly advanced – and well ahead of European state-building for many centuries. However, the Renaissance, the Reformation, the Enlightenment, and the Industrial Revolution (and much social, political, economic, and scientific development too often powered by (or in response to) the most terrible wars) changed all this dramatically. Thus, by the time the Age of European Exploration was powerfully underway, China came to discover just how far it had slipped behind across so many areas of human collective endeavour – not least in state-craft. (These matters are discussed in depth in Chapter 9.)

Just how far was evident from the remarks made by the "Father of Modern China", Sun, Yat-sen. In 1924, he argued that:

31 The overall savings rate in Hong Kong is typically around 25% of Gross Domestic Product (GDP). This rate is well below that in Mainland China (50% of GDP in 2012) but well above the rate applying in the US (13% of GDP in 2012). This relatively high savings rate sits alongside quite low savings held by the worst-off in Hong Kong, however (see, Chen, Te-ping, "Two Thirds of Hong Kong Breadwinners Lack Savings", *The Wall Street Journal,* November 20, 2012, available at: http://blogs.wsj.com/chinarealtime/2012/11/20/two-thirds-of-hong-kong-breadwinners-lack-savings/ (accessed October 1, 2019). This article does not take into account, though, two key factors bolstering individual security in Hong Kong: very wide access to confined but secure and effective, low-rent public housing (see Chapter 5); and the (comparatively) very strong Chinese family support networks in place. Savings rates in Hong Kong have remained much the same since 2012 and also in China. In the US, they had dropped to about 2.4% of GDP by 2017. See "Gross Domestic Savings (% of GDP) 1960–2017", *World Bank*, available at: https://data.worldbank.org/indicator/NY.GDS.TOTL.ZS (accessed October 1, 2019); and "Personal Savings Rates in the United States from 1960 to 2017", *Statista,* available at: https://www.statista.com/statistics/246234/personal-savings-rate-in-the-united-states/ (accessed October 1, 2019).

32 For further discussion of such features, see Bond, *Beyond the Chinese Face*, Chapters 6 and 8, and Lau, *Society and Politics in Hong Kong,* 68–72. The review above provides a summary of factors which have had a marked influence on the way Chinese societies tend to organize themselves and engage with the world about them. The review is not meant to imply the Chinese social and cultural values are somehow saintly or blemish-free. Traditionally, Chinese culture is highly patriarchal with a wretched history of female oppression. This problem remains dreadfully real (see Xinran, *The Good Women of China: Hidden Voices* (Vintage, Toronto, 2003)). Chinese culture also places great pressure on individuals to "fit" within family and other social structures. It is a culture which historically has frowned powerfully on the (sole) pursuit of individual goals or indulgence. As it happens, the Chinese family structure also appears to be a remarkable facilitator of (parasitic) gambling and other financial excesses. Within this sort of close-knit family structure, it remains commonplace for family members caught by a gambling addiction or engaged in other money wasting pursuits to return, repeatedly, to various family members for "loans" – loans which are far too infrequently refused and far too frequently, never repaid.

> The Chinese people have only family and clan solidarity; they do not have national spirit ... they are just a heap of loose sand. ... Other men are the carving knife and the serving dish; we are the fish and the meat.[33]

He was reported also to be significantly impressed by the achievement of the British Government in Hong Kong, not least by the good drainage system. This experience convinced him, still further, of the backwardness of China – and the need to overthrow the Qing Imperial Dynasty.[34]

Hong Kong experience, by then, had shown how fundamental concepts, arising from Diceyan Constitutionalism, such as the free and lawful citizen (whose status was institutionally protected), had remarkable potential to mesh productively with the entrenched, collective, self-organizing aspects of Chinese Familialism in Hong Kong.

33 Sun Yatsen, Wikiquote, available at: https://en.wikiquote.org/wiki/Sun_Yat-sen (accessed October 1, 2019).

34 England, Vaudine, "Hong Kong Rediscovers Sun Yat-sen", *The New York Times,* September 17, 2007, available at: http://www.nytimes.com/2007/09/17/arts/17iht-sun.1.7531495.html?_r=0 (accessed October 1, 2019).

3 Assessing legitimacy

This chapter introduces certain theoretical bases for assessing the legitimacy – or lack thereof – of authoritarian governance systems. These perspectives are employed in the closing chapters. My principal emphasis is on the work of John Rawls with an additional note on the work of Joseph Weiler.

There is a need for such assessments given the primary focus of this book. China has created the largest and most successful authoritarian state the world has seen and in Hong Kong, the Authoritarian Legality (AL) foundations laid down in the BHK era remain a central component within the political structure of the HKSAR.

Advanced liberal democratic societies are demonstrably more concerned with and congenial to individual autonomy than any other societies – this is where their claim to superiority is most clearly grounded. But this is not a basis for any sort of "end of history" argument that only liberal democracies can claim an overriding, pre-eminent legitimacy regardless of wider circumstances.[1]

John Plamenatz noted, in 1973, how the case is commonly made:

> That all men everywhere, merely by virtue of being men, have certain fundamental rights, and among these is the right not to be governed by anyone who has not acquired authority over them by their consent.

1 This *apex-of-political-development* viewpoint took clear shape in a 1989 essay and then in a 1992 book, each written by the US political scientist Francis Fukuyama. Fukuyama argued in the 1989 essay that: "What we may be witnessing is not just the end of the Cold War, or the passing of a particular period of postwar history, but the end of history as such: that is, the end point of mankind's ideological evolution and the universalisation of Western liberal democracy as the final form of human government". See Fukuyama, Francis, *The End of History* (1989), *The National Interest*, available at: http://www.wesjones.com/eoh.htm#source (accessed October 1, 2019); and Fukuyama, Francis, *The End of History and the Last Man* (Free Press, New York, 1992). See further discussion in the closing chapters.

He argued that this position was absurd, however, because:

> If we are to make a realistic case for democracy we must be content to argue that it is the best form of government only when certain conditions apply.[2]

In *A Theory of Justice*,[3] John Rawls argued that the justice or otherwise of inequality is determined by what he called the "difference" principle: inequality is to be permitted to the extent that "it is to everyone's advantage", essentially by increasing economic welfare.

The possibility of allowing significant, continuing inequality (as a means to a good end) emerges from a trade-off conducted according to what Rawls called the "general conception of justice":

> All social values – liberty and opportunity, income and wealth, and the social bases of self-respect – are to be distributed equally unless an unequal distribution of any, or all, of these values is to everyone's advantage. Injustice, then, is simply inequalities that are not to the benefit of all.[4]

In the general conception, the difference principle applies, precisely, generally. Equality might in (almost) all its aspects and to (almost) any extent be sacrificed to economic welfare. But in a liberal democratic society in which legitimacy rests on "justice as fairness", the difference principle is but the second of two principles of justice:

> First principle: Each person is to have an equal right to the most extensive total system of equal basic liberties compatible with a similar system of liberties for all.
>
> Second principle: social and economic inequalities are to be arranged so that they are … reasonably expected to be to everyone's advantage.[5]

The order of these two principles is not arbitrary but expressive of a most important priority of the first over the second. Rawls' fundamental ethical commitment is to the (rationality and) autonomy of human beings as it is established by Kant, and justice as fairness is, he believes, the principle of a political arrangement that

2 Plamenatz, John, *Democracy and Illusion* (Longman, London, 1973), 8.

3 References here will usually be to Rawls, John, *A., Theory of Justice* (rev. edn.) (Oxford University Press, Oxford, 1999), hereinafter cited as TJ. Certain passages of the first edition are arguably superior to the revised edition, certainly in terms of focusing on our concerns here, and I will refer to these passages, noting when I do so. Rawls, John, *A., Theory of Justice* (Belknap Press, Cambridge, MA, 1971) is hereinafter cited as TJ1.

4 TJ, 54.

5 TJ, 53. The difference principle is revised as the argument of TJ progresses and in its final formulation "reasonably expected to be to everyone's advantage" becomes "to the greatest benefit of the least advantaged": TJ, 266. The aspect of the principle of interest here is clearer in its first formulation.

is essential for such autonomy,[6] though it is intrinsic to the persuasiveness of his argument that he goes a long way towards accommodating the difference principle's consideration of total economic welfare within that arrangement.

The plausibility of the difference principle rests upon what, in later work, Rawls called the "realistic utopianism" of his approach.[7] The stability of an economy requires an acceptance that, on any plausible philosophical anthropology of economic action, there is a trade-off between equality and output.

Rawls regarded justice as fairness as a "special case" of the general conception.[8] If we put the abstract philosophical points to one side, justice as fairness is a special case in that it normally can have purchase only in affluent societies, and of these it usually applies only to the liberal democracies because they are the only societies where there is the possibility of consensus over the value of autonomy. In the first instance, it is only affluent societies that can provide, say, social security adequate to sustain a person's autonomy during periods of incapacity or unemployment. But, more than this, it is only affluent societies that can frequently refuse to exploit possible trade-offs between increasing economic welfare and preserving autonomy.

It is actually easier to accept the sacrifice of basic liberties than it will at first seem to those who are members of liberal democratic societies because, in a sense, there is little to sacrifice. In societies which are not sufficiently affluent to provide primary goods adequately, the formal existence of basic liberties may count for little as, in the absence of the requisite primary goods, a person may well lack the capacity to exercise those liberties.[9] This argument draws upon the strength of Rawls' concept of the basic structure and its provision of primary goods. As T.H. Marshall put it in one influential formulation,[10] legal and political rights of citizenship will tend to be merely formal without a "social citizenship"

6 TJ, 452.

7 Rawls, John, *The Law of Peoples* (Harvard University Press, Cambridge, MA, 1999), 4–5.

8 TJ1, 63. In the second edition of *A Theory of Justice*, this language was somewhat altered as part, it would seem of Rawls' retreat from a general theory of justice to an even greater focus on the political theory of liberal democracy culminating in Rawls, John, *Political Liberalism* (Columbia University Press, New York, 1993) and Rawls, John, *Justice as Fairness: A Restatement* (2nd.edn.) (Harvard University Press, New York, 2001).

9 India, the world's second largest nation by population, is also the world's largest democracy, with strong, judicially enforceable individual rights embedded in the Indian Constitution. In 2012, more than 37% of the population (more than 400 million) were still living in absolute poverty making up one third of the world's most poor. Between 1981 and 2012, extreme poverty in China (the world's paramount authoritarian state) fell from 88% to 6.5% of the population according to the World Bank. See Banik, Dan, "The Hungry Nation: Food Policy and Food Politics in India" (2016) 1 *Food Ethics*, 29, available at: https://link.springer.com/article/10.1007/s41055-016-0001-1 (accessed October 1, 2019); and Allison, Graham, "Beijing's Anti-Poverty Drive Has Lessons for Us All", *The Telegraph /China Daily*, August 28, 2018, available at: https://www.telegraph.co.uk/news/world/china-watch/society/decreasing-chinas-poverty/ (accessed October 1, 2019).

10 Marshall, T. H., "Citizenship and Social Class", in Marshall and Bottomore (Eds.), *Citizenship and Social Class* (Pluto, London, 1992).

conveying the capacity to exercise the otherwise formal rights. Rawls' argument implies that in a poor society, increases in economic welfare may be pursued in accordance with the general conception through trade-offs unacceptable in liberal democratic society, but only so as to get to a position where the formerly poor society can provide primary goods and thus really establish an extensive system of total basic liberties. This is to say that economic policies may be justified by the general conception in societies other than liberal democracies because the result of those policies is that those societies will eventually become capable of transforming themselves so as to prioritize protection of individual autonomy.[11]

If one accepts Rawls' Kantian commitment to autonomy, then it is arguable, and I believe it is indeed the case, that he furnishes us not only with a conception of a workable relationship of liberty and economic welfare in liberal democratic society but also with a workable approach to the evaluation of undemocratic and illiberal policies adopted in societies at a lower level of advancement (in the Rawlsian sense) than in developed liberal democracies. Such policies can be justified if they are to everybody's advantage, which is mainly a question of economic welfare, and if they prepare the way for the development of a society in which justice as fairness then prioritizes basic liberties over the pursuit of economic welfare.

Finally, Joseph Weiler deploys a resonant understanding of what he terms the political DNA of a given polity when analyzing the crisis besetting the European Union (with its non-democratic, elite leadership structure) over recent decades. Professor Weiler sets out three types of governance legitimacy, which can fairly be summarized as process or input (democratic) legitimacy; performance or output legitimacy; and messianic or vision legitimacy.[12]

11 TJ1, 152. The changes to this passage made in the revised edition, TJ, 132, seem to make Rawls' argument less clear.

12 Weiler, Joseph H. H., "Europe in Crisis – On Political Messianism, Legitimacy and the Rule of Law" (2012) *Singapore Journal of Legal Studies,* 248.

4 British Hong Kong

Foundational developments

Prior to the British acquiring Hong Kong Island in 1842 under the Treaty of Nanking (now Nanjing),[1] it was an outpost within Imperial China and home to a number of small fishing communities.[2] The Treaty of Nanking and almost all other "Treaties" signed by the Chinese under (mainly) European pressure, particularly during the nineteenth century, were all regarded as "unequal" and therefore not recognized by China as proper Treaties.[3]

The British took possession of Hong Kong Island after what is known as the First Opium War (1839–1842). The British, as a result of their success in this war, were able to force Imperial China to open its doors to much increased trade and, especially, to substantial trade in opium.[4] The British were able to provide the opium from India. They needed a new item of trade as there was much they wanted from China (tea, porcelain, silk, for example).[5] Opium is addictive, so,

1 The romanized versions of Chinese place names vary in their spelling. This is the result of historical practice.

2 Tsang, Steve, *A Modern History of Hong Kong* (I. B. Tauris, London, 2007).

3 See Wesley-Smith, Peter, *Unequal Treaty 1898–1997: China, Great Britain and Hong Kong's New Territories* (Oxford University Press, Hong Kong, 1983). Imperial Japan also invaded and increasingly colonized much of China over the period from 1895 to 1945. See *Oxford Paperback Encyclopedia* (Oxford University Press, Oxford, 1998), 730. See also Kimura, Ehito, "The New Unequal Treaties", *The Bangkok Post*, January 22, 1998, available at: https://scholar.google.com/citations?user=eD0HbnEAAAAJ&hl=en#d=gs_md_cita-d&u=%2Fcitations%3Fview_op%3Dview_citation%26hl%3Den%26user%3DeD0HbnEAAAAJ%26citation_for_view%3DeD0HbnEAAAAJ%3AeQOLeE2rZwMC%26tzom%3D-660 and also at: http://www.geocities.com/rainforest/7813/0206_imf.htm (accessed October 1, 2019).

4 Initially, this opium trade was, officially, mainly from India, through Hong Kong, to North America, Europe, and Australia (at a time when such trade was quite legal and opium was used extensively as a primary pain-killer (pre-aspirin)). Unofficially, there was very substantial trade into China using smuggling methods. Eventually, that trade with China was legalized about 20 years after the establishment of British Hong Kong. See, further, Cullen, Richard and Tso, Kevin K. S., "Using Opium as a Public Revenue Resource – Not as Easy as It Looks: The British Hong Kong Experience" (2012) *British Tax Review*, 226.

5 Florek, Stan, "The Mechanics of Opium Wars", *Australian Museum*, available at: https://australianmuseum.net.au/learn/cultures/international-collection/chinese/the-mechanics-of-opium-wars/ (accessed October 1, 2019).

once its sale became established, demand increased.[6] There was also, as one might expect, an ample supply of local merchants within China happy to profit from the trade. The established view is that the war was fought by the British to put a stop to Chinese attempts to curtail the British export of opium to China. At the height of this trade, opium was said to be the largest single article of commerce in the world.[7]

Professor Stephen Platt maintains that:

> [T]he war was incredibly controversial in its own time, far more so than I expected when I started my research. For the proponents, it was a matter of framing. They denied any connection to opium and argued that the war was entirely about defending Britain's national honor and protecting their countrymen from alleged atrocities in China. But the involvement of opium was inescapable – thus the name "Opium War", as the *London Times* and other papers called it. To many people in Britain the notion of going to war to advance the interests of drug dealers, against a country that had always been friendly to Britain, was abhorrent. As William Gladstone [who first became Prime Minister in 1868] wrote in his diary at the time, "I am in dread of the judgments of God upon England for our national iniquity towards China". The collision between those two sides came to a head in the spring of 1840 with a huge debate in the House of Commons over a motion to stop the war by forcing the resignation of the ministers who started it. After three full nights of debate, with impassioned speeches that in some cases went on for hours, the motion failed by a razor's margin.[8]

American traders also swiftly seized the opportunities arising from the Sino-opium trade. The grandfather of one of the most famous US Presidents, Franklin Delano Roosevelt, was a Boston trader, Warren Delano, made rich by the opium trade.[9]

This First Opium War is often referred to as the beginning of China's *Century of Humiliation*, a term which has been used by the current President of the PRC, Xi Jinping, as he has argued the case for the *Chinese Dream* of national rejuvenation.[10]

6 It is claimed that up to 90% of people suffered directly or indirectly from the addiction impact of opium in certain coastal areas of south-west China (ibid.).

7 Morris, Jan, *Hong Kong: Epilogue to an Empire* (Penguin, London, 1990), 22. For an alternative view of the role of the opium trade in triggering the war, see "China and British Imperialism: Revenge Is Sweet", *The Economist*, September 4, 1993, 91–92. See also Hampton, Mark, *Hong Kong and British Culture* (Oxford University Press, Oxford, 2015).

8 See Ramzy, Austin, "How Britain Went to War with China over Opium", *New York Times*, July 3, 2018, available at: https://www.nytimes.com/2018/07/03/world/asia/opium-war-book-china-britain.html (accessed October 1, 2019).

9 Meyer, Karl E., "The Opium War's Secret History", *New York Times*, June 28, 1997.

10 Ramzy, "How Britain Went to War".

Hong Kong became a Crown Colony within the British Empire with a constitution provided in the Letters Patent and Royal Instructions,[11] issued through the Privy Council in London.[12] This was the customary method the British used for providing constitutional underpinnings to colonies like Hong Kong.[13] Such colonies remained subject to the operation of the direct application of UK law in certain circumstances and their own law-making powers were limited, normally to laws having effect within the specific colony. Other larger, usually "white" dependencies within the British Empire, like the Australian colonies, were provided with Westminster-enacted constitutions and full parliamentary systems of elected government.[14] The Letters Patent for Hong Kong, which were subject to a number of amendments, remained Hong Kong's primary constitutional document until the change of sovereignty in 1997.[15]

The Second Opium War was fought by the British from 1856 to 1860 after further Chinese resistance to the opium trade (though triggered by a particular, incidental military clash). In 1860, the British took possession of the Kowloon Peninsula and Stonecutters Island, directly north of Hong Kong Island under the First Convention of Peking. As in the case of Hong Kong Island, the area was ceded, under this new Treaty, to the UK in perpetuity. The British now enjoyed much more complete control of Hong Kong's Victoria Harbour.

In 1894–1895, modernizing, highly militarized Japan inflicted another defeat on China. Japan took control of Taiwan at this time and various European powers (including the UK) moved in to obtain further concessions from China. In 1898, the British obtained a 99-year lease of the "New Territories" under the Second Convention of Peking. This added a large area north of the Kowloon Peninsula plus a number of nearby islands to the existing Crown Colony. The land area of Hong Kong was increased to around 1,100 km^2. The population at this time was about 250,000.[16]

In 1911, the decaying Qing Dynasty finally collapsed and the Republic of China was established under its new President and pre-eminent "founding father", Sun Yat-sen. Overall, British Hong Kong continued to prosper, though it endured difficult periods during the 1920s and 1930s.[17] Over the same period, the Japanese extended their control and influence in Mainland China dramatically.

11 Ghai, Yash, *Hong Kong's New Constitutional Order* (2nd ed.) (Hong Kong University Press, Hong Kong, 1999).

12 The history and important operational aspects of Hong Kong's constitutional documentation under British rule are explained well in Chapter 1, ibid.

13 See "Letters Patent", LegCo Info. Pack, available at: http://www.legco.gov.hk/general/english/library/infopacks/yr11-12/1112infopacks-lc-04-e.pdf (accessed October 1, 2019).

14 For a typical example of such a Constitution, see the Victoria Constitution Act 1855 (UK), available at: http://foundingdocs.gov.au/item-sdid-19.html (accessed October 1, 2019).

15 Ghai, *Hong Kong's New Constitutional Order.*

16 Morris, *Hong Kong*, 35.

17 Miners, Norman, *The Government and Politics of Hong Kong* (5th ed.) (Oxford University Press, Hong Kong, 1991), 4.

Almost at the same time, as the Japanese bombed Pearl Harbour on December 7, 1941, they attacked Hong Kong from their base in Guangdong Province directly to the north. They overran the colony with ruthless speed. By Christmas Day 1941, all of Hong Kong was in Japanese hands.

After the defeat of Japan in 1945, the Civil War in China between Chiang Kai-Shek's Kuomintang (KMT) and the Communist Party of China (CPC) led by Mao Zedong resumed. By 1949, the defeated KMT had retreated to the island of Taiwan. The new PRC was proclaimed on October 1, 1949.

Although the People's Liberation Army (PLA) (of the CPC) was on the border with Hong Kong by 1949, no attempt was made to invade. By 1950, China had entered the war on the Korean Peninsula on the side of North Korea. This made any near-term invasion of Hong Kong unlikely for several reasons. First, the limited resources of the new PRC were already stretched by the war in the north-east. Also, the British were, by then, well dug in, in Hong Kong. Next, the Korean War demonstrated, to Beijing, the advantage of having this British enclave in the south. Following the outbreak of the Korean War, the Western powers placed an embargo on the export of strategic goods to the PRC. China was, nonetheless, able to obtain important supplies through Hong Kong.[18]

Out of this experience grew a largely unspoken, mutual understanding between Beijing and London. The essence of this understanding was that, provided Hong Kong did not become any sort of strategic threat to the PRC, the British presence there would be tolerated *pro tempore*. The key elements of this *modus vivendi*, according to Norman Miners, included no significant moves towards democracy in Hong Kong; no operational Taiwanese (that is, KMT) political presence in Hong Kong; and no impediments to China participating in and profiting from the Hong Kong economy.[19]

Under this arrangement, Hong Kong enjoyed a near continuous, significant growth in prosperity for a period of five decades following the end of World War II. In 1945, Hong Kong's per capita gross domestic product (GDP) was, by some estimates, lower than that of India and Kenya.[20] By 1992, Hong Kong's per capita GDP had overtaken that of the UK. By 2004, Hong Kong was ranked at 23 in a global, "highest GDP per head" table, ahead of Canada and Australia.[21] Wealth distribution in Hong Kong remains very uneven; significant poverty persists. Nevertheless, Hong Kong materially transformed itself in the decades after 1945 from a war-ravaged colony of less than 800,000 to a leading international finance and service centre with a population of over 7 million. Hong Kong also

18 Ibid., 4.

19 Ibid., 6.

20 Bartholomew, James, *The Welfare State Made Britain Poor* – extract (dated October 31, 2005) from book at: http://moneyweek.com/the-welfare-state-made-britain-poor/ (accessed October 1, 2019).

21 *Pocket World in Figures 2005* (The Economist – Profile Books, London, 2004), 28.

became one of the world's busiest container ports and became the most popular tourist destination in Asia after the PRC.[22]

Over the period from 1945 to 1997, Hong Kong experienced (or was caught up in to some degree) various regional crises, including the Korean War; the upheaval and famine of Mao's infamous "Great Leap Forward" (1958–1962)[23]; Mao's even more ill-famed, "Great Proletarian Cultural Revolution" (1966–1976)[24]; and the Vietnamese War. In all these and other cases, Hong Kong absorbed the impact, recovered, and, usually with remarkable swiftness, returned to a path of strong growth.

Formative values

Diceyan Constitutionalism

Chapter 2 articulates how Diceyan Constitutionalism shaped the creation and maintenance of a strong, largely constructive, and consistent public institutional framework in Hong Kong. It also powerfully influenced operational procedures for the officers of these institutions.

Many defects remained within this scheme. Thus, the British governance system applying during this era has been portrayed as "systematically biased against Chinese and other non-European defendants".[25] Peter Wesley-Smith describes the Rule of Law as being, throughout this period, "[a British] ideal more dramatically subverted than any other".[26]

Although the record is clear that the colonial Rule of Law system in Hong Kong steadily fell short of always working in accordance with its foundational better principles, two high profile cases, one from the nineteenth century and another from the twentieth century, do show how well, when put to the test, it could live up to those values.

22 Tsang, A., *Modern History of Hong Kong*. Broad, current HKSAR Statistics are set out at: https://www.gov.hk/en/about/abouthk/facts.htm (accessed October 1, 2019).

23 *Cambridge Paperback Encyclopedia* (3rd ed.) (Cambridge University Press, Cambridge, 1999), 365.

24 Ibid., 228. The Cultural Revolution is normally said to have lasted from 1966 to 1976 (the year Mao Zedong died). During this time, virtually all laws and the entire legal system were either mainly ignored or simply destroyed and China endured years of terrible social, political, and economic disruption often spilling over into murderous chaos. A range of factors led to its inception but, above all, Mao Zedong fostered the (lawless) Cultural Revolution as he fought, with characteristic complete ruthlessness, to regain his supreme authority within the CPC, following the disastrous "Great Leap Forward" (1958–1959) which Mao had also fostered. See, further, Chen, Jianfu, *Chinese Law: Context and Transformation* (Brill, Leiden, 2015), Chapter 2; and "GDP Growth in China: 1952–2015", *Chinability,* available at: http://www.chinability.com/GDP.htm (accessed October 1, 2019).

25 Munn, Christopher, *Anglo-China: Chinese People and British Rule in Hong Kong, 1841–1880* (Curzon Press, Richmond, 2001), 251.

26 Wesley-Smith, Peter, "Book Review: Munn, Christopher, *Anglo-China: Chinese People and British Rule in Hong Kong, 1841–1880*" (2003) (Jan.–Feb.) *China Perspectives*, 74.

As noted above, the Second Opium War began in October 1856. It was triggered, above all, by (a) European – and especially British – imperial demands that China must open up still more to trade, not least in opium, and (b) lethal but futile Chinese resistance. The French actively joined the British in pursuing the war. It was concluded with victory against a completely outgunned China in October 1860. The war was resolved in 1860 (where France, Russia, the UK, and the US were all parties, with China, to various treaties). Outcomes of the war included legalization of the trade in opium to China; agreement to British involvement in the "coolie trade" (shipping indentured Chinese labourers to the Americas); sacking of the Chinese Imperial Summer Palace (as punishment); massive indemnity payments; and the granting of a part of Outer Manchuria to the Russians, where the new port city of Vladivostok ("Ruler of the East") was established.[27]

In Hong Kong, the outbreak of this war prompted strong reactions, conspicuously from a certain baker. Cheong Ah-lum was the principal of a business supplying bread to expatriates in BHK. It is widely believed that in 1857 he (possibly with accomplices) laced bread with arsenic in a bid to decimate a significant section of leading members of the British population in Hong Kong. In almost all cases, those who ate the bread soon after vomited and thus failed to ingest much arsenic. Still, Governor Bowring saw his wife fall badly ill. She soon after returned to England and died about a year later. Attorney-General Anstey favoured a "drumhead court martial". As the UK was at war with China by then, this was a legally available option. Anstey favoured such a trial the better to secure a swift verdict of death by hanging. The Governor rejected this option and insisted on a civilian trial by jury (some of whose members had been poisoned). Chief Justice Hulme advised the jury that no matter how angry they felt, "hanging the wrong man will not further the ends of justice". Based on the evidence presented, Cheong was acquitted by the jury. He swiftly relocated to Macua and then to Vietnam and died, aged 70, in 1900.[28]

The paramount leader of the Vietnamese revolution against French occupation was Ho Chi Minh. This is the name by which he is best known, but he had many aliases during his remarkable life (he died in 1969 in Hanoi, aged 79). In 1929, he was sentenced to death in absentia by the French in Indochina. He came to BHK in 1930 to escape the French, to spread his belief in communism, and to work to overthrow French rule in Indochina. The French discovered his

27 Goldfinger, Shandra, "The Second Opium War", Mount Holyoke College, available at: https://www.mtholyoke.edu/~goldf20s/politics116/secondwar.html (accessed October 1, 2019).

28 See Schoonakker, Bonny, "Racial Tensions Mixed with a Dash of Arsenic and Yeast", *South China Morning Post*, January 15, 2007, available at: https://www.scmp.com/article/578666/racial-tensions-mixed-dash-arsenic-and-yeast (accessed October 1, 2019); and Tso Kevin, K. S., "Fundamental Political and Constitutional Norms: Hong Kong and Macau Compared" (2012) 13 *Australian Journal of Asian Law*, available at: https://papers.ssrn.com/sol3/papers.cfm?abstract_id=2159544 (accessed October 1, 2019).

presence in Hong Kong and alerted the British authorities. Ho was detained in Victoria Gaol in 1931. He refused to admit his real identity. The British nevertheless made ready to deport him to Indochina on a French ship.[29]

Francis Loseby, Ho's lawyer in Hong Kong (and the then President of the Hong Kong Bar Association) successful prevented this (with a writ of *Habeas Corpus*). After the High Court in Hong Kong ordered Ho's deportation, Loseby lodged an appeal with the Privy Council in London. In 1932, the matter was settled outside of the Privy Council.[30] It is understood that the British Colonial Office had an internal rule that a prisoner of the British should not be deported to face a death penalty (especially one handed down in absentia).

Ho suffered from both tuberculosis and dysentery. A cover story was leaked, to deflect the French, that he had died in Hong Kong of tuberculosis. In the meantime, Ho was eventually put on a ship out of Hong Kong to Amoy (now Xiamen) in China. Ho retained a friendship with Loseby who visited him (as President of North Vietnam) in Hanoi in 1960.[31]

The governance system which evolved within British Hong Kong was, taken as a whole, rational, predictable, coherent, and, for the time, primarily measured rather than arbitrary. It was also resilient and successful. Its enduring merits were more central than its continuing drawbacks and those merits stood up well, comparatively. Hong Kong came to experience an operational governance system of qualified integrity.[32]

It is a basic argument of this book that this was a "necessary condition" underpinning political-economic success in the particular case of BHK. It was not, however, a sufficient condition. Proof of this is plain enough: Diceyan Constitutionalism was implanted in a wide range of colonies throughout the

29 Chan, Samson, "Ho Chi Minh in Victoria Gaol", *Hong Kong Memory*, available at: https://www.hkmemory.hk/collections/victoria_prison/Ho_Chi_Minh_in_Victoria_Gaol/index.html (accessed October 1, 2019).

30 Ibid.

31 Kwok, Yenni, "Liberating the Past", *South China Morning Post*, May 13, 2008, available at: https://www.scmp.com/article/637331/liberating-past (accessed October 1, 2019). This article outlines the details of a monologue play written by Peter Wesley-Smith (former Professor and Dean of Law in the Faculty of Law at Hong Kong University). The play is entitled "Ho Chi Minh in Hong Kong: His Persecution and the Triumph of the Glorious Rule of Law". Wesley-Smith notes that the barrister representing the Hong Kong Government at the Privy Council Appeal, Stafford Cripps, was a socialist. He was also a nephew of a famous UK socialist, Sydney Webb, one of the founders (with his wife Beatrice) of the London School of Economics. It was Cripps, Wesley-Smith says, who suggested the compromise which led to Ho being released to China (and the French being deceived).

32 See Tso, Kevin K. S., "Fundamental Political and Constitutional Norms: Hong Kong and Macau Compared" (2012) 13 *Australian Journal of Asian Law*, available at: http://papers.ssrn.com/sol3/papers.cfm?abstract_id=2159544 (accessed October 1, 2019). This article evaluates the core values, continuity of policy development, and relative autonomy established within BHK and compares this to the notably more changeable governance patterns evident of the comparable period in Portuguese-run Macau.

British Empire. Only in a few of those colonies (especially where no natural resources were at hand) did outcomes such as one finds in BHK emerge.[33]

Chinese Familialism

The population of Hong Kong is predominantly Chinese (over 95%). As explained in Chapter 2, the Chinese have created and maintained the largest, most enduring civilization on the planet. Briefly restated, the end result is a culture of immense depth and, despite its complexity, a culture which has displayed a set of clear hallmarks over many centuries deeply influenced, above all and for over 2,000 years, by the seminal writings of the venerated philosopher Confucius (551–479 BC).[34]

Simon Leys argued lucidly that:

> It is only when we contemplate China that we can become exactly aware of our own identity and that we begin to perceive which part of our heritage truly pertains to universal humanity, and which part merely reflects Indo-European idiosyncrasies.[35]

Professor Allison explains how Confucius placed the family at the centre of the system of human values he articulated. Mencius confirmed and amplified this viewpoint. Allison concluded that:

> For the Chinese mind, the value of the family is self evident. It is not simply an ingredient in an overall [Hegelian] proof structure such that the entire world can be seen as fitting into an overall organic whole. What makes for this difference between East and West? If my general theory of at-homeness is correct, then, for the Chinese mind, the family represents a *natural* extension of oneself. There is no need to prove the priority of the family. It is accepted as a given fact.[36]

The process of socialization of Chinese children typically involves much loving care but also (a) early restrictions on movement; (b) early schooling commencement; and (c) a firm corrective regime.[37] The crucial socio-economic role of the family is as deeply embedded in Hong Kong as in other Chinese societies.[38] Another historical, abiding concern in Chinese societies is the maintenance of

33 Singapore, clearly, provides a like example. Once again one finds, there, an advantageous linking of Diceyan Constitutionalism and Chinese Familialism.

34 See Chapter 2.

35 Leys, Simon, *The Burning Forest* (Paladin, London, 1988), 42.

36 Allison R. E. (ed.), *Understanding the Chinese Mind* (Oxford University Press, Hong Kong, 1995), 19.

37 Bond, Michael Harris, *Beyond the Chinese Face* (Oxford University Press, Oxford), Chapter 2.

38 Lau, Siu-kai, *Society and Politics in Hong Kong* (Chinese University Press, Hong Kong, 1991), Chapter 3.

social order. The family rather than the State has been seen (and experienced) as the most important hedge against chaos.[39]

Leo Goodstadt provides penetrating (regularly scathing) criticism of the governance of BHK (and the HKSAR) in his book, *Uneasy Partners*, published in 2005.[40] He also acutely notes how cooperative, stable, and law-abiding the Hong Kong population was:

> There was never any need for the rulers to keep the people of Hong Kong at a distance or to exclude them from participation from government. … It would have been hard to find anywhere a society more socially responsible and tolerant, more politically mature and self-reliant, or a people easier to serve and rule. They were ideal constituents, the secure foundations on which Hong Kong's success had been built despite the economic turbulence and political uncertainty.[41]

There is here, in my view, a reflection of the way in which the collectively self-reliant and self-regulating aspects of Chinese Familialism engaged so productively with the predictable, essentially rational, colonial governance institutions shaped by Diceyan Constitutionalism. Fundamental concepts, arising from that constitutional thinking, such as the free and lawful citizen (whose status was institutionally protected), had, it transpired, remarkable potential to mesh with the entrenched, positive, collectivist aspects of Chinese Familialism.

Goodstadt also observes the way in which Hong Kong emerged so swiftly from the terrible post-war poverty arising from the brutal, often horrific, Japanese occupation from 1941 to 1945.[42] A confirming product, in my view, of the fruitful engagement just outlined. Moreover, Goodstadt notes how it was argued "that the British came close to matching the standards of acceptable government set by Chinese traditional norms".[43]

The *single track* mode of civil society regulation

A pivotal aspect of Diceyan Constitutionalism was the belief in and the requirement for there to be a single set of courts to adjudicate all legal disputes. Specialist

39 Han, Suyin, *The Crippled Tree* (Triad/Panther, London, 1984), 71.

40 Goodstadt, Leo, *Uneasy Partners: The Conflict between Public Interest and Private Profit in Hong Kong* (Hong Kong University Press, Hong Kong, 2005), "Conclusions, The Ideal Constituents".

41 Ibid., 228.

42 Ibid. As noted earlier, Hong Kong's per capita GDP was by some estimates, in 1945, lower than that of India and Kenya. In less than 40 years, by 1992, Hong Kong's per capita GDP had overtaken that of the UK. See Bartholomew, James, *The Welfare State Made Britain Poor* – extract (dated October 31, 2005) from book at: http://moneyweek.com/the-welfare-state-made-britain-poor/ (accessed October 1, 2019).

43 Goodstadt, *Uneasy Partners*.

courts mediating the relationship between State and citizen, such as existed in France in Dicey's time, were reviewed comparatively and adversely as a way of demonstrating the benefits – to the citizen above all – of the British approach.[44]

A concurrent understanding was that the law regulating the State–citizen relationship should be the product of transparent (normally non-retrospective) law making by Parliament. Moreover, in the case of enforcing institutions, even when there was a perceived need for clandestine surveillance, the general rule was that such operations should be housed within primary institutions notwithstanding their covert role.

The fundamental precepts of modern British policing date back to the statutory reforms introduced by Sir Robert Peel in 1829, when he was Home Secretary. The "Peelian Principles", as they have become known, rely on the key concept of policing by consent.[45] The Police Historian Charles Reith argued, in 1956, that this conception of a Police Force was:

> [U]nique in history and throughout the world because it derived not from fear but almost exclusively from public cooperation with the police, induced

44 Schwartz, Bernard, *French Administrative Law and the Common-Law World* (New York University Press, New York, 1954), Chapter 2. The author argues that Dicey ultimately backed away from the level of severity of his original criticism of the Droit Administratif.

45 "Principles of Good Policing", Civitas, available at: http://www.civitas.org.uk/research/crime/facts-comments/principles-of-good-policing/ (accessed October 1, 2019). The nine principles of policing: (1) To prevent crime and disorder, as an alternative to their repression by military force and severity of legal punishment; (2) To recognize always that the power of the police to fulfil their functions and duties is dependent on public approval of their existence, actions, and behaviour and on their ability to secure and maintain public respect; (3) To recognize always that to secure and maintain the respect and approval of the public means also the securing of the willing co-operation of the public in the task of securing observance of laws; (4) To recognize always that the extent to which the co-operation of the public can be secured diminishes proportionately the necessity of the use of physical force and compulsion for achieving police objectives; (5) To seek and preserve public favour, not by pandering to public opinion but by constantly demonstrating absolutely impartial service to law, in complete independence of policy, and without regard to the justice or injustice of the substance of individual laws, by ready offering of individual service and friendship to all members of the public without regard to their wealth or social standing, by ready exercise of courtesy and friendly good humour; and by ready offering of individual sacrifice in protecting and preserving life; (6) To use physical force only when the exercise of persuasion, advice, and warning is found to be insufficient to obtain public co-operation to an extent necessary to secure observance of law or to restore order, and to use only the minimum degree of physical force which is necessary on any particular occasion for achieving a police objective; (7) To maintain at all times a relationship with the public that gives reality to the historic tradition that the police are the public and that the public are the police, the police being only members of the public who are paid to give full-time attention to duties which are incumbent on every citizen in the interests of community welfare and existence; (8) To recognize always the need for strict adherence to police executive functions and to refrain from even seeming to usurp the powers of the judiciary of avenging individuals or the State and of authoritatively judging guilt and punishing the guilty; (9) To recognize always that the test of police efficiency is the absence of crime and disorder and not the visible evidence of police action in dealing with them.

> by them designedly by behaviour which secures and maintains for them the approval, respect and affection of the public.[46]

France, with whom Britain had been at war for over 20 years from 1793 was seen, at that time, to have the most efficient Police Force in Europe. But it relied heavily on both secret and regular policing. There was, thus, notable opposition to setting up a professional, highly organized Police Force in Britain early in the nineteenth century for fear that it would replicate the dangers seen in the French system of policing. Sir Robert Peel's approach overcame these deep concerns.[47]

The first "Special Branch", responsible for assuring national security and controlling political violence, was formed in London in 1883 as a unit *within* the London Metropolitan Police Force.[48] In the interests of clarity, it should be noted that in the early twentieth century, shortly prior to World War I (as the threat of war with Germany grew), a National Security Service was created, by Executive Order, outside of the Police Force. Briefly, the Secret Intelligence Service (SIS) was established to collect intelligence covertly overseas (by a branch commonly known as "MI6") and to undertake internal intelligence gathering (by a branch commonly known as "MI5"). The SIS now operates within a statutory framework. SIS officers have extensive investigative powers but, unlike the Police (including Special Branch), they do not have direct powers to arrest suspects.[49]

Given the AL system which applied throughout the British era, Hong Kong has been subject to *Authoritarian Policing* from the outset.[50] But that policing system has been formed according to the essential policy precepts of Peelian, British policing.

The Guangdong–Hong Kong strike of 1925, organized by the relatively new CPC, threatened the security of Hong Kong. The first precursor to the Special Branch in Hong Kong was established within the Hong Kong Police Force by 1930, as an Anti-Communist Squad. By 1933, it had become the Special Branch of the Hong Kong Police.[51] Special Branch was formally disbanded prior to the

46 Reith, Charles, *A New Study of Police History* (Oliver and Boyd, London, 1956), 140.

47 "Sir Robert Peel and the Metropolitan Police", *The National Archives*, available at: http://www.nationalarchives.gov.uk/education/candp/prevention/g08/g08cs2.htm (accessed October 1, 2019).

48 Steele, John, "End for Special Branch after 122 years", *The Telegraph,* September 9, 2005, available at: http://www.telegraph.co.uk/news/uknews/1497979/End-for-Special-Branch-after-122-years.html (accessed October 1, 2019).

49 Rimington, Stella, "Intelligence, Security and the Law", *MI5 News and Speeches,* November 3, 1994, available at: https://www.mi5.gov.uk/news/intelligence-security-and-the-law (accessed October 1, 2019).

50 A major conference entitled, "Authoritarian Police and Legality in Asia", was held at Hong Kong University in February 2019. The comprehensive papers presented covered: Mainland China; Hong Kong; Japan; Singapore; South Korea; Taiwan; and Vietnam. A book based on these papers has been agreed to. The submitted papers are on file with the author.

51 Fu, H. L. and Cullen, Richard, "Political Policing in Hong Kong" (2003) 33 *Hong Kong Law Journal,* 201.

handover of BHK to China in 1997. The activities which it undertook have, not surprisingly, been taken up by other units within the Hong Kong Police Force.[52] For our purposes, we should distinguish how political policing was and remains a project housed within the general policing system of Hong Kong.

The Special Branch system was designed to undertake political policing, not least in Hong Kong. That is, a primary function was to watch out for and control security threats arising from politicized sources (rather than from mainstream criminal sources). Such work involved much spying and could lead to abusive investigation methods. What it did not set out to do, however, was to "politicize the Police". The ideal – if not always the reality – was that of a professional law enforcement system operating within a clear legally stated framework. Moreover, the police were not, under this sort of understanding, to be significantly militarized. Members of this professional force were subject to strict discipline and were in uniform – but they were civilians still, not members of or *de facto* part of the British military establishment. Although the anti-riot units which emerged after the mid-1950s were organized in a notably more military way, they remained operationally – like the Special Branch – within and under the command of the Hong Kong Police Force.

The option not chosen as a result of this British–Diceyan approach is the "two-track" mode where the State creates a separated set of laws (or "laws beyond law") – with a separated institutional enforcing system – to mediate, if not all, all seriously hostile State–citizen interactions. With this option, one secures not just political policing but a specialized, often para-military police force which, institutionally, is trained to understand their criminal-political foes as direct (and personal) political enemies. Such a police force has an expressly partisan approach to its duties.

Many examples demonstrate this alternative operational scheme to different degrees. Post-war South Korea, under US control and tutelage, provides one stark example:

> In postwar South Korea, the focus of this article, the United States helped to empower former Japanese colonial agents and consolidated the rule of Syngman Rhee, an anti-communist who deployed police against leftists seeking a transformation of the political economy and reconciliation with the North. While praising the principle that police in a democratic nation should be impartial and nonpartisan, American advisors mobilized police primarily along political lines and built up a constabulary force which provided the backbone of the South Korean Army (ROKA). Counter-Intelligence Corps

52 Ibid. The Hong Kong Police Force became the Royal Hong Kong Police Force (RHKPF) in 1969. The Royal Charter was granted in recognition of the work of the Police in containing the very serious labour-related and political (Cultural Revolution spillover) violence (see below). Upon the reversion of sovereignty on July 1, 1997, the RHKPF became the Hong Kong Police Force once more.

(CIC) officers used the programs to recruit agents for clandestine missions in the North, which was an important factor precipitating the Korean war. Political policing operations continued through the 1950s and 1960s, resulting in significant human rights violations. The South Korean police became known for torture and brutality, and the US bore important responsibility for this development.[53]

Political-legal developments: post–World War II

In this part, I review, in greater detail, aspects of the more recent political experience in BHK. It is sensible to recall, first, the fundamentals of the broad political-constitutional structure which the British deployed in Hong Kong, however.

Like many other similarly ranked jurisdictions within the Empire, Hong Kong used a form of government structurally based on the classical, pre-Parliamentary Government model such as applied during the reign of George III (1760–1820). By this time, there were clear personnel linkages between the British Government headed by the King and the Parliament. Although Lord North, a member of the House of Commons notwithstanding his title, never referred to himself as the "Prime Minister", he was a member of the King's ministry or cabinet and was regarded as the King's leading Minister by George III.[54] The King actively led his own government, especially during the earlier years of his reign and he chose his ministry from within and outside of Parliament. At this time, the Kingdom of Great Britain thus retained a strong Executive Government outside of Parliament.[55]

In Hong Kong, from 1842 to 1997, there was, in keeping with this "George III model", a strong Executive Government, headed by the Governor, which in essence, governed from outside of the Legislature. LegCo was a separated (from the Executive) component of the colonial governance structure. It was fully appointed by the Governor for close to 150 years.

53 Kuzmarov, Jeremy, "Police Training, 'Nation Building' and Political Repression in Postcolonial South Korea" (2012) 10 *The Asia Pacific Journal*, available at: http://apjjf.org/2012/10/27/Jeremy-Kuzmarov/3785/article.html (accessed October 1, 2019). For a full review of the meaning of the concept of "laws beyond law", in the context of (irregular) policing in China, see Fu, Hualing, "The Varieties of Law in China", *Human Rights in China,* July 18, 2011, available at: http://www.hrichina.org/en/crf/article/5422 (accessed October 1, 2019). For a thorough discussion of the President of China's serious, post-2013, anti-corruption campaign (including the many irregular/non-lawful/abusive enforcement methods deployed), see Fu, Hualing, "Wielding the Sword, President Xi's New Anti-Corruption Campaign" in (Rose-Akerman and Lagunes (eds.) *Greed, Corruption and the Modern State* (Edward Elgar, Cheltenham, 2015).

54 Black, Jeremy, "King George III and His Prime Ministers", *History of Government – The National Archives,* April 24, 2013, available at: https://history.blog.gov.uk/2013/04/24/george-iii-and-his-prime-ministers/ (accessed October 1, 2019).

55 Ibid.

When first established in 1843, LegCo had four Official Members (that is, three Civil Service members plus the Governor). By 1984, total LegCo membership had reached 61 (29 Official Members – 4 of whom were ex-officio and 32 Unofficial Members, that is, members appointed from outside of the Civil Service – from commerce, industry, and the professions). The British introduced limited, LegCo, "Functional Constituency" (FC) elections for the first time in 1985. The number of Official Members was reduced to 11 (including four ex-officio) and the number of Unofficial Members was raised to 46 in the same year. Of those Unofficial Members, a total of 23 were, for the first time, indirectly elected (from limited professional and commercial constituencies and from certain electoral colleges – all collectively referred to as Functional Constituencies). The first directly elected Legislators took office in 1991 when 18 LegCo members were elected by geographical constituencies. The 1991 LegCo comprised 61 members in total: 4 ex-officio; 18 appointed members, and 39 elected members (18 directly elected plus 21 FC members). By 1993, the Governor, who remained an ex-officio member, absented himself and gave up his role as President of LegCo. The Deputy President took over this role.[56]

Combined with these two institutions, the Governor (and his Civil Service/Bureaucratic Government) and LegCo, was the independent Judiciary – supported by the also independent Legal Profession.

Despite the lack of democracy, Hong Kong was allowed, post–World War II, to develop, under British rule, into the freest society in East Asia. The press and the media generally were able to flourish[57] and the Rule of Law, implemented primarily through an independent judiciary, put down deep roots.[58] Meanwhile, the task of governing Hong Kong remained in the hands of a London-appointed Governor working with a Civil Service notable for its very high level of political engagement.[59]

Politically, BHK remained mainly stable during the decades after World War II. But there were periods of violent political disruption with the worst of

56 "History of the Legislature", *Legislative Council, HKSAR,* available at: http://www.legco.gov.hk/general/english/intro/hist_lc.htm (accessed October 1, 2019). These post-1985 developments – and the later, BHK 1995 LegCo elections – are dealt with further below.

57 Bonnin, Michel, "The Press in Hong Kong – Flourishing but under Threat" (1995) 1 (September) *China Perspectives*, 48.

58 See Ghai, Yash, "Praise Is Not enough", *South China Morning Post*, March 22, 1998. See also Jones, Carol, "Politics Postponed" in (Jayasuriya (ed.)) *Law, Capitalism and Power in Asia* (Routledge, London, 1999).

59 As someone once said about Hong Kong, "Nowhere in the world combines so much civic freedom with so much political restriction". See Ko, Vanessa, "Hong Kong's Non-Election: A 'Rotten' System on Show", *Time,* March 19, 2012, available at: http://content.time.com/time/world/article/0,8599,2109397,00.html (accessed October 1, 2019).

these arising in 1967, after the Cultural Revolution[60] began in the Mainland (in 1966).[61]

In fact, the first case of serious post-war, political rioting in Hong Kong occurred in 1956, when supporters of the KMT (the (1949) losing side in the Chinese Civil War) and CPC supporters clashed violently in Tsuen Wan in the New Territories. The rioting commenced during the celebration of the "Double 10" anniversary.[62] There were 59 deaths, including a murdered Swiss national and much property damage. British military personnel were used to reinforce the Hong Kong Police Force.[63]

The next serious, post-war riots, from April, 1966, are commonly referred to as the "Star Ferry Riots". The dissatisfaction with British rule in Hong Kong at this time was high. Richard Hughes, the long-experienced Australian journalist based in Hong Kong at this time, put it this way:

> Life, as in most of Asia, is hard and cruel for many. There are gross extremes of wealth and poverty reminiscent of Shanghai in the thirties and forties. The hanging gardens and golden roofs of terraced villas on The Peak overlook the diseased scabs of squatters' huts corroding distant hillsides, the fleets of junks and sampans that are the floating homes of 100,000 people and the huddled packed tenements where another 80,000 subsist illegally on the rooftops, and which succumb so often to typhoon and fire or collapse from old age.[64]

60 For a succinct overview of the (Maoist) foundations and unfolding of the Cultural Revolution, see Watkins, Thayer, "The Great Proletarian Cultural Revolution in China, 1966–1976", San Jose State University, Department of Economics, available at: http://www.sjsu.edu/faculty/watkins/cultrev.htm (accessed October 1, 2019).

61 Wei, Christina, "1967 Leftist Riots", *Hong Kong in Transition,* available at: https://www.mtholyoke.edu/~wei20c/classweb/wp/66riots.html (hard copy retained by author). See also "Photography, the 1967 Hong Kong Riots", available at: http://hongwrong.com/1967-hk-riots/ (accessed June 19, 2016).

62 October 10, 1911 was the day the Wuchang Uprising began in Hubei Province in China. It is regarded as the start of the Chinese Revolution, which saw the overthrow of the last Imperial (Qing) Dynasty and the establishment of the (KMT) Republic of China. It remains the National Day of the Republic of China – in Taiwan. See "Double Tenth National Day", available at: http://www.taiwan.gov.tw/ct.asp?xItem=44786&CtNode=2503&mp=1008 (accessed October 1, 2019).

63 See Lee, Connie Hong-nee, *Society and Policing in Hong Kong: A Study of the 1956 Riot,* Master of Social Science Dissertation – 1995, available at: https://hub.hku.hk/bitstream/10722/27467/1/FullText.pdf (accessed June 19, 2016). The author notes that, after the 1956 riot, the Police created more military-styled units (for the first time) to deal with large-scale disturbances. See also "Hong Kong 1956 Riots", available at: https://en.wikipedia.org/wiki/Hong_Kong_1956_riots (accessed October 1, 2019).

64 Hughes, Richard, *Borrowed Place, Borrowed Time* (2nd ed.) (Andre Deutsch, London, 1976), 13. See also Wei, Christina, "1966 Star Ferry Riots", *Hong Kong in Transition,* available at: https://www.mtholyoke.edu/~wei20c/classweb/wp/66riots.html (hard copy retained by author).

A special hostility was reserved for the extensive corruption which had grown apace in the 1950s and 1960s and which the British had done little to contain. Indeed, the corruption was most insidious within the then Hong Kong Police Force. (Within ten years, a major programme to tackle corruption through the creation of the Independent Commission Against Corruption (ICAC) would achieve notable success (see further below).) The announcement of fare increases in 1966 on the vital (especially for the "grass roots"[65]) Star Ferry service across Victoria Harbour (which presaged other public transport fare increases) triggered the rioting. The rioting, concentrated in Kowloon, lasted for several days. One protester died, there was extensive property damage and many arrests – with many protesters sent to jail.[66]

The "1967 Leftist Riots", as they are known, were far more serious. They began in May 1967 and lasted until December 1967. This major political disturbance began with a minor labour dispute, but it was significantly fuelled by the spillover from the early stages of the Cultural Revolution, which was fomenting rampant turmoil in China. Over 50 people were killed during the riots or as a result of the regular bombings which took place (including some assassinations). Thousands of fake and real bombs were manufactured. Property damage was far more extensive than in 1966. The disturbances spread across Hong Kong with strong concentrations in Kowloon and on Hong Kong Island. Initially, the PRC Government in Beijing supported the rioters with "The People's Daily" in Beijing backing the uprising. There was increasing anxiousness in BHK that the PRC might consider invading and occupying Hong Kong. The Commander of the People's Liberation Army Guangzhou Military Region was said to have favoured such an invasion. It is claimed that the Chinese Premier, Zhou Enlai (2nd to Mao Zedong), vetoed this plan. Zhou is also said to have ordered the end to bomb-making and rioting by all leftist groups in late 1967.[67]

For the clear majority of the post-war period, BHK operated primarily as an "economic city" rather than as a "political city", however. Certain small groups within the growing middle class had a keen interest in politics. And left-wing activists remained even after the Cultural Revolution–driven tumult subsided. Hong Kong retained a small, core community of KMT–Taiwan sympathizers also. The British actively – and successfully – discouraged mass interest in greater

65 This is the term most commonly used in Hong Kong to refer to the mass of non-elite, ordinary working people. See *Cambridge Dictionary*, "Grassroots", available at: https://dictionary.cambridge.org/dictionary/english/grassroots (accessed October 1, 2019).

66 Wei, ibid. See also "Hong Kong 1966 Riots", available at: https://en.wikipedia.org/wiki/Hong_Kong_1966_riots (accessed October 1, 2019).

67 Wei, Christina, "1967 Leftist Riots", *Hong Kong in Transition,* available at: https://www.mtholyoke.edu/~wei20c/classweb/wp/66riots.html (hard copy retained by author). See also "Photography, the 1967 Hong Kong Riots", available at: http://hongwrong.com/1967-hkriots/ (accessed October 1, 2019). See also "Hong Kong 167 Leftist Riots" available at: https://en.wikipedia.org/wiki/Hong_Kong_1967_Leftist_riots (accessed October 1, 2019).

politicization of Hong Kong, however.[68] This complied with the unwritten provisions in their "pact" with Beijing,[69] which endured until the early 1990s.[70] It also suited Hong Kong's Chinese and non-Chinese business elites. They typically felt that the lack of electoral politics was good for trade and business. And they were, throughout this period, highly influential with the Government.[71]

The ordinary mass of people remained largely apolitical. Elite views had some influence in this regard. But other factors were also important in explaining this comparative lack of interest in politics. The vast majority of the post-war population had migrated from – mostly fled – the PRC. Many of them saw Hong Kong as a staging post – their aim was to migrate (or at least see their children migrate) usually to a range of Western, English-speaking countries. They saw themselves as "sojourners".[72] Another important factor was the rapid economic growth in Hong Kong. Although people often lived in very difficult circumstances, with many new migrants from the earlier post-war period having to live in hillside shantytowns, they had entered an economy which was, year after year, growing at a prodigious rate. This reality offered hope. It created a more positive general mood than one would normally encounter in such a poverty-ridden environment. It helped create an atmosphere where concentrating on family economic betterment rather than on politics made good sense to many. The Government also re-emphasized a policy, particularly after the political turmoil of the 1960s, of

68 Sing, Ming, *Hong Kong's Tortuous Democratization* (Routledge-Curzon, London, 2004), Chapters 3 and 4.

69 In 1958, there were discussions between the UK and BHK Governments about the introduction of full democratic governance institutions in BHK. The CPC let the UK know that it opposed any such political reforms being implemented in Hong Kong, however, and the proposal did not proceed. See Guilford, Gwynn, "The Secret History of Hong Kong's Democratic Stalemate", *The Atlantic*, October 14, 2014, available at: http://www.theatlantic.com/international/archive/2014/10/the-secret-history-of-hong-kongs-democratic-stalemate/381424/ (accessed October 1, 2019). See also Miners, Norman, *The Government and Politics of Hong Kong* (5th ed.) (Oxford University Press, Hong Kong, 1991).

70 The UK appointed a professional politician, Chris Patten, as the last Governor of Hong Kong in 1992. Patten attempted, ultimately with limited success, to introduce greater democratization over the period 1992–1997. Beijing reacted strongly and adversely to these political initiatives. Beijing replaced the 1995 LegCo with a Provisional LegCo which operated for a year after July 1, 1997. Despite these tensions, the handover ultimately proceeded fairly smoothly. See, further, Ghai, Yash, *Hong Kong's New Constitutional Order* (2nd ed.) (Hong Kong University Press, Hong Kong, 1999); and Cullen, Richard, "Revenue Law in Hong Kong: The Future", in (Wacks (ed.)) *The New Legal Order in Hong Kong* (Hong Kong University Press, Hong Kong, 1999), Chapter 12.

71 Goodstadt, Leo, *Uneasy Partners*. See also Littlewood, Michael, "Taxation without Representation: The History of Hong Kong's Troublingly Successful Tax System" (2002) 3 *British Tax Review*, 212.

72 See Lau, Siu-kai, *Society and Politics in Hong Kong* (Chinese University Press, Hong Kong, 1991); and Lau, Siu-kai, "Chinese Familism in an Urban-Industrial Setting: The Case of Hong Kong" (1981) 43 *Journal of Marriage and the Family*, 181.

consulting widely by providing institutional avenues for community leaders and others to express views on policy development and implementation.[73]

If one had to pick a single initiative of the Government which did most (a) to reinforce Hong Kong's adherence to the Rule of Law; (b) to buttress acceptance of benevolent-autocratic government; and (c) to enhance social stability, it would be the establishment of the Independent Commission Against Corruption in 1974. As the ICAC explains:

> Hong Kong was in a state of rapid change in the sixties and seventies. The massive growth in population and the fast expansion of the manufacturing industry accelerated the pace of social and economic development. The Government, while maintaining social order and delivering the bare essentials in housing and other services, was unable to satisfy the insatiable needs of the exploding population. This provided a fertile environment for the unscrupulous. In order to earn a living and secure the services which they needed the public was forced to adopt the "backdoor route". "Tea money", "black money", "hell money" – whatever the phrase – became not only well-known to many Hong Kong people, but accepted with resignation as a necessary evil.[74]

Within around a year of the ICAC commencing operations, major inroads were made into the massive level of corruption prevailing. The Hong Kong Police Force (previously regarded as "the best police force money could buy") was brought to account with numbers of corrupt police going to jail. In particular, the ICAC was successful in extraditing and prosecuting Chief Superintendent Godber who was jailed for four years in 1975.[75] Ever since the ICAC broke, the back of corruption in Hong Kong, the City-State has enjoyed an enviable reputation for being a "clean" city and a good place to do business. In 2018, Hong Kong ranked 14th in a worldwide Corruption Perceptions Index, level with Austria and Iceland, and ahead of Belgium, Ireland, and Japan.[76]

The confluence of the factors noted above produced (a) a generally stable political climate; (b) government by an elite-influenced civil service; and (c) poor prospects for the growth of party politics.[77] The system was intrinsically unreceptive to the growth of popular lobbying groups seeking government assistance.

73 Young, Simon N. M. and Cullen, Richard, *Electing Hong Kong's Chief Executive* (Hong Kong University Press, Hong Kong, 2010), Chapter 3.

74 "[ICAC] Brief History", available at: http://www.icac.org.hk/mobile/en/about_icac/bh/index.html (accessed October 1, 2019). Hong Kong was strongly influenced in its move to establish the ICAC by the earlier, successful, experience of Singapore in drastically reducing corruption (see Goodstadt, *Uneasy Partners,* 141).

75 "Brief History", ibid.

76 Transparency International, *Corruption Perceptions Index 2018,* available at: https://www.transparency.org/cpi2018 (accessed October 1, 2019).

77 Sing, *Hong Kong's Tortuous Democratization*, Chapters 7 and 8.

The Government also helped deflect community disaffection and agitation by moving to address many key problems on its own initiative. The Government also instituted comprehensive programmes (particularly from the 1970s) addressing housing (building one of the world's most massive public housing systems within a single city), education, health, and infrastructure development.[78]

From the late 1970s, however, Beijing increasingly became a focus of concern and anticipation. The final acquisition Treaty signed by the UK and China in 1898 related to the area of Hong Kong known as the "New Territories". The New Territories comprise by far the majority of the area of modern Hong Kong. This final Treaty, unlike the earlier Treaties, only granted a 99-year lease over the New Territories to the UK. It was the approaching expiry of this New Territories, Lease Treaty which prompted the UK to initiate discussions with the PRC in the late 1970s on the future of Hong Kong. In these negotiations, the PRC held almost all the "high cards". Beijing, early on in the negotiations, made it clear that Hong Kong was to revert to PRC sovereignty on July 1, 1997 – the day after the expiry of the New Territories Lease Treaty.[79]

These negotiations led to the signing of the Joint Declaration between London and Beijing in 1984, which set out the agreement for the return of full sovereignty over BHK to the PRC from July 1, 1997.[80] The Joint Declaration provided that the essence of the economic, social, and political systems which had developed and been applied in BHK were to be retained for 50 years (in the sense of *at least* – no change after 50 years is mandated by the Joint Declaration). The Joint Declaration also promised that a Basic Law would be established for the new HKSAR, to take effect on July 1, 1997.[81] This Basic Law, founded significantly on the Joint Declaration, was passed by the National People's Congress (NPC) in Beijing in April 1990.[82] The Basic Law does not have any *sunset clause*. That is, it is worded, on the face of it, to apply indefinitely. (The Basic Law is discussed in detail in Chapter 6.)

On June 4, 1989, the planning for a "smooth transition" was profoundly disrupted when the PRC Government used battlefield weapons, including tanks, to

78 See, further, Chapter 5.

79 Hong Kong consists of Hong Kong Island, the Kowloon Peninsula situated on the Mainland opposite Hong Kong Island, the New Territories comprising the area north of Kowloon up to the Shenzhen River, and 235 islands.

80 Joint Declaration of the Government of the United Kingdom and Northern Island and the Government of the People's Republic of China on the Question of Hong Kong (1984). The PRC declared in the Joint Declaration that it had decided to resume the exercise of sovereignty over Hong Kong (the leased territories, together with Hong Kong Island and Kowloon) with effect from July 1, 1997. The UK declared that it would restore Hong Kong to the PRC with effect from July 1, 1997. The Joint Declaration entered came into force on May 27, 1985, when the two governments exchanged instruments of ratification. It was registered as a treaty at the United Nations by the Chinese and British governments on June 12, 1985. The timing, process, and Chinese dominance of negotiations are described in detail in Ghai, *Hong Kong's New Constitutional Order*, 36–56.

81 Ibid.

82 The Basic Law of the Hong Kong Special Administrative Region of the People's Republic of China.

end a massive, long-running demonstration for political reform by thousands of its own citizens in and around Tiananmen Square in Beijing.[83]

This terrible incident swiftly led to what were the largest ever public demonstrations seen in BHK. Over 1 million people are reported to have marched, firstly in support of the protesting students, in May 1989, and then in protest, against Beijing, on June 5, 1989.[84] Notwithstanding their massive size, the protests were peaceful and not, in themselves, disruptive of the economic, social, and political order within BHK. They were fundamentally galvanizing, politically, however. And they were a marker of the deep anxiety now abroad across a clear majority of the Hong Kong Chinese population. That nervousness triggered an upsurge in emigration and some real market trembling. It also played a major role in ensuring the remarkably positive outcome for the newly emerging Pan-Democrat (PD) movement in the 1991 LegCo Elections.[85]

The 1991 LegCo Elections were the first time any direct election system applied to LegCo Elections. In essence, a dual-member, First Past the Post (FPP) system was used for the 18 directly elected seats out of the total of 60 seats (including the Governor as President of LegCo).[86] The PDs won 16 of the new, directly elected seats.[87]

The BHK Government responded rapidly to this deeply worrying and bloody turn of events by launching certain measures to try and restore some calm and reassurance within BHK. Four key measures were announced: the go-ahead of the construction of a huge new airport (with much additional, related new infrastructure – cost US$20 billion approximately[88]); the provision of full British passports for thousands of more senior bureaucrats (and their families); the rapid expansion of tertiary education facilities within Hong Kong; and the enactment

83 "Tiananmen Square", *Cambridge Paperback Encyclopedia* (3rd ed.) (Cambridge University Press, Cambridge, 1999), 862. Tiananmen Square, which covers 98 acres, is the largest public square in the world.

84 Beatty, Bob, *Democracy, Asian Values and Hong Kong: Evaluating Political Elite Beliefs* (Praeger, Westport, 2003), Chapter 1.

85 Ibid.

86 Briefly, in an FPP system, the member with the most votes wins; thus, in a three-cornered contest, anyone who secures at least one-third – plus one – of the votes cast will win.

87 This partial democratization of LegCo Elections had been agreed to in negotiations between London and Beijing. There is a sound review of the lead up to and the outcome of the 1991 LegCo Elections in Louie, Kin-Shuen, "Political Parties" in (Sung and Lee (eds.)) *The Other Hong Kong Report 1991* (Chinese University Press, Hong Kong, 1991), Chapter 4. The 1991 LegCo was made up of 18 directly elected members; 21 Functional Constituency members; 17 Governor-appointed members; 3 ex-officio members, and the Governor as President of LegCo.

88 This massive project (called the Airport Core Project) included the construction of extensive new road and rail lines (including very large bridges); massive reclamations; the building of an entire new satellite city; and the building of two new container ports. Total cost, in 1997, was estimated to be around US$20 billion (see Wong, Raymond, "A Technical and Project Review of 10 Airport Core Projects and Their Influence on Current Developments", *City University of Hong Kong Archive,* available at: http://www6.cityu.edu.hk/construction_archive/major_reference_pdf.aspx?id=350 (accessed October 1, 2019).

of a Hong Kong Bill of Rights Ordinance (BORO) – which largely incorporated the UN International Covenant on Civil and Political Rights into the domestic law of BHK.[89]

The BORO was both entrenched and given overriding status by an amendment to the effective Constitution of BHK, the Letters Patent. Thus, the BHK Courts were now empowered to apply the BORO not only in the interpretation of all existing BHK Ordinances but also in the interpretation of Ordinances not yet passed. Technically, this new power on constitutional review (that is, the power now given to the BHK Courts to strike down legislation found to be not in compliance with the BORO) applied only until June 30, 1997. As we will see below, however, the authorizing power of the BORO has been incorporated as a part of Hong Kong's post-1997 constitutional framework via the Basic Law.[90]

The BHK Courts moved fairly swiftly to recognize their new powers and to apply them in a series of cases, often related to the Criminal Law. As Professor Jones notes:

> Between 1991 and 1997 the BORO proved a formidable weapon, used repeatedly to bring the government and its agencies to account.[91]

Prior to June 4, 1989, the Government in BHK had not been minded to introduce any sort of specific legislation to protect individual rights. Although in BHK, LegCo was, constitutionally, a subordinate legislature to the Parliament at Westminster, within those confines, a localized form of Dicey's doctrine of Parliamentary Sovereignty applied: the Courts of BHK could not actually strike down validly enacted LegCo laws. As Dicey had said:

> Parliament has … the right … to make or unmake any law whatever. … English judges do not claim or exercise the power to repeal a Statute, whilst Acts of Parliament may override and constantly do override the law of the judges.[92]

I discuss the introduction of the BORO – and the Basic Law – and how they fit, or do not, within a Diceyan constitutional framework in Chapter 6.

89 Cullen, Richard, "Hong Kong Revenue Law: The Present, 1997 and Beyond" (1993) *Tax Notes International*, 1109.

90 Yap, Po Jen, *Constitutional Dialogue in Common Law Asia* (Oxford University Press, Oxford, 2015), Chapter 3.

91 Jones, Carol A. G., *Lost in China: Law Culture and Identity in Post-1997 Hong Kong* (Cambridge University Press, Cambridge, 2015), Chapter 2.

92 Dicey, A. V, *Introduction to the Study of the Law of the Constitution* (MacMillan, London, 1885) 39ff. See also Blackshield, Tony, "The Constitution and Judicial Review" (1999) 74 *Australian Law Reform Commission Reform Journal*, 40, available at: http://www.austlii.edu.au/au/journals/ALRCRefJl/1999/8.html (accessed October 1, 2019).

5 Revenue and the Rule of Law

Introduction

Discussions about the role of a significantly free media in maintaining the Rule of Law are frequent – and pertinent. The essence of this argument is that:

> The Rule of Law requires freedom of speech and the media. People must be free to comment and assemble without fear and be able to criticize the actions of government. The role of journalists in this process is pivotal. The media remains an effective means of promoting accountability in government, and journalists play an essential role in upholding the Rule of Law. If their sources of information are not protected, and they themselves are open to legal action which prevents them from reporting in the public interest, the Rule of Law is threatened.[1]

It is much less common to ask, though, how much does the Rule of Law cost?[2] That is, what are the overall costs of establishing and running a long term, thriving Rule of Law system – and where does the money to fund such a system come from? These are plainly relevant questions. One working assumption appears to be that it is enough for a jurisdiction to aim to establish the Rule of Law at the

1 See "Free Speech and the Media", *Rule of Law Institute of Australia*, available at: https://www.ruleoflaw.org.au/priorities/free-speech-and-the-media/ (accessed October 1, 2019). See also Tso Kevin K. S., "Fundamental Political and Constitutional Norms: Hong Kong and Macau Compared" (2012) 13 *Australian Journal of Asian Law*, available at: https://papers.ssrn.com/sol3/papers.cfm?abstract_id=2159544 (accessed October 1, 2019).

2 A Google search of "How much does the Rule of Law cost? and "Paying for the Rule of Law" generate results looking at litigation costs or the need for legal aid but no articles looking at the funding of the Rule of Law generally which explain why this is important. A US book (Holmes, Stephen and Sunstein, Cass R., *The Cost of Rights: Why Liberty Depends on Taxes* (Norton, New York, 1999) investigates the "cost of rights" in the sense that rights, not least social welfare entitlements, need to be funded. However, the focus is not on funding the general infrastructure needed for a successful Rule of Law regime.

core of its governance system. If that aim is essentially sincere, then somehow, this being a "good thing", funding should materialize.[3]

Over 800 years ago, however, at the time of the creation of what many regard as the most important foundational Rule of Law document, the Magna Carta,[4] a connection between funding and the Rule of Law was strikingly clear, in the sense that the grave need for increased public finances helped impel the creation of this seminal Common Law document:

> King John, known as John Lackland (Norman French, Johan sanz Terre), ruled what has come to be known as the Angevin Empire from 1199 to 1216. That Empire included England, certain Provinces in the West of France (bordering the Atlantic Ocean) and the Eastern half of Ireland. John was an unpopular King both in reality, at the time, and in literature since (King John was the "bad King" who features in the (still popular) tales of the folklore hero "Robin Hood", who, with his "Merry Men" became famous by defying the King as they "robbed from the rich to give to the poor"). Despite having administrative competence, John was disliked for his spitefulness and cruelty. Worse still, he was notably unsuccessful in his battles in France, which were meant to regain lands lost there earlier. These attempts to recover French parts of the Angevin Empire proved to be as costly as they were fruitless. It was here that a key explanation for the Barons rebellion lies. Much of the financing for the failed battles in France came from extensive taxation of the English Barons. By the Spring of 1215, a core of insurgent Barons, working with Steven Langton, the Archbishop of Canterbury (the highest leader of the Church in England) had sworn support for the Realm and the Church – but renounced their feudal ties to King John. Moreover, they drew up a written list of demands to protect their principal interests, know, in draft, as "The Articles of the Barons". At this time, the Rebel Barons also marched on and took control of London, Lincoln and Exeter.[5]

3 "The rule of law is strong in a country where people can criticise the law and those in power openly, and in public. People should not be afraid of the government and its officials: judges, politicians, police, and other government officers. Appropriate checks and balances on the power of officials ensure that an individual does not feel fearful of being persecuted if they criticise someone who has power". This quotation is taken from the discussion of the Rule of Law in "Free Speech and the Media". That discussion is, within its own limits, concise and comprehensive. There is zero discussion about the cost of establishing and maintaining a robust Rule of Law system, however.

4 Cowdery, Nicholas, "Magna Carta and the Rule of Law", *LexisNexis, Australia*, June 5, 2015, available at: https://www.lexisnexis.com.au/en/insights-and-analysis/rule-of-law/2015/05jun2015-magna-carta-and-the-rule-of-law (accessed October 1, 2019).

5 Cullen, Richard, "Magna Carta 800 Years on: A Sino-Euro Reflection", *HKU Legal Scholarship Blog*, June 7, 2015, available at: http://researchblog.law.hku.hk/2015/06/richard-cullen-marks-800-years-of-magna_7.html (accessed October 1, 2019).

Within about a year, King John (and the Barons) had repudiated the agreement. Soon after, in 1216, King John died. The Magna Carta was reissued, with certain variations, many times after this. Three of the original 63 clauses have survived to this day.[6] It remains both a pivotal source document for the Rule of Law as we still understand it[7] and a document originally agreed to in order to relieve acute stress within the Kingdom's financial system.

I argue in this chapter that it is central to the operation of a successful Rule of Law regime that it be securely well funded. This reasoning applies to both *thin* and *thick* versions of the Rule of Law.[8] The stability and prosperity built during the BHK era demonstrate the enduring economic and social benefits which can be underpinned by such a regime and which can, in turn, reinforce the fundamental success of a Rule of Law system – a success which has continued into the HKSAR era.

Strongly worded arguments are regularly made that the Rule of Law in the HKSAR is being eroded arising from initiatives emanating from Beijing.[9] And there are strong rebuttals of these views.[10] A former Chief Secretary of both BHK and the HKSAR discussed Beijing's intervention in Hong Kong at an invited meeting with the Vice President of the US and in meetings with other US officials

6 Ibid.

7 Cowdery, "Magna Carta and the Rule of Law".

8 As discussed in Chapter 1, Peerenboom draws a distinction between "thin" and "thick" versions of the Rule of Law. The definition used here is the *thin version*. The *thick version* includes additional elements, according to this typology, including certain market-based economic systems, institutions of democratic governance, and conceptions of human rights. See Peerenboom, Randall, *China's Long March toward Rule of Law* (Cambridge University Press, Cambridge, 2002), Chapter 1; and "Thin Rule of Law versus Thick Rule of Law", *Asia Law*, November 26, 2015 (where the difference is concisely discussed), available at: https://asialaw.wordpress.com/2015/11/26/thin-rule-of-law-versus-thick-rule-of-law/ (accessed October 1, 2019).

9 See, for example, Haas, Benjamin, "UK Lawyers Say Hong Kong Rule of Law under Threat after Jailing of Activists", *The Guardian*, October 16, 2017, available at: https://www.theguardian.com/world/2017/oct/16/uk-lawyers-say-hong-kong-rule-of-law-under-threat-after-jailing-of-activists (accessed October 1, 2019); Cheung, Tony, "Ignore People's Aspirations at Your Peril, Hong Kong's Last Governor [Chris Patten] Warns", *South China Morning Post,* November 16, 2016, available at: https://www.scmp.com/news/hong-kong/politics/article/2049434/hong-kongs-last-governor-chris-patten-lauds-rule-law-during (accessed October 1, 2019); and Cheung, Elizabeth, "US Government Stands by Vocal Concern about Hong Kong's Autonomy, after Beijing's Complaints of 'Distortion and Defamation'", *South China Morning Post,* March 2, 2019, available at: https://www.scmp.com/news/hong-kong/hong-kong-economy/article/2188346/hong-kong-has-been-acting-accordance-rule-law-says (accessed October 1, 2019).

10 See Cross, Grenville, "The Rule of Law Stands Firm in Hong Kong", *The Guardian,* October 26, 2017, available at: https://www.theguardian.com/world/2017/oct/25/the-rule-of-law-stands-firm-in-hong-kong (accessed October 1, 2019); and Cross, Grenville, "HK Judiciary Independent, Just, Upholds Rule of Law", *China Daily,* September 13, 2018, available at: https://www.chinadailyhk.com/articles/79/164/72/1536804551458.html (accessed October 1, 2019).

and experts during a visit to the US in March 2019.[11] The Vice President's concern about rights and freedoms in the HKSAR was stressed. A former Director of Public Prosecutions in the HKSAR responded firmly emphasizing how well rights and freedoms are protected in Hong Kong. He relied, inter alia, on the well-regarded, US-based, World Justice Project (WJP) Rule of Law Index for 2019, which placed the HKSAR 16th out of 126 jurisdictions ahead of the US at 20th out of 126.[12]

At this point, it is timely, to recall (from Chapter 1) what the Rule of Law signifies, especially in the context of Hong Kong. Despite the scope for continual debate over the detail of what the Rule of Law means, I take the view that there is a broadly based, sound consensus as to its core meaning and essential elements. I agree with Randall Peerenboom that:

> At its most basic, [the] Rule of Law refers to a system in which law imposes meaningful limits on the state and individual members of the ruling elite, as captured in a notion of a government of laws, supremacy of law and equality of all before the law.

The WJP defines the Rule of Law in similar terms to these with one added rider, that: "Justice is delivered by competent, ethical, and independent representatives and neutrals who are of sufficient number, have adequate resources, and reflect the makeup of the communities they serve".[13]

Assessing the Rule of Law

The British Empire, at its peak, was more widespread than any other. It included huge jurisdictions, such as British India (encompassing modern-day India, Pakistan, and Bangladesh) and small, maritime-trading, city-states like Singapore and Hong Kong. The British brought the Common Law to all of these together with the doctrine of the Rule of Law. This was the *thin version* of the Rule of Law.

India is today the world's largest single democracy (with around four times the population of the US). It has a comprehensive, written Constitution which draws

11 Churchill, Owen, Lum, Alvin, "Hong Kong's Former No 2 Anson Chan Meets Mike Pence in Washington as US Report Criticises Beijing 'Intervention' in City's Affairs", *South China Morning Post,* March 23, 2019, available at: https://www.scmp.com/news/china/diplomacy/article/2188945/huawei-cfo-meng-wanzhou-canadian-court-us-extradition-hearing (accessed October 1, 2019).

12 Cross, Grenville, "Anson Chan, Say It as It Is or Forever Hold Your Peace", *China Daily,* March 29, 2019, available at: http://www.chinadaily.com.cn/hkedition/2019-03/29/content_37452988.htm (accessed October 1, 2019). See also "Rule of Law Index 2019", *World Justice Project* (WJP), available at: https://worldjusticeproject.org/our-work/research-and-data/wjp-rule-law-index-2019 (accessed October 1, 2019).

13 WJP.

on core Common Law principles. The Constitution also has significant human rights protections which are ultimately overseen by an authoritative Supreme Court with powers of final interpretation. Fundamental rights are set out in Part III on the Constitution.[14]

The way in which India manages to run democratic elections on such a scale is, as Robin Jeffrey recently noted, extraordinary. He also explains that the Election Commission of India (ECI) must take much of the credit for this singular achievement. It transpires that this feat throws light on India's strengths and weaknesses all at once; Professor Jeffrey says that the ECI: "[Is] one of the few institutions in India that maintains a reputation for efficiency, toughness and rectitude".[15]

The WJP – Rule of Law 2019 (WJP Index) gave India a Global Ranking of 68 (out of 126 jurisdictions reviewed) for Rule of Law compliance (Denmark was ranked number 1; China's ranking was 82).[16] The Transparency International Corruption Perception Index 2018 (CPI-2018) ranked India at 78th out of 180 jurisdictions for corruption risk (Denmark again ranked number 1; China's ranking was 87).[17]

The WJP Index ranked the HKSAR at 16th out of 126 jurisdictions for Rule of Law compliance and the CPI-2018 ranked the HKSAR at equal 14th out of 180 jurisdictions for perceived corruption risk. The comparable figures for Singapore were as follows: WJP Index 13th out of 126 and CPI-2018 3rd out of 180.[18]

14 *Constitution of India*, National Government Portal of India, available at: https://www.india.gov.in/my-government/constitution-india (accessed October 1, 2019). See also Gettleman, Jeffrey, Kumar, Hari, and Schultz, Kai, "Hundreds of Cases a Day and a Flair for Drama: India's Crusading Supreme Court", *New York Times*, September 27, 2018, available at: https://www.nytimes.com/2018/09/27/world/asia/india-supreme-court-modi.html (accessed October 1, 2019).

15 Jeffrey, Robin, "How India Runs the Biggest Elections in the World", *Australia India Institute, University of Melbourne*, November 1, 2018, available at: https://pursuit.unimelb.edu.au/articles/how-india-runs-the-biggest-elections-in-the-world (accessed October 1, 2019).

16 WJP.

17 *Corruption Perception Index- 2018*, Transparency International, available at: https://www.transparency.org/news/pressrelease/corruption_perceptions_index_2018 (accessed October 1, 2019).

18 Many commentators, especially in the West, have labelled Singapore as being at least a "soft authoritarian" State. For a thoughtful overview of this debate, see Huang, Kun, "Is Singapore an Authoritarian Government", *Quora*, October 7, 2017, available at: https://www.quora.com/Is-Singapore-an-authoritarian-government (accessed October 1, 2019). The very good ranking of Singapore on the WJP Index and the CPI-2018 is interesting. Whatever may be the impact of the Singapore version of AL (with its de facto One-Party governance system (see Huang above)), Singapore still ranks in the top 2% worldwide under the CPI-2018 and within the top 11% under the WJP Index. Comparable figures for the US are as follows: CPI-2018, within top 13%; WJP Index, within top 16%. The introduction to this chapter highlighted the strongly argued need for a free media to support the Rule of Law. Singapore, again, presents an example which questions this position. According to the World Press Freedom Index 2018, Singapore ranks 151 out of 180 jurisdictions. This places it within the lowest 16% for press freedom – yet it is within the top 11% for Rule of

India is, of course, a vastly different jurisdiction with immensely greater governance problems than the HKSAR or Singapore. Just to begin with, it has a population that is about 170 times that of Hong Kong and around 230 times that of Singapore. This, however, supports the key point being made in this chapter: institutional structures supporting the Rule of Law are necessary to establish such a regime, but they are far from sufficient. Without far-reaching, robust funding, they will fail to deliver the Rule of Law effectively for all – for the mass of people or the "grass roots". Lack of adequate funding for the Rule of Law structures will continuously obstruct the proper development of any such regime.

This is the position in which India has found itself for decades and where it still finds itself. India gained its independence in 1947. Around two years later, the CPC overcame the KMT in the Chinese Civil War and established the PRC on October 1, 1949. At that time, the per capita GDP in China was roughly the same as that of India. Today, notwithstanding significant growth in India, the Chinese economy is around five times the size of the Indian economy using a basic GDP per capita measure.[19] India's economic development delay is an important factor underpinning the Rule of Law lag evident in the ranking figures noted above.

Public revenue in Hong Kong: key aspects[20]

One can reasonably claim that Hong Kong is a remarkable tax policy museum. For First World jurisdiction, it has an unusually limited range of taxes – there are no Sales Taxes nor any formal Capital Gains Tax, for example.[21] But one can also argue that this has been a centre of revenue policy innovation.[22] The innovation, above all, has pivoted on successfully accessing non-usual sources of public revenue (especially land-related revenues). This has allowed for the application,

Law compliance according to the WJP Index. The HKSAR ranks 70th out of 180 for press freedom. India ranks 138 out of 180 and China ranks 176 out of 180. See "2018 World Press Freedom Index", *Reporters without Borders*, available at: https://rsf.org/en/ranking (accessed October 1, 2019).

19 See Bhardwaj, Ankit, "What Is the Comparative Picture of Economic Growth of India and China since 1950", *China India Comparisons*, January 6, 2015, available at: https://www.quora.com/What-is-the-comparative-picture-of-economic-growth-of-India-and-China-since-1950 (accessed October 1, 2019).

20 This review is based on an extract from Cullen, Richard, "Hong Kong's Remarkable Land Revenue Regime" (2014) 14 *Asian Business Law*, 193.

21 Cullen, Richard and Wong, Antonietta, "Globalization and the Hong Kong Revenue Regime" in (Cockfield (ed.)) *Globalization and Its Tax Discontents: Tax Policy and International Investments* (University of Toronto Press, Toronto, 2010).

22 Hong Kong has consistently used British terminology to describe its public revenue system, thus the primary taxation statute is the *Inland Revenue Ordinance* (1947). One usually talks of the revenue regime and revenue policy (although the terms tax system and tax policy are also used). As we will see, the varied sources of public revenues which are not, in fact, taxes make this British terminology more apt, overall.

from the creation of British Hong Kong (in 1842) to the present day, of an instinctive version of "Occam's Razor" to system review.[23] The result is that tax reform has been kept to a minimum. Hong Kong thus retains a Revenue Regime (RR) which is (formally) low tax, clearly simple (with low compliance costs), and it has generated revenues (within the special and relevant features of Hong Kong society) sufficient to build excellent infrastructure to often provide first-rate government services, to enable Hong Kong to stay virtually debt free, and to amass huge fiscal reserves. It is a system well equipped to pay for and maintain a robust Rule of Law regime.

The very success of the RR has helped entrench certain problems, however. Maintaining comparatively massive reserves to provide security against future uncertainties has been a paramount concern since the beginning of the BHK era. Given Hong Kong's very strong public finances, the poverty gap is, prima facie, far wider than it should be; and the (revenue policy) planning to cope with the onset of major demographic and other changes is excessively tentative. Fiscal prudence is no bad thing, but Hong Kong has a locked-in tilt towards "over-prudence". Moreover, the cost of doing anything in Hong Kong is conspicuously inflated by the very high cost of land – ultimately provided by a de facto monopoly supplier: the Hong Kong Government. Yet, as we will see, the overall success of land-based funding of public revenue has also provided the basis for some important positive responses to these shortcomings.

From its inception, British Hong Kong was a Free Port, so Customs Duties were not available as a source of revenue. Also from the outset, the British did not allow any sale of freehold land. All land was made available as leasehold land (with strict conditions attached to each particular lease). Landholders wishing to vary the building usage allowed under a particular lease had, on each such occasion, to pay a premium to the Hong Kong Government to secure the variation.[24]

Moreover, the practice grew of restricting the availability of land for development. This tended to drive up the price of land (towards the upper limits of what

23 The test associated with William of Occam (1285–1349 AD) is commonly rendered as Pluralitas non est ponenda sine necessitate or "plurality should not be posited without necessity". See, further, Occam's Razor, at: http://www.skepdic.com/occam.html (accessed August 28, 2019).

24 The Free Port status followed the earlier British Singapore model. Following British acceptance of defeat in the American War of Independence in 1783, British colonial policy emphasized an avoidance of London-imposed, long-distance tax or other imposts and maximum reliance on local sources of income. See, further, Cullen and Wong, "Globalization and the Hong Kong Revenue Regime". The Hong Kong Anglican Cathedral occupies a grant of freehold land. Landholders in the New Territories have also historically been allowed, by the government, to enjoy certain special rights to land based on ancestral rights which derive from membership of long established communities in the New Territories. See Nissim, Roger, *Land Administration and Practice in Hong Kong* (2nd ed.) (Hong Kong University Press, Hong Kong, 2008).

the market would accept) and also revenue receipts.[25] When one factored in the consistent strong, opium-based, growth in the economy over the first 50-plus years of British Hong Kong, the Government found that its land-based revenue regime more than compensated for the shortfall in expected funding from the opium-based revenue stream.[26] Indeed, the colony's fiscal foundations proved to be so sturdy that, within around 40 years of its founding, the Hong Kong Government had already amassed more than one year of total, normal, public expenditure in Fiscal Reserves.[27]

The Hong Kong Government has also historically been able to control expenditure quite effectively. Services were originally limited in keeping with nineteenth

25 In 1995/1996, during the last years of British rule, the Hong Kong government still derived some 32% of total revenues from land-related transactions (including sales, lease modification premiums, and Stamp Duties – but not including Profits Tax and Salaries Tax arising directly from the real estate sector). When one adds in the Profits Tax paid by developers and all the others involved in construction and Salaries Tax paid by those working in the sector, the HKSAR Government relied on land transaction–related revenues for around 50% of its income, see Halkyard, Andrew, "The Hong Kong Tax Paradox" (1998) *Revenue Law Journal*, 1. Twenty years later, these figures have increased. Land-related revenues (land sales and lease modification premiums) accounted for 27% of total revenues in the 2017–2018 financial year and related Stamp Duties made up 15% of total revenues. Once one adds in Profits Tax paid by developers and builders and Salaries Tax paid by their employees, land transaction–related revenues exceed 50% (see *The 2018–19 Budget Speech [Hong Kong]*, available at: https://www.budget.gov.hk/2018/eng/budget10.html (accessed October 1, 2019)). This heavy reliance on land transaction revenues in Hong Kong bears some resemblance to the theories propagated by Henry George, the nineteenth century American economist and social reformer who long advocated the introduction of a single tax on the unimproved value of all land to replace all other taxes. See Smith, J. P., *Taxing Popularity: The Story of Taxation in Australia* (Federalism Research Centre, Canberra, 1993), 18–24; and *Dictionary of American Biography,* (1st. ed.), "George, Henry" (Johnson and Malone (eds.)), Vol. VII (Charles Scribner's Sons, New York, 1931), 211–212. A Henry George follower, Lizzie Magie, created the precursor to the board game Monopoly in 1904 to demonstrate his theories (see Pilon, Mary, "Monopoly's Inventor: The Progressive Who Didn't Pass 'Go'", *New York Times,* February 15, 2015, available at: https://www.nytimes.com/2015/02/15/business/behind-monopoly-an-inventor-who-didnt-pass-go.html (accessed October 1, 2019).

26 See, further, Cullen, Richard and Tso, Kevin K. S., "Using Opium as a Public Revenue Source – Not as Easy as It Looks: The British Hong Kong Experience" (2012) *British Tax Review*, 226.

27 In 1884, Hong Kong was one of the few colonies within the British Empire carrying zero debt. In fact, Hong Kong ran a current account surplus for most of the years from 1873 to 1882 with the surplus in some years reaching close to 20% of total expenditure, thus allowing the accumulation of very significant reserves. See *The Colonial Office List for 1884* (Harrison, London, 1862–1925), 18, 92. This savings habit has persisted; in February, 2019 Hong Kong's public foreign reserves exceeded US$434 billion (see https://tradingeconomics.com/hong-kong/foreign-exchange-reserves (accessed October 1, 2019) of which (in 2018) over US$140 billion are Government Fiscal Reserves (around two years of total current Hong Kong government expenditure.). See *The 2018–2019 Budget*, available at: https://www.budget.gov.hk/2018/eng/budget11.html (accessed October 1, 2019).

century practice, but the remarkable self-reliance of the majority Chinese population has also been a decisive factor in lowering demands on government. This was the case as the British established their Hong Kong colony and it remains the case to a large extent today.[28]

This land-related revenue regime was further strengthened as the total area comprising the Crown Colony increased significantly, initially in 1860 and then in 1898. The expansion of Hong Kong increased the Hong Kong Government's "land-bank" greatly.

The land-related income streams arising from the opium-based, booming economy during the first 50 years of the colony proved to be remarkably strong. The land-based revenue system has proved to be so successful that it remains a mainstay of the Hong Kong fiscal regime to this day. These foundations were also fundamental in allowing the colony to thrive without need to resort to any sort of direct income taxation for around 100 years – and when such taxes came, they were kept low and simple – see below.

A good way to get a feel for just how financially significant this system is, in operation, is to look at an example. In 1995, the Hong Kong Government put a parcel of land (Lot 129) of around 180,000 ft^2 up for sale on Ap Lei Chau, which is an island located to the south of Hong Kong Island. Ap Lei Chau is connected by a causeway bridge to neighbouring Aberdeen on Hong Kong Island. The whole area is densely populated. As is the case across much of Hong Kong, these high-density urban areas are surrounded by wooded mountains and the sea.

Lot 129 is located along the Ap Lei Chau waterfront across the road from numerous small-scale shipyards which service the local fishing fleet and the many pleasure junks and luxury yachts moored in the large Aberdeen Typhoon Shelter. The Government sold the Lot 129 lease – for industrial use – for just under US$30 million in 1995 to a secondary commercial-industrial developer. By 2005, two primary residential property developers had acquired a significant interest in Lot 129 (by now valued at about US$74 million). The two property developers needed to have the lease modified to allow a major, high-end residential development in several modern high-rise tower blocks to proceed. The lease modification premium – paid to the Government – to convert the lease from the original-sale industrial use to the high-end residential use was approximately US$504 million. The Hong Kong Government thus derived US$534 million within around ten years, virtually at two strokes of a pen, from the two Lot 129 transactions.[29]

28 See Goodstadt, Leo F., *Uneasy Partners; The Conflict between Public Interest and Private Profit in Hong Kong* (Hong Kong University Press, Hong Kong, 2005).

29 For a detailed, well-documented analysis of these transactions, see Webb, David, *Larvotto – Do You Know the Boatyard?* March 3, 2010, available at: https://webb-site.com/articles/larvotto.asp (accessed October 1, 2019).

It is important to note that the essence of this land-based revenue system is that the public land revenues are mainly collected "up front". Leases in BHK typically had durations of 75, 99, or (less commonly) 999 years. Since the establishment of the HKSAR on July 1, 1997, almost all new Government leases have been granted for 50 years (there are special 21-year leases for petrol stations, for example). The Joint Declaration speaks of the Basic Policies for the HKSAR listed therein remaining unchanged for 50 years (in Clause 1(12)). The Joint Declaration does not, however, mandate that any change must take place in 2047. Although there is resonance with Clause 1(12) of the Joint Declaration in Article 5 of the Basic Law of the HKSAR, there is no explicit Basic Law "sunset provision".[30] The Basic Law is drafted to operate indefinitely.[31] The Basic Law makes clear, and the HKSAR Government has confirmed, that it has complete power to issue or renew leases beyond 2047. The clear majority of leases include a right to renew. The Government has verified that such renewals will continue to be recognized by law (until and beyond 2047) and that the long-standing policy of charging only a minimal Government rent per annum (where lease-stipulated) will also be maintained. This rent is customarily 3% of a conservatively estimated annual, potential rent value.[32] The drawbacks of relying on this "up front" payment system have been well argued by a number of commentators (for example, it crowds out smaller, less cash-rich developers and thus curbs competition).[33] For successive Hong Kong Governments, this system has proved highly attractive, however. For one thing, the transaction costs associated with collecting very large amounts of public revenue each year are kept remarkably low.

Hong Kong's massive Fiscal Reserves are, today, officially, part of the Exchange Fund. The Exchange Fund essentially comprises (a) the Fiscal Reserves (money saved from revenues raised but not spent over previous decades) of the Government's General Revenue Account (roughly 40% of the Exchange Fund); and (b) the balance of government foreign currency reserves which back the Hong Kong Dollar (HKD) (roughly 60% of the Exchange Fund). The Exchange Fund is managed by the Hong Kong Monetary Authority (HKMA). The HKMA also

30 Rowse, Mike, "Hong Kong's World Won't Stop in 2047, So We'd Better Start Building Bridges", *South China Morning Post*, January 14, 2018, available at: https://www.scmp.com/comment/insight-opinion/article/2127831/hong-kongs-world-wont-stop-2047-so-wed-better-start-building (accessed October 1, 2019).

31 The Basic Law can be amended or interpreted (see Chapter 6) or it could be repealed (a possibility but potentially, politically very difficult).

32 "Land Tenure System and Land Policy in Hong Kong", *Land Department*, February 2017, available at https://www.landsd.gov.hk/en/service/landpolicy.htm (accessed October 1, 2019).

33 For a comprehensive critical review of the land revenue system, detailing its drawbacks, see Webb, David, "Hong Kong Land Lease Reform, Part 1 and Part 2", *Webb-site Reports*, October 2010, available at: https://webb-site.com/articles/leases1.asp (accessed October 1, 2019).

manages the quasi-currency board pegging of the HKD to the US Dollar (USD).[34] The unprecedented heavy reliance on deficit financing by the HKSAR Government over several consecutive years following the Asian Financial Crisis (AFC), which commenced in mid-1997, was paid for out of the Government's Fiscal Reserves in the Exchange Fund. No borrowing was needed to fund deficits which exceeded 20% of Government expenditure in some years following the onset of the AFC. This deficit financing ran for 5–6 years. Within a further five years, the Fiscal Reserves were fully replenished and stronger than ever. Interestingly, as a matter of law, the HKSAR Government does not need to seek LegCo approval to access the Fiscal Reserves (unlike in the case of expenditure based on current year revenues).[35]

Hong Kong's first ever income tax was the War Revenue Ordinance passed by the LegCo in 1940 (and updated in 1941) in response, above all, to the rapidly expanding invasion of China by Japan. It created a system of schedules, establishing three separate taxes on different categories of income – a Property Tax with a flat rate, a Salaries Tax with progressive rates, and a Profits Tax with a flat rate for corporations and progressive rates for unincorporated firms. The Ordinance exempted all offshore income from taxation.[36]

In drafting the Ordinance, the War Revenue Committee copied the schedular British Income Tax system introduced by Prime Minister Addington in 1803, despite the fact that the British system itself had been reformed in 1910 to base tax liability on a taxpayer's total income.[37]

The new, post-war, 1947 tax legislation passed by LegCo, the Inland Revenue Ordinance (IRO), retained the basic schedular structure and the restricted territorial ambit of the War Revenue Ordinance of 1941. Since 1947, the IRO has been formally re-examined on three occasions, in 1954, 1968, and 1976, by Review Committees. No major alterations were made to the IRO, however.[38]

34 See "Fiscal Reserve Account", *Hong Kong Monetary Authority*, available at: https://www.hkma.gov.hk/gdbook/eng/f/fiscal_reserve_account.shtml (accessed October 1, 2019); and "What Is the Hong Kong Monetary Authority", *Comply Advantage*, available at: https://complyadvantage.com/knowledgebase/key-institutions/hong-kong-monetary-authority/ (accessed October 1, 2019).

35 Cullen, "Hong Kong's Remarkable Land Revenue Regime".

36 Ibid. This approach was consistent with the nineteenth century tax policy – favouring source-based taxation in the colonies – adopted by the British as their Empire developed. See Barker, William B., "Expanding the Study of Comparative Tax Law to Promote Democratic Policy: The Example of the Move to Capital Gains Taxation in Post-Apartheid South Africa" (2005) 109 *Pennsylvania State Law Review*, 101.

37 Littlewood, Michael, "Taxation without Representation: The History of Hong Kong's Troublingly Successful Tax System" (2002) *British Tax Review* 212. See also Littlewood, Michael, "Tax Reform in Hong Kong in the 1970s: Sincere Failure or Successful Charade?" in Tiley, John (ed.), *Studies in the History of Tax Law* (Hart, Oxford, 2004); and Littlewood, Michael, *Taxation without Representation: The History of Hong Kong's Troublingly Successful Tax System* (Hong Kong University Press, Hong Kong, 2010).

38 Littlewood, 2002 and 2010, ibid.

The RR in the HKSAR today encompasses the following key features[39]:

- A formally narrow taxation base;
- Significant reliance on land-related revenues;
- Low taxation rates;
- Separate schedules applying separately identified taxes to different classes of income – no general income tax;
- No taxation of income derived from outside of Hong Kong regardless of the residence status of the taxpayer (source-based taxation);
- No formal Capital Gains Tax;
- No General Consumption Tax;
- Simple and relatively stable taxation laws;
- Retention of Stamp Duties in the system;
- No Death or Gift Duties since 2006;
- The use of a range of other fees and taxes (including Betting Duty and duties on tobacco, (some) alcohol, and petroleum products);
- Until recently almost no use of Double Taxation Treaties (DTTs)[40];
- Comparatively constrained government spending;
- Very little government borrowing;
- Infrequent deficit budgeting; and
- Massive accumulated Fiscal Reserves.

The three (source-based) taxes imposed (using separate schedules) by the IRO are Profits Tax, Salaries Tax, and Property Tax.

One crucial role of the Basic Law is to provide for the highest degree of fiscal separation of the HKSAR from the Mainland (Two Systems) within the PRC (One Country). Particular effort has been put into drafting provisions in the Basic Law which are designed to install a constitutional, "fiscal firewall" between the two Tax Systems.

Article 106 of the Basic Law provides that Hong Kong is to have its own independent finances and prohibits the PRC from raising taxes in Hong Kong or sharing the HKSAR's tax revenue. Article 108 further provides that:

> The Hong Kong Special Administrative Region shall practise an independent taxation system. The Hong Kong Special Administrative Region shall, taking the low tax policy previously pursued in Hong Kong as reference, enact laws on its own concerning types of taxes, tax rates, tax reductions, allowances and exemptions, and other matters of taxation.

39 This outline of the current Hong Kong revenue system summarizes a more comprehensive review of the taxes applying in the HKSAR, which can be found in Cullen and Wong, "Globalization and the Hong Kong's Revenue Regime".

40 Hong Kong's approach to DTTs has been changing since 1997, however. As a result of external pressures and international campaigns against Tax Havens, the HKSAR has now signed up to many DTTs. See, further, Liu, Irene Jay, "HK Seeking Tax Treaties to Silence Tax Haven Claims", *South China Morning Post,* March 31, 2012.

Underwriting the Rule of Law

Primary funding

No Rule of Law system is ever faultless: individual operational failures are inevitable. The complex regulatory demands faced by BHK ensured that it would be no exception. Nevertheless, a comparatively robust, well-funded system, which worked, was established in Hong Kong. The foundations were good and it has continued to work long term.

What, though, needs to be paid for in order to underwrite a successful Rule of Law system? The Hong Kong experience shows that there are two broad areas of required funding: primary institutional funding and secondary, stability funding. In a large densely populated city like modern Hong Kong, both are crucial.

By primary institutional funding, I mean establishing and maintaining the "software" and "hardware" for a Rule of Law system at durable, fit-for-purpose levels. One needs strongly qualified, independent judges and lawyers and a well-trained and disciplined Police Force. You need to pay to ensure the required levels of education and training. You need to pay to provide proper premises to house both the judicial system and the Police Force and to provide needed uniforms and equipment, etc. You must maintain payment rates which work powerfully to dissuade corruption. Having a very well-funded, independent anti-corruption authority is also good: the ICAC proved to be vital in securing the Rule of Law in post-war BHK and it continues to play this role.

Further key aspects required within the primary framework include well-funded, high-quality Law Schools to train future lawyers and judges and a stoutly funded system of legal aid primarily designed to assist those defending themselves within the criminal justice system, where needed, and to enable access to civil litigation for those with a good case but lacking financial means.

The Rule of Law which prevailed in BHK over the first 100 years was a measurably "thin" version, but it did work well for its time. And, from the outset, funding was at least adequate. There were no local Law Schools and no ICAC in that era, but judges and lawyers were well educated and trained in the principles of the Common Law in the UK. Policing, too, was governed by the essential protocols of British (Peelian) policing (see Chapter 4). The basic understanding of what a Rule of Law system meant became well grounded. The brutal period of Japanese occupation from 1941 to 1945 confirmed what the Rule of Law, as it stood then, meant by showing, in horrifying detail, how much was lost with the overthrow of the BHK system. It was a terrible experience for Hong Kong and a time which saw the Hong Kong population shrink drastically (from 1.6 million) as around one million fled from the Japanese.[41]

41 Apart from regularly using cruel, often terrifying, and lethal modes of law enforcement, the Japanese renamed many main roads and landmarks in Hong Kong and there was enforced teaching of the Japanese language and history. See "Three Years and Eight Months: Hong Kong during the Japanese Occupation", *Hong Kong University of Science and Technology*

In the post-war period, the Rule of Law in BHK was re-energized as the Hong Kong economy took off (from an impoverished base). The British spent significantly to rebuild the judicial and policing systems and by 1969, BHK gained its first Law School at Hong Kong University.[42] As explained in Chapter 4, the establishment of the ICAC in 1974 was another key turning point. Professor Yash Ghai noted in 1999 that:

> [A]lthough not perfectly, the Hong Kong legal system was based on the essential principles of the common law. There was equality before the law. Individuals and groups aggrieved by a decision of a government official or public agency could go to the courts for redress.[43]

Demands for increased legal aid are regular in Hong Kong as are criticisms of reduced public funding for judicial review applications.[44] It is possible, however, that legal aid provision in Hong Kong has become, over time, better funded and more open than in most other developed world jurisdictions. The total Legal Aid Department (LAD) budget for 2018–2019 was over US$175 million, including funding for over 500 LAD staff and provision of aid.[45] In 2016, legal aid funding in the HKSAR was, according to one report, about 50% higher than in the EU (US$15 per capita compared to around US$10 per capita).[46]

Public funding for a very wide range of judicial review applications to challenge government decisions and laws passed by LegCo has been extensive, but it has, more recently, fallen significantly (from a fairly high level in 2015 when over 20% of such applications were funded).[47] A former Permanent Judge of the CFA, Henry Litton (a prominent lawyer in Hong Kong since the 1960s), has been scathing in his criticism of the over-acceptance by HKSAR courts of judicial

---

Library, available at: https://library.ust.hk/exhibitions/japanese-occupation/?page=Intro (accessed October 1, 2019).

42 See "About Us", *Faculty of Law, The University of Hong Kong*, available at: https://www.law.hku.hk/faculty/index.php (accessed October 1, 2019).

43 Ghai, Yash, *Hong Kong's New Constitutional Order* (2nd ed.) (Hong Kong University Press, Hong Kong, 1999), 24.

44 See Carvalho, Rachel, "Alarm at Drop in Legal Aid for Judicial Review Applications", *South China Morning Post*, May 13, 2018, available at: https://www.scmp.com/news/hong-kong/hong-kong-law-and-crime/article/2145874/alarm-drop-legal-aid-hong-kong-judicial (accessed October 1, 2019); and Lam, Jeffie and Lum, Alvin, "Bill for Outside Legal Help on Politics-Related Cases Hits HK$17 Million", *South China Morning Post*, March 12, 2019, available at: https://www.scmp.com/news/hong-kong/law-and-crime/article/3001410/hong-kongs-justice-department-spends-70-cent-more (accessed October 1, 2019).

45 See *Legal Aid Department – Head 94*, available at: https://www.budget.gov.hk/2018/eng/pdf/head094.pdf (accessed October 1, 2019).

46 Kwok, Tony, "Hong Kong Should Grant Legal Aid Only to Deserving Cases", *South China Morning Post*, April 12, 2016, available at: https://www.scmp.com/comment/insight-opinion/article/1935458/hong-kong-should-grant-legal-aid-only-deserving-cases (accessed October 1, 2019).

47 Carvalho, "Alarm at Drop in Legal Aid for Judicial Review Applications".

review applications (not infrequently funded by legal aid). Too many such applications are without merit, in his view, and should be dismissed without a hearing. Litton is also highly critical of the tendency of HKSAR courts to turn, as he sees it, straightforward matters into constitutional (usually rights-based) disputes.[48]

Secondary funding

Secondary stability funding covers a wide area, but certain key components stand out. Government and especially its Civil Service operational arms must be well funded to secure clean, comprehensive, and efficient governance as far as is reasonably possible. Government, either directly through the public sector or by subsidies and regulation, needs to ensure the widely available provision of a range of vital livelihood benefits, including medical, hospital, aged-care, and educational services. Government also needs to develop and shape community-focussed transport and communications systems and to pay serious attention to environmental concerns.

Most vital of all, in ensuring foundational stability for a durable and effective Rule of Law system especially within any sizeable jurisdiction, however, is housing. This crucial need was made starkly clear to the BHK Government on the evening of Christmas Day, December 25, 1953, when a devastating fire swept through the Shek Kip Mei squatter area in Kowloon. Some 53,000 immigrants from the Mainland were made homeless overnight. The BHK Governor Sir Alexander Grantham launched what was to become one the most massive public housing projects in any large city worldwide. Grantham was able to commence this project because the BHK Government could fund it. Initial temporary housing was erected within two months. Between 1954 and 1964, the Government built more than 140 multi-storey "Resettlement Blocks" as they were known. In 1971, the then new Governor, Sir Murray Maclehose, announced a still bigger public housing programme to house close to 2 million people in flats (small as they were) fitted with decent facilities. The then Housing Society and the Housing Authority (working on longer term solutions) were primarily responsible for implementing this ***housing revolution***.[49]

The remarkable outcome has been the creation of Hong Kong's vast stock of Public Rental Housing (PRH) (now over 800,000 flats) and the mass provision of subsidized Home Ownership Scheme (HOS) residences (now in excess

48 Buddle, Cliff, "Out of Touch, Not Fit for Purpose, Hong Kong Judiciary Savaged by a Former Top Judge and Lawyer", *South China Morning Post*, February 19, 2019, available at: https://www.scmp.com/lifestyle/arts-culture/article/2186737/out-touch-not-fit-purpose-hong-kong-judiciary-savaged-former (accessed October 1, 2019). See also Litton Henry, *Is Hong Kong Sleepwalking to 2047* (Sherriff Books, 2019).

49 "Memories of Home – 50 Years of Public Housing in Hong Kong", *The Heritage Museum – Hong Kong*, available at: https://www.heritagemuseum.gov.hk/documents/2199315/2199693/Public_Housing-E.pdf (accessed October 1, 2019).

of 400,000 flats).[50] All such flats are small with average living space per person at around 11 m^2 (or less). Older PRH estates are often conveniently located and even new estates normally have good public transport access. Rents average less than US$250 per month or 10–15% of disposable income (with such income normally being below the taxable threshold[51]). Thus, the large majority of low-income Hong Kong residents are comparatively well housed, though in small flats. A system exists, too, for passing on a PRH flat from one generation to the next, subject to a means test regime. Almost 30% of Hong Kong residents live in PRH with about another 20% living in subsidized, privately-owned housing.[52]

We need to consider how this housing revolution was funded when private market residential flats prices have long been, per square foot, among the highest in the world. Because the Government in Hong Kong has always owned the freehold title of virtually all land, the land used to build PRH and HOS flats came at zero nominal cost as the scheme was implemented. And all those revenues from (high value) land-related transactions and activity have, historically, readily funded public housing expenditure.

The completed flats have then been let at low rent to stable, reliable tenants, on the whole, so that bad debt and excessive wear-and-tear problems are minimized. As Leo Goodstadt noted: "It would have been hard to find anywhere a society more socially responsible and tolerant, more politically mature and self-reliant, or a people easier to serve and rule".[53]

The very worst off, amongst those living below the Poverty Line in the HKSAR, are the poor who do not yet have access to PRH. Stuck in low-income jobs (if that fortunate), families of four or more can find themselves with no choice but to rent (an often non-legal) "subdivided unit" of 10 m^2 or even less. This is where the poverty gap in Hong Kong is evident at its worst. Almost 210,000 people are

50 These HOS flats are sold at a discount as the Government does not charge the land cost ("land premium") to eligible (mainly sitting-PRH tenant) buyers upon initial purchase. Owners can resell, subject to certain conditions and, at that time, usually the land premium must be paid. As a consequence, many thousands of (ex-)HOS flats are now counted as part of the private market.

51 About 60% of wage and salary earners fall outside the Salaries Tax net.

52 See "Hong Kong: The Facts – Housing", *Transport and Housing Bureau*, available at: https://www.thb.gov.hk/eng/psp/publications/housing/hongkongthefacts/index.htm (accessed October 1, 2019). See also *Public Housing in Hong Kong: Past Present and Future*, available at: http://www.cih.org.hk/event_speaker_dnload/events2006100801/Public%20Housing%20in%20Hong%20Kong-%20Presentation%2024-9-06(insert%20photo).pdf (accessed October 1, 2019).

53 Goodstadt, *Uneasy Partners*, 228.

estimated to live in more than 90,000 such subdivided units.[54] The PRH waiting list for such people varies from three to five years.[55]

Some comparative context is useful to add perspective on these difficult housing problems facing Hong Kong. New Zealand and Australia do not face the very constrained land availability problems of Hong Kong (see below). Both are wealthy First World jurisdictions blessed with significant natural resources.[56] Yet, according to widely recorded measures, homelessness is a significantly greater problem in both jurisdictions compared to Hong Kong.

The official Hong Kong homelessness rate was under 1,200 in 2018. Academic studies, looking at street-sleepers, say that the real rate is at least 2,000. In a population of 7.7 million, this is equivalent to a rate of 0.015% to 0.026%.[57] Homelessness estimates for New Zealand range from an official government figure of 4,000 to an academic study figure of 41,000 in a population of almost 4.8 million, equivalent to a rate ranging from 0.083% to 0.85%.[58] In Australia, homelessness was estimated by the Australian Bureau of Statistics at over 115,000 in 2018 in a population of around 25 million, which translates to a rate of 0.46%.[59] It is true that different measuring methods may be being used, but these figures are at least indicative. Using the minimum comparative figure, New Zealand has a homelessness rate which is more than three times the higher estimate for the HKSAR. Using the highest New Zealand and Hong Kong estimates, the New Zealand rate is over 32 times higher. In Australia, the rate is almost 18 times higher.

54 Cheng, Kris, "209,700 People Live in Subdivided Flats in Hong Kong, 2016 Census Reveals", *Hong Kong Free Press*, January 19, 2018, available at: https://www.hongkongfp.com/2018/01/19/209700-people-live-subdivided-flats-hong-kong-2016-govt-census-reveals/ (accessed October 1, 2019).

55 "Hong Kong: The Facts – Housing", *Transport and Housing Bureau*, available at: https://www.thb.gov.hk/eng/psp/publications/housing/hongkongthefacts/index.htm (accessed October 1, 2019).

56 In 2017, according to the World Bank, New Zealand, GDP per capita was US$42,940 and Australia's was US$53,799. In the same year, the figures for the HKSAR and the US were US$46,193 and US$59,931, respectively. See "GDP Per Capita (Current US$ – 2017), *The World Bank*, available at: https://data.worldbank.org/indicator/NY.GDP.PCAP.CD?locations=NZ (accessed October 1, 2019).

57 Siu, Phila, "Number of Registered Hong Kong Homeless Soars as Sky-High Rents Force People to Sleep Rough", *South China Morning Post*, May 2, 2018, available at: https://www.scmp.com/news/hong-kong/community/article/2144384/number-registered-hong-kong-homeless-soars-sky-high-rents (accessed October 1, 2019).

58 Davison, Isaac, "Fact of Fiction; NZ's 41,000 Homeless", *New Zealand Herald*, August 22, 2017, available at: https://www.nzherald.co.nz/nz/news/article.cfm?c_id=1&objectid=11908336 (accessed October 1, 2019).

59 Crothers, Joanna, " Homelessness Growing Worse in Australia, Census Data Shows", *ABC News*, March 14, 2018, available at: https://mobile.abc.net.au/news/2018-03-14/homelessness-in-australia-jumps-14pc-over-five-year-period/9547786 (accessed October 1, 2019).

Some other comparative statistics related to the provision of PRH in New Zealand and Australia are worth noting. Housing New Zealand has about 62,000 PRH units available for rent – a ratio of units to total population of 1.3%.[60] The figure in Australia is somewhat higher than that for New Zealand at 1.7%.[61] Just looking at PRH flats in Hong Kong (not including HOS flats), the comparative ratio is 11.4% – almost nine times higher than in New Zealand and almost seven times higher than in Australia. In both New Zealand and Australia, rents for PRH are typically about 25% (or more) of total income compared to 10–15% in Hong Kong.[62]

The Hong Kong Government has now run up against major land shortage problems, making it more difficult, still, to build badly needed additional PRH flats and HOS flats. Briefly for political-historical (and hilly geography) reasons, well under 30% of the total HKSAR area (today) of some 1100 km^2 is subject to high-density development. Around 75% is designated as "countryside", which includes farmland and remarkably expansive "country parks".[63] For political-environmental reasons, land reclamation, a consistent practice from 1842 and throughout the BHK era, became increasingly difficult to implement. The Government has ambitious plans to increase the supply of housing by 450,000 public and private units (70% public and 30% private) over the ten years period until 2029 – using, inter alia, re-zoned farmland and low-density areas and so-called "brownfield" sites (without reclaiming areas in country parks).[64] The Government is also planning a massive reclamation to create around 1,700 hectares of new land (in essence, a new island) close to the eastern end of Lantau

60 "Housing Statistics – Managed Stock", *Housing New Zealand*, February 2019, available at: https://www.hnzc.co.nz/publications/housing-statistics-managed-stock/ (accessed October 1, 2019).

61 "Housing Assistance in Australia – 2016", *Australian Institute of Health and Welfare*, June 2, 2016, available at: https://www.aihw.gov.au/reports/housing-assistance/housing-assistance-in-australia-2016/contents/social-housing-dwellings (accessed October 1, 2019).

62 See "Housing Assistance in Australia 2018", *Australian Institute of Health and Welfare*, available at: https://www.aihw.gov.au/reports/housing-assistance/housing-assistance-in-australia-2018/contents/housing-in-australia (accessed October 1, 2019); and "Applying for a Government-Subsidized Home", *Citizens Advice Bureau*, August 25, 2017, available at: http://www.cab.org.nz/vat/hle/sh/Pages/Applying-to-HNZ.aspx (accessed October 1, 2019).

63 "Hong Kong: The Facts – Country Parks and Conservation", *Agriculture, Fisheries and Conservation Department*, available at: https://www.afcd.gov.hk/english/country/cou_lea/the_facts.html (accessed October 1, 2019).

64 Vetter, David, "Why Public Housing Shortfall Will Remain a Thorn in Hong Kong's Side", *South China Morning Post*, January 19, 2019, available at: https://www.scmp.com/news/hong-kong/society/article/2182106/why-public-housing-shortfall-will-remain-thorn-hong-kongs (accessed October 1, 2019). See also *Chief Executive's 2018 Policy Address, Chapter III, Housing and Land Supply*, available at: https://www.policyaddress.gov.hk/2018/eng/pdf/PA2018.pdf (accessed October 1, 2019).

Island, not so far from Kowloon and Hong Kong Island. Housing could be provided here for over 1 million people by 2035.[65]

The Lantau Tomorrow Vision – which includes the East Lantau Metropolis project[66] – is, predictably, controversial, though in my view, many of the criticisms amount to making *the perfect and enemy of the good*. There are no *silver bullet* solutions to the land supply problems facing Hong Kong. Few places have had greater, successful experience with land reclamation than Hong Kong. Only the Government can "build" new land. With new land, the "NIMBY" (Not In My Back-Yard) problems are far less acute and by building its own new land, the bargaining power of the Government will be enhanced as it deals with the leasehold-owners (often major developers) of farmland and related sites. Moreover, this new large-scale reclamation has significant potential to assist in ways no other proposals can, for example, by allowing complete relocation and redevelopment of large, ageing PRH estates while retaining "neighbourhood" characteristics.[67] One conservative estimate suggests that the value of the land created should exceed the reclamation cost by 14% (US$145 billion vs. US$128 billion).[68]

Other views are significantly critical and negative, claiming that this project will effectively wipe out all of Hong Kong's savings (that is, all of the Fiscal Reserves – around US$140 billion). The cost is great and there are risks. Completing the project may involve *spending* much of the Fiscal Reserve fund. This would reduce the *cash* reserves but the land reclaimed would create a potentially more valuable asset reserve (see above).[69]

Summary

This chapter began with a commentary on the significance of a free media in developing and sustaining the Rule of Law. I made reference to how India has struggled to build a Rule of Law system not just for its middle class but for all and how its economic lag and independent Rule of Law and corruption measures show – and confirm – how this has come to pass. On the other hand, Singapore,

65 *Policy Address*, Ibid.

66 Ibid.

67 Wong, Martin, "HK$1 Trillion Reclamation Project Is the Answer to Future Land Needs, *South China Morning Post*, March 19, 2018, available at: https://www.scmp.com/business/article/3002198/benefits-proposed-east-lantau-metropolis-outweigh-estimated-reclamation (accessed October 1, 2019).

68 Ibid.

69 For an interesting, strongly critical assessment of the project, see Harris, Richard, "To Win Hongkongers' Support for the Lantau Reclamation Plan, Officials Should Improve Their Maths – or Their Spin", *South China Morning Post*, March 29, 2019, available at: https://www.scmp.com/comment/insight-opinion/article/3003607/win-hongkongers-support-lantau-reclamation-plan-officials (accessed October 1, 2019). It would take some doing to spend the amount envisaged on reclamation and then end up with a reclaimed area of no measurable worth in a city with some of the highest land values in the world, which is the outcome one would presumably need to achieve a genuine *wiping out* of all the reserves.

argued by many to be *soft-authoritarian*, does very well according to international Rule of Law measures and conspicuously well in terms of low-corruption assessments. Yet Singapore is rated within the lowest 16% according to a leading international media-freedom index. I agree that the role of the media is significant, but I have argued here that adequate, substantial funding is, on balance, measurably more important to create and sustain a robust Rule of Law system.

A detailed case study of the Hong Kong experience is set out above. From the BHK era until the present, Hong Kong has provided an unusual but remarkably good example of how to establish and maintain a successful, prudent (over-prudent to a degree) public financial system. As it happens, Singapore provides another excellent, similar example.[70]

Hong Kong has relied on what has proved to be an exceptionally good scheme to buttress its entire, low tax, public financial system: it has created continuing access to rich flows of land-related revenues. It has been able to do this because, over the last almost 180 years, the Government has retained a perpetual, core proprietorial interest in virtually all land within Hong Kong. Despite all sales being fixed-term leasehold-based, the system has come to be fully accepted by vendors, purchasers (local and offshore), and bankers. That the authorities have undertaken to retain low yearly rents and to commit to penalty-free lease renewals explains much of why this is so.

Interestingly, Singapore is now providing some fresh evidence of the long-term (stability-maintaining) wisdom of the Hong Kong approach. In notable respects, the Singapore public housing system is superior to that in Hong Kong. In particular, living space is clearly better and Singapore uses an "owner-occupier" model where almost all occupiers (over 80% of the population) live in flats which are *owned* under a 99-year lease. However, these leases do not have any renewal rights. In fact, it is a long-standing policy of the Singapore Government that such leased flats are to be handed back to the Government after 99 years to allow redistribution to future generations. As some leases now have less than 50 years to run, owners are finding that their primary asset is beginning to depreciate in value and reselling to other eligible buyers is made more difficult. The Singapore Government is trying to explain that owning such a flat was never meant to be an indefinitely secure, appreciating investment and to convince owners that it is in the public interest that this is so – not an easy task.[71]

70 See Purves, Andrew, *No Debt, High Growth, Low Tax* (Shepheard-Walwyn, London, 2015).

71 See Philemon, Ravi, "The Ticking Time Bomb of the 99-Year-Leashold HDB Flats", *Yahoo Finance,* April 5, 2018, available at: https://sg.finance.yahoo.com/news/ticking-time-bomb-99-leasehold-131753337.html (accessed March 25, 2019); Ong, Justin, "NDR 2018: Why Are HDB Leases 99 Years Long? PM Lee Explains", *Channel News Asia,* August 21, 2018, available at: https://www.channelnewsasia.com/news/singapore/ndr-2018-hdb-lease-99-years-flat-national-day-rally-10631442 (accessed March 25, 2019); and Kok, Xinghui, "Singapore Homeowners Have 99 Problems (and the Lease is No 1), *South China Morning Post,* August 22, 2018, available at: https://www.scmp.com/week-asia/

The Hong Kong system created a major problem in that it was pricing even basic, decent housing far beyond the reach of the lower paid and, indeed, was making it unaffordable for a clear majority of residents. This was a result of the system's inherent tendency to push land prices higher combined with policies producing a shortage of available land for high-density usage and the almost always steady growth in demand.[72] For more than six decades, however, successive Hong Kong Governments have been working on a special solution which has involved creating one of the most extensive systems for providing public housing (or social housing as it is now often called in some jurisdictions) seen anywhere on this scale. The Government has used land over which it had so prudently retained ultimate ownership and ample funds, not least from the land-related revenue streams, to bring about this housing revolution.

The massive spending on public housing enabled by Hong Kong's super-solvency has, in turn, provided a crucial foundation for the dominant, long-term social stability which has prevailed since the end of World War II. That stability has been regularly tested by intense, sometimes deadly, political protesting – as detailed in Chapters 4 and 7. After each such ordeal, Hong Kong has collectively righted itself often quite swiftly – though we are yet to see this outcome following the exceptional level of political rioting in 2019. That so many – and especially the least well-off – have small but decent, low-cost, well-maintained homes to go to is the key explanatory factor for this. Hong Kong has stuck to a fundamentally wise, experience-proved public housing policy. As a result, Hong Kong, as we have seen, does a much better job of providing decent basic housing for the widest possible number than other former British Empire colonial possessions like Australia or New Zealand, both of which are better endowed rich nations.

The interaction between the primary and secondary spending outlined above has been immensely beneficial to Hong Kong. The public (and general) housing model that has evolved is less good than that in Singapore in some ways. But it is

politics/article/2160662/singapores-homeowners-have-99-problems-and-their-lease-no-1 (accessed March 25, 2019).

72 Population growth through immigration, above all from Mainland China, has been a constant since the end of World War II. It intensified greatly after the victory of Mao, Zedong, and the CPC in the Chinese Civil War in 1949 followed, over the next three decades, by the Great Leap Forward famine and the awful horrors of the Cultural Revolution. The population growth pressure has continued. Around 50,000 Mainland Chinese per year come to the HKSAR under a scheme established by the British during the BHK era. There is also increased internal home-seeking within Hong Kong. Due to the extraordinary growth in the Chinese economy, there are now many active Mainland buyers in the Hong Kong market. Policies introduced by the HKSAR Government to dampen prices have had some effect, but demand is so strong that the impact is limited. See Cullen, Richard, "Real Estate Price Inflation: Lessons from Hong Kong" *TLRP Tax Comments,* June, 2016, available at: http://www.law.hku.hk/aiifl/wp-content/uploads/file/TLRP-TaxComments-No_3.pdf (accessed March 25, 2019); and Chen, Jianlin, "The Yet to be Effective but Effective Tax: Hong Kong's Buyer's Stamp Duty as a Critical Study of Legislation by Press Release Case" (2014) 10 *University of Pennsylvania East Asia Law Review*, 1.

better in other ways in that it has avoided creating the duration (and, thus, investment) uncertainties now emerging in Singapore.

In January 1941, the President of the US, Franklin D. Roosevelt, delivered what came to be known as the Four Freedoms Speech. These freedoms were freedom of speech, freedom of worship, freedom from want, and freedom from fear.[73] Freedom from want stressed the right to a healthy peacetime life for people everywhere. Freedom from fear stressed (in the context of World War II which had begun over a year earlier in Europe) an international order made free from the ability of one nation to threaten any neighbour. Freedom from fear can also be read, however, as a basic Rule of Law freedom to live your life peacefully *within* a given jurisdiction without threat to life, limb, or property across all public (and private) spaces. Albert Camus once said that he found it impossible to imagine the rebirth of Europe (after World War II) without taking into account the work of the remarkable French philosopher Simone Weil.[74] One of the closely explored "Needs of the Soul" which Weil explained in her book *The Need for Roots* was "security" which is described as freedom from fear or terror.[75]

Hong Kong can clearly improve, but it has done much to secure freedom from want for most residents. With respect to freedom from fear, as defined in Rule of Law terms above, Hong Kong has also done remarkably well. Homicide rates provide one useful indicator of the general threat to freedom from fear. According to one comprehensive review, Hong Kong has a murder rate which places it in the lowest 5% worldwide, ranked at 209 within 217 jurisdictions with a rate of 0.4 per 100,000 persons. Other rankings include Australia, 183 (1.1/100,000); New Zealand, 193 (0.9/100,000); and the US, 111 (4.7/100,000). The murder rate in Australia is about 3 times that in Hong Kong, while New Zealand has a rate about double the rate in Hong Kong and the US has a murder rate over 11 times that in Hong Kong.[76]

One leading international "Safe City" index is produced by the *Economist Intelligence Unit* (EIU). The EIU safety perspective is that of international professionals (bankers, lawyers, and the like) rather than the perspective of ordinary local residents. Hong Kong still rates very well on the EIU index, within the

73 "FDR and the Four Freedoms Speech", *FDR Library and Museum*, January 2018, available at: https://fdrlibrary.org/four-freedoms (accessed March 25, 2019).

74 Zaretsky, Robert, "Why French Conservatives' New Favorite Philosopher Is Simone Weil", *Foreign Policy*, July 30, 2018, available at: https://foreignpolicy.com/2018/07/30/frances-far-right-claims-a-left-anarchist-martyr-as-its-own/ (accessed March 30, 2019).

75 Weil, Simone, *The Need for Roots* (Routledge, & Kegan Paul, London, 1952) (first translation), Part 1 (available at: https://www.docdroid.net/rKuInyQ/simone-weil-the-need-for-roots-prelude-to-a-declaration-of-duties-towards-mankind.pdf#page=5 (accessed March 30, 3019).

76 Pariona, Amber, "Murder Rate by Country", *World Atlas*, January 11, 2018, available at: https://www.worldatlas.com/articles/murder-rates-by-country.html (accessed March 25, 2019).

top 10 (at number 9).[77] In fact, within the top 10, all but two cities listed have a population below 6 million, sometimes well below – only Tokyo and Hong Kong have populations above this figure. Certain similar surveys are still more positive. Hong Kong was recently rated as the safest travel jurisdiction worldwide (ahead of Singapore and Japan) according to a US assessment, one where "[A] woman or a man can walk any street at any time of day or night without fear".[78] The US Department of State also has Hong Kong listed as one of the world's safest cities.[79] In the Gallup 2018 Global Law and Order survey, which puts its questions about city safety to local residents, Hong Kong was ranked sixth out of 142 countries.[80]

An important topic long discussed is what are Hong Kong's core values? A commonly presented list of core values identified by successive Hong Kong Governments is freedom, human rights, democracy, the Rule of Law, and clean governance. Which of these have the highest priority varies according to political standpoints (for example, pro-democracy vs. pro-establishment), but most agree that all are validly included in this list. The Rule of Law is one of the widely shared core values.[81] The crux of the argument made in this chapter is that Hong Kong has, since 1842, equipped itself extraordinarily well to apply sufficient *primary and secondary funding* to build an enviable Rule of Law regime – one which has been much shaped in its creation by principles derived from Diceyan Constitutionalism. (The way in which this regime has been acutely tested in 2019 is reviewed in the closing chapters.)

77 "The Safe Cities Index 2017", *The Economist Intelligence Unit,* available at: http://safecities.economist.com/safe-cities-index-2017 (accessed March 25, 2019).

78 "Hong Kong Is the Safest Country to Travel in the World", *Asia Correspondent,* November 2017, available at: https://asiancorrespondent.com/2017/11/hong-kong-safest-city-travel-world/ (accessed March 25, 2019).

79 Nip, Amy, "SAR Listed as One of the World's Safest Cities", *The Standard,* January 12, 2018, available at: http://www.thestandard.com.hk/section-news.php?id=191660&sid=4 (accessed March 25, 2019).

80 "2018 Global Law and Order Index", *Gallup Analytics,* available at: file:///D:/Data/My%20Documents/Downloads/Gallup_Global_Law_And_Order_Report_2018.pdf (accessed March 25, 2019).

81 Huen, Jenny and Yip, Paul, "Hong Kong Must Treasure and Protect Its Core Values, Including 'One Country Two Systems'", *South China Morning Post,* November 7, 2016, available at: https://www.scmp.com/comment/insight-opinion/article/2043650/hong-kong-must-treasure-and-protect-its-core-values (accessed March 26, 2019).

6 The HKSAR

Introduction

On July 1, 1997, the Royal Yacht "Britannia" departed Hong Kong's Victoria Harbour following the formal reversion of sovereignty over Hong Kong to the People's Republic of China (PRC) in accordance with the provisions of the Joint Declaration signed in 1984. More than 150 years of British rule came to an end. Hong Kong moved beyond the dominion of long-since, fully democratic Britain and took on, as its new sovereign, not only the world's most populous nation but the world's largest ever and most successful One-Party State (OPS).[1] Beijing became Hong Kong's focus, Beijing where the PRC Government had used battlefield weapons, including tanks, to break up, with significant loss of life, a massive, long-running demonstration for political reform by thousands of its own citizens in and around Tiananmen Square on June 4, 1989.

This was a fundamental turning point. Hong Kong has since become an increasingly "political city". This process of politicization gained especially strong momentum in 2003 when the second HKSAR Government tried to enact new anti-subversion laws even while the Severe Acute Respiratory Syndrome (SARS) epidemic remained a serious threat.[2]

Since July 1, 1997, the HKSAR has enjoyed a Special Administrative Region status within the PRC under the "One Country – Two Systems" (OCTS) formula. The Basic Law of the HKSAR, enacted by the National People's Congress

1 In fact, the CPC is not the sole political party in the PRC – there are eight other small approved political parties. It is, however, the overwhelmingly dominant political party in China and it is the only political party involved in the substantial running of the PRC. At its heart, China is, thus, a One-Party State. See, further, Wang, Xiaofeng, "What Do China's Democratic Parties Do?" *The Diplomat*, March 3, 2018, available at: https://thediplomat.com/2018/03/what-do-chinas-democratic-parties-actually-do/ (accessed September 14, 2019).

2 Chen, Albert H. Y., "The Rule of Law under 'One Country Two Systems': The Case of Hong Kong 1997–2010" (2011) 6 *National Taiwan University Law Review*, 269. See also Fu, Petersen and Young (eds.), *National Security and Fundamental Freedoms: Hong Kong's Article 23 under Scrutiny* (Hong Kong University Press, Hong Kong, 2005). These and other related developments are discussed in detail below.

(NPC) of the PRC, is now the most significant document regulating the relationship between Hong Kong and Beijing.[3]

The discussion below is premised on the valid understanding that the Basic Law is the directly operative Constitution of the HKSAR. There is, however, a vital aspect of the constitutional order in Hong Kong that has never been widely discussed but which will have to be studied in coming years because it is bound to assume increasing importance. At the most fundamental level and inescapably, the Basic Law draws its lifeblood from the PRC Constitution of 1982. It is Article 31 of that Constitution that has sanctioned the creation of the Basic Law. This is the ultimate basis of the oft-stated claim that the Basic Law is a Constitution. To a measurable degree there is a tension between two *grundnorms* here.[4] There is, however, a clear paramount grundnorm which is embedded in the PRC Constitution.

The Basic Law

Overview

Hong Kong's Basic Law was described, unequivocally, by Hong Kong's Court of Final Appeal (CFA) in 1999, in *Ng Kar Ling & Others v. Director of Immigration* as the Constitution of the HKSAR.[5] Although the Basic Law does not incorporate and entrench the Rule of Law by name, it does emphasize that the HKSAR Government must only act in accordance with the law and that residents are entitled to seek judicial review of acts of the executive authorities.[6] Article 8 of the Basic Law also provides that:

> The laws previously in force in Hong Kong, that is, the common law, rules of equity, ordinances, subordinate legislation and customary law shall be

3 The Basic Law of the Hong Kong Special Administrative Region of the People's Republic of China, a law of the NPC of the PRC, was promulgated and adopted by the NPC on April 4, 1990. It came into force on July 1, 1997. For a thorough overview of the operational track record of OCTS and the Basic Law, since 1997, see Chen, ibid. The definitive single text commentary on the Basic Law remains; Ghai, Yash, *Hong Kong's New Constitutional Order* (2nd ed.) (Hong Kong University Press, Hong Kong, 1999). The primary multi-author text on the Basic Law is Chan and Lim (eds.), *Law of the Hong Kong Constitution* (2nd ed.) (Sweet & Maxwell, Hong Kong, 2015). See also Lo, Pui Yin, *The Judicial Construction of Hong Kong's Basic Law: Courts, Politics and Society after 1997* (Hong Kong University Press, Hong Kong, 2014). The ultimate constitutional instrument of the PRC is the PRC Constitution of 1982. That Constitution has nothing specifically and directly to say about the Hong Kong–Beijing relationship, however. Amending it to take on such a task was politically impossible for a range of macro-political reasons. Thus, this responsibility was assigned to the Basic Law.

4 Grundnorm is a German word meaning "fundamental norm". The legal philosopher Hans Kelsen coined the term to refer to the fundamental norm, order or rule that forms an underlying basis for a legal system. See, *Definitions – US Legal*, available at: https://definitions.uslegal.com/g/grundnorm/ (accessed August 31, 2019).

5 *Ng Kar Ling & Others v. Director of Immigration* (1999) HKLRD, 315, at 337.

6 See Articles 64 and 35 of the Basic Law. See also Ghai, *Hong Kong's New Constitutional Order*, 266.

> maintained except for any that contravene this Law, and subject to any amendment by the legislature of the Hong Kong Special Administrative Region.

As discussed in Chapter 5, the Joint Declaration provides, in Clause 1(12), that the Basic Policies for the HKSAR listed therein are to remain unchanged for 50 years (from July 1, 1997). The Joint Declaration does not, however, mandate that change must take place in 2047. Although there is resonance with Clause 1(12) of the Joint Declaration in Article 5 of the Basic Law of the HKSAR, there is no explicit Basic Law "sunset provision". The Basic Law is drafted to operate indefinitely.[7]

The Basic Law also guarantees a wide range of fundamental rights and freedoms in Chapter III, including freedom of speech (Article 27), freedom of the person (Article 28), freedom from unlawful or arbitrary entry (Article 29), freedom and privacy of communication (Article 30), freedom of movement (Article 31), freedom of conscience and religion (Article 32), freedom of choice of occupation (Article 33), freedom to engage in research (Article 34), and freedom to access confidential legal advice and to sue the executive authorities (Article 35). Additionally, Article 39 incorporates into the Basic Law the provisions of the United Nations, International Covenant on Civil and Political Rights (ICCPR) – as enacted in 1991, in BHK, through the Bill of Rights Ordinance (BORO). The ICCPR (through the BORO) applies a wide set of rights which reinforce those set out in Chapter III of the Basic Law.

Further relevant provisions are: Article 2 (where the National People's Congress (NPC) of the PRC authorizes the HKSAR to enjoy independent judicial power) and Article 17. Although Article 17 allows the Standing Committee of the National People's Congress (SCNPC) to invalidate HKSAR laws if they are not considered to be in conformity with the Basic Law, there is no power in Article 17 allowing SCNPC invalidation on the grounds of non-conformity with the Constitution of the People's Republic of China (1982).[8]

Other Basic Law provisions which stress the separateness of the HKSAR include: Articles 82 and 92 (foreign judges may be made members of the CFA and appointed to the HKSAR judiciary), Article 111 (the HKSAR shall maintain a separate currency), Article 116 (the HKSAR shall maintain a separate customs territory, and Articles 106–110 (which stress the separateness of the taxation system and the fiscal autonomy of the HKSAR).

The Basic Law thus goes a considerable way towards embedding not just the Common Law system but also the Rule of Law, within the Constitution

7 The Basic Law can be amended or interpreted (see below) or, most radically, it could be repealed at some future point after 2047 (see discussion in Chapter 5 re Article 5 of the Basic Law).

8 See discussion by Ghai, Yash, in (Chan, Fu, and Ghai (eds.)) *Hong Kong's Constitutional Debate: Conflict over Interpretation* (Hong Kong University Press, Hong Kong, 2000), 48–49.

of the HKSAR. As part of this process, it stresses a fundamental aspect of the Rule of Law: judicial review of (most[9]) executive acts. Were the HKSAR legal system either self-contained (like the Australian or Canadian systems now are, for example[10]) or linked to a similar Common Law system (as Hong Kong was prior to 1997[11]), this would amplify the prima facie, convincing substance of the guarantees in the Basic Law.

Article 158 of the Basic Law

Since July 1, 1997, the Hong Kong legal system has had to function beneath the umbrella of the PRC legal system or, to be more frank, under both the protection *and guidance* of the PRC political-legal system.[12] The primary constitutional reason for this may be found in Article 158 of the Basic Law. It sits alongside the guarantees supporting the Rule of Law in the HKSAR. Article 158 provides, inter alia, that:

> The power of interpretation of this Law shall be vested in the Standing Committee of the National People's Congress ...

Article 159 goes on to set out a process for amending the Basic Law, but it is Article 158 which has turned out to be the crucial provision as the intricate process of accommodating Hong Kong's Common Law system within the PRC political-legal tradition has unfolded. Since the change of sovereignty, the SCNPC has interpreted the operation of the Basic Law five times. Each interpretation has been controversial and has raised questions about the complete sturdiness of the Rule of Law in the HKSAR.

The first Basic Law Interpretation was controversial for a range of reasons, including: being the first, because of the nature of the interpretation, and due to

9 In all Rule of Law systems, exceptions to judicial review are allowed in special cases, for example, with respect to certain defence and national security issues and in relation to the dissolution of Parliament. The range of possible exceptions applying in the UK was set out by the House of Lords in *Council of Civil Service Unions and others v. Minister for the Civil Service* (1984) 3 All ER 935, a case which has had wide influence beyond the UK. In general, the range of exceptions to the application of judicial review of executive action continues to narrow.

10 In the case of both Australia and Canada, the final legal recourse, in each case, is now to either the High Court of Australia or the Supreme Court of Canada. Final appeals to a court embedded within another legal system, the Judicial Committee of the Privy Council (JCPC), in the UK are no longer available.

11 And as New Zealand was until 2004, where the ultimate court of appeal was (as was the case in Hong Kong until mid-1997) the JCPC. See http://www.justice.govt.nz/courts/privy_council.html.

12 Ghai, *Hong Kong's New Constitutional Order*.

the issues involved. In the *Right of Abode Litigation*, in January 1999[13], the CFA, relying on its own analysis of the Basic Law, concluded amongst other things, that:

(A) The CFA (and other Hong Kong courts) had an obligation to examine legislation of the HKSAR to ensure that it was not in conflict with the Basic Law;
(B) The Basic Law had been implemented to establish key PRC policies with respect to the HKSAR for the 50 years subsequent to 1997 [and beyond (see note above regarding Article 5 of the Basic Law)];
(C) The old interpretive restrictions on the powers of the Hong Kong courts under the British colonial system did not apply to the HKSAR post-1997 as the Basic Law now conferred ultimate power on the courts of Hong Kong and any restrictions on their powers of interpretation had to be found within the Basic Law; and,
(D) It followed from the above that the CFA and courts of Hong Kong enjoyed a jurisdiction to examine, in certain cases, if legislative acts of the NPC were consistent with the Basic Law.[14]

The CFA also concluded that the Basic Law was the fundamental instrument governing the constitutional operation of the HKSAR. On the substantive issues in dispute, the CFA found that a number of the key provisions in the HKSAR Immigration Ordinance[15] restricting the right of certain Mainland persons[16] to

13 There were two linked Right of Abode cases: *Ng Kar Ling & Others v. Director of Immigration* (1999) 1 HKLRD, 315; and *Chan Kam Nga & Others v. Director of Immigration* (1999) 1 HKLRD, 304. The linked cases are also referred to hereinafter, as the *Right of Abode Litigation*. The latter case dealt with certain separate aspects of the Right of Abode claimants, including a key finding that those born *before* a parent became a Hong Kong permanent resident enjoyed the Right of Abode. For a full discussion of all the issues involved, including the constitutional matters and the substantive Right of Abode claims, together with transcripts of all the relevant cases and key documents and details of the public debate, see Chan, Fu and Ghai (eds.) *Hong Kong's Constitutional Debate: Conflict over Interpretation* (Hong Kong University Press, Hong Kong, 2000).

14 *Ng Kar Ling & Others v. Director of Immigration* (1999) 1 HKLRD, 315; and *Chan Kam Nga & Others v. Director of Immigration* (1999) 1 HKLRD, 304, 337.

15 The Ordinances in question were the Immigration (Amendment) (No. 2) Ordinance (1997) (the No. 2 Ordinance) and the Immigration (Amendment) (No. 3) Ordinance (1997) (the No. 3 Ordinance). They each amended the Immigration Ordinance (Cap. 115). Both the No. 2 Ordinance and the No. 3 Ordinance had been passed by the legislature the PRC appointed with effect from July 1, 1997, the Provisional Legislative Council (PLC) after Beijing's dispute with the UK about the composition of the 1995, Hong Kong LegCo. The CFA found, in the *Right of Abode Litigation*, that the creation of the PLC was consistent with the Basic Law (and laws it passed were thus prima facie valid).

16 "Mainland persons" refers (for practical purposes) to Chinese persons normally resident in Mainland China – that part of Greater China excluding the HKSAR, the MacauSAR, and Taiwan.

claim a Right of Abode in Hong Kong were invalid because they were inconsistent with the relevant Right of Abode–related provisions in the Basic Law.[17]

Following this decision, the HKSAR Government, Beijing, and many Hong Kong residents all expressed serious apprehension about the impact of the potential, major, migration-based uplift in the population of Hong Kong, sanctioned by the CFA decisions. The upper estimates of those Mainland Chinese made eligible to seek the Right of Abode in the HKSAR suggested a Hong Kong population increase of up to 25% arising from the CFA decisions. In late February 1999, about one month after the decision was handed down in the *Right of Abode Litigation*, the CFA offered an extraordinary "clarification". In *Ng Ka Ling & Others v. Director of Immigration (No. 2)*, the CFA advised that notwithstanding any commentary in the *Right of Abode Litigation*, (a) it agreed that its power of interpretation of the Basic Law was derived from authorization by the SCNPC under Article 158 of the Basic Law; (b) it was *not* questioning the authority of the SCNPC to offer an interpretation under Article 158 of the Basic Law; and (c) it was *not* questioning the authority of the SCNPC and NPC to do any act which was in accordance with the provisions of the Basic Law.[18]

Subsequently, the SCNPC issued, at the request of the Chief Executive of the HKSAR, its first Interpretation under Article 158 of the Basic Law on June 26, 1999. This significantly reversed the findings with greatest practical impact arising from the *Right of Abode Litigation* so as to reduce the categories of persons entitled to claim Right of Abode in the HKSAR considerably. The Interpretation is short. It principally claims that the CFA interpretation was not in accord with the "intent" of the Basic Law without providing any detailed reasons. The Interpretation also says that the CFA should have sought an Interpretation of the SCNPC under Article 158 on the matters in issue.[19] In the *Right of Abode Litigation*, the CFA set down a two-stage test for when the CFA should refer a matter under Article 158 to the SCNPC. In essence, the CFA stipulated that it would be necessary to find that a HKSAR–Mainland matter was the dominant concern in particular litigation to mandate a CFA referral. The CFA found that this high-threshold test was not satisfied in the *Right of Abode Litigation* and, thus, a referral was not required.[20]

17 *Right of Abode Litigation.*

18 *Ng Kar Ling & Others v. Director of Immigration (No. 2)* (1999) 1 HKLRD, 577. See also Kellogg, Thomas, "Excessive Deference or Strategic Retreat: The Impact of Basic Law Article 158" (2008) (Spring) *Hong Kong Journal*, obtained from http://www.hkjournal.org/archive/2008_spring/5.htm (hard copy retained by author). The clarification offered little substantive change in the views so far expressed by the CFA. The claimed right of the CFA to review acts of the NPC or SCNPC in certain circumstances was not stated directly but restated indirectly.

19 "Interpretation of the Basic Law", *Government of HKSAR/Basic Law Committee, 15th Anniversary Review* – 2012, available at: https://www.basiclaw.gov.hk/en/publications/book/15anniversary_reunification_ch2_3.pdf (accessed May 7, 2019).

20 This reasoning resonates with some test setting, over time, by the High Court of Australia (HCA). Sir Anthony Mason, former Chief Justice of the HCA, was a part of the CFA panel

One interesting aspect of the findings, not disturbed by the first Article 158 Interpretation of the SCNPC, is that the politics, the wording of Article 24(3) of the Basic Law, and some HKSAR case law support the view that a person of Chinese nationality born in *Taiwan* – with one parent holding the Right of Abode in the HKSAR at the time of birth – would also be eligible to apply for the Right of Abode in the HKSAR. This is because although the PRC regards Taiwan as being a "renegade province", it still regards Taiwan as being a part of China, thus someone born there should acquire Chinese nationality within the meaning of Article 24(3). This article, combined with Article 24(1), provides, "that persons of Chinese nationality born outside of Hong Kong to a Chinese citizen born in Hong Kong before or after the establishment of the HKSAR" are in a position to apply for the Right of Abode in Hong Kong.[21]

When the *Right of Abode Litigation* judgements were first handed down, they were affirmed by a number of commentators for the way they strengthened the Rule of Law in Hong Kong – and this shortly after the change of sovereignty. However, in December 1999, less than 12 months after the initial judgements, the CFA conceded that the limits imposed by the SCNPC on its powers of constitutional interpretation were consistent with the Basic Law. In *Lau Kong Yung & Others v. Director of Immigration*,[22] the CFA accepted that it was bound by the SCNPC Interpretation of June 1999, which it applied to the facts in this particular case. The CFA sanctioned the removal (to the PRC Mainland) of a number of Right of Abode applicants (who may otherwise have had a "legitimate expectation" that they could apply for the Right of Abode and stay in the HKSAR). The CFA also found, in effect, that the SCNPC enjoyed a plenary power to deploy

(as a Non-Permanent (external) CFA Judge) which forged the decisions in the *Right of Abode Litigation*. See, for example, the reasoning of Mason J (as he then was) in *Western Australia v. Commonwealth* (1975) 134 CLR, 201; and also Sloane, Michael, "Representation of Commonwealth Territories in the Senate", *Parliament of Australia,* available at: http://www.aph.gov.au/About_Parliament/Senate/Powers_practice_n_procedures/pops/pop64/c07 (accessed October 1, 2019).

21 Chinese persons born in Taiwan would be regarded by Beijing as "persons of Chinese nationality born outside of Hong Kong" within Article 24 of the Basic Law. See, further, "Nationality Law of the People's Republic of China", *Immigration Department of the HKSAR,* available at: https://www.immd.gov.hk/eng/residents/immigration/chinese/law.html (accessed May 14, 2019); and *Commissioner of Registration v. Registration of Persons Tribunal* (2015) 5 HKC 209 (CFI), para 28. This case indicates that a son born in Taiwan to a qualifying Hong Kong mother has been granted the Right of Abode in the HKSAR. If a Taiwanese person with one Hong Kong parent who held the Right of Abode at the time of that person's birth secured the Right of Abode in the HKSAR, this also could open the door for such a person to obtain both a HKSAR Passport and a *Home Entry Permit* allowing easy access to the Mainland. With respect to advising on/changing nationality in the HKSAR, see https://www.immd.gov.hk/eng/services/chinese_nationality/Declaration_of_Change_of_Nationality.html (accessed May 13, 2019).

22 (1999) 4 HKC 731.

Article 158 – on its own initiative, where it felt the need – to interpret all parts of the Basic Law.[23]

The second SCNPC Article 158 Interpretation came over four years later, in April 2004. This Interpretation was designed to put a stop to momentum building within Hong Kong to accelerate discussion about a significant move towards increased democratization in 2007 (when a Chief Executive Election was due) and 2008 (when a LegCo election was due).[24] Under the relevant provisions in the Basic Law,[25] the SCNPC had a key role to play but that role arose at the end of any (2007–2008 or later) possible democratic reform process.[26] What the Interpretation did was stipulate that the SCNPC would need (a) to consider a (newly required) report from the HKSAR Chief Executive explaining any claimed need to amend the methods for selection of the Chief Executive and/or the formation of LegCo and (b) then determine if any reform were needed.[27] This Interpretation turned the SCNPC from being a final arbiter under the Basic Law, as drafted, into being an entry-point gatekeeper.[28] The SCNPC, even more than in 1999, effected an amendment to the Basic Law with this Interpretation, which attracted significant adverse commentary.[29] (However, see the comparative discussion below highlighting the wide use of constitutional interpretations to effect constitutional amendments in certain major Common Law jurisdictions.)

The third SCNPC Interpretation of Article 53 (and Article 46) of the Basic Law was delivered in April 2005. Article 53 provides, inter alia, that, in the event of the position of Chief Executive of the HKSAR becoming vacant midterm, a new Chief Executive must be chosen within six months of the relevant Chief Executive stepping down. Article 46 provides that each Chief Executive is to serve for five years and shall not serve for more than two consecutive terms. Mr. C.H. Tung, Hong Kong's first Chief Executive, was reselected for a second five-year term commencing from July 1, 2002. In March 2005, he announced he was stepping down approximately halfway through this second term. Beijing made it known that it wished for the HKSAR Chief Secretary, Donald Tsang (Mr. Tung's

23 Ibid.

24 See, Articles 45 and 68 and Annex 1 and Annex 2 of the Basic Law.

25 Ibid.

26 See Article 7 of Annex 1 and Part 3 of Annex 2 of the Basic Law.

27 "Interpretation of the Basic Law", *Government of HKSAR/Basic Law Committee, 15th Anniversary Review* – 2012, available at: https://www.basiclaw.gov.hk/en/publications/book/15anniversary_reunification_ch2_3.pdf (accessed May 7, 2019).

28 The fundamentals of this second Interpretation reminds one of a story (possibly apocryphal) related to Sydney and Beatrice Webb (the Fabian Socialists who together helped found the London School of Economics) which highlights the advantages of entry-point gate-keeping. Beatrice was reportedly criticized for dominating her husband. She responded by explaining that Sydney made all the important decisions in their work. She just decided which decisions were important and which were not.

29 See Yang, Xiaonan in (Young and Ghai (eds.)) *Hong Kong's Court of Final Appeal: The Development of the Law in China's Hong Kong* (Cambridge University Press, Cambridge, 2014), Chapter 3.

effective deputy), to take over from Mr. Tung. Beijing also made it plain that it only wished Mr. Tsang to serve out the remainder of Mr. Tung's second term, until June 30, 2007. This was, it would seem, in accord with established practice in the PRC Mainland when a senior government official steps down midterm.[30] The problem was that the Basic Law makes no provision for a term shorter than five years for any Chief Executive, including any new Chief Executive replacing an incumbent who leaves office midterm. This time Beijing demonstrated some initial reluctance to use the Article 158 power to solve this problem with another Interpretation. But as it became clear that any attempt to solve the problem by a simple amendment to the Chief Executive Election Ordinance[31] would attract an application for judicial review, Beijing decided it needed to act. On April 27, 2005, the SCNPC handed down its third Interpretation stating, inter alia, that a replacement Chief Executive is to serve the remainder of the term of the previous Chief Executive.[32]

The fourth SNCPC Interpretation arose in 2011 as a result of the first direct referral of a case, under Article 158, from the CFA to the SCNPC. The matter involved, chiefly, a commercial law dispute between the Democratic Republic of Congo (DRC) and a US "Vulture Fund", which was seeking to enforce certain debts owed by the DRC, which the US fund had purchased at a significant discount. The facts were rather complex but involved the Vulture Fund seeking access to money being paid by a Chinese Rail company to the DRC (in a Hong Kong–based transaction) to settle the debt the fund had purchased.[33] The key issue in the case (*Democratic Republic of Congo & Others v. F G Hemisphere Associates LLC*[34] *(Congo case)*) was whether a Qualified State Immunity Rule (which applied in BHK and was argued to apply in the HKSAR post-1997) or an Absolute State Immunity Rule (the rule in the PRC) applied in Hong Kong. In resisting the action, the DRC (which was said to have waived immunity by

30 Mr. Tsang went on to serve a full second term. As a Chief Executive who had to be chosen and appointed with some alacrity, in the circumstances applying, it was clear that Beijing wanted his first term to operate as a shorter "probationary" appointment. It is reasonable to assume that similar reasoning underpins the PRC Mainland practice in such cases.

31 Cap. 569.

32 "Interpretation of the Basic Law", *Government of HKSAR/Basic Law Committee, 15th Anniversary Review* – 2012, available at: https://www.basiclaw.gov.hk/en/publications/book/15anniversary_reunification_ch2_3.pdf (accessed May 7, 2019). See also Cheung, Jimmy, "Beijing May Settle Chief's Term Row", *South China Morning Post*, March 21, 2005, A1. "Beijing's View on HK's New Chief", *South China Morning Post*, April 28, 2005, A3. For a telling criticism of this resort to Article 158, see Ghai, Yash, "Just What Can Beijing Teach Us", *South China Morning Post*, April 13, 2005, A17.

33 For a succinct explanation of the facts and the law, see Crossley, Kathryn, "Case Analysis: *Democratic Republic of the Congo and Others v. FG Hemispheres Associates LLC*", *Asian Legal Business*, June 17, 2011, available at: https://www.legalbusinessonline.com/news-analysis/case-analysis-democratic-republic-congo-and-ors-v-fg-hemisphere-associates-llc/64049 (accessed September 14, 2019).

34 (2011) HKCFA 43.

submitting previously to an arbitration agreement) proposed that the (PRC) Absolute State Immunity Rule applied. The case involved a consideration of Basic Law Article 13 (governing Foreign Affairs related to the HKSAR) and Article 19 (governing "Acts of State").[35]

The CFA stated that:

(A) The HKSAR cannot, as a matter of legal and constitutional principle, adhere to a doctrine of State Immunity which differs from that adopted by the PRC. The doctrine of State Immunity practised in the HKSAR, as in the rest of China, is accordingly a doctrine of Absolute Immunity.
(B) There is no basis in law for holding that the 1st defendant (the Congo government) has waived its immunity before the courts of the HKSAR.
(C) Prior to rendering a final judgment in this matter, the Court is under a duty pursuant to Article 158(3) of the Basic Law to refer, and does hereby refer, the questions set out in Section G of this judgment to the [NPCSC], [because] Articles 13 and 19 [are excluded provisions], [and] the Interpretation sought being necessary for the Court's adjudication of the present case.[36]

Both the CFA, in the Provisional Judgement it chose to offer, and the SCNPC agreed with the fundamental claim to Absolute State Immunity argued by the DRC Government. Li, Guangxiang summarizes the outcome in this way:

> Finally, for the sake of completing the story, it is convenient to note that the NPCSC has, at the request of the Hong Kong CFA, given its interpretation in respect of Articles 13(1) and 19(1) of the Basic Law. The NPCSC confirmed the CFA's provisional decision. It confirmed that the doctrine or principle of Absolute Sovereign Immunity applies in Hong Kong, as it does in the Mainland. Shortly after the NPCSC issued its interpretation, the CFA handed down its final judgment in the Congo case, merely affirming the provisional judgement it had reached prior to the making of the reference.[37]

The case was a focus of significant academic debate within the HKSAR, but it did not evince much general criticism. Presumably, this was because of the dominant

35 See "Judgment Update: *Democratic Republic of Congo & Others v. F G Hemisphere Associates LLC*", *Department of Justice, HKSAR,* available at: https://www.doj.gov.hk/eng/public/basiclaw/basic14_3.pdf (accessed May 10, 2019).

36 Ibid. See also Li, Guangxiang, *Constitutional Review under the "One Country, Two Systems Framework": An Inquiry into Establishment, Justification and Scope,* PhD Thesis – Durham University, UK, available at: http://etheses.dur.ac.uk/6966/1/Constitutional_Review_in_Hong_Kong.pdf?DDD19+ (accessed October 1, 2019). This thesis, in Chapter 4, Section 3.5, provides a well-informed review of the *Congo Case.*

37 Li, ibid. See also "Interpretation of the Basic Law", *Government of HKSAR/Basic Law Committee, 15th Anniversary Review* – 2012, available at: https://www.basiclaw.gov.hk/en/publications/book/15anniversary_reunification_ch2_3.pdf (accessed May 7, 2019).

commercial (rather than direct Public Law) nature of the dispute and the fact that Article 13 (governing Foreign Affairs related to the HKSAR) and the relevant part of Article 19 (governing "Acts of State") involved areas, according to the Basic Law, within the dominion of Beijing.[38]

The fifth Article 158 Interpretation of the Basic Law occurred in 2016 under circumstances which were measurably more controversial. After each LegCo election, all the members-elect of the new LegCo must swear an oath of office before taking their seat in LegCo. Since the 2004 LegCo election, certain Pan-Democrat (PD) members had used the oath-taking ceremony to include expressions of political opposition on matters such as the lack of progress with democratic reform in the HKSAR and enmity towards Beijing.

The Oaths and Declarations Ordinance sets out the required LegCo oath:

> I swear that, being a member of the Legislative Council of the Hong Kong Special Administrative Region of the People's Republic of China, I will uphold the Basic Law of the Hong Kong Special Administrative Region of the People's Republic of China, bear allegiance to the Hong Kong Special Administrative Region of the People's Republic of China and serve the Hong Kong Special Administrative Region conscientiously, dutifully, in full accordance with the law, honestly and with integrity.

After the 2016 LegCo election, a number of PD members-elect (including "localist" members[39]) again used the oath-taking ceremony, in October 2016, to make sometimes profane and offensive (to many in Hong Kong) political statements. Most offensive was the use of the term "Chee-na" to refer to China. This term was originally used in China during the early Tang Dynasty (618–906 AD). It came to signify the geographic location of China during the Imperial Era. This was how the word was originally regarded in Japan, but after the rise of industrializing, militarist Japan, following the Meiji Restoration in 1868, the term began to be used within Imperial Japan as a derogatory term which helped justify Japan's brutal expansion within China after World War I. The word is now inseparably associated with the appalling horrors of Japanese aggression within China which lasted until 1945.[40]

38 Li, ibid, 158.

39 "Localism" in the HKSAR now typically involves taking a position which is actively hostile to perceived excessive numbers of Mainland visitors and general Mainland incursions into the HKSAR; which seeks a right of self-determination for Hong Kong to decide on whether it remains or stays within the PRC; or which seeks actions to secure Hong Kong independence from the PRC. Localists stress that they are committed to protecting the interests and identity of Hong Kong. See, further, Kaeding, Malte Phillip, "The Rise of 'Localism' in Hong Kong" (2017) 28 *Journal of Democracy*, 157.

40 Chow, Chung-yan, "The C-Word: Why Hong Kong Localists Have Offended All Chinese", *South China Morning Post*, October 30, 2016, available at: https://www.scmp.com/week-asia/

Shortly after the series of controversial oath-taking incidents, which undermined the commitments contained within the required oath, the HKSAR Government took action in October 2016 to seek judicial review requesting that two of the pro-independence, LegCo-elect members be disqualified from taking office for failing to take their oaths in the proper manner.

While the case was still being resolved, the SCNPC invoked Article 158 to issue an interpretation of Article 104 of the Basic Law which mandates that the Chief Executive, the Principal Officials (Ministers), Executive Council Members, and all members of the Judiciary must all swear allegiance in the form (in essence) set out above. This Interpretation said that any person who intentionally uses words not in accord with the prescribed wording or who takes an oath in a manner which is not sincere or solemn is barred from taking public office and they cannot retake the oath.[41]

On November 16, 2016, after the Interpretation was handed down, Judge Thomas Au Hing-Cheung found that the first two legislators should lose their seats based on his interpretation of the Oaths and Declarations Ordinance. About two weeks later, the Court of Appeal (CA) confirmed this decision and ruled that the legislators could not retake their oaths. The court also specifically referred to the Interpretation. About a year later, the CFA, in effect, confirmed the validity of the decision of the CA (and at first instance) when it refused leave to appeal, to challenge the disqualifications.[42]

Subsequently, four more PD LegCo-elect members were disqualified in July 2017 after the HKSAR Government, in December 2016, requested a judicial review of the validity of their oath-taking earlier that year.[43] They were found to have failed to have taken their oaths in a proper manner in conformity with relevant legislation and the SCNPC Interpretation of Article 104 of the Basic Law.

One claim made in favour of those disqualified was a variation on a "legitimate expectations" argument: the use of oath-taking as a vehicle for political point making (at times grand-standing) had become established as an accepted political-legal norm. It was true that this practice dated back to 2004. Yet it

opinion/article/2040978/c-word-why-hong-kong-localists-have-offended-all-chinese (accessed May 6, 2019).

41 *Interpretation of Article 104 of the Basic Law of the Hong Kong Special Administrative Region of the People's Republic of China by the Standing Committee of the National People's Congress (Adopted by the Standing Committee of the Twelfth National People's Congress at its Twenty-Fourth Session on 7 November 2016)*, available at: https://www.basiclaw.gov.hk/en/basiclawtext/images/basiclawtext_doc25.pdf (accessed May 6, 2019).

42 Lau, Chris, "Why Did Top Court Strike Down Final Appeal over Oath Taking Saga?" *South China Morning Post*, September 2, 2017, available at: https://www.scmp.com/news/hong-kong/law-crime/article/2109404/explainer-why-did-hong-kongs-top-court-strike-down-final (accessed May 6, 2019).

43 Hass, Benjamin, "Hong Kong Pro-Democracy Legislators Disqualified from Parliament", *The Guardian*, July 14, 2017, available at: https://www.theguardian.com/world/2017/jul/14/hong-kong-pro-democracy-legislators-disqualified-parliament (accessed May 6, 2019).

can be safely said that no one in Hong Kong would accept that HKSAR Judges could ever swear an oath other than in a proper way. That is, solemn oath-taking is rightly regarded as a key mode of grounding the institutional integrity of the judicial system in the HKSAR. For the courts, it was clear that once the matter came before them, they had to take the view that oath-taking within the legislature is also a fundamental part of the process of securing LegCo institutional integrity. One cannot have solemn oaths and depreciated oaths.

Finally, we need to consider what might best be called an SCNPC *Advisory Interpretation* issued in late 2017. This Chinese jurisprudential innovation was triggered by the intense debate, which surfaced that year, about establishing joint Hong Kong and Mainland immigration facilities at the new Hong Kong High Speed Rail (HSR) station in Kowloon which connected Hong Kong to the extensive HSR network on the Mainland (co-location).[44]

Supporters of this arrangement relied significantly on the Statement of Validity – on co-location – issued in December 2017 by the SCNPC. This perspective stresses the sovereign authority of the SCNPC within the OCTS political-legal hierarchy governing the status of the HKSAR within the PRC. Note, however, this was not an Article 158 Interpretation, but rather a stand-alone Statement of Validity.[45] Critics focused on the claimed lack of Basic Law foundations to support co-location – and the unorthodox reliance on this SCNPC Statement.[46] These critical assessments used an interpretive emphasis derived from Hong Kong's Common Law system. Yet a broad examination of Public Law interpretive methods in Common Law jurisdictions reveals a notably expansive approach (discussed directly below in the context of interpretations effecting constitutional amendments). This Common Law tradition lends significant weight to arguments made in favour of the organic evolution of the Basic Law to address new circumstances – a view which underpins the SCNPC advice on the validity of co-location. Li Fei, a leading PRC expert on the Basic Law and Chair of the Basic Law Committee established under the SCNPC, confirmed that a Chinese version of adaptive constitutionalism (consistent with the *Living Constitution* theory – see below) applied to the Basic Law when he said that there was no single article that the SCNPC had relied on to make its decision, as the Basic Law, drafted over 20 years earlier, could not have envisaged future developments such as the HSR. He went on to say that:

> [T]he "one country two systems" principle was unprecedented [and] the Basic Law ... cannot be so clear as to explain everything, and to foresee everything that could happen.[47]

44 The HSR network is now approximately 25,000 km in length.

45 Siu, Phila and Chung, Kimmy, "Controversial Joint Checkpoint Plan Approved for High-Speed Rail Link", *South China Morning Post*, December 27, 2017, available at: https://www.scmp.com/news/hong-kong/politics/article/2125820/chinas-top-body-approves-plan-enforce-mainland-laws-joint (accessed May 7, 2019).

46 Ibid.

47 Ibid.

The Living Constitution theory was developed in the US about 100 years ago by constitutional scholars, judges, and political leaders who stressed that a Constitution is notably more akin to a living organism than to a complex machine.[48] Australia presents an informing case study of how a Common Law jurisdiction may set about adapting its fundamental Public Law to fit significantly changed circumstances – in keeping with the spirit of this Living Constitution theory.[49]

Australia arose as a new nation on January 1, 1901. The Australian Federal Constitution created a new, central Commonwealth Government and converted the then six colonies into six new Australian States. Section 128 (the prescribed amendment provision) made it very difficult to amend the Constitution in a formal way. The original Australian drafters of the Constitution envisioned a set of relatively powerful State Governments coexisting with the new Commonwealth Government, which would largely confine itself to looking after matters such as defence, foreign affairs, a new monetary union, and maintaining free trade within Australia.

Within 20 years, the High Court of Australia began to turn this political order on its head through a constitutional interpretation handing extensive powers over industrial relations to the Commonwealth Government.[50] That process has continued almost without let-up ever since. The Commonwealth now dominates public policy making in areas such as taxation, public borrowing, corporate regulation, competition law, labour regulation, welfare, education, healthcare, and major infrastructure development.

Australia is, consequently, a profoundly different political entity today compared to the Australia which endured until 1920. Almost all of this massive change has been secured by the High Court of Australia relying on adaptive, constitutional interpretative norms. Meanwhile, the formal wording of the Australian Constitution has remained largely intact. This remarkable constitutional transformation was set running by events never foreseen by the original drafters, including the outbreak of World War I.

Over 20 years ago, the CFA laid down a set of primary principles designed to shape the interpretation of the Basic Law of the HKSAR. In the *Right of*

48 See, for example, Strauss, David, A., *The Living Constitution* (Oxford University Press, New York, 2010); and Strauss, David A. "The Living Constitution", *University of Chicago Law School,* September 22, 2010, available at: https://www.law.uchicago.edu/news/living-constitution (accessed May 7, 2019).

49 This analysis draws significantly on: Cullen, Richard, "Opponents of Co-Location Ignore 'Living Law' Model", *China Daily,* February 2, 2018, available at: http://www.chinadaily.com.cn/hkedition/2018-02/02/content_35630779.htm (accessed May 7, 2019).

50 *Amalgamated Society of Engineers v. Adelaide Steamship Co. Ltd* (*Engineers Case*) (1920) 28 CLR 129. See Galligan, Brian, *The Politics of the High Court* (University of Queensland Press, St. Lucia, 1987) for a comprehensive analysis of how the High Court, using an ostensibly "narrow reading" of the relevant provision in the Australian Constitution, created the basis for a remarkable enhancement of Commonwealth powers at the expense of the States.

Abode Litigation, Chief Justice Li stipulated that, with the Basic Law, a purposive approach is needed as gaps and ambiguities are bound to arise in such an instrument given its necessary generality. He also cautioned against using a technical, narrow, or rigid approach when considering the language of the Basic Law. These CFA formulations are in harmony with Living Constitution theory – and the comments made by Li Fei, above.

The feasibility study for the first HSR line in China did not commence until several years after the promulgation of the Basic Law and well after its drafting had been concluded. There was, thus, zero consideration given in the Basic Law to the linkage of the HKSAR to this HSR network. These fresh *facts on the ground* are different in their particular nature to those rapid economic, technical, and political factors which have driven such massive, interpretative change to Australia's fundamental Public Law over the last 100 years. But they share the quality of changing, unforeseen circumstances applying pressure for rational, organic constitutional evolution.

Those arguments which say that co-location has not specifically been shown to be permitted by the Basic Law rely, above all, on a lack of explained particular authority in the Basic Law for co-location (a previously unforeseen need) and the Basic Law protections against the general application of Mainland Law in the HKSAR. These arguments are serious but they are, when viewed within a Living Constitution context (coupled with the cautionary words from the CFA), narrow and quite technical. In fact, although there are no provisions in the Basic Law which explicitly authorize a co-location initiative, neither are there any explicit prohibitions.[51] Had similar narrow arguments prevailed (and they were made) in Australia about 100 years ago, this would have conspicuously restrained Australia's development and adaptation to a constantly changing world.

There is one further aspect of the SCPNC Statement of Validity on co-location which should be addressed: the point that it was, in effect, an Advisory Interpretation. The SCNPC was quite clear about the weight to be given to this special Statement. Li Fei said that:

> The co-location arrangement, which complies with the Constitution and the Basic Law, carries constitutional authority ... it is an important constitutional judgment which cannot be challenged.[52]

From a Common Law perspective, the SCNPC Statement looks most like an *Advisory Opinion*. The Common Law developed a general doctrine that precluded courts from giving any sort of advance opinions. A Common Law court, it was argued, should, by its nature, not decide abstract questions (with finality)

51 I am indebted to an astute Master of Common Law student at Hong Kong University for pointing this out in 2018.

52 Siu and Chung, "Controversial Joint Checkpoint Plan Approved for High-Speed Rail Link".

but should only adjudicate where there was a justiciable dispute between two or more contesting parties.[53]

As it happens, this general prohibition on Advisory Opinions has been measurably reduced in Common Law jurisdictions in more recent years. Thus, the CA in the HKSAR confirmed in 2006, in *Leung TC William v. Secretary for Justice*,[54] that the courts could hear what it termed "academic cases" in certain exceptional circumstances. In Britain, the United Kingdom Supreme Court (UKSC) has arguably become even more radically open to providing advance opinions. In 2016, Lady Hale, the then Deputy President (now the President) of the UKSC, indicated in a public lecture what her view would likely be in the ongoing Brexit litigation, a month before that litigation reached the UKSC. That is, she spoke publicly about a case she was about to hear.[55]

In the *Northern Ireland Abortion case*, in mid-2018, the UKSC found by a majority that the Northern Ireland Human Rights Commission did not have *standing* (the necessary authority) to bring the particular case – which argued that certain abortion-related legislation in Northern Ireland was not compatible with the UK Human Rights Act (HRA). Normally, following a *no-standing* decision, that would be the end of judicial discussion on the particular matter. In this case, however, a majority of the UKSC went on to offer a view on the substance of the case, namely that the relevant Northern Ireland legislation appeared to be incompatible with the HRA.[56]

Five applications were lodged seeking judicial review (with legal-aid assistance) of the constitutionality of the co-location arrangement. The HKSAR High Court (Court of First Instance) held, in December 2018, that the arrangements, by then operating, were constitutional. The court found that none of the aspects of the co-location arrangement were prohibited by the Basic Law and that it was

53 *In re Judiciary Act* (1921) 29 CLR, 257. See also Shrubb, William, "Advisory Opinions and the Rule of Law", *Rule of Law Institute of Australia*, May 16, 2016, available at: https://www.ruleoflaw.org.au/advisory-opinions-rule-law/ (accessed May 7, 2019). One jurisdiction which provides a constitutional exception to this general rule is Canada, which allows "References" on certain legal issues to be brought by an Attorney-General before superior courts. See, further, Cullen, Richard, "Canada and Australia: A Federal Parting of the Ways" (1989) 18 *Federal Law Review*, 53.

54 (2006) 4 HKLRD,211.

55 Campbell, David and Allan, James, "Adjudication in Advance: Are UK Judges Out of Control? *The Spectator*, July 7, 2018, available at: https://www.spectator.co.uk/2018/07/adjudication-in-advance/ (accessed May 5, 2019).

56 See *In the Matter of an Application by the Northern Ireland Human Rights Commission for Judicial Review (Northern Ireland) Reference by the Court of Appeal in Northern Ireland Pursuant to Paragraph 33 of Schedule 10 to the Northern Ireland Act 1998* (2018) UKSC 27 *(Northern Ireland Abortion Case)*; and Campbell and Allan, ibid.

open to LegCo to pass the relevant supporting legislation. The court also admitted the SCNPC Advisory Interpretation as an aid to its elucidation of the Basic Law.[57]

As a practical matter, the co-location system provides a far better mode of transiting between the HKSAR and the Mainland than had previously been available. Hong Kong passengers can now complete all formal immigration and customs procedures for both the HKSAR and the Mainland at a single entry–exit point. Passengers leaving Hong Kong by HSR can now travel to any point in the Mainland without need of further border-crossing procedures and their return to the HKSAR from anywhere in the Mainland (by HSR) is made equally more straightforward. These are options not open to air or bus travellers to and from the Mainland. Operationally, the system is like that applied to trains running in the English Channel Tunnel and at certain airports handling flights between Canada and the US. The co-location policy has enjoyed wide public support. Interestingly, Kurt Tong, a former US Consul-General in the HKSAR, suggested in 2019 that it could be good to establish a US Customs and Immigration co-location facility at Hong Kong Airport.[58]

In summary, although there is much in the text of the Basic Law which provides significant underpinning to the Rule of Law in Hong Kong, the deployment of Article 158, in particular, has given cause for serious concern about the long-term impact of SCNPC Interpretations on the Rule of Law. We know, now, from the unfolding of the Interpretations and the related case law that Article 158 Interpretations may be initiated: by the CFA, the SCNPC itself, or by the Chief Executive of the HKSAR.

When the then new Secretary for Justice was appointed in late 2005, he went on record to state that the use of Article 158 should be avoided as far as possible.[59] In fact, Article 158 interpretations have been used sparingly – five times in over two decades. The SCPNC also enjoys the right to interpret PRC laws which apply only in the Mainland. This power also has been used in a limited manner – and with caution.[60]

57 *Co-Location Judicial Reviews* (2018) HKCFI 2657. See also "Court of First Instance Upholds Constitutionality of Co-Location Arrangement", *Parkside Chambers*, December 17, 2018, available at: http://www.parksidechambers.com.hk/court-of-first-instance-upholds-the-constitutionality-of-the-co-location-arrangement/ (accessed May 7, 2019); and Yap, Po Jen and Jiang, Zixin, "Co-Location is Constitutional" (2018) 48 *Hong Kong Law Journal*, 37.

58 See Delaney, Robert and Magnier, Mark, "Showdown with Beijing Looms as More US Lawmakers Back Hong Kong Democracy Bill", *South China Morning Post,* September 14, 2019, available at: https://www.scmp.com/news/hong-kong/article/3027215/showdown-beijing-looms-more-us-lawmakers-back-hong-kong-democracy (accessed September 14, 2019).

59 See Wong, Yan-long, "One Country Two Systems", *Chatham House Speech,* June 9, 2006, available at: http://www.info.gov.hk/gia/general/200606/09/P200606080140.htm (October 1, 2019).

60 See Yang, Xiaonan, "Legislative Interpretations by the Standing Committee of the National People's Congress in China" (2008) 38 *Hong Kong Law Journal*, 255.

It is important to note, too, that in the case of each Interpretation, the focus of the SCNPC has been on "solving" perceived and rather immediate practical, policy problems: controlling apprehended, excessive migration to the HKSAR from the Mainland; taking a tighter grip over the initiation of political reforms in Hong Kong; applying a Mainland principle to the novel problem of replacing a Chief Executive of the HKSAR, midterm; resolving a commercial Conflict of Laws dispute with finality; and vigilantly stipulating the elements of an acceptable oath of office in the HKSAR. The SCNPC has not, in its Interpretations, generally concerned itself with spelling out wider principles of Public Law to apply in the HKSAR. This is not part of the "problem solving" thrust evident in the SCNPC use of Article 158 over the last two decades. Thus, broad, definitive statements from the CFA about (for example) the constitutional status of the Basic Law, the importance of purposive (or generous) interpretation, and the CFA, Article 158 referral test, have not, thus far, been specifically contradicted within any of the Interpretations.

Constitutional amendment by interpretation (discussed above) is the rule rather than the exception across a number of leading Common Law jurisdictions. Both Australia and the US provide conspicuous examples. In both these jurisdictions, the rigid formal constitutional change mechanisms have not stood in the way of radical changes being made – by *judicial interpretation* – to the once settled constitutional order. In Australia, although the wording on the Australian Constitution has been little changed, as a result of High Court of Australia interpretations the Federal Constitution has been hugely centralized over the last 100 years.[61] In the US, it is interpretations by the United States Supreme Court (USSC) which have, for example, ended segregation in schools (and beyond), legalized abortion rights and gay marriage rights, radically reformed defamation law, and effectively legalized the vast US pornography industry (in the interests of protecting free expression under the US Bill of Rights).[62] The UK, with its

61 Allan, James and Aroney, Nicholas, "An Uncommon Court: How the High Court of Australia Has Undermined Australian Federalism" (2008) 30 *Sydney Law Review*, 245.

62 See, for example, Holland, Kenneth M., "Judicial Activism in the United States" in (Holland ed.) *Judicial Activism in Comparative Perspective* (Palgrave Macmillan, London, 1991; Cullen, Richard and Tso, Kevin K. S. Tso, "Commercial Free Speech: A Critical Reconsideration" (2016) 17, *Australian Journal of Asian Law*, available at: https://papers.ssrn.com/sol3/papers.cfm?abstract_id=2939388 (accessed May 5, 2019); and "An Overview of Past Pornography Rulings by the U.S. Supreme Court", Public Broadcasting Service, available at: https://www.pbs.org/wgbh/pages/frontline/shows/porn/prosecuting/overview.html (accessed May 5, 2019). One estimate put the revenue of the US pornography industry at $15 billion in 2018 over 30% more than total revenues for Hollywood in the same year; "Estimated US Entertainment Industry Revenue in 2018", *Quartz Index*, available at: https://index.qz.com/1310708/porn-could-be-worth-more-to-the-us-economy-than-netflix-the-nba-or-the-nfl/ (accessed May 5, 2019).

unwritten Constitution, is now catching up with recent decisions by the UKSC confirming a significant lifting of Diceyan constraints on judicial activism.[63]

It was expected, prior to 1997, that there may well be conflicts between the two legal traditions. After more than two decades, the pattern which has emerged from these interpretations can be summarized as follows:

1. The SCNPC, acting as the Basic Law constitutional umpire, can employ Article 158 at the request of the CFA, at the request of the HKSAR Government, or on its own initiative.
2. The SCNPC's power to interpret the Basic Law is unqualified and can be used to clarify and supplement provisions and is binding on local courts.[64]
3. There are significant differences in how the SCNPC functions within the Mainland system and how superior courts operate in Common Law jurisdictions.
   a. In the Common Law world, there is a deep understanding (i.e. custom) which accepts that supreme courts enjoy powers to reconstruct primary legal principles by applying new interpretations in particular leading cases. In a range of jurisdictions, courts at this level regularly use such powers to change how constitutions operate in fundamental ways (these interpretations are typically set out in lengthy, carefully written judgements). The constitutional text is not changed – but the courts give fresh meaning to existing words – often with long-term dramatic consequences, in light of changing political-economic circumstances.
   b. The SCNPC, as the principal legislative-judicial organ, within a civil law OPS has no such comparable role. Its interpretations do have long-term impact, but interpretations are typically short and have a narrow focus

63 See Campbell, David, "*Marbury v. Madison* in the UK: Brexit and the Creation of Judicial Supremacy", available at: http://eprints.lancs.ac.uk/124104/2/Marbury_v_Madison_in_the_UK.pdf (accessed May 5, 2019); and Campbell and Allan, "Adjudication in Advance: Are UK Judges Out of Control?"

64 For a well-argued, alternative view, see Chan Cora, "The Legal Limits on Beijing's Powers to Interpret Hong Kong's Basic Law", *HKU Legal Scholarship Blog*, November 3, 2016, available at: http://researchblog.law.hku.hk/2016/11/cora-chan-on-legal-limits-of-beijings.html (accessed May 6, 2019). Professor Chan argues in favour of a Common Law influenced, quite stringent test to establish when the SCNPC ought, legitimately, to be able to issue an Article 158 Interpretation. Under this test, subject matters and who may refer are regulated by tightly argued restrictions. Moreover, Interpretations, it is argued, should not spill over into being Amendments (where Article 159 applies) of the Basic Law. There are, though, two difficulties with this approach. First, in *Lau Kong Yung & Others v. Director of Immigration* (1999) 4 HKC 731, the CFA accepted that it was bound by the SCNPC Interpretation of June, 1999. The CFA also found, in effect, that the SCNPC enjoyed a plenary power to deploy Article 158 – on its own initiative where it felt the need (in addition to the initiative of the HKSAR Government and that of the CFA) – to interpret all parts of the Basic Law. Next, as argued above, constitutional amendment by interpretation is the norm across a range of major Common Law jurisdictions. The SCNPC Interpretations thus far are not radical or lacking in legitimacy, bearing this long-standing context in mind.

– the primary task is to solve immediate, practical policy problems (it is fair to identify this as a constitutional convention in China).

c. The Article 158 Interpretations to date reflect this essential distinction. This custom applies a certain measure of control over the NPCSC interpretation power (compared to superior Common Law courts).

4. SCNPC interpretations are a part of the wider Mainland political-legal tradition. They are employed with other Mainland laws (under Article 67(4) of the Constitution of the PRC), though Article 158 Interpretations are the most significant.
5. The arguments favouring some form of Living Constitution interpretive approach to the Basic Law are consistent with the use of this approach (however named) in certain major Common Law jurisdictions and with CFA comments on the Basic Law.
6. The creation and use of an Advisory Interpretation option to help resolve the co-location disputation is consistent with the relaxation in major Common Law jurisdictions (including the HKSAR) of the earlier Common Law rejection of Advisory Opinions.
7. The fact remains, however, that Article 158, not least, as understood by the CFA, confers very great powers over the Basic Law (and therefor over the HKSAR) on the SCNPC. (Moreover, these powers are underpinned by the central role given to the SCNPC under the PRC Constitution of 1982.) The chief risk that Article 158 may be used both more radically and more frequently arises from any heightened perceptions in Beijing that events in the HKSAR present significant dangers to PRC sovereignty – especially to Chinese national security. The law can be used effectively to regulate, sometimes insistently, the political and social space within a given jurisdiction. One can see how Article 158 might be used to deploy more of that model within the HKSAR, if Beijing feels that need.[65] Moreover, the Advisory Interpretation approach used to resolve the co-location dispute could also be used to assist in such a project.

The former Chief Justice of the HCA, Sir Anthony Mason, has, in his capacity as a Non-Permanent Judge (NPJ) of the CFA, influenced the shaping of the Basic Law jurisprudence of the CFA significantly. He delivered a strong and essentially positive assessment in 2011 after the first four Article 158 Interpretations had

65 See, further, Zhu, Han, "Beijing's 'Rule of Law' Strategy for Governing Hong Kong: Legalisation without Democratisation" (2019) *China Perspectives*, 23. This paper "examines the evolution of legal strategies that the central government has used in managing Hong Kong affairs in the past three decades. It demonstrates that the Beijing government appears to have successfully employed the tactic of "legalisation without democratisation" to neutralise political resistance, to resolve thorny issues, and to stifle pro-independence voices. … Legalisation without democratisation has given rise to a worrying trend of rising authoritarian legalism in Hong Kong."

been delivered. His concluding summation explains the standing of the Basic Law within the OCTS framework well:

> [T]he closer the attention I give to the provisions of the Basic Law, the greater the respect I have for the people who put it together. They were confronted with the task of constructing a Constitution which bridged two different systems of government, two different economic systems and two different legal systems. From a technical viewpoint, their well-crafted Constitution appears to have identified the potential difficulties and to have provided solutions to them. Only the future will determine how successful these solutions are. Despite the tensions which it may generate from time to time, Article 158 is an ingenious link between the two legal systems. Whether it is viewed from a constitutional, legal or political perspective, Article 158 is central to the Hong Kong conception of the Rule of Law. Debate about the Rule of Law in Hong Kong must recognise and proceed from the centrality of Article 158. In the words of Professor Vernon Bogdanor, "[f]or believers in the rule of law ... power should lie ... with the Constitution". Recognition of that centrality in a Constitution which seeks to bridge two systems of law and jurisprudence enables us to see more clearly that the Basic Law's distinction between the power of authoritative interpretation and the power of final adjudication leaves the Hong Kong courts in a position where their decisions are respected and prevail, even if their interpretations of the Basic Law may give way on occasions to different interpretations based on a different system of law. It must be acknowledged, however, that in other common law legal systems the power of final adjudication ordinarily includes the power of final interpretation. That is not so in Hong Kong. The power of final adjudication in Hong Kong does not include the power of final interpretation.[66]

The Basic Law and individual rights

The courts in the HKSAR, including the CFA, have by now built up a substantial body of jurisprudence arising from cases (including the *Right of Abode Litigation*) establishing protections of a wide range of individual or human rights under complementary safeguards contained within the BORO and Chapter III of the Basic Law: *Fundamental Rights and Duties of the Residents.*[67]

66 Mason, the Honourable Sir Anthony, "The Rule of Law in the Shadow of the Giant" (2011) 33 *Sydney Law Review*, 623, available at: http://www.austlii.edu.au/au/journals/SydLawRw/2011/27.pdf (accessed October 1, 2019). Professor Ghai has argued that a set of agreed rules for the use of Article 158 is required and that securing this would benefit both Hong Kong and Beijing – see Ghai, *Hong Kong's New Constitutional Order*.

67 A good analytical summary of the HKSAR individual rights case law can be found in Chan, Johannes and Kaufman, Christine, "The Protection of Human Rights under the Hong Kong Basic Law", *The University of Zurich, Faculty of Law*, available at: http://www.ivr.uzh.ch/dam/jcr:ffffffff-ec76-c8f9-ffff-ffff9e8d0d07/Furrer_Nicole.pdf (accessed October 1, 2019).

The case law includes (for example) decisions in relation to sex discrimination (2006) and sexual orientation (2006) – in both cases favouring protection of the rights of individuals,[68] the right to property (2006) – favouring the Government,[69] the rights of indigenous inhabitants of the HKSAR (2000) – limiting the scope of these rights,[70] and privacy and surveillance (2006) – favouring protection of individual rights.[71] There is no space here to review all of the human rights decisions of the HKSAR. It is important, however, to discuss several of the leading cases dealing with freedom of expression and freedom of assembly.[72]

The Flag case

Not long after the *Right of Abode Litigation*, the CFA was called on, in 1999, to consider the protection of freedom of expression rights in *Ng Kung-Siu & Anor v. HKSAR (Flag case)*.[73] The *Flag case* involved the validity (under Article 27 of the Basic Law) of HKSAR laws criminalizing the defacing of either the PRC flag or the HKSAR flag. The CFA ultimately held that the particular laws were valid, in summary because only one mode of expression was restricted (defacing either flag) and others remained available (for example, denigrating either flag in writing or verbally). The Chief Justice of the CFA, Andrew Li, in the course of his judgement, expressed that:

> Freedom of expression is a fundamental freedom in a democratic society. It lies at the heart of civil society and of Hong Kong's system and way of life. The courts must give a generous interpretation to its constitutional guarantee. This freedom includes the freedom to express ideas which the majority may find disagreeable or offensive and the freedom to criticise governmental institutions and the conduct of public officials.[74]

68 See *Secretary for Justice v. Yau Yuk Lung Zigo* (2006) 4 HKLRD 211 (CFA); and *Leung T. C. William Roy v. Secretary for Justice* (2006) 4 HKLRD 211 (CA); and Article 25 of the Basic Law (equality rights) and the BORO.

69 See *Fine Tower Associates Ltd v. Town Planning Board* (2008) 1 HKLRD 553 (for example); and Articles 6 and 105 of the Basic Law (property rights).

70 See *Secretary for Justice v. Chan Wah* (2000) 3 HKCFAR 459; and Article 40 of the Basic Law (indigenous inhabitant rights) and the BORO.

71 See *Leung Kwok Hung v. Chief Executive of the HKSAR*, CACV 73 and 87/2006 (unreported) – (2006) Hong Kong Electronic Cases (HKEC) 816; and Article 30 of the Basic Law (privacy rights) and the BORO. For a thorough review of the related series of cases here, see Lo, P. Y. "Levitating Unconstitutional Law" (2006) 36 *Hong Kong Law Journal*, 433.

72 A comprehensive review of key HKSAR individual rights cases may be found in Chan and Lim (eds.), *Law of the Hong Kong Constitution* (2nd ed.) (Sweet & Maxwell, Hong Kong, 2015) especially in Part 5, *Fundamental Rights and Freedoms.*

73 (1999) 3 HKLRD 907.

74 Ibid. For a critical review of this decision and certain related decisions, see also Ning Y. M. "One Court, Two Rulings? Freedom of Expression in Post-1997 Hong Kong" (2001) *Asia Pacific Media Educator*, 11.

There is an interesting aspect of the *Flag case*, which is not often mentioned. Article 18 of the Basic Law provides that no PRC National Law is to be applied directly in the HKSAR, but certain such laws may be added to Annex III of the Basic Law and they may then be applied within the HKSAR by the HKSAR itself – either by promulgation or by local, HKSAR legislation. The relevant National Law, protecting the PRC flag, was applied in the HKSAR using this method. It was first listed in Annex III and then locally enacted by the Provisional Legislative Council (PLC), which was appointed by Beijing and which operated for one year from July 1, 1997 in reaction to the Patten Reforms, which had changed key aspects of the election system used for choosing members of the (pre-handover) 1995 LegCo (see further below).

In the *Right of Abode Litigation*, the CFA, controversially, argued that:

> The CFA and courts of Hong Kong enjoyed a jurisdiction to examine, in certain cases, if legislative acts of the NPC were consistent with the Basic Law.

Although this claim has been firmly disapproved of, this "power" has never been explicitly overruled in any SCNPC Article 158 Interpretation. The legislation under review in the *Flag case* was, indirectly but clearly, a law of the NPC, which had been included in Annex III of the Basic Law. Thus, the CFA in the *Flag case* did, in this sense, examine a legislative act of the NPC to ensure that it was consistent with the Basic Law. The CFA did, of course, find that the examined law was valid. There is some resonance here with the seminal 1803, USSC case of *Marbury v. Madison*[75] (where the USSC assigned to itself the power to review legislative acts of Congress, inter alia, to ensure compliance with the US Constitution) in the sense that the USSC court ultimately found in favour of the then US Government in that case.[76]

The Falun Gong case

In May 2005, the CFA handed down its decision in *Yeung May Wan & Others v. HKSAR.*[77] In this case, the CFA took a generous approach when examining the right of Falun Gong practitioners to demonstrate peacefully in Hong Kong. The court found that these demonstrators enjoyed a right to demonstrate protected by Article 27 of the Basic Law (which protects freedom of speech, press, assembly, association, and demonstration). The CFA said these freedoms were core values at the heart of Hong Kong's system. In quashing the original public place obstruction convictions, the CFA found that the minor obstructions were not unreasonable, especially in the light of Article 27, and the convictions could not stand. Some protesters also resisted arrest when the Police eventually moved

75 5 US (1 Cranch) 137 (1803).
76 Ibid.
77 (2005) 8 HKCFAR 137.

them on (after more than a year of protesting[78]). The CFA also found that, as the protest was protected by the Basic Law, the protesters were not resisting what were fully lawful arrests and so these convictions were also quashed. The judgement was welcomed for the way it strengthened the protection of human rights in Hong Kong and also the Rule of Law.[79]

The public procession case

Shortly after this, in 2005, the CFA handed down another key judgement on freedom of assembly in *Leung Kwok Hung v. HKSAR*.[80] The argument here was against the regime set down in the Public Order Ordinance (POORD) requiring prior notification of both public processions (marches) and public assemblies in almost all cases where more than 30 persons take part (public procession) or more than 50 persons gather (public meetings).[81] On this occasion by a majority of 4:1, the CFA held that almost all the notification scheme in the POORD was valid.[82] Notwithstanding the finding that the regulatory scheme was constitutional, the majority observed at the beginning of their judgement that:

> The freedom of peaceful assembly is a fundamental right. It is closely associated with the fundamental right of the freedom of speech. The freedom of speech and the freedom of peaceful assembly are precious and lie at the foundation of a democratic society.
>
> These freedoms are of cardinal importance for the stability and progress of society for a number of inter-related reasons. The resolution of conflicts, tensions and problems through open dialogue and debate is of the essence of a democratic society. These freedoms enable such dialogue and debate to take place and ensure their vigour. A democratic society is one where the market place of ideas must thrive. These freedoms enable citizens to voice criticisms, air grievances and seek redress. This is relevant not only to institutions exercising powers of government but also to organizations outside the public sector which in modern times have tremendous influence over the lives of citizens. Minority views may be disagreeable, unpopular, distasteful

78 Poon, Patrick, "Falun Gong 16 Plead Not Guilty to Obstruction", *South China Morning Post*, June 18, 2002, available at: http://www.scmp.com/article/382501/falun-gong-16-plead-not-guilty-obstruction (accessed October 1, 2019). The protestors kept their numbers under 30 apparently to avoid triggering any of the relevant provisions of the Public Order Ordinance (discussed in the next CFA case).

79 See Hogg, Chris, "HK Quashes Falun Gong Convictions", *BBC News*, available at: http://news.bbc.co.uk/2/hi/asia-pacific/4515503.stm (accessed October 1, 2019); and Ghai, Yash, "Great Guardian of Human Rights", *South China Morning Post*, May 10, 2005, A19.

80 (2005) HKCFA 41.

81 See Part III of the POORD.

82 One provision, conferring what the CFA majority thought was an excessive administrative discretion, was "severed" (or read down), see (2005) HKCFA 41 para 67 ff.

> or even offensive to others. But tolerance is a hallmark of a pluralistic society. Through the exercise of these freedoms minority views can be properly ventilated.[83]

The literature commenting on the protection of individual rights in the HKSAR is large and always growing. The erosion of those protections is a frequently recurring theme in much of what is written. A quite comprehensive report on the extent of this deep-rooted, disconsolate view of freedoms within the HKSAR, written by David Matthews, was published in the Times Higher Education online in September 2015. The article summarizes a number of key concerns as follows:

> Fears that Hong Kong's special, ambiguous status was under attack from the Chinese administration helped draw more than 100,000 protesters to the streets last year, with key parts of the city's business district occupied for months [by the Occupy Central Movement]. The immediate flashpoint was an announcement by Beijing in August 2014 that a nominating committee, which critics expected to be packed with loyalists, would screen candidates for the election for Hong Kong's chief executive in 2017. The protesters' tent cities were cleared by December, without the Tiananmen-style massacre that some feared at the height of the occupation. But the city is still as politicised as ever and anxiety about mainland encroachment runs high. Academic freedom and university autonomy is guaranteed by law in Hong Kong. Nevertheless, a number of scholars who are not "politically correct" – that is, they are too critical of Beijing – believe that they are being targeted by media smear campaigns from pro-communist newspapers, passed over for jobs, or blocked from taking senior management positions by university councils loyal to Beijing.[84]

The focus in this and many similar articles is on what might be termed the "operational rights environment" – that is the general perceptions of freedoms beyond the judicial setting we have focused on above.

83 Ibid., para 1 and 2.

84 Matthews, David, "Unsafe Harbour: Academic Freedom in Hong Kong", *Times High Education,* September 10, 2015, available at: https://www.timeshighereducation.com/features/academic-freedom-in-hong-kong-unsafe-harbour (accessed October 1, 2019). See also Lam, Jeffie, "Rights Campaigner Bids Hong Kong a Reluctant Farewell" (Interview with Professor Michael Davis), *South China Morning Post,* July 23, 2016, available at: http://www.scmp.com/news/hong-kong/politics/article/1993469/rights-campaigner-bids-hong-kong-reluctant-farewell (accessed October 1, 2019). For a different perspective on the topic of academic freedom in the HKSAR, see Carty, Tony, "What Exactly Does Academic Freedom Mean to Johannes Chan and His Supporters?", *South China Morning Post,* October 7, 2015, available at: http://www.scmp.com/comment/insight-opinion/article/1864887/what-exactly-does-academic-freedom-mean-johannes-chan-and (accessed October 1, 2019).

A rather less alarming summary was offered by Professor Albert Chen in 2011 – in this case, far more directed towards the judicial protection of rights in the HKSAR:

> [I]n the post-1997 era the courts of Hong Kong have flourished as the guardian of the rule of law, constitutionalism, human rights and civil liberties. Increasing numbers of major issues of social and public policy have been litigated in the courts, as members of the public become more aware of the possibilities of judicial review of governmental and legislative measures and more conscious of their rights. The discourse of the law has become more powerful than ever before in Hong Kong society. At the same time, the courts have been careful not to over-extend their jurisdiction in a manner that would upset the delicate balance of judicial, executive and legislative powers in the SAR and the even more delicate power relationship between the SAR courts and the Central Authorities in Beijing.[85]

More recently, concerns have been expressed in relation to matters raising fresh questions about the protection of rights within the HKSAR.

Extra-legal rendition

Controversy arose over the case of five booksellers who ran into trouble with Mainland authorities. They published and sold books about Mainland politics in Hong Kong, including gossipy works on Mainland leaders. Three of them were detained when they were on the Mainland and one appeared to have been taken from Thailand. The controversy arose in Hong Kong when one of them, a Hong Kong permanent resident, was apparently abducted by Mainland officials in Hong Kong and taken to the Mainland for interrogation and detention.[86] He was subsequently released back to Hong Kong. The Basic Law plainly does not allow Mainland officials to exercise any such direct powers in the HKSAR.

The Mainland authorities regarded the booksellers as Chinese nationals who have violated Mainland law on the mainland. A Chinese official comment is illuminating:

> [T]he books published aren't about Hong Kong affairs … but about the Mainland's affairs … [He] publishes … books in Hong Kong and brings

85 Chen, "The Rule of Law".

86 Siu, Phila, Ng, Kang-chung, and Fung, Owen, "Bookseller Lam Wing-kee Reveals Explosive Details of His Mainland China Detention, Claims Lee Po Told Him He Was 'Taken Away from Hong Kong'", *South China Morning Post,* June 16, 2016, available at: https://www.scmp.com/news/hong-kong/politics/article/1976489/bookseller-lam-wing-kee-reveals-explosive-details-his (accessed May 13, 2019).

> them back to sell on the Mainland. This is his understanding of "one country, two systems" – this "one country, two systems", we'd rather not have it.[87]

There was another case of a Mainland billionaire businessman being taken from a hotel in Hong Kong back to the Mainland supposedly to assist the authorities in investigating the Mainland stock market crash in 2015.[88]

These two cases represent warnings, likely directed at certain Mainland Chinese above all. The message is that Hong Kong's more liberal environment should not be exploited – using Hong Kong as a refuge – for overt political activism directed against Beijing. Hong Kong is right to complain that the general rule is very clear: Mainland authorities cannot exercise their jurisdiction in the HKSAR and this is a line that Hong Kong must insist should not be crossed. Mainland authorities deny being involved in any improper "snatching". Although this denial may not be credible, it indicates that Beijing realizes that the Basic Law forecloses any claim that acknowledged powers to detain and transfer exist.

Hong Kong National Party

In July 2018, there was a response to another perceived national security risk. The HKSAR Secretary for Security demanded that the Hong Kong National Party (HKNP), a political group formed by young (localist) activists in 2016, respond to detailed questions on the party's support for Hong Kong independence. The Secretary for Security subsequently determined that the HKNP was an unlawful organization under the Societies Ordinance. This action involved the application of the (British enacted) Societies Ordinance in the interests of national security, an explicit basis for invoking the Societies Ordinance.

These executive actions limiting prima facie rights of political participation (on particular legal grounds) remain subject to ultimate judicial review. An initial review by a panel appointed by the HKSAR Executive Council confirmed the ban.[89]

87 Ngo, Jennifer, and Lam, Jeffie, "Followed by Strangers, Bookseller Lam Wing-kee Pulls Out of July 1 March Fearing 'Serious Threat' to Personal Safety", *South China Morning Post,* July 1, 2016, available at: https://www.scmp.com/news/hong-kong/politics/article/1983958/followed-strangers-bookseller-lam-wing-kee-pulls-out-july-1 (accessed May 13, 2019). For a detailed, measured review of the Hong Kong booksellers case (inter alia), see Lo Sonny, "'New' Cross-Border Crime between Hong and China", *China Policy Institute, University of Nottingham,* obtained from: https://cpianalysis.org/2016/08/02/new-cross-border-crime-between-hong-kong-and-china/ (hard copy retained by author).

88 Yeung, Raymond, Choi, Chi-yuk, Leung, Christy, Lo, Clifford, and Siu, Philla, "Missing Chinese Billionaire Xiao Jianhua 'Last Seen at Hong Kong's Four Seasons Hotel' Before Entering Mainland", *South China Morning Post,* January 31, 2017, available at: https://www.scmp.com/news/china/policies-politics/article/2066744/missing-chinese-billionaire-xiao-jianhua-last-seen-hong (accessed May 13, 2019).

89 Lum, Alvin and Chung, Kimmy, "Hong Kong National Party Ban Upheld by Panel Which Says It Doesn't Trust Group Not 'to Resort to Violence' in Independence Bid", *South China*

Prior to the declaration that the HKNP was an unlawful organization but after notice of action under the Societies Ordinance to ban the party was served, the Foreign Correspondents Club (FCC) in Hong Kong hosted a lunch-time address by the leader of the HKNP where he advocated Hong Kong independence from China. This proved to be controversial. Adding to the controversy, the British journalist who was the vice-chairman of the FCC and who hosted the event, subsequently failed to secure renewal of his HKSAR work visa (which coincidentally needed renewing at about the same time).[90]

Rendition and extradition

A further cause of serious concern and the focus of intense lobbying internationally as well as locally arose from the introduction of a set of proposed amendments to the Fugitive Offenders Ordinance (FOO) in 2019, which were designed to allow rendition of fugitives from the HKSAR to the other parts of Greater China, namely Mainland China, the Macau SAR, and Taiwan – and extradition to another 174 countries around the world.[91] There is a clear gap in the operational provisions of the criminal law in Hong Kong and it is a gap which has steadily been taken advantage of by fugitives from Macau, the Mainland, and Taiwan since 1997: the HKSAR has become a de facto haven for a number of such fugitives. The task of remedying this lack of additional, needed rendition (and extradition) provisions has been delayed, now, for over 20 years. The FOO Amendments proposed significant safeguards but the issue of rendition of fugitives, especially those who are HKSAR residents, to the Mainland is contentious.[92] The protests and riots which arose following the attempt to enact these amendments are discussed in detail in Chapter 7.

The HKSAR–Beijing relationship

In July 1997, the memory of June 1989 was still vivid. Nevertheless, Hong Kong and Beijing had, by then, settled down to the task of making the new relationship work. The PRC's former "paramount leader", Deng Xiao-Ping, was the

Morning Post, February 21, 2019, available at: https://www.scmp.com/news/hong-kong/politics/article/2187174/hong-kong-national-party-ban-upheld-panel-which-says-it (accessed May 13, 2019).

90 "Hong Kong Rejects Visa for FT Editor Victor Mallet", *BBC News*, October 6, 2018, available at: https://www.bbc.com/news/world-asia-china-45769811 (accessed May 13, 2019).

91 See Cross, Grenville, "New US Commission Report Makes Flawed Assessments on HK for Political Reasons", *China Daily*, May 15, 2019, available at: https://www.chinadailyhk.com/articles/45/7/154/1557854326514.html (accessed May 15, 2019).

92 See Tong, Ronny, "Hong Kong Should Trust Its Own Judiciary on All Extradition Requests – Whether or Not They Come from Mainland China", *South China Morning Post*, April 3, 2019, available at: https://www.scmp.com/comment/insight-opinion/article/3004273/hong-kong-should-trust-its-own-judiciary-all-extradition (accessed May 14, 2019).

primary architect of the OCTS political philosophy, which underpinned the Joint Declaration and Hong Kong's reversion to China. OCTS is also meant to provide the framework for an eventual rapprochement between the PRC and the "renegade province" of Taiwan.[93] The former Portuguese colony of Macau reverted to Chinese sovereignty (after almost 450 years) under the same formula on December 20, 1999, when it became the Macau Special Administrative Region of the PRC.[94]

Despite Hong Kong's post-1997 economic and political problems (including the collapse, from 1998, of a huge property bubble which formed over the last few years of the BHK era; a run on the US dollar-pegged HK dollar; political and policy tensions on a range of issues; and the onset, in 2003, of SARS), popular attitudes within Hong Kong towards Beijing largely remained neutral or positive for some years after the handover.[95]

The majority of Hong Kong residents, though watchful about their new national identity, accepted the reality with a pragmatic mixture of positive and negative assessments. China's remarkable economic growth and related achievements continued to provide special opportunities for Hong Kong. Beijing also

93 From the perspective of Taiwan (the Republic of China on Taiwan (ROC on Taiwan)), Taiwan is clearly not the "renegade province" which Beijing perceives. Taiwan is a separate, self-governing jurisdiction which operates beyond any formal aegis of the PRC. It has done so ever since the final defeat, in 1949, on the Chinese Mainland, of the KMT by the CPC in the Chinese Civil War. Taiwan's status internationally is that it is largely no longer recognized as a separate Sovereign State. This has been the case since 1971, when the ROC on Taiwan was replaced at the UN by the PRC as the State representing China. Attempts at that time to secure some sort of "double membership" for China within the UN to accommodate both the PRC and the ROC on Taiwan were opposed by *both* Beijing and Taipei. The literature on the status of Taiwan is extensive. There is some useful more recent discussion in Turton, Michael and Benedictus, Brian, "US Policy and International Law", *The Diplomat,* July 17, 2014, available at: http://thediplomat.com/2014/07/us-policy-and-international-law-taiwans-friend/ (accessed October 1, 2019); Sheu, Gary, "No, Taiwan's Status Is Not Uncertain", *The Diplomat,* August 8, 2014, available at: http://thediplomat.com/2014/08/no-taiwans-status-is-not-uncertain/ (accessed July 10, 2016); and Winkler, Sigrid, "Taiwan's UN Dilemma, To Be or Not To Be", *Brookings Institute,* June, 2012, available at: http://www.brookings.edu/research/opinions/2012/06/20-taiwan-un-winkler (accessed October 1, 2019).

94 See "Macau", *The CIA World Factbook,* available at: https://www.cia.gov/library/publications/the-world-factbook/geos/mc.html (accessed October 1, 2019). In Macau, the transition to becoming the MacauSAR has proved to be significantly more smooth than in the case of the HKSAR. A number of factors help explain this. First, the Portuguese administration was widely seen as being significantly less competent than the British administration in Hong Kong – it was, thus, an "easier act to follow" (see Lo, Shiu Hing, *Political Development in Macau* (Chinese University Press, Hong Kong, 1993)). Next, Macau chose, as Chief Executive, Edmund Ho, who proved to be politically adept. Macau is also much smaller than Hong Kong, with a population of less than 700,000 and its gambling-dependent economy has (mainly) flourished as never before since 1999 (see "Macau", *The CIA World Factbook* (above). See, further, Chapter 10.

95 See "The First Five Years", *The Hong Kong Transition Project,* obtained from: http://hktp.hkbu.edu.hk/5years/5years.pdf (page 21ff) (hard copy retained by author).

stepped in to assist the HKSAR economically in significant ways after 1997 (for example, during the AFC and to assist recovery after the SARS crisis). Moreover, successive HKSAR Governments were seen to be most responsible for the broad negative experiences encountered post-1997.

Over the last ten years, however, an increasingly hostile attitude towards Beijing amongst a sizeable, active minority in the HKSAR has asserted itself. This group includes a significant number of concerned and frustrated members of professional elites, students (tertiary and secondary), alienated youth, and those harbouring long-standing, experienced-based antagonism towards Beijing. The discontent manifested itself in a deep opposition often verging on constant antagonism towards the HKSAR Government, led by Chief Executive C.Y. Leung, which took office (for five years) on July 1, 2012 and its successor led by Chief Executive Carrie Lam. This resulted in the most seriously disruptive protests the HKSAR has ever seen: the 2014 Occupy Central Movement (OCM), the 2016 Mong Kok Riot, and the 2019 Protests and Riots, all of which are discussed in detail in Chapter 7.

There is, thus, today a continuing, rancorous aspect embedded within the relationship between the HKSAR and Beijing. This aggrieved activism is sustained from within the significant, hostile group outlined above (which grouping is prone to internal disputation). It is also sustained by real and perceived examples of the undermining of the autonomy of the HKSAR by Beijing both directly and indirectly.

It is fair to say that the HKSAR has entered into a (delayed) period of postcolonial insecurity. Some sort of BHK "rear-view" perception[96] may have applied across the first decade after 1997 so as to help delay a coming-to-terms with the full reality of the change of sovereignty for those Hong Kong residents who found that this posed a challenge. Many of those most discontented today may have, during the second decade after 1997, come to realize more sharply that the era of BHK is now a part of Hong Kong history and the future is squarely within the PRC.[97] This appears to have amplified feelings of alarm about the future of Hong Kong.

96 That is, there was, for many, some kind of collective delay in recognizing how certain, significant, and final the change of sovereignty was. This misconception was providential in an important way for Beijing and the HKSAR Government in so far as it helped maintain a lower level of radical political activism (than now obtains) during the first decade of the HKSAR. For an energized minority, there is still a mixture of wishful, wilful, and gaze-avoiding reluctance to accept the finality aspect of this change (see further below). Amongst this group, the quest for *true democracy* often takes on an existential significance.

97 In 1968 and again in 1976 in the second edition of his best-known book, the long time, China watcher, BHK-based Australian journalist, and reputed member of the British Intelligence Service (MI6), Richard Hughes, argued that "Hong Kong Is China". See Hughes, Richard, *Borrow Place, Borrowed Time: Hong Kong and Its Many Faces* (Andre Deutsch, London, 1976), 9.

HKSAR political reform

I have discussed above how BHK used a form of Government structurally based on the classical, UK Government model that applied during the late eighteenth century.[98] There was, from 1842 to 1997 in BHK, a strong Executive Government, headed by the Governor, which, in essence, governed from outside of the Legislature. LegCo was, in keeping with this model, fully appointed by the Governor for close to 150 years. These two institutions were combined with the independent Judiciary.

In the post-war period, there had been discussions, in 1958, between the UK and BHK Governments about the introduction of full democratic governance institutions in BHK. The CPC let the UK know that it opposed any such political reforms being implemented in Hong Kong, however, and the proposal did not proceed.[99]

As July 1997 approached, a key influence on the intensifying discussion about enhanced political reform after the establishment of the HKSAR was the Basic Law. In particular, Article 45 of the Basic Law provides (with respect to the selection of the Chief Executive) that:

> The Chief Executive of the Hong Kong Special Administrative Region shall be selected by election or through consultations held locally and be appointed by the Central People's Government.
>
> The method for selecting the Chief Executive shall be specified in the light of the actual situation in the Hong Kong Special Administrative Region and in accordance with the principle of gradual and orderly progress. The ultimate aim is the selection of the Chief Executive by universal suffrage upon nomination by a broadly representative nominating committee in accordance with democratic procedures.
>
> The specific method for selecting the Chief Executive is prescribed in Annex I: Method for the Selection of the Chief Executive of the Hong Kong Special Administrative Region.

The relevant part of Annex I provides that:

> If there is a need to amend the method for selecting the Chief Executives for the terms subsequent to the year 2007, such amendments must be made

98 For an outline, see "British History: Government in the 18th Century", *Legal Studies Program – University of Wisconsin*, available at: https://www.ssc.wisc.edu/~rkeyser/?page_id=760 (accessed May 14, 22019).

99 Guilford, Gwynn, "The Secret History of Hong Kong's Democratic Stalemate", *The Atlantic*, October 14, 2014, available at: http://www.theatlantic.com/international/archive/2014/10/the-secret-history-of-hong-kongs-democratic-stalemate/381424/ (accessed October 1, 2019). See also Miners, Norman, *The Government and Politics of Hong Kong* (5th ed.) (Oxford University Press, Hong Kong, 1991).

> with the endorsement of a two-thirds majority of all the members of the Legislative Council and the consent of the Chief Executive, and they shall be reported to the Standing Committee of the National People's Congress for approval.[100]

Article 68 of the Basic Law provides (with respect to LegCo) that:

> The Legislative Council of the Hong Kong Special Administrative Region shall be constituted by election.
>
> The method for forming the Legislative Council shall be specified in the light of the actual situation in the Hong Kong Special Administrative Region and in accordance with the principle of gradual and orderly progress. The ultimate aim is the election of all the members of the Legislative Council by universal suffrage.
>
> The specific method for forming the Legislative Council and its procedures for voting on bills and motions are prescribed in Annex II: "Method for the Formation of the Legislative Council of the Hong Kong Special Administrative Region and Its Voting Procedures.

The relevant part of Annex II provides that:

> With regard to the method for forming the Legislative Council of the Hong Kong Special Administrative Region and its procedures for voting on bills and motions after 2007, if there is a need to amend the provisions of this Annex, such amendments must be made with the endorsement of a two-thirds majority of all the members of the Council and the consent of the Chief Executive, and they shall be reported to the Standing Committee of the National People's Congress for the record.

These Basic Law provisions collectively created a level of anticipation that significant democratic reform could be achieved in the HKSAR looking ten years ahead, in view of the stipulations, above, with 2007 being a possible turning-point year.

We will come back to this anticipation, the reform debates – and the outcomes – shortly. Before this, however, we need briefly to review the final set of democratic reforms (the Patten Reforms) put into effect for the 1995 LegCo Elections by the last British Governor of BHK, Chris Patten. Governor Patten took up his new appointment in Hong Kong in 1992. The key democratizing reform which he introduced for the 1995 LegCo Elections expanded the then franchise of FCs from around 180,000 to over 2 million.[101]

100 Annex 1, Clause 7.

101 For a detailed analysis of the FCs, see Loh, Christine (ed.), *Functional Constituencies* (Hong Kong University Press, Hong Kong, 2005).

These Patten Reforms were seen by many supporters as both supporting and adding weight to the "2007-Anticipation" just noted. Beijing rejected these proposed reforms almost as soon as they were announced. Beijing declared that the LegCo "through train" (from 1995 to 1999 – the normal four-year LegCo term) would no longer apply and that that PLC would be created to replace the 1995 LegCo, from July 1, 1997.[102]

The 1995 LegCo was replaced, from July 1, 1997, by the PLC. The PLC only lasted for one year and, as it transpired, it had a limited legislative agenda.[103] There were fresh elections for LegCo in 1998 – but only for a two-year LegCo, to 2000, to serve out the remaining two years (approximately) of the annulled, 1995 LegCo. The Patten Reforms were overturned with effect from July 1, 1997 by the PLC and the number of FC voters was greatly reduced for the 1998 LegCo Elections.[104] The LegCo voting system was also changed significantly. Multi-member (usually five in number) electorates were created and a new, rather basic form of Proportional Representation (PR) was introduced to replace the previous FPP electoral system (with dual-member electorates) used in BHK.[105]

The wisdom of pushing ahead with the Patten Reforms after Beijing had made known its complete opposition has been much debated. It is fair to say that, although these reforms did not flout the letter of the Basic Law, they did not, either, plainly observe the spirit of the Basic Law – as set out above in Article 68 and Article II.[106] Their ultimate, post-1997 impact was to slow the reform project

102 There is a detailed discussion of how the "through train" (the continuation of the 1995 LegCo across the 1997 Handover until 1999) was put a stop to by Beijing; in Carol, John Mark, *A Concise History of Hong Kong* (Rowman & Littlefield, Lanham, 2007), Chapter 8.

103 The constitutionally valid standing of the PLC was confirmed by the CFA in the course of the *Right of Abode Litigation*.

104 Ma, Ngok and Choy, Chi-keung, "The Evolution of the Electoral System and Party Politics in Hong Kong" in (Sing, Ming (ed.)) *Hong Kong Government and Politics* (Oxford University Press, Hong Kong, 2003).

105 Briefly, in an FPP system, the member with the most votes wins; thus, in a three-cornered contest, anyone who secures at least one-third – plus one – of the votes cast will win. With a PR voting system, seats are awarded proportionately (across a multi-seat electorate) to each candidate who secures the minimum "quota" required. Under the HKSAR PR system, where candidates typically appear on a Party List, any excess votes beyond a quota are discarded – they cannot be transferred to another Party List. Under this system, the "last member" elected may secure their seat on, effectively, a residual FPP basis, which can mean being voted into LegCo based on a relatively low number of votes. This system has been of important assistance in facilitating the election of more radical candidates to LegCo.

106 Cullen, Richard, "Hong Kong Revenue Law: The Present, 1997 and Beyond", *Tax Notes International*, November 1, 1993, 1109. In fact, Governor Patten is on record, from 1992 (just after he arrived in Hong Kong as the last BHK Governor), as saying that his Patten Reforms would need to conform not only with the Joint Declaration but also with the Basic Law (see Lim, Chin Leng, "Hong Kong's Basic Law and Political Reform", *The Straits Times*, October 17, 2014, available at: http://www.straitstimes.com/opinion/hong-kongs-basic-law-and-political-reform (accessed October 1, 2019).

to a measurable degree. For Governor Patten, they did secure an enhancement of his political reputation.[107]

Despite the acrimony arising from this belated push for greater democracy during the final years of BHK, discussion about further political reform continued. In 2005, the first post-1997, official political reform discussion was launched by the then fairly new, second Chief Executive, Donald Tsang.[108] The Government Reform Proposal related to both the 2007 Chief Executive Election and the 2008 LegCo Elections.[109] The Government argued that they were constrained by the SCNPC detailed ruling, associated with the second Article 158 Interpretation establishing the SCNP "gate-keeping" role (2004-Ruling). This 2004-Ruling stipulated that these elections in 2007 and 2008 could not be conducted on the basis of full universal suffrage. The Reform Proposal, in essence, was (a) to expand the Electoral College (in Basic Law terms, the Election Committee – see Annex 1, Clause 2 of the Basic Law)[110] for (s)electing the Chief Executive by including (mainly but not exclusively) elected District Councillors[111]; and (b) to raise the number of LegCo members from 60 to 70. Five of the new members would be directly elected and the other five would be elected by District Councillors. (The 2004-Ruling also stipulated that a 50/50 balance between directly elected members and FCs should be maintained in LegCo.)

The broad PD group, including PD LegCo members, supportive academics, PD party members, PD supporters from a range of Civil Society organizations (including Christian Churches), and supporters from within the general public eventually declared their opposition to the Government proposals (initially they had shown a willingness to negotiate – for example, to accept the proposals if *appointed* District Councillors were excluded from voting within the relevant Electoral Colleges). More radical elements within the PD movement then successfully campaigned against any compromise. The proposals were duly voted down within LegCo when presented by the Government in late December 2005. (The broad PD grouping in LegCo held over one-third of the LegCo seats, thus giving them a reform veto power under the Basic Law (see the relevant excerpts above from the Basic Law).)

107 See, for example, Dimbleby, Jonathan, *The Last Governor: Chris Patten and the Handover of Hong Kong* (Little, Brown, New York, 1998).

108 See discussion above, related to the third Article 158, SCNPC Interpretation.

109 The history and development (up until 2010) of the basis for selecting the Chief Executive of the HKSAR is fully discussed in Young, Simon and Cullen, Richard, *Electing Hong Kong's Chief Executive* (Hong Kong University Press, Hong Kong, 2010).

110 *The Cambridge Advanced Learner's Dictionary and Thesaurus* defines an *Electoral College* as "A group of people whose job is to choose a political or religious leader", available at: http://dictionary.cambridge.org/dictionary/english/electoral-college (accessed October 1, 2019).

111 District Councils in Hong Kong provide a form of limited Local Government under the Home Affairs Bureau of the HKSAR Government. At the time of these proposed reforms, they were largely directly elected – but more than 20% were appointed by the Chief Executive.

The HKSAR Government, under Chief Executive Donald Tsang, set a further political reform initiative, related to both the Chief Executive Election and the LegCo Elections, in train in late 2009. Briefly, this proposal recommended enlarging the Electoral College to choose the Chief Executive from 800 to 1200 members (for the 2012 Chief Executive Election) and enlarging the size of LegCo from 60 to 70 members (split between five directly elected and five new FCs (to represent District Councils)). This change was also to apply in 2012 as, in that year, it transpired that there would be elections for both the Chief Executive (five-year term) and LegCo (four-year term). The proposal was, thus, very similar to that put forward in 2005.

Five PD members attempted to create a "referendum" on the proposal by one PD member standing down, in January 2010, in each of the five multi-member LegCo constituencies. Each then re-stood in the five resulting By-Elections. This was meant to be a test of the general acceptability of the 2010 reform proposal. It was attacked by Beijing as demonstrating radicalism and having no legal basis (as a referendum). The largest party within the PD group, the Democratic Party (DP), led by Albert Ho, did not participate in this scheme – the party voted against participation. Those resigning were either members of Radical Pan-Democrat (RPD) parties or the middle class, lawyer-dominated, Civic Party. Pro-Government–pro-Beijing parties boycotted the By-Elections, so there was no significant opposition. All the resigning LegCo members were easily re-elected. As a referendum, it was a political failure, however. Only around 17% of eligible voters bothered to vote, compared to just over 45% in the 2008 LegCo Elections.[112]

Divisions within the broad PD group were already increasing by 2010. The By-Election strategy amplified these internal divisions with bitter attacks being launched by some RPDs against more moderate PDs due to their failure to support the project. Those campaigning for the project used Chinese four-character posters which stressed the idea of an "uprising", which also generated increased censure from Beijing.[113]

This time, however, real change was achieved, possibly in part due to the separating, divisiveness of the By-Election campaigning, the DP, applied itself with energy to try and achieve significant progress on political reform, by negotiation. The Chief Executive also worked to secure a compromise agreement with Beijing. The key to achieving this was the agreement by Beijing (and the HKSAR Government) that, although the five new FCs (representing District Councils) would remain "FCs", these FC members would be voted into office by *all* HKSAR registered voters who did not belong to another specific FC constituency. In effect, all the ten new LegCo members in 2012 would be elected by

112 See, further, Lo, Sonny, *Hong Kong's Indigenous Democracy: Origins Evolution and Conventions* (Palgrave Macmillan, Basingstoke, 2015, Chapter 3; and "By-Elections in Hong Kong: Protest vote", *The Economist*, May 20, 2010, available at: http://www.economist.com/node/16167654 (accessed October 1, 2019).

113 Lo and *The Economist*, ibid.

universal suffrage – five members via new directly elected seats and five members in the District Council "super-seat" FCs. (To stand for election in a "super-seat", one had first to be a duly elected District Councillor.). The other Government-proposed reforms, including those related to the composition of the Electoral College for Chief Executive Elections, were also passed in June 2010.[114] Soon after the passage of these reforms, the divisions within the broad PD group grew more bitter, with most hostility direct at the DP.[115]

At this point, we should note that the electoral law was amended in June 2012 so that a "By-Election Referendum" of the sort conducted in early 2010 could not run again in the same way. Any LegCo member who resigned and triggered a By-Election cannot, now, stand for re-election to LegCo within six months of resigning.[116]

The SCNPC repeated, in 2007, what it had stipulated in the 2004-Ruling, that universal suffrage was not to apply to the coming 2012 Chief Executive and LegCo Elections. It did, however, also provide a provisional timetable for the introduction of universal suffrage in the HKSAR: in 2017 for the Chief Executive Election and in 2020 for the LegCo Elections.[117] Implementation of this universal suffrage plan was subject to an operative consensus being achieved within the HKSAR (based on a framework to be provided from Beijing) and final approval by the SCNPC. This was the context in which the most recent project to achieve further political reform in Hong Kong was to unfold.

The political reform stalemate

The SCNPC timetable for potential, though conditional, political reform set down in 2004 was politically smart in the sense that (by tracking the natural election cycle) it separated the timing for reform of Chief Executive Elections (2017) and LegCo Elections (2020). This meant that the process of reform discussion would be spared the incapacitating confusion of trying to argue, in full, through two sets of reforms over the same period. Moreover, though no easy task, reform of the Chief Executive Election system is, prima facie, the less demanding of these two projects. To begin with, one is dealing with the election of a single person – rather than 70 LegCo members. Next, the structural changes needed

114 Martin, Michael F., "Prospects for Democracy in Hong Kong: The 2012 Election Reforms", *Congressional Research Service, Washington,* February 1, 2011, available at: https://www.fas.org/sgp/crs/row/R40992.pdf (accessed October 1, 2019). The agreed reforms to LegCo Elections – introducing a very wide franchise for the new District Council FCs – had clear resonances with a pivotal feature of the Patten Reforms (see above). Wisely, perhaps, none of those involved in building the breakthrough mentioned the provenance of this approach to political reform.

115 Ibid.

116 Section 39(2A), which was added to the Legislative Council Ordinance (Cap. 542) in June 2012, now so provides.

117 Li, Joseph, "NPCSC Empowered to Set Out Roadmaps for Election: Chen", *China Daily,* June 30, 2015, available at: http://www.chinadailyasia.com/leaders/2015-06/30/content_15284605.html (accessed October 1, 2019).

are demanding and contentious – but less severely so than is the case with LegCo electoral reform. (There was discussion of reform of the LegCo Election system during the 2014–2015 political reform debate, but the principal focus was on reform of the Chief Executive Election system.)

The third HKSAR Government took office on July 1, 2012.[118] C.Y. Leung won a rather bitterly fought Chief Executive contest (under the 2012 revised rules passed by LegCo in mid-2010 – see discussion directly above).[119]

The Leung Administration established a Task Force on Constitutional Development in October 2013 to begin a new consultation and review process aimed at achieving a consensus on a system of universal suffrage to be used for the 2017 Chief Executive Election. Much fervent, bitter – and more rational – discussion ensued.

Before we turn to what was in contention and why, it is sensible to summarize the reform timetable, however. The First Consultation concluded in May 2014, following which the Chief Executive submitted his Report to the SCNPC. A Second Consultation period ran from January 2015 to March 2015. In April 2015, the Government advised its formal proposals for reform. In June 2015, the broad PD group in LegCo, as expected, vetoed the reform proposals (by denying the two-thirds majority needed under Article 45 and Annex I of the Basic Law).[120]

Many submissions were made during the First Consultation with a wide range of proposals offered: (a) how persons wishing to stand in the 2017 Chief Executive Election were to be selected as eligible candidates; (b) how the new universal suffrage, voting system should work. The first question rapidly came to be seen as the core issue in the debate.[121] The primary concern for moderate PDs, especially, was that the system for nominating eligible candidates should be sufficiently open so as to allow a clear possibility of at least one PD candidate being able to participate in the actual election. For RPDs (and in due course,

118 The first Chief Executive, C.H. Tung, was selected in 1997 and then in 2002. He stepped down about midway through his second term, in 2005. Donald Tsang, his former Chief Secretary (Deputy), led the next HKSAR Government for the balance of Mr. Tung's second term. The Tsang Government continued through until June 30, 2012, after Tsang was chosen at the 2007 Chief Executive Election. See the discussion about the third SCNPC Article 158 Interpretation above. See also Young and Cullen, *Electing Hong Kong's Chief Executive.*

119 "The Worst System, Including All the Others", *The Economist,* March 31, 2012, available at: http://www.economist.com/node/21551482 (accessed October 1, 2019).

120 See, further, with respect to the timetable and related matters: "Method for Selecting the Chief Executive by Universal Suffrage: Questions and Answers", *HKSAR Government,* June 24, 2015, available at: http://www.2017.gov.hk/en/liberal/faq.html (accessed October 1, 2019). See also review of the process written in January, 2015 by the HKSAR Chief Secretary, Carrie Lam, "2017: Seize the Opportunity", *News HKSAR Government,* January 8, 2015, available at: http://www.news.gov.hk/en/record/html/2015/01/20150107_153831.shtml (accessed October 1, 2019).

121 Martin, Michael E., "Prospects for Democracy in Hong Kong: The 2017 Election Reforms", *US Congressional Research Service,* June 9, 2015, available at: https://www.fas.org/sgp/crs/row/R44031.pdf (accessed October 1, 2019).

most PDs) more was wanted – in particular, a right to secure a place on the ballot paper using a method of Civil (or Public) Nomination (typically, a nomination from 35,000 to 100,000 registered voters). With respect to the second question, the debate was mainly focused on whether, assuming more than two candidates stood, there should be a second-round, two person run-off Election (as applies, for example, in French Presidential Elections) or a so-called "instant run-off" election (as applies, for example, in most Australian Parliamentary Elections – where such systems are referred to as Preferential Voting).[122]

In fact, quite rigid boundary lines, within which reform would be permitted, were set down by the SCNPC as the debate unfolded. A "five-step" (some say "six-step"[123]) broad procedure to be followed in the reform discussion had also been fixed by the SCNPC in 2004. It can be summarized as follows:

1. The Chief Executive submits a Report to the SCNPC as to whether relevant political reform is needed (and thus amendment of electoral laws in accord with – *and amendment of* – Annex I).
2. The SCNPC determines if there is a need for such an amendment.
3. Assuming the answer at 2 is "yes", the Chief Executive submits the relevant amending legislation to LegCo.
4. LegCo must approve any such proposed legislative amendment by a two-thirds majority, in accord with Annex I.
5. The Chief Executive consents to the approved new amendment.
6. The SCNPC approves the new amendment in accord with Annex I.[124]

After the Chief Executive submitted his Report (Step 1) in July 2014,[125] the SCNPC issued its Decision of August 31, 2014, which set out seven requirements to move to a universal suffrage system for the election of the Chief Executive of the HKSAR in 2017. These requirements were, in essence, as follows:

1. "A broadly representative nominating committee shall be formed. The provisions for the number of members, composition and formation method of the nominating committee shall be made in accordance with the number of

122 The Occupy Central Movement (discussed further below) produced a good summary of a wide range of 28 submitted proposals which detail, inter alia, the points noted. See "Summaries: Proposals on Nomination and Electoral Procedures for Election of Hong Kong's Chief Executive by Universal Suffrage", *Occupy Central with Love and Peace (OCLP)*, available at: http://oclp.hk/image/data/Classification_Chief%20Executive%20Election%20Methods%20(Eng)_041714.pdf (accessed October 1, 2019).

123 The HKSAR Government normally combines Steps 5 and 6 in this list into a single Step 5.

124 See "Consultation Document: Let's Talk and Achieve Universal Suffrage", *HKSAR Government*, December, 2013, available at: http://www.legco.gov.hk/yr13-14/english/panels/ca/papers/ca1209-cdoc20131204-e.pdf (accessed October 1, 2019). See also Martin, "Prospects for Democracy in Hong Kong".

125 "Chief Executive's Report to the SCNPC", *HKSAR Government*, July, 2014, available at: http://www.2017.gov.hk/en/npcsc/ (accessed October 1, 2019).

members, composition and formation method of the Election Committee for the Fourth Chief Executive" (the Election Committee that selected C.Y. Leung).

2. "The nominating committee shall nominate two to three candidates for the office of Chief Executive in accordance with democratic procedures".
3. "Each candidate must have the endorsement of more than half of all members of the nominating committee" (more than 600 members).
4. "All eligible electors in the Hong Kong Special Administrative Region have the right to vote in the election of the Chief Executive and elect one of the candidates for the office of Chief Executive in accordance with the law".
5. "The Chief Executive-elect, after being selected through universal suffrage, will have to be appointed by the Central People's Government" (the Chinese Government in Beijing).
6. "The specific method of universal suffrage for selecting the Chief Executive shall be prescribed in accordance with legal procedures through amending Annex I of the Basic Law".
7. "If the specific method of universal suffrage for selecting the Chief Executive is not adopted in accordance with legal procedures, the method used for selecting the Chief Executive for the preceding term shall continue to apply".[126]

The stipulations handed down on August 31, 2014, plainly ruled out any form of Civil Nomination. They also provided that the proposed new Chief Executive Nominating Committee would retain the (mainly pro-Beijing) membership profile of the former Chief Executive Election Committee) – and that any person initially nominated as a candidate for the 2017 Chief Executive Election would have to be endorsed by at least 50% plus 1 of the Nominating Committee. Moreover, the total number of candidates allowed to run was limited to three. In sum, this meant that it was most likely that only broadly pro-establishment candidates would make the final cut (of two to three candidates).

In one particular respect, this most recent push for political reform in the HKSAR does stand out: it has provided the context for what is, comfortably, Hong Kong's most rancorous debate over political reform since 1997. This polarization led, inter alia, to the OCM massed protesters taking over key intersections and roads in the HKSAR for several months from September 2014, a major political riot in Mong Kok in February 2016, and the extended 2019 protests and riots (all of which are discussed in Chapter 7).

126 This summary is drawn from Martin, "Prospects for Democracy in Hong Kong". See also "Full Text: NPC Standing Committee Decision of Hong Kong 2017 Election Framework", *South China Morning Post,* August 31, 2014, available at: http://www.scmp.com/news/hong-kong/article/1582245/full-text-npc-standing-committee-decision-hong-kong-2017-election (accessed October 1, 2019).

As the debate intensified, it is clear that the RPDs increasingly set the agenda. This was an agenda which was both radical and often antagonistic to opposing views – including more moderate PD views. That this happened is not surprising. Levels of frustration within the broad PD movement about the slow pace of democratic reform in the HKSAR were high and intensifying.[127] This was even more the case within the RPDs who not infrequently found themselves competing with one another to demonstrate the greatest fervour aimed at achieving full or true democracy. This zeal meant that the RPDs were barely constrained, if at all, by questions of "political possibility". The RPDs could project the sort of resolve that grows from a sense of *militant virtue*.

The rigid position taken by Beijing and the HKSAR Government was confirmed and reconfirmed. A mood of bitter polarization settled across the entire reform process. The PDs boycotted the Government Second Consultation on reform (which ran from January to May 2015) prior to rejecting, in LegCo, the complete proposed reform package in June 2015 – vetoing that package in accord with the provisions in Annex 1 of the Basic Law.[128]

Professor Chen of Hong Kong University argued that this vetoing outcome had taken away the people's right to vote (in 2017). He also noted that the heavily advocated proposal(s) for Civil Nomination were obviously inconsistent with Article 45 of the Basic Law and that the PDs preferred to see retention of the current "small circle" Chief Executive Election system rather than allow a pro-establishment Chief Executive gain a popular mandate through a nomination-vetted, Chief Executive Election.[129]

The stalemate achieved looks to be one which may remain locked in place for years to come. Neither side has secured any of the advantages each sought. At worst, what has happened may mean, as Professor Lim puts it, "the demise of a shared framework for public-political debate which has been credited for post-handover Hong Kong's spectacular success".[130]

The highly physical "debates", in 2019, within a LegCo Bills Committee reviewing planned rendition and extradition amendments to the FOO (discussed

127 This frustration was also understandable. Almost ten years after the disappointed aspirations with respect to 2007 (see above), only limited change had been achieved (increasing the effectively, directly elected seats in LegCo to 40 out of 70 – and that reform was controversial (see above)).

128 In fact, the (defeated) broadly pro-establishment supporters of the package managed to portray significant disarray when the time for the vote came. See "Hong Kong Reform Package Rejected as Pro-Beijing Camp Walk Out in 'Miscommunication'", *South China Morning Post,* June 18, 2015, available at: http://www.scmp.com/news/hong-kong/politics/article/1823398/hong-kong-political-reform-package-voted-down-legco-leaving (accessed October 1, 2019).

129 These comments are contained in an interview article from mid-2015, see Li, Joseph, "NPCSC Empowered to Set Out Roadmaps for Election: Chen", *China Daily,* June 30, 2015, available at: http://www.chinadailyasia.com/leaders/2015-06/30/content_15284605.html (accessed October 1, 2019).

130 Lim, "Hong Kong's Basic Law and political reform".

earlier and also below) were unprecedented. These disruptions – and the protests and riots which followed them – almost certainly have left the reform door still more firmly closed.

Comparative governance dysfunction

The role within BHK and, then, the HKSAR of the three key governance institutions in Hong Kong (the Executive Government, LegCo, and the Judiciary) has each already been reviewed in some detail. My purpose here is to investigate more generally, to what degree each of these political-legal centres of authority may support or undercut the quality of governance in the HKSAR today.

The World Governance Indicators (WGIs) compiled by the World Bank Review: Voice & Accountability; Political Stability and Absence of Violence/ Terrorism; Government Effectiveness; Regulatory Quality; Rule of Law; and Control of Corruption.[131] The WGIs cover the period 1996–2017. All WGIs show that the HKSAR remains well ranked in terms of overall good governance, compared to all jurisdictions (more than 200) surveyed over this period. In the case of the 2017 indicators, the HKSAR scored more than 90/100. The lowest rankings in 2017 were for Voice & Accountability (61/100) and Political Stability (75/100 – down from 90/100 in 2007).[132] The key indicators show steady, strong performance and, in some instances, an improved comparative performance by the HKSAR over the total period and compared with the BHK era.[133]

Nonetheless, the HKSAR has found it increasingly difficult to implement many new major policies and programmes over the last decade.[134] The reasons why this is so are complex, but it is clear that the elevated level of social and political polarization already noted is a significant factor increasing dysfunction at the level of major policy development and implementation.

Among the three key institutions noted, the Judiciary in the HKSAR is the one widely regarded as functioning most successfully – especially at the highest levels. Like Judiciaries everywhere, it is burdened with challenges related to general capacity and effectiveness in meeting demands but the superior Courts, not least the CFA, have continued to deliver effective, benchmark judgements of high quality. Sir Anthony Mason, NPJ of the CFA from 1997 to 2015, made his respect for the work of his colleagues on the CFA clear in 2013 when he said:

131 "Worldwide Governance Indicators: Hong Kong SAR, China", *World Bank – 2018*, available at: http://info.worldbank.org/governance/wgi/index.aspx#reports (accessed May 14, 2019).

132 Ibid.

133 Ibid.

134 Yeung, C. K., "Let Hong Kong Think Its Way Out of Its Governance Problems", *South China Morning Post*, November 25, 2014, available at: http://www.scmp.com/comment/insight-opinion/article/1648532/let-hong-kong-think-its-way-out-its-governance-problems (accessed July 16, 2016).

> In conclusion, it remains for me to say that it has been a great honour and a great pleasure to serve as an NPJ of the CFA. I have enjoyed every minute of it or, to be more accurate, most minutes of it. And I have immense respect for my colleagues on the Court.[135]

The WGIs noted above point out that the Rule of Law Indicator stood at 93.75% in 2017 (placing the HKSAR within the top 7% across 214 jurisdictions worldwide on this (core value) indicator). In 1996, the final year of British rule in Hong Kong, this WGI stood at 70%.[136] A QC from London, also a member of the House of Lords, who has visited and worked in Hong Kong regularly, spoke at Hong Kong University in early 2014. Concerns were expressed by some attending the talk about the erosion of the authority of the Judiciary – and the Rule of Law – in the HKSAR. His response was that, overall, the Judiciary was in very sound health in Hong Kong. He observed that that part of the governance structure which looked to be in the least good condition was LegCo.[137]

It is noteworthy that the foundations of the Hong Kong Judiciary, as we have seen in Chapter 4, were comparatively quite robust from the outset. This nineteenth-century groundwork has been a major factor in building the long-term level of strong institutional integrity one can see still today in the HKSAR Judiciary.

Governments worldwide struggle to maintain popular support in the current era. Increasing aspirations and expectations, a growing wealth-gap, and societal divisions plus ageing populations and environmental concerns, to name several key factors, encounter shrinking public revenues leading, in many jurisdictions, to growing public debt. When this is coupled with the growing role of social media, with its remarkable capacity to shape and shift public opinion, the result is frequently amplified, popular distemper.[138] The HSKSAR Government is

135 Mason, the Honourable Sir Anthony, "Sitting as a Non-Permanent Judge in the Court of Final Appeal for the Past 16 years", *Speech to Hong Kong Judicial Institute,* October 25, 2013, available at: http://www.hkcfa.hk/filemanager/speech/en/upload/78/20131025%20Mason%20-%20Sitting%20as%20Non-Permanent%20Judge%20in%20the%20Court%20of%20Final%20Appeal%20for%20the%20past%2016%20years.pdf (accessed July 16, 2016). See also Mason, "The Rule of Law in the Shadow of the Giant".

136 "Worldwide Governance Indicators: Hong Kong SAR, China: 1996–2014", *The World Bank,* available at: http://info.worldbank.org/governance/wgi/pdf/c97.pdf (accessed July 16, 2016).

137 Detailed notes on file with Richard Cullen. See also Cullen, Richard, "Lawmakers Escaping Media Scrutiny", *Letters to the Editor – South China Morning Post,* August 12, 2013, available at: http://www.scmp.com/comment/letters/article/1296052/letters-editor-august-12-2013 (accessed July 16, 2016).

138 See Phillips, Angela, "Social Media Is Changing the Face of Politics – And It's Not Good News", *The Conversation,* February 9, 2016, available at: http://theconversation.com/social-media-is-changing-the-face-of-politics-and-its-not-good-news-54266 (accessed July 21, 2016); and "What's Gone Wrong with Democracy", *The Economist,* March 1, 2014 http://www.economist.com/news/essays/21596796-democracy-was-most-successful-

certainly no exception. The conventional (regularly high-pitched) print media in the HKSAR remains more numerous than the print media in almost any other part of the developed world. Inadequate or incompetent Government performance is swiftly and invariably highlighted – often with great colour. The popularity of the HKSAR Government remains lower than it would prefer.[139]

Yet, when we refer to those WGIs from the World Bank, *Governance Effectiveness* achieved a level of 98% in 2017. That is, in terms of effective governance, according to the World Bank, the HKSAR was within the top 3% of jurisdictions worldwide.[140]

An important explanation for the relatively, still sound ranking of the HKSAR Government is, as with the Judiciary, to be found in the long-term historical profile of successive Governments in BHK. In particular, the Colonial Service which provided the backbone of these Governments, had a reputation for comparative competence and integrity. Officers for the Colonial Service were chosen on the basis of ability to a significant degree. This was a professional Civil Service. Officers entered service with their eye on a lifetime career – provided they were competent, diligent, and stayed out of serious trouble. This system was meant to provide a notable level of professional continuity in governance. The system tended to engender, in the Colonial Officials, some real sense of the worth of both personal and institutional integrity.[141]

None of this is meant to disguise any of the failings of the system, which have also been noted above.[142] As it happened, there was a good point of nearby comparison – the far older (than BHK) Portuguese Colony of Macua. There the emphasis with colonial governance was far less on professional continuity.

---

political-idea-20th-century-why-has-it-run-trouble-and-what-can-be-do (accessed July 16, 2016).

139 The HKSAR Government popularity – and that of the Chief Executive and his Principal Officials – are continuously monitored by various opinion polls operating in the HKSAR, the leading one being the Public Opinion Programme at the University of Hong Kong (HKU POP). HKU POP regularly surveys the popularity of the Chief Executive and the Principal Officials (Ministers). See "Press Releases", *HKU POP Site*, available at: https://www.hkupop.hku.hk/english/release/index.html (accessed July 16, 2016).

140 See Ho, Lok-sang, "Facts Clash with Lies in Discussion of Hong Kong Protests", *China Daily*, September 10, 2019, available at: http://www.chinadaily.com.cn/hkedition/2019-09/10/content_37508944.htm (accessed September 10, 2019).

141 This perspective is argued well in Tso, Kevin K. S., "Fundamental Constitutional and Political Norms: Hong Kong and Macau Compared" (2012) 13 *Australian Journal of Asian Law*, available at: http://papers.ssrn.com/sol3/papers.cfm?abstract_id=2159544 (accessed July 16, 2016).

142 See, further, on these failings: Munn, Christopher, *Anglo-China: Chinese People and British Rule in Hong Kong – 1841–1880* (Curzon Press, Richmond, 2001); and Wesley-Smith, Peter, "Book Review: Munn, Christopher, *Anglo-China: Chinese People and British Rule in Hong Kong – 1841–1880*" (2003) (Jan.-Feb.) *China Perspectives*, 74.

Selecting who would serve in Macua was decided more according to elite connections and the patronage system within Portugal.[143]

When we look at LegCo, the "report card" is the least good of all three of the primary institutions under review. In LegCo, the broad PD grouping (including PDs and RPDs) comprised more than one-third of all members until 2016[144]. In the polarized political atmosphere already reviewed, LegCo has become a primary seat of battle. The problems with securing political reform within LegCo have already been analyzed. Of greater day-to-day concern for effective governance, however, have been the delaying and obstructive measures, especially filibustering and quorum calls,[145] used to frustrate or stop a very wide range of new legislative and funding measures introduced by the Government.[146]

The first post-1997 filibuster in LegCo happened in 1999 and was organized by pro-establishment lawmakers to delay a vote on a bill where insufficient of their numbers were on hand to vote in favour. Since then, until late 2017 when reforms were effected,[147] (after the loss of the broad PD veto power) filibusters were used in LegCo almost continuously by the RPDs, usually supported by all PDs in order to delay (and stop, if possible) funding of major public-funded projects; introduction of amendments governing By-Elections in the HKSAR; and copyright law amendments; to give examples. Filibustering has been used before the LegCo Finance Committee (and its subcommittees) as well. More recently,

143 Tso, "Fundamental Constitutional and Political Norms: Hong Kong and Macau Compared".

144 As explained above, after the oath-taking incidents, following the 2016 LegCo Elections, altogether six (broadly) PD LegCo members were found to be ineligible to take their seats by the courts. The initial outcome of the 2016 LegCo elections resulted in the broad PD movement (including PD and RDP members) holding more than enough seats to retain their veto power on a range of key issues. Following the disqualifications, the PD movement lost significant ground in the resulting by-elections and, in particular, they lost the veto power they previously held. See, further, Cheung, Tony, Lam, Jeffie, and Sum, Lok-kei, "Hong Kong Democrats Fail to Win Back LegCo Veto Foothold in By-Election", *South China Morning Post*, March 12, 2018, available at: https://www.scmp.com/news/hong-kong/politics/article/2136762/pan-democrats-look-set-regain-power-veto-rivals-moves-hong (accessed May 14, 2019); and Lo, Alex, "Pan-dems Ruin LegCo Reform for Everyone", *South China Morning Post,* April 12, 2019, available at: https://www.scmp.com/comment/insight-opinion/article/3005973/pan-dems-ruin-legco-reform-everyone (accessed May 14, 2019).

145 "Filibustering" means "the practice of obstructing legislative business by dilatory tactics" (from the Dutch for "freebooter"). "Quorum Call" means checking if the necessary number of persons required for a particular meeting are present. See, in both cases, Walker, David M. *The Oxford Companion to Law* (Oxford University Press, Oxford, 1980).

146 Ip, Regina, "When Politics Trumps Reason; Continual Filibustering by Hong Kong's Pan-Democrats Has Gone Too Far", *South China Morning Post,* January 16, 2016, available at: http://www.scmp.com/comment/insight-opinion/article/1901291/when-politics-trumps-reason-continual-filibustering-hong (accessed July 16, 2016).

147 He, Shusi, "LegCo Passes Anti-Filibuster Rule Amendments", *China Daily,* December 16, 2017, available at: https://www.chinadailyhk.com/articles/60/215/129/1513387573200.html (accessed May 14, 2019).

repeated quorum calls have been used to the same end.[148] Filibusters have also been used by RPDs to delay, if not stop, approval of annual recurring funding under the HKSAR Budget by proposing almost 2,000 amendments.[149]

The time and money costs of these measures are significant. For example, the filibustering to try and stop the By-Election amendment involved the review of 1,000 proposed amendments, which claimed almost 86 hours of debating time spread over five weeks.[150] In the course of less than a month, where the update of the Copyright Ordinance was being debated yet again (this amendment has been a project since 1997), a check of the relevant quorum was requested 101 times. The Government eventually gave up on proceeding with the amendment as this "log-jam" item was holding up other important legislative items from being advanced.[151] The total cost of quorum calls – that is, the cost of repeated head-counting – from 2012 to 2016 was over HK$45 million (almost US$6 million) with more than 220 hours spent doing the counting.[152]

Altogether, filibusters are another harmful idea largely copied from established practice within the US Congress, where they have also done significantly more harm than good, but where they are unfortunately, for all practical purposes, entrenched.[153]

Another measure stopped was a Government plan to reform the Medical Council of the HKSAR – the medical watchdog responsible for overseeing many key aspects of the medical profession in Hong Kong. The reforms, strongly supported by the main patients' rights group, were designed to enhance lay membership and reduce the delay for hearings from 58 months to 30 months. The then

148 Ibid. See also Ho, Wai Kei, Lee, Chun Kit, Ng, Kai Yin, N, Vincent, and Wong, Ka Yiu, "Filibustering in Hong Kong", *S. K. H. Lam Woo Memorial School Liberal Studies Project,* May 27, 2013, obtained from: http://www.lamwoo.edu.hk/subject/info/ls/work/student%20work%204.pdf (hard copy retained by author).

149 Fung, Owen, "Itching to Filibuster: Radical Hong Kong Lawmakers Submit Nearly 2,000 Amendments to Halt City's 2016–2017 Budget", *South China Morning Post,* April 14, 2016, available at: http://www.scmp.com/news/hong-kong/politics/article/1935776/itching-filibuster-radical-hong-kong-lawmakers-submit-nearly (accessed July 16, 2016).

150 Ip, "When Politics Trumps Reason."

151 Ibid. See also Hawthorne, Luke, "The Fragrant but (Un)Safe Harbour: What Happened to Hong Kong's Copyright Amendment?, *Lexology,* March 23, 2016, available at: http://www.lexology.com/library/detail.aspx?g=69507875-1fed-46e1-b1a4-752664558ee2 (accessed July 17, 2016).

152 Ng, Kang-chung and Fung, Owen, "'A Colossal Waste of Time and Money': LegCo Quorum Calls Cost Hongkongers HK$45.6 Million", *South China Morning Post,* July 15, 2016, available at: http://www.scmp.com/news/hong-kong/politics/article/1990207/colossal-waste-time-and-money-legco-quorum-calls-cost (accessed, July 16, 2016).

153 Cullen, Richard, "Filibusters: Flawed in Principle and Bad for Hong Kong", *IPP Review,* March 9, 2018, available at: https://ippreview.com/index.php/Blog/single/id/667.html (accessed May 14, 2019).

Chief Secretary, Carrie Lam, described the coalition of doctors and PDs who thwarted passage of the reform measures as "the tyranny of the minority".[154]

Apart from these delaying measures, rowdy behaviour by RPDs and PDs within LegCo is now commonplace and can include throwing items at Government Officials within the LegCo chamber (including a glass).[155] In early 2015, one RPD had apparently obtained some fake faecal matter, which he threw at the Chief Executive (running towards him to do so) as the Chief Executive was addressing LegCo. It was witnessing this action, combined with an awareness of the entrenched filibustering, which moved one respected commentator from the UK to comment that, in his view, the dysfunctional governance institution in the HKSAR appeared to be LegCo.[156] He further noted his surprise that the media in the HKSAR did not seem to recognize that this was so – and that it was a significant problem.[157]

Events in LegCo in May 2019 confirmed that it lacks a sense of fundamental, collective institutional integrity. PD LegCo members insisted on the right to maintain a filibuster (which had already run for many weeks) within a Bills Committee (looking at the proposed rendition/extradition amendments to the FOO discussed above) after the LegCo Secretariat established, in effect, a replacement Bills Committee in order to move review of the relevant bill forward. This behaviour is discussed in more detail in Chapter 7.

It is important to note that there are institutional factors which amplify the operational frustration of LegCo members – and especially PD members. The rules set down in the Basic Law in essence make it almost impossible for members to introduce their own Bills for debate. They are thus left with little beyond having a primary role which involves discussing and approving (or not) those Bills which the Government introduces. Moreover, the Government has ultimate control over the timetabling of new laws and amendments. (This frustration is

154 Cheung, Elizabeth and Tsang, Emily, "'Tyranny of the Minority' Hong Kong Medical Reform Bill Fails as Filibuster Blocks Legislative Council Vote on Final Day", *South China Morning Post*, July 15, 2016, available at: http://www.scmp.com/news/hong-kong/health-environment/article/1990164/tyranny-minority-hong-kong-medical-reform-bill (accessed July 16, 2016).

155 Chan, Kahon, "CE Condemns Radicals Unruly Behaviour", *China Daily*, May 23, 2014, obtained from: http://www.chinadailyasia.com/hknews/2014-05/23/content_15136603.html (hard copy retained by author). An RPD LegCo member was charged with common assault after throwing a glass at the Chief Executive in LegCo, see Mak, Adeline, "Battling It Out in Court", *The Standard*, April 20, 2016, obtained from: http://www.thestandard.com.hk/section-news.php?id=168481 (hard copy retained by author).

156 Detailed notes on file with Richard Cullen. See also Cullen, Richard, "Lawmakers Escaping Media Scrutiny", *Letters to the Editor – South China Morning Post*, August 12, 2013, available at: http://www.scmp.com/comment/letters/article/1296052/letters-editor-august-12-2013 (accessed July 16, 2016).

157 The contrast between LegCo and the Parliament at Westminster is stark in terms of behaviour regulation and self-control. See Cullen, Richard, "LegCo Rule Book Can Learn from Westminster", *China Daily*, July 16, 2018, available at: http://www.chinadaily.com.cn/hkedition/2018-07/16/content_36579824.htm (accessed May 14, 2019).

further elevated for the PDs by their deep sense of grievance with respect to political reform (discussed above).) Some of the explanation for the level of dysfunction now experienced within LegCo arises from these role-limiting factors.[158]

I have explained how the Judiciary and the HKSAR Government (to a lesser extent) both retain a collective awareness of the importance of maintaining institutional integrity. This enduring awareness, in each case, draws on strong, institutional BHK foundations. LegCo was, for most of its life in BHK, an attenuated legislature appointed by the Governor. The sense of institutional integrity was, thus, significantly less strong compared to the other two arms of government. This has left LegCo more vulnerable to further erosion of its own collective understanding of its core public purpose.

In sum, the Judiciary in Hong Kong (particularly the CFA) continues to maintain very high standards (and independence) and to display the highest competence regularly. The HKSAR Government has far wider responsibilities and it struggles at times to measure up well. Those WGI ratings from the World Bank are, however, indicative, at least, that it is comparatively proficient. LegCo can do much in a proper and positive manner. But it is beset by serious operational problems, sourced from within, which lower its performance level measurably and continuously. It is fair to say that LegCo has, unfortunately, become the (comparative) pivot of governance dysfunction in Hong Kong.

158 See Article 62 (Government LegCo related powers) and Article 73 (powers and functions of LegCo) of the Basic Law. See also Horlemann, Ralph, *Hong Kong's Transition to Chinese Rule* (Routledge, London, 2003), Chapter 5.

7 Stress testing Authoritarian Legality in Hong Kong

Introduction

The term *stress testing* originally designated the process of deliberately operating a mechanical product beyond normal limits to determine what might be its failure point. The concept is now far more widely put to use, for example, in relation to health care improvement and to try and check institutional risks within financial systems. Here we are looking at serious stresses applied, over many decades, to the broadly contiguous "through train" political systems of BHK and the HKSAR. Although the testing here is not experimental but drawn from real life, it is nonetheless possible to observe, analyze, and draw certain conclusions as to how well these co-joined, AL political systems have coped with the manifest stresses they have repeatedly encountered.

Early tests

The creation of BHK in 1841–1842[1] was a direct product of warfare between Britain and Qing Dynasty China. Successive Chinese Governments (Imperial, to 1911, Republican, from 1912, and Communist, from 1949) all refused to accept the validity of the three Treaties whereby the UK came to acquire the full extent of BHK (which now comprises the HKSAR).[2] Significant potential stress thus

1 The First Opium War ran from 1839 to 1842. In 1841, Captain Charles Eliot of the Royal Navy and Captain Anthony Blaxland Stransham of the Royal Marines occupied Hong Kong Island. Hong Kong Island was ceded to the UK by China in 1842 under the Treaty of Nanking (the first of the "Unequal Treaties"). See, further, Ghai, Yash, *Hong Kong's New Constitutional Order* (Hong Kong University Press, Hong Kong, 1999), Chapter 1. See also Wesley-Smith, Peter, *Unequal Treaty 1898–1997: China, Great Britain and Hong Kong's New Territories* (Oxford University Press, Hong Kong, 1983).

2 Subsequent to the Treaty of Nanking in 1842 were the Convention of Peking 1860 (following the conclusion of the Second Opium War, where the UK acquired the Kowloon Peninsula and Stonecutters Island), and the Convention of Peking 1898 (following the further decline of the Qing Imperial Government, where the rest of what became BHK, the "New Territories" were granted to the UK under a 99-year lease). This extended BHK to its final full size of 1,100 km^2 approximately. See Ghai, ibid.

applied from the outset. However, all those Chinese Governments were either incapable of taking any direct action to redress the perceived injustices imposed by the Treaties (Imperial); far too distracted by the need to survive within a context of continuous armed conflict with internal and external forces (Republican); or essentially minded to adopt a pragmatic *modus vivendi* (Communist[3]).

Real pressure on BHK stability was experienced during the first decades after the fall of the Qing Dynasty and the establishment of the fledgeling, unstable, Republic of China in 1912. In 1925, on May 30, Sikh Police under British command opened fire on Chinese demonstrators in Shanghai killing around ten and wounding many others. Less than a year later, foreign troops killed another 50-plus Chinese demonstrators at Shamian Island in Guangzhou. Shamian Island, a small sandbank island within the Pearl River, had been used as an "internal outpost" for foreigners trading with China since the Song Dynasty (960–1279 AD) and was long the headquarters for all the busy, main European trading institutions focussed on south-west China. It remained so, after 1912 (until 1949).[4]

Following these lethal incidents, the KMT instigated a strike and boycott directed against British interests, primarily in Guangzhou and Hong Kong. The BHK economy was very badly affected for some months and many Hong Kong Chinese fled the Crown Colony seeking sanctuary in adjacent Guangdong Province. By 1926, the worst of the strike had passed, BHK resumed normal trading, and the BHK economy (and stability) recovered. London had intervened, as matters were swiftly growing very grim, providing BHK with a trade loan of more than 3 million pounds which prevented the economy from sliding further towards ruin.[5]

Post-war tests

Development of the broad BHK Political System after World War II has already been discussed in some detail in Chapter 4. It is convenient to assist the narrative and analysis in this chapter to recapitulate that earlier review, in brief.

The first case of serious post-war, political rioting in Hong Kong occurred in 1956, when supporters of the KMT and CPC supporters clashed violently in Tsuen Wan in the New Territories. There were 59 deaths and much property damage. British military personnel were used to reinforce the Hong Kong Police Force.[6]

3 Loh, Christine, *Underground Front: The Chinese Communist Party in Hong Kong* (2nd ed.) (Hong Kong University Press, Hong Kong, 2018), Chapter 5.
4 Carroll, John Mark, *A Concise History of Hong Kong* (Rowman & Littlefield, Lanham, 2007).
5 Ibid.
6 See Lee, Connie, Hong-nee, *Society and Policing in Hong Kong: A Study of the 1956 Riot,* Master of Social Science Dissertation – 1995, available at: https://hub.hku.hk/bitstream/10722/27467/1/FullText.pdf (accessed October 1, 2019). The author notes that, after the 1956 riot, the Police created more military-styled units (for the first time) to deal with

The next serious, post-war riots, in April 1966, are commonly referred to as the "Star Ferry Riots". The dissatisfaction with British rule in Hong Kong at this time was high. There was a special hostility to the extensive corruption which had grown apace in the 1950s and 1960s, especially within the Hong Kong Police Force, which the British had done little to contain. The announcement of fare increases on the Star Ferry service across Victoria Harbour triggered the rioting. The rioting, concentrated in Kowloon, lasted for several days. One protester died and there were extensive property damage and many arrests.[7]

The "1967 Leftist Riots", as they are known, were far more serious. They lasted from May to December 1967. This major political disturbance was significantly fuelled by the spillover from the early stages of the Cultural Revolution. Over 50 people were killed. Thousands of fake and real bombs were manufactured. Property damage was far more extensive than in 1966. Initially, the PRC Government in Beijing supported the rioters. There was increasing anxiety in BHK, that the PRC was considering invading and occupying Hong Kong. It is said that the Chinese Premier, Zhou Enlai (second to Mao Zedong), vetoed this plan. Zhou is also said to have ordered the end to bomb-making and rioting by all leftist groups in late 1967.[8]

Despite these very serious examples of political unrest, the ordinary mass of people remained largely apolitical. The vast majority of the post-war population had migrated from – mostly fled – the PRC. Many of them saw Hong Kong as a staging post – their aim was to migrate (or at least see their children migrate) usually to a range of Western, English-speaking countries. They saw themselves as "sojourners".[9] Another important factor was the rapid economic growth in Hong Kong. Although people often lived in very difficult circumstances, they had entered an economy which was, year after year, typically growing at a prodigious rate. This reality offered hope. It created a more positive general mood than one would normally encounter in such a poverty-ridden environment. It helped create an atmosphere where concentrating on family economic betterment rather than on politics made good sense to many. The Government also re-emphasized a policy, particularly after the political turmoil of the 1960s, of consulting widely

---

large-scale disturbances. See also, "Hong Kong 1956 Riots", available at: https://en.wikipedia.org/wiki/Hong_Kong_1956_riots (accessed October 1, 2019).

7 Ibid. See also "Hong Kong 1966 Riots", available at: https://en.wikipedia.org/wiki/Hong_Kong_1966_riots (accessed October 1, 2019).

8 Wei, Christina, "1967 Leftist Riots" Hong Kong in Transition, obtained from: https://www.mtholyoke.edu/~wei20c/classweb/wp/66riots.html (hard copy retained by author). See also "Photography, the 1967 Hong Kong Riots", available at: http://hongwrong.com/1967-hkriots/ (accessed October 1, 2019). See also "Hong Kong 1967 Leftist Riots" available at: https://en.wikipedia.org/wiki/Hong_Kong_1967_Leftist_riots (accessed October 1, 2019).

9 See Lau, Siu-kai, *Society and Politics in Hong Kong* (Chinese University Press, Hong Kong, 1991); and Lau, Siu-kai, "Chinese Familism in an Urban-Industrial Setting: The Case of Hong Kong" (1981) 43 *Journal of Marriage and the Family*, 181.

by providing institutional avenues for community leaders and others to express views on policy development and implementation.[10]

The important initiative of the Government which did most (a) to reinforce Hong Kong's adherence to the Rule of Law, (b) to buttress acceptance of benevolent-authoritarian government, and (c) to enhance social stability was the establishment of the highly successful ICAC in 1974. Within a year or so of the ICAC commencing operations, major inroads were made into the massive level of corruption prevailing. After the ICAC broke the back of corruption, Hong Kong has since enjoyed an enviable reputation for being a "clean" city and a good place to do business – and to live securely.[11]

The confluence of the factors noted above produced (a) a generally stable political climate, (b) government by an elite-influenced civil service, and (c) poor prospects for the growth of party politics.[12]

On June 4, 1989, the planning for a "smooth transition" (of sovereign control over Hong Kong from London to Beijing) was profoundly disrupted when the PRC Government used battlefield weapons, including tanks, to end a massive, long-running demonstration for political reform by thousands of its own citizens in and around Tiananmen Square. This terrible incident swiftly led to what were the largest ever public demonstrations seen in BHK. Over 1 million people are reported to have marched, firstly in support of the protesting students, in May 1989, and then in protest against Beijing, on June 5, 1989.[13] Notwithstanding their massive size, the protests were peaceful and not, in themselves, disruptive of the economic, social, and political order within BHK. They were fundamentally galvanizing, politically, however. And they were a marker of the deep anxiety now abroad across a clear majority of the Hong Kong Chinese population. The PDs won 16 out of the 18, of the new, directly elected seats in the 1991 LegCo Elections (see Chapter 4).

The British Hong Kong Government worked, with notable success, to restore stability and growth launching certain reassuring measures within BHK. These included the construction of a huge new airport (with much additional, related

10 Young, Simon N. M. and Cullen, Richard, *Electing Hong Kong's Chief Executive* (Hong Kong University Press, Hong Kong, 2010), Chapter 3.

11 See, for example, the WJP Index 2018, which ranked the HKSAR at 16th out of 126 jurisdictions for Rule of Law compliance, and the CPI-2018, which ranked the HKSAR at equal 14th out of 180 jurisdictions for perceived corruption risk. *WJP Rule of Law Index 2017–2018,* World Justice Project, available at: https://worldjusticeproject.org/our-work/research-and-data/wjp-rule-law-index-2017%E2%80%932018 (accessed October 1, 2019); and *Corruption Perception Index- 2018*, Transparency International, available at: https://www.transparency.org/news/pressrelease/corruption_perceptions_index_2018 (accessed October 1, 2019

12 Sing, Ming, *Hong Kong's Tortuous Democratization* (Routledge-Curzon, London, 2004), Chapters 7 and 8.

13 Beatty, Bob, *Democracy, Asian Values and Hong Kong: Evaluating Political Elite Beliefs* (Praeger, Westport, 2003), Chapter 1.

new infrastructure – cost US$20 billion approximately[14]), the provision of full British passports for thousands of more senior bureaucrats, the rapid expansion of tertiary education facilities within Hong Kong, and the enactment of the BORO.[15]

HKSAR tests

In 2006, according to Hong Kong Police statistics, the total number of what are termed *Public Order Events* (meetings and processions) in the HKSAR was 2,228 for the year. These numbers peaked in 2016 at 13,158. By 2018, the total number had eased to 11,880 per annum.[16] Each year 20%–25% are processions or marches and rest (more static) meetings or protests. Over the last several years of the BHK era, comparable figures averaged a little less than 1,200 per year. In 1998, the first year after the handover, the figure roughly doubled and has grown from there.[17] These Public Order Events include notified public meetings, public processions approved, notified public processions, non-notifiable public meetings, and non-notifiable public processions.[18] (The rules governing which processions and meetings need to be notified under the POORD have been outlined in Chapter 6.)

Since 1997, the number of protests, as broadly defined above, has built from around 3 per day to over 30 per day, peaking at around 36 per day in 2016. These are just raw figures and they can be read in different ways. First, there has been a major lift in the level of protesting since 1997 and the closing of the BHK era. The figures also suggest (as does the analysis above) that there has been a steady political awakening, especially after June 1989. Finally, it is inescapable that the figures demonstrate that the HKSAR is a society which remains remarkably open to public protests based around public gatherings and processions. It may be that

14 This massive project (called the Airport Core Project) included the construction of extensive new road and rail-lines (including very large bridges), massive reclamations, the building of an entirely new satellite city, and the building of two new container ports. Total cost, in 1997, was estimated to be around US$20 billion (see Wong Raymond, "A Technical and Project Review of 10 Airport Core Projects and Their Influence on Current Developments", *City University of Hong Kong Archive,* available at: http://www6.cityu.edu.hk/construction_archive/major_reference_pdf.aspx?id=350 (accessed October 1, 2019).

15 Cullen, Richard, "Hong Kong Revenue Law: The Present, 1997 and Beyond" (1993) *Tax Notes International*, 1109.

16 "Public Order Event Statistics", *Hong Kong Police Force*, available at: https://www.police.gov.hk/ppp_en/09_statistics/poes.html (accessed May 30, 2019).

17 "No. of Public Order Events", *Hong Kong Council of Social Services*, available at: http://www.socialindicators.org.hk/en/indicators/political_participation/2.5 (accessed October 1, 2019).

18 Ibid.

the HKSAR allows more protest per capita in a given year than any other comparably developed, First-World city.[19]

The focus here is on the several primary, turning-point mass protests: in 2003 (the first massive July 1 march); in 2012 (the education reform protest); in 2014 (the Occupy Central (OCM) multi-month protest); the 2016 Mong Kok Political Riot; and the 2019 Protests and Riots. But it is important to note the several regular, often annual, major protest events which draw medium to very large crowds: the June 4 Vigil, the July 1 National Day March, and the New Year's Day March.[20]

July 1, 2003

In 2003, early in the second term of the first HKSAR Government (under Mr. C.H. Tung), the Government tried to enact new national security laws under Article 23 of the Basic Law. The enactment of such laws remains an obligation of the HKSAR Government under the Basic Law. These laws are meant to replace the (still operative) British national security regime.[21] As presented in 2003, the draft proposals did, in fact, improve on the BHK regime, but they also contained a number of controversial measures.[22] As this Article 23 project commenced, the SARS outbreak (which had its immediate source (in late 2002) in Guangdong Province, adjacent to the HKSAR) posed an increasingly lethal threat to the HKSAR. The SARS epidemic eventually killed almost 300 people in the HKSAR and left many more debilitated, some very badly.[23]

Even while the SARS epidemic remained a serious threat, the HKSAR pressed ahead with the, by now, highly controversial Article 23 project. Civil society

19 Clear statistics like those provided in Hong Kong are rather more difficult to find for other cities. The Metropolitan Police in London (which has a population roughly comparable to that of Hong Kong – 8.136 million:7.4 million) just say that there are "thousands of events and processions across the country" ("Events and Processions", *The Met*, available at: https://www.met.police.uk/advice/advice-and-information/e/events-and-processions/ (accessed May 30, 2019).

20 See Lo, Sonny, *Hong Kong's Indigenous Democracy* (Palgrave-Macmillan, Basingstoke, 2015) where, inter alia, these important, embedded-regular mass demonstrations are reviewed. The June 4 Vigil commemorates the June 4, 1989 crushing of the Tiananmen Square student protests by the CPC. July 1 is a Public Holiday in the HKSAR, to mark the handover from the UK to the PRC. The date also became the day for a – if not the – major annual protest event from 2003 (see below). New Year's Day has been used, as desired, to organize further smaller, still significant, anti-government/anti-Beijing protests since 2010.

21 Fu, Hualing and Cullen, Richard, "National Security Law in Hong Kong: Quo Vadis – A Study of Article 23 of the Basic Law of Hong Kong" (2002) 19 *UCLA Pacific Basin Law Journal*, 185.

22 See (Fu, Petersen, and Young (eds.)) *National Security and Fundamental Freedoms: Hong Kong's Article 23 under Scrutiny* (Hong Kong University Press, Hong Kong, 2005).

23 A comprehensive review of the SARS epidemic can be found in Loh, Christine (ed.), *At the Epicentre: Hong Kong and the SARS Outbreak* (Hong Kong University Press, Hong Kong, 2004).

resentment grew apace, amplified by significant popular media expression of this antipathy.[24] The ultimate response was a mass demonstration on the largest scale since the 1989 marches. Over 500,000 people are reported to have rallied and advanced through the spinal centre of Hong Kong Island on July 1, 2003, the National Reunification Day Holiday. It was a clearly focussed, entirely peaceful protest which dispersed without incident on the same day. The extent of antagonistic feeling took both the HKSAR Government and Beijing by surprise. Very soon after the march, the Hong Kong Government announced that it was dropping the Article 23 proposals entirely. Within less than two years, the Chief Executive, Mr. Tung, had stepped down early and the two key Government Principal Officials (Ministers) responsible for security and health had also stepped down.[25]

2012 – education reform protest

In 2001, the then Manpower and Education Bureau of the HKSAR Government (which became the Education Bureau in 2007) identified *Moral and Civic Education* (MCE) as an essential element for whole-person education in Hong Kong aimed at fostering positive and constructive attitudes.[26] The expressed, broad aim was that *Moral and National Education* (MNE) would replace MCE, with a notable lift in teaching of the PRC (and CPC) context of social, economic, and political life in the HKSAR.[27] The teaching of any significant Chinese context had never been a strength during the BHK era.[28]

The proposal to develop a full MNE teaching profile and explain how it would be framed and introduced to reform the MCE approach was always going to be controversial. This project proceeded both within the bureaucracy and during the initial consultations without arousing any high-temperature opposition. The second HKSAR Administration, under Donald Tsang, seems to have taken a deliberately unhurried approach, the better to avoid the potential for a political

24 Ibid. There is a good short reflection, in this book, on the ethics of the "advocacy journalism" which came to play such a significant role in fostering the July 1 march – see Chapter 12.

25 See Fu et al., *National Security and Fundamental Freedoms*. See also Chen, Albert H. Y., "The Rule of Law under 'One Country Two Systems': The Case of Hong Kong 1997–2010" (2011) 6 *National Taiwan University Law Review*, 269, available at: http://www.law.ntu.edu.tw/ntulawreview/articles/6-1/09-Article-Albert%20H.%20Y.%20Chen_p269-299.pdf (accessed October 1, 2019).

26 "Moral and National Education Guide: Curriculum Guide (Primary 1 – Secondary 6)", *Curriculum Development Council*, April 2012, available at: http://www.edb.gov.hk/attachment/en/curriculum-development/moral-national-edu/MNE%20Guide%20(ENG)%20Final_remark_09102012.pdf (accessed October 1, 2019).

27 See Cheng, Angel Oi Yee, "The Controversies of Moral, Civic and National Education in Hong Kong" *Education Policy Talk*, April 7, 2014, available at: https://educationpolicytalk.com/2014/04/07/the-controversies-of-moral-civic-and-national-education-in-hong-kong/ (accessed October 1, 2019).

28 Ibid.

storm over this matter.[29] The third HKSAR Administration, under C.Y. Leung, opted to announce a commitment to MNE implementation shortly after taking office in July 2012.[30]

A protest, which was led by secondary student activists and widely supported by teachers and parents groups and the PD movement besieged the headquarters of the HKSAR Government for 10 days. It swelled in numbers to almost 30,000 (police estimate) or 100,000 (protester estimate). The siege was called off after the new Chief Executive C.Y. Leung announced, under pressure, that introduction of the new MNE curriculum would no longer be mandatory.[31]

2014 – Occupy Central Movement

The Occupy Central Movement (OCM) had its origins in a journal article published in January 2013 by Professor Benny Tai Yiu Ting from the Faculty of Law at Hong Kong University (HKU). In this article, he proposed that residents of the HKSAR should plan a civil disobedience occupation of the Central Business District on Hong Kong Island to put pressure on the HKSAR Government and Beijing in the event that the expected 2014–2015 Political Reform proposals offered only "fake" democracy.[32] The concept of this protest – its purpose and its methodology – aroused significant general interest. Professor Tai was joined by two other persons who formed a three-person leadership team: Dr. Chan Kin-man (from the Chinese University of Hong Kong) and the Reverend Chu Yiu-ming (OCM Trio).[33]

After the Chief Executive submitted his Report (on Political Reform) in July 2014,[34] the SCNPC issued its Decision of August 31, 2014, which set out seven requirements to move to a universal suffrage system for the election of the Chief Executive of the HKSAR in 2017.[35] These stipulations plainly ruled out any form of Civil Nomination. They also provided that the proposed new Chief Executive Nominating Committee would retain the (mainly pro-Beijing) membership profile of the former Chief Executive Election Committee – and that any person initially nominated as a candidate for the 2017 Chief Executive Election would

29 Ibid.

30 Ibid.

31 Lau, Stuart, Nip, Amy, and Wan, Adrian, "Protest against National Education to End after Government Climbdown", *South China Morning Post,* September 9, 2012, available at: http://www.scmp.com/news/hong-kong/article/1032535/protest-against-national-education-end-after-government-climbdown (accessed October 1, 2019).

32 Tai, Benny, "Occupy Central with Love and Peace", *Archive,* available at: https://oclphkenglish.wordpress.com/tag/benny-tai/ (accessed October 1, 2019).

33 "Hong Kong's Occupy Central Founders Surrender to Police", *BBC News,* December 3, 2014, available at: http://www.bbc.com/news/world-asia-china-30305473 (accessed October 1, 2019).

34 "Chief Executive's Report to the SCNPC", *HKSAR Government,* July 2014, available at: http://www.2017.gov.hk/en/npcsc/ (accessed October 1, 2019).

35 See discussion in Chapter 6.

have to be endorsed by at least 50% plus one of the Nominating Committee. Moreover, the total number of candidates allowed to run was limited to three. In sum, this meant that it was most likely that only broadly pro-establishment candidates would make the final cut (of two to three candidates). The chances of any mainstream PD candidate being approved to run in the 2017 Chief Executive Election were, thus, exceptionally slim.

The OCM was notably active in the months before the SCNPC Decision. In particular, the OCM held a series of public consultation meetings which led to the holding of what came to be called a Civil Referendum, run by the Hong Kong University Public Opinion Programme (HKU POP). It was clear that the consultation meetings were dominated by representatives from the RPD sector of the PD movement. The OCM Trio seemed to have limited control over how these consultations meetings ultimately worked. HKU POP agreed to proceed with running the Civil Referendum, notwithstanding the fact that the RPDs had succeeded in eliminating all but the more radical options (each including Civil Nomination) from the Civil Referendum list.[36] The Civil Referendum run by HKU POP attracted around 800,000 self-selecting participants (from a total HKSAR *registered* voting population of around 3.8 million – the total *potential* HKSAR voting population was around 5 million[37]). Unsurprisingly, there was strong support for including a Civil Nomination system as part of the mechanism to select who could stand in the 2017 Chief Executive Election.[38]

Within three weeks of the SCNPC Decision on August 31, 2014, a student protest strike was announced. By the end of September, mass protests had commenced outside of the HKSAR Government Complex; Benny Tai announced that Occupy Central had been launched. Riot Police unsuccessfully used tear gas, inter alia, to break up the OCM protest. The Police swiftly retreated from using such methods. Many more joined the OCM protest after the use of tear gas. A very large tent-based encampment soon occupied a range of key thoroughfares on Hong Kong Island and also key arterial junctions around Mong Kok in Kowloon. The total number protesting fluctuated, but it ranged up to 50,000 taking part in the various occupations.[39]

36 Cheung, Tony and Chong, Tanna, "Occupy Central Accused of 'Disenfranchising' Moderate Views in Vote", *South China Morning Post,* May 7, 2014, available at: http://www.scmp.com/news/hong-kong/article/1506490/occupy-central-founder-denies-deliberation-day-vote-was-hijacked (accessed October 1, 2019).

37 See "Voter Registration Statistics – 2016", *HKSAR Government,* available at: http://www.voterregistration.gov.hk/eng/statistic20161.html#1 (accessed October 1, 2019); and "Percentage of Population Registered to Vote", *Hong Kong Council of Social Services,* available at: http://www.socialindicators.org.hk/en/indicators/political_participation/2.1 (accessed October 1, 2019).

38 "6.22 Civil Referendum", *HKU POP Site*, obtained from: https://www.hkupop.hku.hk/english/release/release1164.html (hard copy retained by author).

39 "What Is Occupy Central: 10 Key Facts About Hong Kong's Pro-Democracy Movement", *South China Morning Post,* September 30, 2014, available at: http://www.scmp.com/article/1604649/what-occupy-central-10-things-you-need-know (accessed October 1, 2019).

The social and economic disruption, for ordinary residents and all manner of businesses, resulting from the OCM occupations was immense. The occupations lasted almost three months, from late September until mid-December 2014, formally ending on December 15, 2014. Some public bus surface travel was made impossible for weeks and some was disrupted over the entire period. Many businesses were adversely affected and access to all manner of services, including schools and hospitals, was made far more difficult for many.[40]

Two other particular and remarkable *outcome aspects* of the OCM occupations should also be noted. First, notwithstanding the extensive scale of the occupations and their highly disruptive impact, the behaviour of the protesters was, with a few exceptions, very well disciplined and mainly non-violent even in the midst of ample, rousing speech-making from within the OCM itself. Next, again, with some exceptions, the approach, discipline, and evolved strategy and tactics of the Hong Kong Police (who were placed under immense ongoing pressures) in managing the occupations were all (comparatively) commendable.[41] I say *comparatively* because this is the most rational way to consider the performance of the Police. Managing an occupation protest of this sort, which shut down key thoroughfares in a major First-World city for almost three months, presents an extraordinary policing challenge. That it ran its course and still ended with such minimal direct physical harm and property damage is remarkable. Both Police and the mass of protesters share the credit for this outcome – but the Police plainly had the far harder part to play in achieving this outcome.[42]

Not surprisingly, a number of commentators (and protesters) were far more critical about the performance of the Hong Kong Police in managing the OCM

40 For a measured and detailed review of the OCM, including the political context of its emergence, its development, and its various impacts, see Lim, Tai Wei and Ping, Xiaojuan, *Contextualizing Occupy Central in Contemporary Hong Kong* (Imperial College Press, London, 2015). The authors are academics based in the East Asian Institute at the National University of Singapore.

41 The primary exception involved police violence against one (Civic Party) PD protester. This protestor was jailed for five weeks. Seven members of the Hong Kong Police were charged with serious assault offences against the same protestor. They were each jailed for two years (these sentences remained under appeal at the time of writing). See Ng, Ellie, "Police Officers Jailed for 2 Years for Assault against Occupy Activist Ken Tsang", *Hong Kong Free Press*, February 17, 2017, available at: https://www.hongkongfp.com/2017/02/17/police-officers-jailed-for-assault-against-occupy-activist-ken-tsang/ (accessed May 30, 2019); and Siu, Jasmine, "Activist Ken Tsang Gets Five Weeks in Jail for Assaulting Police and Resisting Arrest during Occupy Protest", *South China Morning Post*, May 30, 2016, available at: http://www.scmp.com/news/hong-kong/law-crime/article/1959354/activist-ken-tsang-gets-five-weeks-jail-assaulting-police (accessed October 1, 2019). Altogether around 1,700 complaints had been filed against the Hong Kong Police arising out of the OCM protests. See Ng, Roydon, "Umbrella Movement", available at: http://www.roydonng.net/blog/category/occupy-central/3 (accessed October 1, 2019).

42 See Lim and Ping, *Contextualizing Occupy Central.*

occupations.[43] To all those who put such views directly to the author, a single question was asked: *Can you name any Police Force, anywhere which could have done a better job during the OCM occupations than the Hong Kong Police?* In every case, the response was either silence or, after a pause: *They should have done better.* Whatever we do, we can all do better, including the Hong Kong Police – and the OCM protesters. But, in effect, making "the perfect an enemy of the good" is rarely an apt way to evaluate human individual or collective performance under complex and demanding pressures.[44]

The popular media commentary on the OCM and the occupations is now immense. The comments range from positively in favour (and not infrequently celebratory) of the entire OCM project through measured reviews to quite hostile evaluations. In general, the international Western media were sympathetic (often robustly) with respect to the OCM project.[45] The majority of the media within the HKSAR were similarly inclined, especially during the early phase of the occupation – with the pro-Beijing, Chinese press in the HKSAR starkly opposed. The views expressed both negative and positive on the performance of the Hong Kong Police often resonated with the views supportive or critical of the OCM project itself.[46]

Operationally, the OCM occupations were beset, almost from the outset, by a lack of clear leadership. The two younger, academic members of the OCM Trio remained involved in the running of the occupation protests, but many other

43 See, for example, "Umbrella Movement", *Fulbright*, available at: https://vsmyanhk.wordpress.com/umbrella-movement/ (accessed October 1, 2019).

44 This aphorism, which counsels against applying extreme or excessive standard setting to measure or guide human behaviour has been noted in various related ways over many centuries by, for example, Aristotle, Confucius ("better a diamond with a flaw than a pebble without"), Shakespeare ("striving to be better, oft we mar what's well", *King Lear,* Act 1, Scene 4), and Voltaire (who first popularized it in 1770). See *Perfect Is the Enemy of Good*, available at: https://en.wikipedia.org/wiki/Perfect_is_the_enemy_of_good (accessed October 1, 2019).

45 Cullen, Richard, "The Credibility of Far East Political Reporting", *IPP Review*, October 24, 2017, available at: https://ippreview.com/index.php/Blog/single/id/575.html (accessed May 30, 2019).

46 There is no space to provide a comprehensive summary of this now extensive commentary. But some indicative materials can be mentioned: Pepper, Suzanne, "Posts Tagged Occupy Central – HK", *China Elections Blog*, obtained from: http://chinaelectionsblog.net/hkfocus/?tag=occupy-central-hk (hard copy retained by author); Ong, Larry, "Hong Kong's Trust in Police Shattered by Protest Violence", *Epoch Times,* December 9, 2014, obtained from: http://www.theepochtimes.com/n3/1133036-hongkongers-trust-in-police-shattered-by-protest-violence/full/ (hard copy retained by author); "Occupy Central", *The Conversation* (around 10 reflective articles covering a wide spectrum of views), obtained from: https://theconversation.com/au/topics/occupy-central (hard copy retained by author); "Hong Kong Protests; Timeline of the Occupation", *BBC News,* December 11, 2016, obtained from: http://www.bbc.com/news/world-asia-china-30390820 (hard copy retained by author); "Occupy Central", *HKU Legal Scholarship Blog* (most taking a sympathetic view of the OCM), obtained from: http://researchblog.law.hku.hk/search/label/Occupy%20Central (hard copy retained by author); and Lim and Ping, *Contextualizing Occupy Central.*

usually younger (student) competing voices were offering leadership at the same time.[47] The role of the RPDs, both student-based and LegCo-related, within the OCM, has already been noted. A direct consequence of this split leadership with varying agendas was a lack of lucidity in the demands being made. One demand was clear from the outset and remained so: that the SCNPC Decision of August 31, 2014 not be accepted. What should replace it or how it should be modified was only clearly articulated in so far as Civil Nomination (for selection as a candidate for the 2017 Chief Executive Election) was a baseline stipulation. As the OCM occupations proceeded, a new ***key demand*** fairly swiftly emerged for many within the (competing) leadership group: C.Y. Leung, the Chief Executive, should step down forthwith. This was not a realistic demand – and it had not been a condition of the originally conceived purpose of the OCM (which was to say no to "fake" democracy of any sort).[48] This demand was, however, made with increasing stridency. As one commentator put it, all this frustrated and resentful zeal "clouded and confused the protest leaders' main cause: the right to genuine universal suffrage".[49]

As the OCM occupations wore on, popular and business frustration with the project (and its tangled goals) also grew. Around seven weeks after the OCM protest began, 83% of HKSAR residents polled wanted the occupations to stop, according to a HKU POP poll. Almost 55%, by then, opposed the OCM and support for the OCM had dropped to 28%.[50]

By this time, certain bus and taxi operators notably affected by the OCM occupations had successfully launched legal actions seeking *ex parte* Interlocutory Injunctions to clear obstructions from the public roads and areas which they normally used. Space does not allow a full discussion of the interesting legal arguments involved – but we should briefly consider the basis of this novel approach. The relevant injunctions were sought, granted (and confirmed on appeal) on the basis that the plaintiffs (taxi drivers, mini-bus drivers, and/or their representatives) had a triable case in ***public nuisance.*** (Criminal convictions based on public nuisance were subsequently secured against nine key OCM persons – see Section "Related criminal actions".)

The claimed (and sustained) public nuisance was the shutting down of free access to various public roads and areas by the OCM occupations. Securing a remedy based on public nuisance at Common Law is difficult. It is not enough

47 See "Hong Kong Protests: The Key Players", *BBC News,* December 2, 2014, available at: http://www.bbc.com/news/world-asia-china-29408476 (accessed October 1, 2019).

48 Horesh, Niv, "How Hong Kong Democracy Protesters Overplayed Their Hand", *The Conversation,* November 27, 2016, available at: https://theconversation.com/how-hong-kongs-democracy-protesters-overplayed-their-hand-34722 (accessed October 1, 2019).

49 Ibid.

50 Cheung, Gary, "Overwhelming Majority of Hong Kongers Want Occupy Protests to End: Survey", *South China Morning Post,* November 19, 2016, available at: http://www.scmp.com/news/hong-kong/article/1643998/overwhelming-majority-hongkongers-want-occupy-protests-end-survey (accessed October 1, 2019).

to be adversely affected by a public nuisance – along with the public in general. A plaintiff needs to show particular, substantial, and direct damage suffered by that plaintiff.[51] It was found that the plaintiffs did have cases which were at least triable, based on the test just outlined, where the losses involved were beyond what the general public had suffered. Those potential losses were also found to be substantial and not "fleeting or evanescent".[52] The basis for issuing certain interlocutory injunctions was, thus, established.[53]

Any refusal to comply with the court orders to clear the areas specified would amount, prima facie, to civil contempt of the court. Various protesters, including certain senior, legally qualified protesters, questioned whether the court orders needed to be obeyed given the fact that the protesters were engaged in a mass civil disobedience, political protest. The Hong Kong Bar Association (HKBA) responded with a swift and strong statement which said that:

> Occupy protesters' defiance of injunctions to clear the streets is eroding the rule of law and sets a bad precedent. The HKBA viewed "with dismay" recent calls for open defiance of the injunctions to clear protest sites in Mong Kok and Admiralty. It said that deliberate defiance of a court order committed en masse would result in a direct affront to the rule of law. "Some prominent politicians – several of whom are legally qualified – have contemptuously dismissed criticisms of prolonged occupation in breach of court orders", it said. "The HKBA must strongly disagree with them". The law underlying the injunctions was not "evil" and by violating it protesters had "overstepped the mark", it added.[54]

In view of the extent to which certain protesters had made it clear that they would likely refuse to comply with the (civil) court orders, the court, on November 10, 2014, added bailiff directions and a police (enforcement) authorization directive to the relevant injunction applying in Mong Kok. Anyone who obstructed bailiffs or the police in the course of enforcing that injunction would now also be liable to a charge of criminal contempt of court.[55] This reality, together with the arguments that the protesters were now plainly undermining the Rule of Law which

51 *Benjamin v. Storr* (1874) LR 9 CP, 400.

52 Ibid.

53 A short, clear review of the basis for these actions can be found in Cary, Jonathan and Sargent, Adrian, "Occupy Central: Civil Disobedience and Civil Remedies", *International Law Office,* December 16, 2014, available at: http://www.internationallawoffice.com/Newsletters/Litigation/Hong-Kong/Smyth-Co-in-association-with-RPC/Occupy-Central-civil-disobedience-and-civil-remedies# (accessed October 1, 2019).

54 Tsang, Emily, Lai, Ying-kit, and Ng, Joyce, "Bar Association Slams Occupy Central for Flouting Injunctions to Clear Streets", *South China Morning Post,* October 29, 2014, available at: http://www.scmp.com/news/hong-kong/article/1627101/bar-association-slams-occupy-central-flouting-injunctions-clear (accessed October 1, 2019).

55 Cary and Sargent, "Occupy Central".

they had all along said was a core value they cherished, saw one of the OCM Trio say that he respected the views of the HKBA and that there was a need to strike a proper balance between the Rule of Law and civil disobedience protests.[56]

What, then, did the OCM occupations achieve? In terms of the specific demands made, not a great deal. There was no withdrawing of the SCNPC Decision of August 31, 2014 in part (still less in whole).[57] The Chief Executive refused to stand down. He remained in office until the end of his first term in mid-2017, though he did not seek a second term as allowed under the Basic Law. The OCM, as a whole, was adamant that any HKSAR Government Political Reform proposals, drawn up in accord with the SCNPC Decision, be vetoed in LegCo. As we know, this happened. Based on PD comments, this was all but bound happen without need of any OCM occupations, however.

The civil disobedience arguments in favour of the OCM occupations were comparatively insubstantial and they grew more so as the occupations continued. Civil disobedience campaigns such as those deployed during the Civil Rights Movement in the US, from the 1950s onwards, were confronting a range of appalling embedded economic, social, and political injustices grounded in over 100 years of brutal slavery[58] and a further 100 years, approximately, of terrible segregation.[59] Levels of deep discrimination had also long applied in South Africa and British India when Mahatma Ghandi began his civil disobedience campaigns.[60] It was true that Beijing was denying access to a system of full democracy. But in no way had Beijing orchestrated, overseen, or tolerated any sort of mass degradation within the HKSAR remotely comparable to that which applied in the US and India. On the contrary, Beijing had recurrently acted to buttress the performance of the HKSAR economy.[61]

56 Tsang et al., "Bar Association".

57 As noted earlier, Professor Chen argues that the heavily advocated proposal (in the course of the OCM occupations) for Civil Nomination was obviously inconsistent with Article 45 of the Basic Law and that the PDs preferred to see retention of the current "small circle" Chief Executive Election system rather than allow a pro-establishment Chief Executive gain a popular mandate through a nomination-vetted, Chief Executive Election. See Li, Joseph, "NPCSC Empowered to Set Out Roadmaps for Election: Chen", *China Daily*, June 30, 2015, available at: http://www.chinadailyasia.com/leaders/2015-06/30/content_15284605.html (accessed October 1, 2019).

58 *History of Slavery in America*, available at: http://www.infoplease.com/timelines/slavery.html (accessed October 1, 2019).

59 *Timeline: Key Moments in Black History*, available at: http://www.infoplease.com/spot/bhmtimeline.html (accessed October 1, 2019).

60 "Civil Disobedience Timeline [Gandhi]", *World History Project*, available at: https://worldhistoryproject.org/topics/civil-disobedience (accessed October 1, 2019).

61 Such assistance has been regular since 1997. Two examples: Assistance was first rendered within months of the handover, when Beijing backed the countermeasures launched by the HKSAR Government to repel predatory attacks on the HK Dollar and the Hong Kong Stock Market; further major assistance came after the SARS crisis with the opening up of the HKSAR to individual tourist visits by Mainland Chinese, inter alia.

In summary, the OCM occupations proceeded on a real but markedly overstated pretext (the proclaimed awfulness of the SCNPC Decision) and the protests themselves ended up being immensely disproportionate, based on that pretext. The lack of clear, coherent, consistent, and firmly rational leadership proved to be a serious shortcoming from the outset. Amongst other things, this allowed more radical elements possessed of uncompromising muscular views (who not infrequently found themselves competing with one another to demonstrate the greatest fervour aimed at achieving true democracy) to become dominant within the OCM even before the occupations began. This zeal meant that such activists were barely constrained, if at all, by questions of "political possibility". Their inherent, bare-knuckle political approach drew yet more strength from (a) the feelings of deep and intensifying frustration within the broad PD movement about the slow pace of democratic reform and (b) the rigid position taken by Beijing and the HKSAR Government on what sort of reform was permissible.

The many Hong Kong people who participated in the OCM occupations or supported them more indirectly (in both cases, mainly with an authentic commitment) gained increased political awareness and a new level of experience in mass political activism, however.[62]

Professor Sonny Lo summed up the impact of the OCM in the following way:

> The 2014 "Occupy Central" movement proved to be politically disruptive to the entire process of trust-building. Instead, it deepened the already profound distrust among the political stakeholders, plunged Hong Kong into a politically and socially unstable environment, and has left deep political wounds on all sides of the ideological spectrum. The movement could be interpreted as a sign of generational change in Hong Kong's opposition politics, but its impact on trust-building was arguably retrogressive.[63]

The criminal charges successfully brought against certain key participants in the OCM and also against particular participants in the Mong Kok Riot of 2016 are discussed below.

2016 – Mong Kok Riot

Chinese – or Lunar – New Year in 2016 ran from Monday, February 8 to Wednesday, February 10 in the HKSAR. On Monday evening (February 8), a major political riot began in the Mong Kok area of Kowloon which lasted for

62 See Fu, Hualing, "Fu on Building Hong Kong's Future", *HKU Legal Scholarship Blog*, November 27, 2014, available at: http://researchblog.law.hku.hk/2014/11/fu-on-building-hong-kongs-future.html (accessed October 1, 2019).

63 Lo, Sonny, "Electoral Reform Hinges on Principles", *China Daily*, July 31, 2016, available at: http://www.chinadailyasia.com/opinion/2016-07/31/content_15470808.html (accessed October 1, 2019).

10–12 hours.[64] Despite serious efforts at recasting what had happened as a non-riot,[65] for those in Hong Kong who sat riveted, watching the live coverage of the awful violence on their television sets, what they saw plainly looked, walked, and "quacked" like a riot.[66]

This argument about *riots not being riots* became particularly intense as the protests and far more extensive rioting unfolded in 2019.[67] The *Cambridge Dictionary* defines a riot as:

> Noisy, violent and uncontrolled behaviour by a group of people in a public place often as a protest.[68]

The legal definition of a riot in Hong Kong is set out in the POORD, the primary law in the HKSAR setting out public order offences. The POORD was consolidated and amended by the British in 1967 and 1970 (and subsequently) prompted by the 1967 political riots (see above). Rioting was added as a specific offence. Despite arguments by the last BHK Governor, that the POORD definition was vague and "open to abuse", neither he nor previous Governors after 1970 affected any amendment of the basic riot provisions in the POORD before the handover in 1997 and, thus, they remain in force. Under the riot stipulations, an unlawful assembly of three persons or more, where a "breach of the peace" is committed becomes a riot and the people assembled will be regarded as riotously assembled. An otherwise lawful assembly will become unlawful if the three or more persons conduct themselves in "a disorderly, intimidating, insulting or provocative manner" which causes any person reasonably to fear that the

64 Lau, Chris, "Timeline and Map; How the Mong Kok Street Hawker Hygiene Clampdown Became a Full-Scale Riot", *South China Morning Post*, February 9, 2016, available at: http://www.scmp.com/news/hong-kong/politics/article/1910858/timeline-and-map-how-mong-kok-street-hawker-hygiene (accessed October 1, 2019).

65 For a detailed view, strongly arguing that the riot was not a riot and that police used excessive means to control the very large-scale disturbance, see Kong, Tsung-gan, "Justice It Ain't: The Repercussions and Implications of Hong Kong's Mong Kok 'Riot' Trials", *Hong Kong Free Press*, June 17, 2018, available at: https://www.hongkongfp.com/2018/06/17/justice-aint-repercussions-implications-hong-kongs-mong-kok-riot-trials/ (accessed May 31, 2019).

66 The *duck test* is a form of abductive reasoning: if it looks like a duck, swims like a duck, and quacks like a duck, then it probably *is* a duck. The test implies that a person can identify an unknown subject by observing that subject's habitual characteristics. See "Duck Test", *Wikipedia*, available at: https://en.wikipedia.org/wiki/Duck_test (accessed August 25, 2019).

67 See, for example, de Blocq van Scheltinga, Daniel, "'Alternative Facts' Cannot Cover Up Actual Damage", *China Daily*, July 5, 2019, available at: http://www.chinadaily.com.cn/hkedition/2019-07/05/content_37488401.htm (accessed August 25, 2019).

68 *Cambridge Dictionary*, available at: https://dictionary.cambridge.org/dictionary/english/rioting (accessed August 25, 2019).

assembled persons will commit a breach of the peace. The maximum penalty for rioting remains ten years imprisonment.[69]

The leading group in the Mong Kok violent unrest identified itself as "Hong Kong Indigenous", a radical "localist" group. These small but active groups in the HKSAR typically have strong general anti-Mainland and specific anti-Beijing governance views which they combine with calls for some form of Hong Kong independence from the PRC.[70] Significant evidence emerged of detailed preparations for the rioting. Shields and weapons (pre-sharpened sticks) were purposely delivered to the riot area and certain group members were uniformly dressed and masked. Groups of demonstrators also gathered to dig up pavement bricks and break them to provide throwing ammunition to the rioters. Later, rioters set a range of fires in the streets affected. A taxi was also attacked and then used as a protest-speaking platform. Police estimated the active number involved in the riot to be between 400–500 persons.[71]

Not surprisingly, the riot attracted saturation media coverage, including continuous live television reporting. Some rioters turned on reporters and camera operators, trying to stop the filming and reporting of riot activities (including the systematic removal of pavement bricks to use as missiles). It was also reported that at least one reporter was hindered and attacked by Police.[72]

The initial Police response came from a limited number of Traffic Police (rather than Riot Police). They were, to a degree, overwhelmed at first, as the television coverage showed. During this period, at around 2 a.m. on Tuesday morning, a policeman fired two shots in the air as highly aroused rioters were closing in towards an injured policeman on the ground. Later the Police Tactical Unit was deployed and the streets were finally cleared by around 8 a.m.[73]

The claimed basis for the protest was to defend the rights of non-licensed street hawkers to sell fishballs as they had traditionally done for many years, in the

69 See Part IV of the POORD: "Unlawful Assemblies, Riots and Similar Offences". See also Lum, Alvin, "A Look at Hong Kong's Rioting Laws after the Jailing of Edward Leung and Lo Kin-man for Their Roles in the Mong Kok Unrest", *South China Morning Post*, June 14, 2018, available at: https://www.scmp.com/news/hong-kong/politics/article/2150640/look-hong-kongs-rioting-laws-after-jailing-edward-leung-and (accessed August 25, 2019).

70 Lau, Stuart, Ngo, Jennifer, Lau, Chris, Kao, Ernest, and Sun, Nikki, "Mong Kok Riot: How Hong Kong's First Night in the Year of the Monkey Descended into Mayhem", *South China Morning Post,* February 10, 2016, available at: http://www.scmp.com/news/hong-kong/article/1911341/mong-kok-riot-how-hong-kongs-first-night-year-monkey-descended-mayhem (accessed October 1, 2019).

71 Ibid.

72 Ibid. See also "Journalists Attacked during Riots in Hong Kong", *International Federation of Journalists*, February 9, 2016, obtained from: http://www.ifj.org/nc/news-single-view/backpid/33/article/journalists-attacked-during-riots-in-hong-kong/ (hard copy retained by author).

73 Lau, "Timeline and Map". Based on my direct observation of television coverage of the riot and later rewatching of that video coverage, it was clear that the injured policeman was in serious danger of a mob attack at the time the warning shots were fired.

Mong Kok area, during the Lunar New Year Festival. Some referred to the riot as the "Fishball Revolution". Others preferred to call the riot a *civil disturbance*.[74] As one report put it, the "radical localists found an outlet to vent their grievances by seizing on the unlikely grassroots issue of hawkers' livelihoods".[75] The hawkers themselves seemed to have had (and wanted) no part in the protest being conducted on their behalf and they reported that they carried on trading fairly well until 3 a.m. and that there were no clashes with Police.[76] The protesters claimed, during the course of the riot, that the demonstration was also an election march (related to the then coming 2016 LegCo Elections).[77]

Over 120 were injured during the riot with 90 of those being police officers.[78] The rioting was widely condemned. As time has passed, the critical view of the riot grew. It was seen as both opportunistic and confused in its purpose and contrary to deeply shared Hong Kong values. A retiring (from LegCo) leader within the RPD group, Albert Chan Wai-yip offered the following comments about the rioters in July, 2016:

> What is their political narrative? Who are they actually against when they hurl bricks at police indiscriminately? What do they want to achieve?[79]

As noted above, some argued very strongly that the riot was not a riot; that some other label should apply.[80] *The Economist*, however, was in no doubt that it was a riot:

> February 8th began as a day of celebration in Hong Kong: it was the start of the Chinese new year (this one influenced by the "fire-monkey", according to Chinese astrology). It ended in the worst outbreak of rioting since the 1960s.[81]

74 This approach was evident amongst PDs and others. PDs generally were rather slow to respond with comments on the riot and when they did comment, they preferred to explain that the *root cause* of the riot was the leadership style of the Chief Executive, C.Y. Leung – a rather bold use of a deterministic analysis in all the circumstances. See Lau, Chris, Lee, Danny, Ng, Joyce, Lo, Clifford, Sun, Nikki, and Lau, Stuart, "Shots Fired and Bricks Thrown: Hong Kong Tense after Mong Kok Mob Violence on First Day of Lunar New Year", *South China Morning Post*, February 9, 2016, available at: http://www.scmp.com/news/hong-kong/law-crime/article/1910845/shots-fired-and-bricks-thrown-hong-kong-tense-after-mong (accessed October 1, 2019).

75 Lau, "Mong Kok Riot".

76 Ibid.

77 Ibid.

78 Lau et al., "Shots Fired".

79 Lau, Stuart, "Radical Hong Kong Lawmaker Reflects on Leaving Office after 31 Years in Political Opposition", *South China Morning Post*, July 18, 2016, available at: http://www.scmp.com/news/hong-kong/politics/article/1991329/radical-hong-kong-lawmaker-reflects-leaving-office-after-31 (accessed October 1, 2019).

80 Kong, "Justice It Aint".

81 "Street Violence and Politics", *The Economist*, February 13, 2016, available at: https://www.economist.com/china/2016/02/13/street-violence-and-politics (accessed May 31, 2019).

2019 protests and riots

The evolution of these protests and riots is explained directly below. Their profound impact on the HKSAR is analyzed in detail within the wider context of the closing chapters.

The FOO Amendments – commonly known as the Extradition Bill – have been summarized in Chapter 6. The Extradition Bill provided the foundations for (rather than being the fundamental cause of) mass protests and rioting which eventually followed its introduction. A primary motivation for introducing the Extradition Bill related to the murder of a young, pregnant Hong Kong woman by her Hong Kong boyfriend in Taiwan in February 2018. The murderer fled back to the HKSAR. He later confessed to the killing but there was no way to try him under the Criminal Law of Hong Kong as the murder was committed outside of the HKSAR.[82] Due to Hong Kong's very weak provisions for allowing extradition, there was no extant instrument under which the killer could be transferred to Taiwan to face trial. The timing of the Extradition Bill was prompted, above all, by this particular, difficult case.[83]

Certain events which preceded the mass protests and the later serial rioting were pivotal in helping to initiate what later unfolded. In May 2019, PD LegCo members insisted on the right to maintain a filibuster (which had already run for many weeks) within a Bills Committee looking at the Extradition Bill. In order to move the review of the bill forward, the LegCo Secretariat established, in effect, a replacement Bills Committee. There was intense resistance to this move by PDs in control of the original committee. The chaotic, forceful physical scenes within LegCo which followed were unprecedented. Members were pushing and shoving with much vigour, snatching at microphones, climbing over the top of other members, shouting critical comments and abuse using portable loudspeaker systems, and so on. One of LegCo's oldest members, who was to chair the replacement committee, was continually intimidated as he tried to carry out his appointed tasks.[84] These developments showed both how angered the PD group were by the Extradition Bill proposal and that they were prepared to adopt extreme modes of opposition.

82 Siu, Jasmine, "Man Who Killed Girlfriend in Taiwan Could Be Free by October, Setting Effective Deadline for Hong Kong Government's Extradition Plan", *South China Morning Post,* April 29, 2019, https://www.scmp.com/news/hong-kong/law-and-crime/article/3008099/sentence-man-who-killed-girlfriend-taiwan-sets.(accessed August 18, 2019).

83 "Transcript of Hong Kong Leader's Leaked 'Quitting' Talk Released", *South China Morning Post,* September 4, 2019, available at: https://www.scmp.com/news/hong-kong/politics/article/3025579/hong-kong-protests-read-full-transcript-carrie-lams-leaked (accessed September 4, 2019).

84 Sum, Lok-kei, Su, Xinqi, and Alvin, Lum, "Hong Kong Government Condemns 'Disorderly and Uncontrollable Conditions' after LegCo Chaos Halts Meeting of Committee Reviewing Extradition Bill", *South China Morning Post,* May 11, 2019, available at: https://www.scmp.com/news/hong-kong/politics/article/3009821/lawmaker-injured-legislative-council-clash-battle-over (accessed August 16, 2019).

Notwithstanding this intense hostility, certain matters related to the Extradition Bill remained clear. First, there is a very serious gap in the criminal justice system in Hong Kong, which has endured since 1997. The HKSAR lacks the level of extradition authority needed to ensure that serious criminals from around the world and from elsewhere in Greater China cannot treat Hong Kong as a safe haven. Next, given plain political realities, legislating to close this gap was destined to be controversial. Third, the proposed amendments, as modified, provided substantial safeguards. However, the topic became the subject of immensely heated debate, notwithstanding the fact that the PRC has signed operative Extradition Agreements with 55 other jurisdictions, including nine EU member states. [85]

Typically, in most jurisdictions, new extradition treaties or agreements, to thwart alleged criminals seeking a safe haven, do not generate great political controversy (still less mass protests) as they are being resolved. They are usually seen as being quite technical and of limited day-to-day relevance for the wider population. Most concerned are those who may be subject to such a treaty (and their lawyers).[86] Here, though, lies the key explanation as to why the Extradition Bill in Hong Kong was so well suited to being portrayed as a cause for serious alarm: this was a bill, it was said, which could – and would – grimly affect the wider population of the HKSAR.

The politically very successful campaign against the proposed Extradition Bill in 2019 relied heavily on amplifying extant, deep general fears and more specifically on overwrought images of predatory criminal prosecution behaviour being visited on the HKSAR by Beijing.[87] The hundreds of thousands first drawn onto the streets of Hong Kong to march against the Extradition Bill were expressing genuinely felt alarm and hostility – they had been persuaded that they or family members might someday be extradited. Those who marched were not "duped" into taking such remarkable mass action, but their motivation was influenced by a substantial and successful, populist, hostile campaign.[88]

85 For a comprehensive comparative analysis of the operative details of the Extradition Bill, including its safeguards, see Cross, Grenville, "Fugitive Surrender: Rights and Responsibilities", *China Daily*, June 12, 2019, available at: https://www.chinadailyhk.com/articles/186/73/64/1560307116859.html (accessed August 25, 2019).

86 "US–UK Extradition: The Law Explained", *BBC News*, April 10, 2012, available at: https://www.bbc.com/news/uk-politics-16041824 (accessed August 18, 2019).

87 One leading US journal incompetently and wrongly claimed that the Extradition Bill "would have allowed virtually anyone in Hong Kong facing criminal charges to be extradited to Mainland China". See Salam, Kathryn, "Will Hong Kong Flare Up or Flame Out?", *Foreign Policy*, August 18, 2019, available at: https://foreignpolicy.com/2019/08/17/will-hong-kong-flare-up-or-flame-out (accessed August 18, 2019).

88 On the negative impact of populist politicking (on left and right), see Remeikis, Amy, "Alastair Campbell on the 'Populist Virus' and Why Bill Shorten Lost, *The Guardian,* July 13, 2019, available at: https://www.theguardian.com/politics/2019/jul/14/alastair-campbell-on-the-populist-virus-and-why-bill-shorten-lost (accessed July 17, 2019). See also Cohen, Dan, "Behind a Made-for-TV Hong Kong Protest Narrative, Washington Is Backing

Under the Extradition Bill, the HKSAR Judiciary was to have a key role in overseeing all extradition or rendition requests (with rights of appeal being incorporated as part of this process). Given Hong Kong's deserved reputation for maintaining the highest quality, independent judiciary in East Asia, these were very important safeguards. Yet, as the alarmist campaigning gathered pace, these protections seemed to count for little. Such views were misguided.[89] But if opinions are, collectively, very strongly held, the desire to look further for evidence and factual information has trouble gaining traction, especially when social media (see Chapter 8) is so critical in shaping opinions. One commentator explained that:

> Realizing the power of social media makes every activist a propagandist and commentator. Harnessing all options, unconstrained by the rules of traditional news outlets, they've delivered their version of events with speed and clarity. Accuracy and truth are secondary to this process but that is not the point.[90]

The recurring violent protests which typically followed on from largely peaceful (at times massive and remarkable to behold) protest marches were shocking to watch.

Most alarming of all was the invasion and ransacking of LegCo by a large mob of violent protesters on July 1, 2019. The damage bill was over US$6 million.[91] The invasion rendered the legislature building unusable for a substantial period. This attack is arguably one of the more serious attacks on a primary legislature since the burning of the pre-war German Parliament, the Reichstag, in 1933 (which was more grave in every respect).[92] Subsequently, on July 21, a

---

Nativism and Mob Violence", *The Grayzone*, August 17, 2019, available at: https://thegrayzone.com/2019/08/17/hong-kong-protest-washington-nativism-violence/ (accessed September 1, 2019).

89 Cross, Grenville, "Hong Kong's Rule of Law Is Alive and Well", *Hong Kong Free Press*, October 28, 2017, available at: https://www.hongkongfp.com/2017/10/28/grenville-cross-sc-hong-kongs-rule-law-alive-well/ (accessed July 17, 2019).

90 "Hearts and Minds – All Warfare Is Based on Deception", *At the Feet of Socrates*, July 30, 2019, available at: https://atthefeetofsocrates.blogspot.com/2019/07/hearts-minds.html (accessed August 5, 2019). Over 300 years earlier, Jonathan Swift warned that *falsehood flies and the truth comes limping after it*. See "A Lie Can Travel Halfway Around the World While the Truth Is Putting on Its Shoes", *Quote Investigator*, available at: https://quoteinvestigator.com/2014/07/13/truth/ (accessed September 15, 2019).

91 He, Shusi, "Repair Bill for Damaged LegCo Complex Put at HK$50m", *China Daily*, July 3, 2019, available at: https://www.chinadailyhk.com/articles/159/47/14/1562089842786.html (accessed July 18, 2019).

92 Boissoneault, Lorraine, "The True Story of the Reichstag Fire and the Nazi Rise to Power", *Smithsonian Magazine*, February 21, 2017, available at: https://www.smithsonianmag.com/history/true-story-reichstag-fire-and-nazis-rise-power-180962240/ (accessed July 18, 2019). Other, more terrifying attacks than that in the HKSAR include the lethal bombardment of the Russian Parliament (or Duma) by tanks in 1993, supporting President Boris Yeltsin against the Parliament. See "Russian Constitutional Crisis of 1993", *McGill University*,

riotous throng of protesters battled Police and attacked the Central Government Liaison Office in Hong Kong using paint bombs to deface, inter alia, the national emblem.[93] Later, radical separatists took down a Chinese flag to throw it into Victoria Harbour.[94] The use of Molotov Cocktails, or petrol bombs, by radical protesters became common as the rioting continued.

On Sunday, July 21, apart from the violent attack on the Central Government Liaison Office, there was a brutal attack that same evening at the Yuen Long, Mass Transit Railway (MTR) Station directed mainly at anti-government protesters (dressed in their characteristic, self-adopted black clothing) who were returning home on the MTR. This attack involved men dressed in white who injured some 45 persons, including protesters and also regular passengers.[95] The attackers included local villagers from the Yuen Long area and a number of Triads or known criminals. The Police were accused of responding too slowly to the attack, which claims became subject to investigation by the ICAC.[96] The Police were, at the same time, still dealing with the violent protests at the Central Government Liaison Office. Speaking about this attack on protesters in Yuen Long, one commentator made these points:

> Within minutes of white-shirted thugs attacking people in Yuen Long on the evening of July 21, edited clips emerged. Then in less than two hours, professional time-stamped photographs with commentary appeared. In an instant, these circulated through chat groups with the assertion that the Police conspired in the attacks. Even without reliable evidence, these claims become the dominant narrative.

available at: https://www.cs.mcgill.ca/~rwest/wikispeedia/wpcd/wp/r/Russian_constitutional_crisis_of_1993.htm (accessed July 21, 2019); for details on the deadly attack on the Indian Parliament in 2001, see Miglani, Sanjeev, "12 Die in Indian Parliament Attack", *The Guardian,* December 14, 2001, available at: https://www.theguardian.com/world/2001/dec/14/kashmir.india (accessed July 21, 2019).

93 Cheung, Tony, "Top Beijing Representative in Hong Kong Condemns Attack on Liaison Office during Extradition Protest, Says Rioters Will Be Punished", *South China Morning Post*, July 22, 2019, available at: https://www.scmp.com/news/hong-kong/politics/article/3019556/top-beijing-representative-hong-kong-condemns-attack (accessed August 18, 2019).

94 "Hong Kong Protesters Rip Down Chinese Flag, Throw It into Iconic Harbor", *Japan Times*, August 3, 2019, available at: https://www.japantimes.co.jp/news/2019/08/03/asia-pacific/hong-kong-braces-four-days-unrest/#.XVkOcdR96XY (accessed August 18, 2019).

95 "At Least 45 Hurt in Yuen Long Attack, One Critical", *RTHK*, July 22, 2019, available at: https://news.rthk.hk/rthk/en/component/k2/1469616-20190722.htm?spTabChangeable=0 (accessed August 25, 2019).

96 Sum, Lok-kei, "Hong Kong Police 'Under Investigation' by Corruption Watchdog over Failure to Protect Public during Yuen Long Attacks", *South China Morning Post*, July 30, 2019, available at: https://www.scmp.com/news/hong-kong/politics/article/3020635/hong-kong-police-officers-call-citys-no-2-clarify-apology (accessed August 25, 2019).

> In no time, the international media – without verifying – repeat the story. Old reports of alleged connivance between the Police and gangs are then rehashed to add weight to the flimsy "facts". This approach gave the innuendo a facade of truth. And many people wanted to believe it.[97]

The responses of the HKSAR Government to the escalating crisis were flexible at the margins (regarding details of the Extradition Bill), but it remained deeply fixed on securing passage of the legislation. This rigidity added further significant fuel to the political confrontation and to the media campaigns being waged with rising intensity against the Extradition Bill. The massive marches and the unprecedented potency and duration of political rioting appeared to leave the HKSAR Government almost immobilized for weeks on end. The Government declared the Extradition Bill was "dead" by July 2019 but struggled badly as it tried to respond to the escalating crisis. A very heavy burden fell on the Police as they fought to control the widespread political lawlessness.[98]

It was stated that five demands had to be met for the mass protesting and, implicitly, the violent demonstrating to be called off: a complete withdrawal of the Extradition Bill; the withdrawal of the "riot" characterization of the June 12 [violent] protests; the unconditional release of all arrested protesters; the formation of an independent commission of inquiry into police behaviour; and the introduction of universal suffrage.[99]

Certainly, both the HKSAR Government and Beijing took the same unbending view towards the serial political rioting: the Extradition Bill had been declared "dead"; there would be no further concessions or compromises while the violence continued; and, above all, the violence, which had become a serious threat to the well-being and the economy of the HKSAR and to the sovereignty of China, had to cease.[100] The possibility of a full enquiry of some sort (presumably with wide terms of reference – see Chapter 9) was left open – after the cessation

97 "Hearts and Minds – All Warfare Is Based on Deception".

98 See Wu, Willa, "Ex-Prosecutor Commends Police Courage, Restraint", *China Daily*, August 7, 2019, available at: http://www.chinadaily.com.cn/a/201908/07/WS5d4ae542a310cf3e35564767.html (accessed August 22, 2019); and Cohen, Colin, "Reasons to Still Believe in Our City", *Newsletter – Boase Cohen & Collins*, August 20, 2019.

99 Cheng, Kris, "All Five Demands Must Be Fulfilled: Thousands of Hong Kong Anti-Extradition Law Protesters Rally in Sha Tin", *Hong Kong Free Press*, July 14, 2019, available at: https://www.hongkongfp.com/2019/07/14/five-demands-must-fulfilled-thousands-hong-kong-anti-extradition-law-protesters-rally-sha-tin/ (accessed August 8, 2019).

100 Chan, Bernard, "To Beijing, the Hong Kong Protest Unrest Is Now a Threat on a National Level", *South China Morning Post*, August 30, 2019, available at: https://www.scmp.com/comment/opinion/article/3024751/beijing-hong-kong-protest-unrest-now-threat-national-level (accessed August 31, 2019).

of all violence.[101] Ultimately, it was announced that the Extradition Bill would be formally withdrawn.[102]

For the major protest marches on April 28, June 9, and June 12, the organizer estimated attendance of 130,000 people, 1.3 million people, and 2 million people, respectively. The Police estimate of peak numbers was 22,800 people, 240,000 people, and 338,000 people, respectively. The estimate by a respected local newspaper, *Ming Pao*, of those attending the April 28 march was 15,000.[103] A later, major protest march held on August 18 was attended by 1.7 million people according to the organizers while the Police estimate was 128,000 people.[104]

The pattern which emerges from the figures above is that the organizer estimates vary between being over 5 times higher to over 13 times higher than Police estimates. Most of the Hong Kong and international media outlets have headlined the organizer's estimates in each of the above cases, usually recording Police estimates in the text, when noted. Different calculation methodologies may account for some of the differences.[105]

The 2019 consecutive political riots have meant that the Hong Kong Police have faced their worst operational pressure in over 50 years.[106] There have been many claims that the reputation of the Police has been significantly harmed as a result of their responses to the extraordinary amount of lawlessness created by the political riots.[107]

101 Chan, ibid. See also Chung, Kimmy and Cheung, Tony, "Hong Kong Protests Have 'Obvious Characteristics of Colour Revolution', Top Beijing Official Warns Amid 'Worst Crisis Since 1997 Handover'", *South China Morning Post*, August 8, 2019, available at: https://www.scmp.com/news/hong-kong/politics/article/3021877/protests-colour-revolution-threatening-hong-kong-abyss-top (accessed August 9, 2019).

102 "Hong Kong Leader Carrie Lam Announces Formal Withdrawal of the Extradition Bill and Sets Up a Platform to Look into Key Causes of Protest Crisis", *South China Morning Post*, September 4, 2019, available at: https://www.scmp.com/news/hong-kong/politics/article/3025641/hong-kong-leader-carrie-lam-announce-formal-withdrawal (accessed September 5, 2019).

103 Ng, Natalie, *2019 Protests Timeline* (on file with the author).

104 "Hong Kong Protesters Defy Ban to Return in Huge Numbers for Peaceful Rally", *ABC News*, August 19, 2019, available at: https://www.abc.net.au/news/2019-08-19/more-than-one-million-hong-kong-protesters-return-to-mass/11426022 (accessed August 26, 2019).

105 Sum, Lok-kei, "Why the Big Difference in Estimates for Crowd Size by Police and Organisers of Sunday's Protest March in Hong Kong?", *South China Morning Post*, April 29, 2019, available at: https://www.scmp.com/news/hong-kong/politics/article/3008182/why-big-difference-estimates-crowd-size-police-and (accessed August 28, 2019).

106 Cross, Grenville, "HK Police Maintaining Fine Traditions in Challenging Times", *China Daily*, August 29, 2019, available at: https://www.chinadailyhk.com/articles/127/14/198/1567080258543.html (accessed August 30, 2019).

107 See Chan, Holmes, "Hong Kong Police Top Brass Face Barrage of Questions over Use of Weapons, Injuries, Undercover Tactics", *Hong Kong Free Press*, August 12, 2019, available at: https://www.hongkongfp.com/2019/08/12/hong-kong-police-top-brass-face-barrage-questions-use-weapons-injuries-undercover-tactics/ (accessed August 27, 2019); and Chan, Holmes, "Hong Kong Police Say Brutality Allegations 'Unfair,' As Gov't Slams

Sir Robert Peel is credited with creating modern policing in Britain around 1829. The "Peelian Principles" of policing embody the idea that the Police Force is not a para-military organization but a civilian law enforcement body which depends on public recognition and acceptance of its role in society to ensure peace and good order (see Chapter 4). This approach to police work has been adapted over time in Britain and beyond. It remains the best basic template one can apply to meet the intense demands of modern policing. It is also a fact of life, however, that the nature of police work is bound to make a number of people unhappy. Police tell you what you can and cannot do and they are authorized to use legitimate force to maintain public peace and order. This can make some people very unhappy and aggressive. It also means that police may have to be very forceful when they are working to resecure public order.

As explained in Chapter 5, one fundamental measure of good policing is how well a society ranks in terms of freedom from fear. If the Rule of Law operates fairly and robustly, individual citizens should be able to move about in any public space day and night without fear of any significant intimidation or threat of crimes against the person. Prior to 2019, the HKSAR was rated as the safest travel jurisdiction worldwide (ahead of Singapore and Japan) according to a US assessment reported by Travel Wire Asia in 2017 – one where, a "woman or a man can walk any street at any time of day or night without fear". The US State Department also lists Hong Kong as one of the world's safest cities. In the Gallup 2018 Global Law and Order report, which puts its questions about city safety to local residents, Hong Kong was ranked 6th out of 142 countries and regions. The US was ranked 35th. The Hong Kong Police Force has made a crucial contribution, over many decades, to help make Hong Kong a very safe, big city.

It is timely to consider how other governments and police forces have dealt with challenges comparable to those faced in the HKSAR in 2019. Most recently, France has encountered serial violent political demonstrations and riots, which began in November 2018 with the "Yellow Vest" protests (named after the road-safety vests worn by protesters). By June, 2019, there had been 11 deaths some 2,500 civilian injuries plus 1,800 injuries amongst the security forces.[108] The number arrested totalled over 8,000 by August 2019 with, typically, more than 25% of those arrested being remanded in custody. Individual searches by

---

'Inconvenience of Peaceful Mass Demo'", *Hong Kong Free Press*, August 19, 2019, available at: https://www.hongkongfp.com/2019/08/19/hong-kong-police-say-brutality-allegations-unfair-govt-slams-inconvenience-peaceful-mass-demo/ (accessed August 26, 2019). See also Kwok, Tony, "Baseless Criticism of Police Must Be Countered", *China Daily*, August 13, 2019, available at: https://www.chinadailyhk.com/articles/77/102/25/1565696439021.html (accessed August 26, 2019).

108 Millar, Joey, "Yellow Vest: Shock Stats Reveal Depth of Macron Chaos – 50,000 on Streets and 11 Dead", *Daily Express*, June 17, 2019, available at: https://www.express.co.uk/news/politics/1141568/yellow-vest-protests-emmanuel-macron-protests-france-news-gilets-jaunes (accessed August 26, 2019).

security authorities were still more extensive.[109] The approach to containing the rioting was aggressively focussed. The Interior Minister said: "We are not going to respond to Molotov Cocktails with nice feelings and we are not going to protect the order of the Republic with soft words".[110] The French media, meanwhile, labelled the smashing of shop windows in Paris as evidence of "mob rage" but the ransacking of LegCo in Hong Kong as "the boldest of operations". The fierce attack on a Mainland journalist by protesters at Hong Kong Airport was "an incident" but the violent menacing of journalists by yellow vest protesters was compared to a "lynching".[111]

After riots in Chicago in 1968, which lasted 48 hours, 11 were left dead, 48 were wounded by police gunfire, and over 2,000 were arrested. The Mayor of the city gave orders to shoot to kill anyone with a Molotov Cocktail in their hand.[112] During a violent Quebec separatist uprising in Canada in 1970, headed by the FLQ (Quebec Liberation Front), Prime Minister Pierre Trudeau implemented the War Measures Act and declared a constitutional emergency. Over 400 FLQ members or suspected sympathizers were rounded up and held without charge and the Canadian Military was used to guard public institutions and public figures. These unprecedented measures succeeded in bringing the separatist insurrection to a fairly swift end.[113]

The Government of Canada, headed by the son of Pierre Trudeau, Justin Trudeau, was a signatory, with the EU, to a Joint Statement in August 2019, urging the HKSAR Government to exercise restraint and to seek dialogue and protect fundamental freedoms during its violent political crisis.[114] In 1970, facing a similar challenge, Pierre Trudeau said in an interview:

109 "Over 1,700 arrested in latest 'yellow vest' protests in France", *France 24*, December 9, 2018, available at: https://www.france24.com/en/20181209-over-1700-arrested-latest-yellow-vest-protests-france (accessed August 26, 2019). See also Cross, Grenville, "Equality of Treatment Necessary for All Criminal Suspects", *China Daily*, September 2, 2019, available at: https://www.chinadailyhk.com/articles/75/125/147/1567429122315.html (accessed September 3, 2019).

110 "Over 1,700", ibid. One commentator observed how the British media had almost blacked-out reporting on the sequential political rioting in France (29 miles from England) whilst focussing inordinately on the political protesting and violence in Hong Kong. See Galloway, George, "Hong Kong Phooey! Would You Like Any Hypocrisy with That?" *RT*, August 13, 2019, available at: https://www.rt.com/op-ed/466396-hong-kong-british-hypocrisy/ (accessed August 26, 2019).

111 Bulard, Martine, "What's Really Behind Hong Kong Protests?" *Le Monde Diplomatiue*, September 2019, available at: https://mondediplo.com/2019/09/02hong-kong (accessed August 31, 2019).

112 "1968 Chicago Riots", *Wikipedia*, available at: https://en.wikipedia.org/wiki/1968_Chicago_riots (accessed August 26, 2019).

113 "The October Crisis", *CBC*, available at: https://www.cbc.ca/history/EPISCONTENTSE1EP16CH1PA4LE.html (accessed August 26, 2019).

114 "Joint Statement by Canada and the European Union on the Situation in Hong Kong", *Government of Canada*, August 17, 2019,available at: https://www.canada.ca/en/global-

circumstances.[120] Under the HKSAR Common Law system, the Police also have to operate without having access to the sort of deterrent provided by convening the prompt-acting, special courts allowable under French Law.

No Police Force ever operates in flawless way – the nature of what each force must do ensures this. The Hong Kong Police Force is no exception. And if its performance is repeatedly reviewed against some textbook portrayal of unblemished policing, shortfalls can be highlighted – and then amplified, as needs be, to launch strong radical attacks.[121] Assessed against robust comparative policing benchmarks drawn from direct policing experience, however, the Hong Kong Police stand out as one of the HKSAR's key public institutional assets.

I have explained why the intense portrayal of the Extradition Bill as a potential danger to all Hong Kong residents was misleading yet most successful. There was an understandable basis for the very large protest marches which followed its announcement. The rolling months of political rioting which then set in were, however, a conspicuously disproportionate and lawless response to the claimed wrongs being objected to.

Related criminal actions

A range of subsequent criminal prosecutions and civil actions were launched in relation to the OCM occupations and the Mong Kok Riot. For the OCM movement alone, the combined total was around 300 (168 criminal and 125 civil actions).[122] Soon after the Mong Kok Riot, over 70 arrests were made and around 50 persons were charged.[123] This section provides an overview of the more important criminal prosecutions arising out of the OCM and the Mong Kok Riot. Criminal prosecutions related to the 2019 Protests and Riots will proceed in due course. Interestingly, the first convictions resulted in swift two- to

120 Yeung, Jessie, Sidhu, Sandi, and Wright, Rebecca, "A Gun Shot, Petrol Bombs and Water Cannons Mark Violent Escalation in Hong Kong Protests", *CNN*, August 26, 2019, available at: https://edition.cnn.com/2019/08/25/asia/hong-kong-protest-aug-25-intl-hnk/index.html (accessed August 27, 2019).

121 The force should be subject to robust public scrutiny, of course, which it is. See the Independent Police Complaints Council Ordinance (Cap. 604); the Independent Police Complaints Council (IPCC) is a key monitoring mechanism – "What is IPCC", *Independent Police Complaints Council*, available at: https://www.ipcc.gov.hk/en/about_us/about_ipcc.html (accessed August 27, 2019). See also Kwok, Tony, "Baseless Criticisms of Police Must Be Countered", *China Daily*, August 14, 2019, available at: http://www.chinadaily.com.cn/hkedition/2019-08/14/content_37501556.htm (accessed August 27, 2019).

122 Lam, Jeffie, "After All the Prosecutions, Was the Occupy Movement in Vain?" *South China Morning Post*, April 10, 2019, available at: https://www.scmp.com/news/hong-kong/law-and-crime/article/3005456/hong-kongs-occupy-protests-five-years-after-all (accessed May 31, 2019).

123 "Mong Kok Riot", *HKSAR Government Press Release*, March 2, 2016, available at: https://www.info.gov.hk/gia/general/201603/02/P201603020594.htm (accessed May 31, 2019).

> Trudeau: There's a lot of bleeding hearts around who don't like t ple with helmets and guns. All I can say is "go ahead and bleed" bu important to keep law and order in this society than to be wor weak-kneed people who don't like the looks of …
>
> Reporter: At what cost? How far would you go? To what extent?
>
> Trudeau: "Well, just watch me".[115]

Soon after Canada and the EU issued their joint statement on Ho France, a key EU member, hosted a G7 (Group of Seven) Summit. Th of France called for "calm and for unity" just before the summit. Mea by France to address possible threats to public order related to the G included deployment of 13,000 police and gendarmes (to deal with ab protesters). Water cannon, rubber bullets, and teargas were all used Magistrates' Court (with 17 Magistrates and dozens of lawyers) was se cent to the summit zone, along with a special holding enclosure for 3 This was to enable those arrested to be held and then charged, tried, if found guilty, and imprisoned, where warranted, without undue dela the Atlantic in the US, almost 600 people were fatally shot by police during 2019, in the space of eight months.[117]

In the HKSAR, in the two to three months after the violent prot rioting began on June 12, hundreds were injured including 180 police Over a thousand were arrested with almost all of those arrested bei on bail.[119] Throughout the course of well over 20 violent political p riots, police officers had, at the time of writing, only drawn their re three occasions, when threatened with serious injury or worse, and o occasions had an officer fired a shot in the air under particularly t

affairs/news/2019/08/joint-statement-by-canada-and-european-union-on-hong-kong.html (accessed August 26, 2019).

115 "The October Crisis".

116 Prerez, Sergio, "French Police Fire Tear Gas, Water Cannons at Anti-G7 Pro Summit", *Reuters*, August 25, 2019, available at: https://www.reuters.c us-g7-summit-protests/french-police-fire-tear-gas-water-cannons-at-anti-g7 idUSKCN1VE0DN (accessed August 27, 2019).

117 Lonsdale, Chris, "Democracy, Yes! But Not the United States Mod *Daily*, August 27, 2019, available at: https://www.chinadailyas cles/92/99/219/1566906524699.html?newsId=93332 (accessed August 28

118 "Hong Kong Protests: 180 Police Officers Injured, Families 'Bullied and In *CNA News*, August 19, 2019, available at: https://www.channelnewsasia. asia/hong-kong-protests-police-injured-families-intimidated-bullied-1181936 August 27, 2019).

119 Leung, Kanis and Lo, Clifford, "Three Men Arrested for Storming Legislativ Hong Kong Police Deny Female Protester's Accusations of Strip-Search", *Morning Post*, August 28, 2019, available at: https://www.scmp.com/news/ politics/article/3024614/three-men-arrested-storming-legislative-council (accessed August 30, 2019).

four-week jail terms for two nominally *pro-government* protesters. Two Mainland men separately protested against claimed US involvement in the 2019 political turmoil by trying to deface the outer wall of the US Consulate in the HKSAR with ink or graffiti and were caught in the act.[124]

OCM criminal matters

Two early criminal prosecutions related to the OCM have already been mentioned. In 2017, seven police officers were each jailed for two years (these sentences remained under appeal at the time of writing) for assaulting one OCM activist.[125] The same activist was jailed, in 2016, for five weeks for assaulting police and resisting arrest.[126]

The most important prosecutions connected to the OCM were launched against nine persons (including the OCM Trio) who were seen to be pivotal in organizing and or maintaining the OCM occupations (OCM-9). This trial, in which all of the OCM-9 stood trial together, was fully argued over almost 20 days. It began in November 2018 and concluded in mid-December. The court delivered its verdict in April 2019. All defendants were found guilty.

The charges brought all were based around the Common Law crime of committing public nuisance. In 2005, the House of Lords in the UK had found that this offence continued to exist, notwithstanding certain overlapping statute-based offences, and that it was compatible with the UK Human Rights Act.[127] The various OCM-related counts were conspiracy to commit public nuisance, incitement to commit public nuisance, and incitement to incite public nuisance.[128] Dating from BHK days, the prosecution chooses where a criminal trial should run in Hong Kong, bearing in mind the gravity of an offence and the possible sentence which may apply. It was expected that applicable sentences in this case would be below seven years imprisonment. The trial ran in the District Court where the

124 Wong, Brian, "Mainland Chinese Taxi Driver Jailed for Two Weeks for Defacing US Consulate in Hong Kong", *South China Morning Post*, August 30, 2019, available at: https://www.scmp.com/news/hong-kong/law-and-crime/article/3025010/mainland-chinese-taxi-driver-jailed-two-weeks-defacing (accessed August 31, 2019).

125 Ng, Ellie, "Police Officers Jailed for 2 years for Assault against Occupy Activist Ken Tsang", *Hong Kong Free Press*, February 17, 2017, available at: https://www.hongkongfp.com/2017/02/17/police-officers-jailed-for-assault-against-occupy-activist-ken-tsang/ (accessed May 30, 2019).

126 Siu, Jasmine, "Activist Ken Tsang Gets Five Weeks in Jail for Assaulting Police and Resisting Arrest during Occupy Protest", *South China Morning Post*, May 30, 2016, available at: http://www.scmp.com/news/hong-kong/law-crime/article/1959354/activist-ken-tsang-gets-five-weeks-jail-assaulting-police (accessed October 1, 2019).

127 *R v. Rimmington and R v. Goldstein* (2005) UKHL 63.

128 Chan, Holmes, "Hong Kong's Leading Umbrella Movement Activists Handed Jail Sentences", *Hong Kong Free Press*, April 24, 2019, available at: https://www.hongkongfp.com/2019/04/24/breaking-hong-kongs-leading-umbrella-movement-activists-handed-jail-sentences/ (accessed May 31, 2019).

maximum sentence which can be imposed is seven years. In the District Court, trial is by judge alone.

In a lengthy judgement, Judge Johnny Chan found all defendants were guilty. He initially handed down sentences to eight of the OCM-9, ranging from 16-month jail terms to a Community Service Order. Some sentences were suspended in view of age and previous good records. In the case of one defendant, sentencing was postponed due to an intervening illness.[129] The Judge dismissed the claims that civil disobedience arguments overrode the claimed criminal conduct. In this case, the Judge said that the OCM had imposed excessive damage and inconvenience over a very long period of time. Moreover, those charged failed to express regret for the suffering and inconvenience they have caused for so many people. The Judge said he was not suggesting that the defendants should give up their political beliefs or demands, but that they should be prepared to apologize to the numerous ordinary people affected, which they were not.[130]

For those firmly opposed to the trial of the OCM-9 and its outcomes, the Government wrongly interfered with the right to protest in the HKSAR and set back rights protection in Hong Kong significantly.[131] It is true that all public protests will likely interfere with others going about their lawful business. And it is right that such protests should be tolerated. As noted above, Hong Kong currently tolerates over 30 such protests every day of the year, on average – arguably more than in any comparably sized city.[132] But any Rule of Law society needs to draw and apply a clear distinction between protests that interfere with the public rights of others incidentally and protests which interfere with the public rights of others as a matter of deliberate intention and over an extended period of time. The latter is a form of protest as coercion. This, in essence, is the distinction which was drawn and applied in the trial of the OCM-9.

It would appear to be a distinction clearly drawn in the UK also. Within eight days of the climate change related *Extinction Rebellion* demonstration commencing in London in April 2019, the Police had arrested 1,056 protesters (not far short of the total OCM-related arrests covering almost three months) and charged over 50 persons.[133]

129 Ibid. At the time of writing, appeals were being prepared by a number of those convicted and sentenced.

130 Ibid.

131 Suzanne Pepper provides a strong, detailed, critical review of the case (see Pepper, Suzanne, "The Umbrella Movement Jailings: How Opportunistic, Made-to-Measure Charges Got the Job Done", *Hong Kong Free Press*, April 27, 2019, available at: https://www.hongkongfp.com/2019/04/27/umbrella-movement-jailings-opportunistic-made-measure-charges-made-mockery-justice/ (accessed June 1, 2019).

132 "Public Order Event Statistics", *Hong Kong Police Force*, available at: https://www.police.gov.hk/ppp_en/09_statistics/poes.html (accessed May 30, 2019).

133 Cross, Grenville, "Rule of Law Must Prevail over 'Occupy' Nine", *China Daily*, April 25, 2019, available at : https://www.chinadailyhk.com/articles/148/72/169/1556128438552.html (accessed June 1, 2019). Cross notes in this article how the last Governor of British Hong Kong, Chris Patten, made no complaint about these London protester arrests

Mong Kok Riot criminal matters

Following the Mong Kok Riot in February 2016, some 90 persons were arrested and a large number ultimately were charged. Many of those were convicted on the serious charge of riot. This is an offence under the POORD which, as enacted under British rule in Hong Kong, carries a maximum sentence of ten years (see above). Some were convicted on other charges, including assault and criminal damage.[134] Two alleged leaders of the riot escaped from Hong Kong to Germany (via Taiwan) after being granted bail (see further below).

Several trials with multiple defendants were held in 2017 and 2018, both in the District Court, before Judge alone, and in the High Court with a jury.[135] Three defendants were convicted of rioting in the first trial in 2017.[136]

In mid-2018, after a case that ran in the High Court for 54 days followed by jury deliberations which took three days, three defendants, including a key advocate of Hong Kong independence and a leader of the Mong Kok Riot, Edward Leung Tin-Kei, were sentenced to imprisonment for terms ranging from three and a half years to seven years.[137] A later jury trial of Leung and three others (where Leung was acquitted of a further riot charge and only one defendant was convicted) ran for 70 days and involved 43 hours of jury deliberations. It concluded in March 2019.[138]

The largest Mong Kok Riot trial, which ran for a year in the District Court, concluded in May 2018. In a 382-page judgement, Judge Kwok concluded that all ten defendants were guilty. One was sent to a Training Centre, but the others were all jailed for terms ranging from two years and four months to three years and nine months.[139]

---

despite many public objections to the use of the law to penalize law-breaking protestor-behaviour in the HKSAR.

134 Kong, "Justice It Ain't".

135 Ibid.

136 Siu, Jasmine, "Three Hong Kong Protesters Become First to be Convicted of Rioting during Mong Kok Clashes", *South China Morning Post*, March 16, 2017, available at: https://www.scmp.com/news/hong-kong/law-crime/article/2079412/three-hong-kong-protesters-become-first-be-convicted (accessed June 1, 2019).

137 See Wu, Venus, "Three Hong Kong Democracy Activists Jailed for Up to Seven Years for Rioting", *Reuters*, June 11, 2018, available at: https://www.reuters.com/article/us-hongkong-court-riot/three-hong-kong-democracy-activists-jailed-up-to-seven-years-for-rioting-idUSKBN1J707U (accessed June 1, 2019); and Lau, Chris and Siu, Jasmine, "Hong Kong Independence Activist Edward Leung Found Guilty of Rioting but Cleared of Incitement over Mong Kok Unrest", *South China Morning Post*, available at: https://www.scmp.com/news/hong-kong/hong-kong-law-and-crime/article/2146806/hong-kong-pro-independence-activist-edward (accessed June 1, 2019).

138 Lau, Chris and Siu, Jasmine, "Former Separatist Leader Edward Leung Found Not Guilty of Additional Mong Kok Riot Charge", *South China Morning Post*, March 22, 2019, available at: https://www.scmp.com/news/hong-kong/law-and-crime/article/3002814/former-separatist-leader-edward-leung-found-not-guilty (accessed June 1, 2019).

139 Siu, Jasmine, "Teenager Jailed for 'Wanton Use of Violence' during Mong Kok Riot", *South China Morning Post*, June 1, 2018, available at: https://www.scmp.com/news/

Evading trial

Two persons charged with rioting, including one alleged leader of the Mong Kok Riot, fled from Hong Kong while released on bail. Ray Wong Toi-Yeung and Alan Li Tung-Sing were members of the localist or independence group, Hong Kong Indigenous. They absconded to Germany, apparently via Taiwan, while they were awaiting trial.[140] It has subsequently been revealed that Germany granted each of them political asylum in 2018, though Germany has been reluctant to confirm the detail of this officially.[141] This appears to be the first time any residents of the HKSAR have sought and gained political asylum.[142]

This is a remarkable case. The two young men had deliberately broken their bail conditions, a serious crime in itself,[143] and they were accused of crimes punishable by many years of imprisonment. Germany could not help but know this. Nor could they not be aware of relevant, significant video evidence implicating the two charged men in the Mong Kok Riot. Germany has given no reasons for granting asylum.[144] Prima facie, the granting of asylum to two clear fugitives from criminal justice coming from a jurisdiction with very strong Rule of Law ranking[145] invites the view that Germany (which also enjoys an excellent Rule of Law ranking[146]) is prepared to assert that political considerations can set aside a primary principle of the Rule of Law, that no one is above the law.

One way of testing the legal soundness of Germany's decision is to consider what may have happened if the Wikileaks founder, Julian Assange, had somehow got himself to Germany after breaching his bail conditions in the UK in 2012, when Sweden was seeking his extradition.[147] Based on this example, Germany

---

hong-kong/hong-kong-law-and-crime/article/2148726/mong-kok-riot-youngest-10-defendants-given (accessed June 1, 2019).

140 See Lo, Alex, When Rioters Pretend to be Dissidents", *South China Morning Post*, May 23, 2019, available at: https://www.scmp.com/comment/insight-opinion/article/3011565/when-rioters-pretend-be-dissidents (accessed June 1, 2019); and Chugani, Michael. "Why Did Germany Feel the Need to Grant Asylum to Hong Kong Riot Fugitives? Ask Carrie Lam", *South China Morning Post,* May 30, 2019, available at: https://www.scmp.com/comment/insight-opinion/article/3012249/why-did-germany-feel-need-grant-asylum-hong-kong-riot (accessed June 1, 2019).

141 Liu, Nicolle, "Hong Kong Activists Gain Refugee Status for the First Time", *Financial Times,* May 22, 2019, available at: https://www.ft.com/content/edd3b148-7c32-11e9-81d2-f785092ab560 (accessed June 1, 2019).

142 In fact, applications for political asylum by US citizens, for example, are regular – 12 were granted asylum in the UK in one year (2015) alone (see Lo, "When Rioters Pretend").

143 "Julian Assange: Wikileaks Co-Founder Jailed over Bail Breach", *BBC News,* May 1, 2019, available at: https://www.bbc.com/news/uk-48118908 (accessed June 1, 2019).

144 Liu, "Hong Kong Activists".

145 Hong Kong ranks 16th out of 126 countries according to the US-based, World Justice Project – see "Rule of Law Index 2019", *World Justice Project*, available at: https://worldjusticeproject.org/sites/default/files/documents/WJP-ROLI-2019-Single%20Page%20View-Reduced_0.pdf (accessed June 1, 2019).

146 Germany ranks sixth out of 126 countries according to the World Justice Project, ibid.

147 "Julian Assange".

would surely have had to grant Assange political asylum had he requested this. Yet it is very hard to imagine that Germany would have done so. In my view, Germany has made an ill-considered political decision in relation to these two men wanted in the HKSAR on very serious criminal charges.[148]

Evidential matters

One dominant feature of all the criminal trials related to the OCM and the Mong Kok Riot has been the heavy reliance on extensive, graphic video evidence. So much alleged wrong-doing has been caught on camera, often in very clear detail, from the beating of the OCM activist by Police Officers to actions and activities of the OCM-9 during the OCM occupations. and even more so in the case of rioting in Mong Kok in February 2016.

Such evidence is not irrefutable, but it has proved itself to be far more telling than the sort of evidence relied upon in days not so long past. Then, the paramount sources of evidence in such cases would have been that given in the

148 The HSAR has encountered another notable instance (already logged) where politics has, prima facie, trumped law. A Hong Kong resident, Chan, Tong-kai, ***admitted*** to unlawfully killing his pregnant Hong Kong girlfriend (a fact recorded in a legal judgement convicting him of another offence) whilst they were holidaying together in Taiwan in early 2017. After killing her and disposing of her body, he fled back to the HKSAR. As noted above, the HKSAR has no system in place to allow extradition or rendition to any other part of Greater China, including Taiwan. The Mainland Affairs Council (MAC) in Taiwan said that Taiwan would not seek extradition/rendition of Mr. Chan to Taiwan under the proposed Extradition Bill: [I]t would not accept any rendition agreement as long as the Hong Kong Government was operating under the "one-China" principle. This seems an even more remarkable potential breach (than in Germany) of the fundamental principle that no one is above the law in a Rule of Law system: here there is willingness to place Mr. Chan above the law of murder in order to make a political point. In fact, apart from Mr. Chan's admission, there is significant CCTV circumstantial evidence. See Siu, Jasmine, "Sentence for Man Who Killed Girlfriend in Taiwan Sets Extradition Deadline", *South China Morning Post*, April 29, 2019, available at: https://www.scmp.com/news/hong-kong/law-and-crime/article/3008099/sentence-man-who-killed-girlfriend-taiwan-sets (accessed June 1, 2019); and Chan, Holmes, "Executive Councillor Ronny Tong 'Very Shocked' as Taiwan Rejects Hong Kong Govt's Extradition Proposal", *Hong Kong Free Press*, February 26, 2019, available at: https://www.hongkongfp.com/2019/02/26/executive-councillor-ronny-tong-shocked-taiwan-rejects-hong-kong-govts-extradition-proposal/ (accessed June 1, 2019). Finally, it should be noted that whilst the MAC has expressed concern over the Extradition Bill rendition amendments, Taiwan itself signed the "Cross Strait Joint Crime-Fighting and Judicial Mutual Assistance Agreement" in May 2009. This was preceded by an earlier version which dates from 1990. Taiwan has thus operated under a criminal justice mutual assistance agreement (which allows for rendition) with Mainland China (with limited safeguards on the face of it) for almost 20 years – apparently without mishap. See "Cross Strait Joint Crime-Fighting and Judicial Mutual Assistance Agreement", *Mainland Affairs Council*, May 22, 2009, available at: https://www.mac.gov.tw/en/cp.aspx?n=FD37619195CF6DA5&s=CED288DC9B1EC576 (accessed June 1, 2019). Had Chan's murdered pregnant girlfriend been a Taiwan resident, it is hard to imagine the MAC and the Taiwan Government would have been so comfortable with allowing Mr. Chan to escape justice.

witness box by police witnesses referring to their notebooks – evidence which could be closely cross-examined by defence lawyers.

One other point should be made. The (multiple defendant) trials noted above have been long, sometimes exceptionally so. Appropriate legal aid has been provided to defendants. It is clear that prior to verdicts being returned, the evidence presented has been extensively tested. By any reasonable measure, these have been fair trials conducted in accordance with clear Rule of Law principles.

Conclusion

The context within which major political protests and riots have developed in Hong Kong since World War II has varied quite dramatically. Through until 2019, however, Hong Kong has reasserted a collective commitment to ongoing basic social – and economic and political – stability.

With the passing of time, more clear views on the OCM occupations have also emerged. Some now feel that what came to be known as the "Umbrella Revolution/Movement" took over from the OCM once the occupations began, with adverse consequences.[149] Other commentators see a mainly polarizing legacy[150] and yet others, a political-deadening legacy.[151]

My own view remains that the OCM occupations proceeded based on a notably overstated pretext; were strikingly disproportionate; were immensely disruptive; and lacked coherence in leadership and in purpose. The claimed civil disobedience basis for commencing the occupations was insubstantial. The great majority in the HKSAR eventually grew weary of the entire project. The main direct achievement which one can see was the large lift in political awareness for many who participated and supported the OCM. The OCM strongly backed the vetoing of the proposed 2017 Chief Executive Election reform package – but this vetoing was all but guaranteed in any event by the collective decision-making of the PDs in LegCo.

This growth in awareness has likely amplified the responses seen during 2019 Protests and Riots. These disruptions, for the reasons explained above, have also been questionably grounded on a populist and alarmist pretext and the responses have been far more violently disproportionate and, in certain ways clearly more disruptive for the mass of people residing in the HKSAR.[152]

149 "Was Occupy Central a Failure (6 Answers)?" *Quora*, available at: https://www.quora.com/Was-Occupy-Central-a-failure (accessed October 1, 2019).

150 Lo, Sonny, "Electoral Reform Hinges on Principles", *China Daily*, July 31, 2016, available at: http://www.chinadailyasia.com/opinion/2016-07/31/content_15470808.html (accessed October 1, 2019).

151 Black, Tim, "Hong Kong: How the Occupy Brand Is Killing Politics", *Spiked*, December 11, 2014, available at: http://www.spiked-online.com/newsite/article/hong-kong-how-the-occupy-brand-is-killing-politics/16332#.V6ahOdR96XZ (accessed October 1, 2019).

152 Cohen, Dan, "Behind a Made-for-TV Hong Kong Protest Narrative".

The entire OCM project was also remarkable in that it went for so long, involved so many participants, police – and OCM opponents – yet the physical harm and property damage suffered was so minimal.[153] To have managed this over a period of almost three months is extraordinary.[154] The dominant, underlying good sense displayed by the clear majority of OCM protesters and the Police – combined with some effective application of the general law by the Judiciary – all crucially helped Hong Kong cope so well with the OCM occupations. What is much less clear is whether the HKSAR can reclaim its previous, deeply shared understanding of the vital need for stability and lawfulness, after the 2019 Protests and Riots. This question is a key focus of the closing chapters.

153 Once again, one only has to think of how anything on the protracted scale (and with the impact) of the OCM occupations might have been handled in any major US city, for example.

154 See the positive review by Joseph Wang in "Was Occupy Central a Failure?" *Quora,* available at: https://www.quora.com/Was-Occupy-Central-a-failure (accessed October 1, 2019).

8 The wider context of political reform

Background

It was shortly after World War II, in late 1947, that Winston Churchill, no longer Prime Minister of the UK, but Opposition Leader, said, in the House of Commons:

> Many forms of government have been tried, and will be tried in this world of sin and woe. No one pretends that democracy is perfect or all wise. Indeed it has been said that democracy is the worst form of government except for all the other forms that have been tried from time to time.[1]

In 1955, following the passage of the Television Act (1954) in the UK (by a Government led by Churchill), the Independent Television Network (ITV), which introduced commercial television advertising to Britain, began broadcasting in competition to BBC Television which had been established in 1932. The passage of the Television Act not only created ITV; it also introduced a complete ban, which has continued to this day (and is replicated in Hong Kong[2]) on paid political broadcast advertising.[3]

The argument made in 1954 (and sustained ever since) justifying this ban was, in essence, that:

> Television broadcasting was a particularly powerful and pervasive medium; Without prohibition there would be an unacceptable danger that political debate would be distorted in favour of those wealthy enough to spend most

1 "Famous Quotes about Democracy", *The Telegraph,* July 12, 2007 (quoting: Hansard, November 11, 1947), available at: https://www.telegraph.co.uk/culture/3673945/Famous-quotes-about-democracy.html (accessed June 2, 2019).

2 "LegCo Paper: Regulating Political Parties by Richard Cullen", *LegCo Hong Kong,* February, 2005, available at: https://www.legco.gov.hk/yr04-05/english/panels/ca/papers/ca0226cb2-911-1e.pdf (accessed June 6, 2019).

3 Monck, Adrian, "British Political TV Ads: Courtesy of Europe?", available at: http://adriamonck.com/2008/12/british-political-tv-ads-courtesy-europe/ (accessed June 2, 2019).

> on broadcast advertising; and to achieve this democracy-protective outcome, the ban must apply to all political advertising regardless of content.[4]

This total ban on paid political broadcast advertising was finally challenged after passage of the UK Human Rights Act (1998), which gives local effect to the European Convention on Human Rights in the UK. Article 10 guarantees the right to freedom of expression and information. In 2008 (in the *Animal Defenders Case*[5]), the House of Lords found unanimously that the total ban was compatible with Article 10 as, in essence, the ban reinforced the democratic process by securing a more level field for political contestation.[6] In particular, Baroness Hale stressed the need to avoid the sort of slanting of the political process arising from unwarranted political broadcast advocacy by wealthy segments in society.[7] In 2013, the European Court of Human Rights confirmed that House of Lords decision, relying on the same sort of reasoning, by a 9 to 8 majority.[8]

In America, the USSC reached an almost completely opposed conclusion, when faced with a series of similar cases. It struck down a number of relevant laws which only regulated campaign expenditure levels and how certain funds might be spent (that is, the laws did not impose any outright ban comparable to that applying in the UK) because, the Court said this was necessary to ensure optimal democratic participation. The USSC reasoning relied on the application of the First Amendment of the US Constitution, which guarantees freedom of speech and freedom of the press (inter alia).[9] Australia is one of the few developed countries in the Common Law world without a comprehensive constitutional Bill of Rights. Nevertheless, the HCA overturned a UK-like legislated ban on paid political broadcast advertising, after the court discovered that a right to political free expression could, in 1992, be deduced from certain wording within the Australian Constitution. The first such action advancing this argument was brought by television station interests who stood to lose most from the introduction of the ban.[10]

4 Ibid.
5 *R (On the Application of Animal Defenders International) v. Secretary for State for Culture, Media and Sport* (2008), UKHL, 15.
6 Ibid.
7 Ibid.
8 *Animal Defenders International v. United Kingdom* (2013), ECHR, 362.
9 See *Buckley v. Valeo*, 424 U.S. 1 (1976); then *Citizens United v. FEC*, 558 U.S. 310 (2010); and then *McCutcheon v. FEC* 572 U.S. 185 (2014).
10 *Australian Capital Television v. Commonwealth* (1992), HCA, 45. As in the US, the HCA had initially become accustomed to wielding powers of constitutional review (of particular statutes) when acting as the "umpire" in Central–State disputes arising out of the Federal system of government. This case provided an opportunity to discover an implied right in the absence of an explicit freedom of expression guarantee in the Australian Constitution. This was an opportunity which appeared to be welcomed by the court. Somewhat ironically, in what is regarded as the primary turning-point case where the HCA began to "rewrite" the Constitution to favour the Federal Government, *Amalgamated Society of Engineers v. Adelaide Steamship Co. Ltd* (*Engineers case*) (1920) 28 CLR 129, the HCA said it was improper

There is, here, a reminder of a crucial political viewpoint discussed in Chapter 2. Dicey saw a fundamental need for an independent judiciary but also the risk that unelected judges, made secure in their tenure to ensure independence, could be tempted to rewrite general laws made by Parliament by overturning them in part or in full: the doctrine of Parliamentary Sovereignty prevented this.[11]

When Churchill made his much quoted observation about democracy in 1947, there was no Internet, let alone social media. But even in that era, political leaders agreed that the rapidly emerging role of television within the popular media sector posed a very significant problem given its perceived scope to prejudice debate related to democratic elections by the use of paid political advertising. Both the US decisions and those in Australia discussed above undergird, in my view, the soundness of the policy reasoning on this matter in the UK. In the US and in Australia, moneyed interests have been the primary litigators, using constitutional arguments, to clear away, as far as possible, all impediments to very high levels of paid political broadcast advertising.

Modern political developments

As the movement towards political reform within BHK began to gather some serious momentum by the early 1990s, many were persuaded by the broad but fundamental political idea that democracy (where not already entrenched) was a no-risk (or at least low-risk) default option for all jurisdictions looking to modernize their political structure. The collapse of Soviet-style Communism from East Germany to Vladivostok and from the Baltic to the Mediterranean happened rapidly – with the great signifying event being the fall of the Berlin Wall in late 1989.

Another marker of the significance and claimed consequences of this historical turning point was first the essay, "The End of History", in1989[12] and then the book, *The End of History and the Last Man*, in 1992,[13] each written by the US political scientist, Francis Fukuyama. Fukuyama argued in the 1989 essay that:

> What we may be witnessing is not just the end of the Cold War, or the passing of a particular period of post-war history, but the end of history as such: that is, the end point of mankind's ideological evolution and the universalisation of Western liberal democracy as the final form of human government.

---

to rely on implications arising from the Constitution to resolve cases (certain such implications had been used by the HCA before 1920 to favour the States).

11 Walker, David M., *The Oxford Companion to Law* (Clarendon Press, Oxford, 1980), "Monarchy", "Parliamentary Government", "Parliament of England", "Parliament of Great Britain", and "Parliament of the United Kingdom".

12 Fukuyama, Francis, "The End of History" (1989) *The National Interest*, available at: http://www.wesjones.com/eoh.htm#source (accessed October 1 2019).

13 Fukuyama, Francis, *The End of History and the Last Man* (Free Press, New York, 1992).

Just on 25 years later, a leading international journal (and long-time champion of Liberal values[14]) *The Economist* was moved to ask, in a major essay: "What's Gone Wrong with Democracy?"[15] This essay explained that "Just a few years ago democracy looked as though it would dominate the world", adding that:

> A report issued by America's State Department declared that having seen off "failed experiments" with authoritarian and totalitarian forms of government, "it seems that now, at long last, democracy is triumphant".[16]

By 2000, over 60% of the total number of countries in the world were classified as democracies. Twenty years later this has changed. *The Economist* essay sets out a catalogue of serious concerns. The collapsed democracies across the now brutally blighted network of most of the "Arab Spring" countries – and Thailand – are discussed as are the compromised democracies in Russia and other parts of Eastern Europe and Central Asia plus South Africa, for example. Within the West, it is argued that "democracy has too often become associated with debt and dysfunction at home and overreach abroad".[17] We are now on the exit side of a period of excessive self-confidence:

> The world applauds the collapse of the regime and offers to help build a democracy. But turfing out an autocrat turns out to be much easier than setting up a viable democratic government. The new regime stumbles, the economy flounders and the country finds itself in a state at least as bad as it was before. This is what happened in much of the Arab spring, and also in Ukraine's Orange revolution a decade ago.[18]

Within about five years of writing the original essay ("The End of History"), Fukuyama was reflecting carefully on what he had said.[19] By 2003, Fukuyama was convinced that "democracy cannot put down roots in stony ground".[20] In 2019, five years after the essay in *The Economist* noted above, that journal was still more gloomy, arguing that Western democracies were being corrupted by widespread

14 See "About Us", *The Economist,* available at: http://www.economist.com/help/about-us#About_Economistcom (accessed October 1 2019).

15 "What's Gone Wrong with Democracy", *The Economist,* March 1, 2014 http://www.economist.com/news/essays/21596796-democracy-was-most-successful-political-idea-20th-century-why-has-it-run-trouble-and-what-can-be-do (accessed October 1, 2019).

16 Ibid.

17 Ibid.

18 Ibid.

19 Fukuyama, Francis, "Reflections on the End of History, Five Years Later" (1995) 34 *History and Theory*, 27.

20 "What's Gone Wrong with Democracy".

cynicism.[21] Andrew Sheng observed, at about the same time, stressing performance rather than process, that:

> If the ultimate outcome of the liberal order is to protest, with no solutions to propose to tackle inequalities, then the liberal order is truly obsolete.[22]

Low-cost access to mass persuasion

Social media have been aptly defined as:

> [W]ebsites and applications that are designed to allow people to share content quickly, efficiently, and in real-time. [23]

Social media continue to play a rapidly increasing role in shaping the way politics works today. This is especially so within technologically open societies. At first hailed as a way to give a greater voice to the widest range of citizens, social media have also progressively begun to look like a gift from the gods to demagogues of all stripes. If you want to build zealous partisan support for particular, typically narrow, political causes, social media are tailor-made for such (usually polarizing) tasks. This is because social media enable swift very low-cost communications – which often build on themselves through continuous resending – to a vast number of recipients all at once. Social media have had, Professor Phillips argues, the most unhelpful impact in jurisdictions, like the US, where broadcast news regulation, to ensure a measure of political neutrality (such as is common in Northern Europe) is largely absent.[24]

Eric Klinenberg, the author of a recent book that analyzes social infrastructure, argued in 2019 that:

> After the 2016 [US] election, Mark Zuckerberg [primary owner of Facebook] wrote a public letter claiming that Facebook would be a crucial social infrastructure that reinvigorates democracy. But since then we have learned that

21 "The Corrupting of Democracy", *The Economist*, August 29, 2019, available at: https://www.economist.com/leaders/2019/08/29/the-corrupting-of-democracy (accessed September 1, 2019).

22 Sheng, Andrew, "Hong Kong, and the Rest of the World, Can't Just Go on Protesting If the Free Market Liberal Order Is to Survive", *South China Morning Post,* July 6, 2019, available at: https://www.scmp.com/comment/opinion/article/3017168/hong-kong-and-rest-world-cant-just-go-protesting-if-free-market (accessed September 1, 2019).

23 See Hudson, Matthew, "What Is Social Media", *The Balance,* May 8, 2019, available at: https://www.thebalancesmb.com/what-is-social-media-2890301 (accessed June 6, 2019).

24 Phillips, Angela, "Social Media Is Changing the Face of Politics – and It's Not Good News", *The Conversation,* February 9, 2016, available at: http://theconversation.com/social-media-is-changing-the-face-of-politics-and-its-not-good-news-54266 (accessed October 1, 2019).

> Facebook is doing much more to promote hate, propaganda and division than to generate the "meaningful communities" that Zuckerberg promised.[25]

Confirming Dean Swift's observation from over 300 years earlier ("falsehood flies while truth limps along behind"[26]), another commentator explained in 2019 that:

> Realizing the power of social media makes every activist a propagandist and commentator. Harnessing all options, unconstrained by the rules of traditional news outlets, they've delivered their version of events with speed and clarity. Accuracy and truth are secondary to this process but that is not the point.[27]

The powerful political impact of social media has been closely studied, accompanied by strong predictive success, by Professor Bela Stantic of Griffith University in Australia.[28] By monitoring the vast, relevant traffic across social media, he and his team were able to predict the vote in favour of *Brexit* in 2016, the victory of Donald Trump in the US Presidential Election in 2016, and the equally unexpected electoral victory of the conservative Federal Government (over the Australian Labor Party (ALP)) in 2019. In the last case, all the regular opinion polls wrongly predicted, up until the election, an ALP victory by a margin of 2–4%.[29] Some analysts argue that the response of the mainstream media, especially the print media, to social media has been to become drawn towards partisan position-taking, particularly in the US, or to become more hasty and less professionally conscientious.[30]

25 "Open Future: Book Excerpt and Interview with Eric Klinenberg, Author of 'Palaces for the People'", *The Economist*, May 31, 2019, available at: https://www.economist.com/open-future/2019/05/31/populism-can-be-beaten-back-by-libraries-really (accessed June 6, 2019).

26 "A Lie Can Travel Halfway around the World While the Truth Is Putting on Its Shoes", *Quote Investigator*, available at: https://quoteinvestigator.com/2014/07/13/truth/ (accessed September 15, 2019).

27 "Hearts and Minds – All Warfare Is Based on Deception", *At the Feet of Socrates*, July 30, 2019, available at: https://atthefeetofsocrates.blogspot.com/2019/07/hearts-minds.html (accessed August 5, 2019).

28 Koslowski, Max, "The Expert Who Predicted Trump, Brexit – and Scott Morrison", *Sydney Morning Herald*, May 19, 2019, available at: https://www.smh.com.au/federal-election-2019/the-expert-who-predicted-trump-brexit-and-scott-morrison-20190519-p51owf.html (accessed June 7, 2019).

29 Ibid.

30 See, for example, Luo Michael, "The Urgent Quest for Slower, Better News", *Newyorker*, April 11, 2019, available at: https://www.newyorker.com/culture/annals-of-inquiry/the-urgent-quest-for-slower-better-news (accessed June 7, 2019); Boxwell, Robert, "After Robert Mueller's Report, the US Press Must Reflect on How It Has Played into China's Hands", *South China Morning Post*, March 30, 2019, available at: https://www.scmp.com/comment/insight-opinion/article/3003826/after-robert-muellers-report-us-press-must-reflect-how-it (accessed June 7, 2019); and Wagner, Kurt, "Three Major Ways Social Media

Next, there is clear evidence that access to live-steaming social media has greatly enhanced the connectivity of those set on committing mass murder in order to make some monstrous political point.[31] Lynching in India has been linked to social media messaging, too.[32] And the scope for swift, low-cost character assassination has risen sharply.[33]

Government responses to these acute developments have varied. Academics at Southampton University in the UK identified an emerging typology of regulatory approaches:

- Libertarian – bare minimum regulation (which they say does not work);
- Commercial self-regulation (dominated by a handful of very large tech-companies);
- European-style, tough, detailed regulation (gaining appeal);
- Authoritarian-style regulation as found in China and a range of other jurisdictions.[34]

Singapore passed a law in 2019 which relies on the third approach but which critics claim is also heavily influenced by the last (authoritarian) approach.[35]

Is Changing Journalism", *Illuminate – SCU,* March 22, 2017, available at: https://www.scu.edu/illuminate/thought-leaders/kurt-wagner-12/three-major-ways-social-media-is-changing-journalism.html (accessed June 7, 2019).

31 See Bogost, Ian, "Social Media Are a Mass Shooter's Best Friend", *The Atlantic,* March 15, 2019, available at: https://www.theatlantic.com/technology/archive/2019/03/how-terrorism-new-zealand-spread-social-media/585040/ (accessed June 7, 2019). See also Ellis-Petersen, Hannah, "Social Media Shut Down in Sri Lanka in Bid to Stem Misinformation", *The Guardian*, April 21, 2019, available at: https://www.theguardian.com/world/2019/apr/21/social-media-shut-down-in-sri-lanka-in-bid-to-stem-misinformation (accessed June 2019).

32 Singh, Prakash, "Death by 'Fake News': Social Media-Fuelled Lynchings Shock India", available at: https://www.nation.co.ke/news/world/Death-by-fake-news-social-media-fuelled-lynchings-India/1068-4662332-sf64lcz/index.html (accessed June 7, 2019).

33 Murray, Douglas, "The Scruton Tapes: An Anatomy of a Modern Hit Job", *The Spectator*, April 27, 2019, available at: https://www.spectator.co.uk/2019/04/the-scruton-tapes-an-anatomy-of-a-modern-hit-job/ (accessed June 7, 2019).

34 Capri, Alex, "Social Media Abuses Threaten Asia's Democratic Elections", *Nikkei Asian Review,* April 9, 2019, available at: https://asia.nikkei.com/Opinion/Social-media-abuses-threaten-Asia-s-democratic-elections (accessed June 7, 2019).

35 See Jaipragas, Bhavan, "Singapore Introduces Anti-Fake News Law to Counter Falsehoods Aimed at 'Exploiting' the City's 'Fault Lines'", *South China Morning Post,* April 1, 2019, available at: https://www.scmp.com/week-asia/politics/article/3004196/singapore-introduces-anti-fake-news-law-counter-falsehoods-aimed (accessed June 7, 2019); Staff and Agencies, "Singapore Fake News Law a 'Disaster' for Freedom of Speech, Says Rights Group", *The Guardian*, May 9, 2019, available at: https://www.theguardian.com/world/2019/may/09/singapore-fake-news-law-a-disaster-for-freedom-of-speech-says-rights-group (accessed, June 7, 2019); and Ng, Huiwen, "Parliament: 7 Things to Know about Singapore's Proposed Law to Combat Online Fake News", *The Straits Times*, April 1, 2019,

Closing observations

When Churchill made his remarks about the comparative superiority of democracy as a time-tested least bad option to establish enduring, fair, stable, and effective government, he did so soon after the most terrible foe liberal democracy had ever faced, Nazism, had been defeated, at very great cost. He also did so at a time when throughout the advanced, liberal-democratic world, the information flows which shaped democratic decision-making were still mainly provided and moulded by the print media where serious, professionally written newspapers dominated the setting of political agendas.

With the coming of commercial television in the mid-1950s, the UK Government, led by Churchill, enacted a law to ban paid broadcast political advertising, so concerned were they about the power of the electronic media to distort proper political discussion.

Following a surge in the establishment of democratic governance systems after the fall of the Berlin Wall and the collapse of the USSR, an unravelling of that surge began within about a decade.[36] Even more troubling, the so-called "Arab Spring", which was meant to usher in widespread democratization across a range of Mediterranean States with Islamic majorities, has given rise to a series of terrible, ongoing conflicts and/or a reversion to militarized rule. One writer put it this way in 2016:

> Five years [after the start of the Arab Spring] it is clear that the result of the uprisings has been calamitous, leading to wars or increased repression in all but one of the six countries where the Arab Spring principally took place. Syria, Libya and Yemen are being torn apart by civil wars that show no sign of ending. In Egypt and Bahrain autocracy is far greater and civil liberties far less than they were prior to 2011. Only in Tunisia, which started off the surge towards radical change, do people have greater rights than they did before.[37]

Since that time, the noted conflicts and outcomes largely continue or have become worse.

---

available at: https://www.straitstimes.com/politics/7-things-to-know-about-singapores-proposed-law-to-combat-online-fake-news (accessed June 7, 2019).

36 See Bubnova, Natalie (ed.), *20 Years without the Berlin Wall: A Breakthrough to Freedom* (Carenegie Moscow Centre, Moscow, 2011), Conclusion; and Svetlik, Michael, "Two Decade Later Democratic Progress and the Fall of the Berlin Wall", *The Electoral Knowledge Network*, available at: http://aceproject.org/today/feature-articles/two-decades-later-democratic-progress-and-the-fall (accessed June, 2019).

37 Cockburn, Patrick, "The Arab Spring Five Years On: A season That Began in Hope, but Ended in Desolation", *The Independent*, January 8, 2016, available at: https://www.independent.co.uk/news/world/middle-east/the-arab-spring-five-years-on-a-season-that-began-in-hope-but-ended-in-desolation-a6803161.html (accessed June 7, 2019).

Although the operation of social media in a basic form dates back around 20 years, it was not until the turn of the century that social media began to grow exponentially and to create a system where a massive number of people could be contacted simultaneously and directly very swiftly at little or no cost.[38] Collectively, social media is, today, a crucial new mass communication fixture comparable in impact to the coming of the telephone well over 100 years ago. It has swiftly become a key zone of political discussion, disputation, and polarization. By 2011, social media provided a well-established, new means of mass, instant communication which helped shape the unfolding of the Arab Spring.

One of those whose social media work helped trigger the uprising in Egypt which led to the downfall of President Hosni Mubarak later outlined the frightening levels of social media polarization which then followed:

> The euphoria soon faded … We failed to build consensus, and the political struggle led to intense polarization. Social media only amplified the polarization by facilitating the spread of misinformation, rumours, echo chambers and hate speech. The environment was purely toxic. The online world became a battleground filled with trolls, lies, hate speech.[39]

What might Churchill say if he were speaking today on the topic he addressed in 1947? Certainly, he would recognize the much greater complexity of and the far less moderated political discussion and disputation with which democracies must now contend: very high levels of anonymous, insistent exchanges dominate, rarely tempered by any form of impulse control.[40]

The HKSAR is a highly developed, compact, First World jurisdiction. Hong Kong is clearly not held back, in terms of its political reform potential, by its political history or economic weakness. Until 2019 (see Chapter 7), one would also have said that neither was the HKSAR beset by entrenched social polarizations in ways which are comparable to Ukraine or Thailand, for example.[41]

The broad context within which the project of political reform in the HKSAR can proceed today has changed. By the early 1990s, as this reform project gathered

38 Hendricks, Drew, "The Complete History of Social Media", *Small Business Trends,* May 8, 2013, available at: https://smallbiztrends.com/2013/05/the-complete-history-of-social-media-infographic.html (accessed June 7, 2019).

39 Wael Ghonim, quoted in Lo, Alex, "Our Social Media Warriors Are Reaching a Dead End", *South China Morning Post*, September 11, 2019, available at: https://www.scmp.com/comment/opinion/article/3026771/our-social-media-warriors-are-reaching-dead-end (accessed September 12, 2019).

40 Murphy, Katherine, "Truth Decay: Why Personal Values Are Poisoning Australians' News Consumption", *The Guardian,* June 12, 2019, available at: https://www.theguardian.com/media/2019/jun/12/truth-decay-why-personal-values-are-poisoning-australians-news-consumption (accessed September 1, 2019).

41 Liu, Luis, "Social Media Are Polarizing Our Society and Instigating More Radicals", *China Daily*, August 25, 2019, available at: https://www.chinadailyhk.com/articles/73/227/151/1566747605386.html (accessed September 1, 2019).

momentum in BHK, a wide consensus had developed to the effect that, *in general*, democratization was the best low-risk political structure reform option. Within ten years that confidence was ebbing. Twenty years later, it continues to falter. Part of why this is so is that so many attempts to secure democratic *regime change*, across a range of diverse jurisdictions, since 1989, have not gone well and sometimes they have gone very badly. Another part of the explanation can be found in the rise of social media and how they have both raised expectations of enhanced democracy and distorted the operation of the broad liberal-democratic legacy forged during the twentieth century. Finally (and cursorily at this point), another central change over the last 20 years has been the way that the HKSAR has slipped from being about 20%, in size, of total Mainland GDP in 1997 to being less than 3% compared to total Mainland GDP by 2017.[42] The regional and global geopolitical contexts have altered dramatically since 1997. Hong Kong's ranking within China has faded distinctly. The remarkable success of the PRC has amplified the city's "identity crisis".[43] These matters are discussed in depth in the closing chapters.

42 "Hong Kong vs. China GDP: A Sobering Reality", *ejinsight*, June 9, 2017, available at: http://www.ejinsight.com/20170609-hk-versus-china-gdp-a-sobering-reality/ (accessed June 7, 2019).

43 Fu, Yu, "The Hong Kong Demonstrations and Identity Crisis", *IPP Review*, August 26, 2019, available at: https://ippreview.com/index.php/Blog/single/id/1063.html (accessed September 1, 2019).

9 China then and now

Introduction

It is beneficial to quote Simon Leys from Chapter 2 once more:

> From a western point of view, China is simply the other pole of the human mind. All the other great cultures are either dead (Egypt, pre-Columbian American and so on), or too exclusively absorbed by the problem of surviving in extreme conditions (primitive cultures), or too close to us (Islamist cultures, India) to present a contrast as total, a revelation as complete, an "otherness" as challenging, an originality as illuminating as China. It is only when we contemplate China that we can become exactly aware of our own identity and that we begin to perceive which part of our heritage truly pertains to universal humanity, and which part merely reflects Indo-European idiosyncrasies.[1]

This chapter provides an overview of China's imperial history before discussing the interaction of the West with China (after the onset of the Age of Discovery). Next, the reawakening of China is reviewed. This resurgence dates back over 40 years. One can argue that it was delayed for some 30 years following the creation of the PRC in 1949, until the central influence of *Maoism* was curtailed following the death of Mao Zedong in 1976. The changing interaction of the US with China after the *open door* policy began in 1978 is reviewed prior to discussing how Hong Kong fits within this significant broad narration.

As Professor Wang Gungwu explained in 2019, understanding Chinese history and its particular significance to the Chinese State and to the Chinese People is of central importance. Relying on theoretical frameworks when analyzing China's new (rising) relationship with the world and especially with the US cannot be a substitute.[2] This historical understanding is also substantially relevant when analyzing the Hong Kong–Beijing relationship.

1 Leys, Simon, *The Burning Forest* (Paladin, London, 1988), 42.

2 "Ancient Past and Modern Ambitions: Wang Gungwu on China's Delicate Balance", *South China Morning Post*, September 7, 2019, available at: https://www.scmp.com/week-asia/

Imperial China

What is striking, when one reflects on the European experience of the rise and fall of the Roman Empire prior to the onset of what became known as the Middle Ages,[3] is how different were the circumstances which shaped the fundamental features of China's large-scale, agrarian political-economy.

Feudalism,[4] as it advanced and was practised in Europe for over 500 years from at least the ninth century, had been, in all material respects, entirely displaced and replaced with the system of bureaucratic government by the First Emperor, Qin Shi Huang, after he came to power and established the Qin Dynasty (221–210 BC).[5] A level of bureaucratic governance had been established during the preceding Zhou Dynasty (1027– 256 BC). This lessened the power of the Feudal Lords of that era but a powerful nobility compensated by grants of feudal estates still remained. The Zhou administrative system has been described as "proto-bureaucratic" by the German-American Sinologist, Professor Franz Michael.[6]

As Professor Michael notes, the previous two millennia of early Chinese history established the foundations for the revolutionary transformation of China's governance systems under the short-lived, draconian, controversial (and ultimately self-destructing) but pivotal Qin Dynasty (the dynasty that also gave rise to the name China). Under the Qin, feudal power was transferred to the now centralized State and the peasants were formally freed from feudal serfdom. Most significantly, the Qin system of governance based on a trained, professional bureaucracy loyal to the new State-Empire was firmly established as the crucial replacement for the previous, feudal-based governance structures.[7]

---

politics/article/3026041/ancient-past-modern-ambitions-historian-wang-gungwus-new-book (accessed September 7, 2019).

3 Sometimes also known as the "Dark Ages". See "Middle Ages", *History*, available at https://www.history.com/topics/middle-ages (accessed July 6, 2019).

4 I use the generally accepted Western/European understanding of feudalism in this chapter in analyzing both the development of China's transition from a largely feudal to a bureaucratic Imperial governance system and the system of feudal governance which developed in Europe after the fall of the Western Roman Empire. According to the *Cambridge Dictionary*, feudal relates "to the social system of Western Europe in the Middle Ages or any society that is organized according to rank. In a feudal society, people at one level of society receive land to live and work on from those higher than them in rank and in return have to work for them and fight for them if necessary, sometimes giving them some of the food they produce". *Cambridge Dictionary*, available at: https://dictionary.cambridge.org/dictionary/english/feudal (accessed June 26, 2019). There is much debate about the precise aspects of feudalism, but this broad definition remains in wide use (see, for example, Newman, Simon, "Government in the Middle Ages", *The Finer Times – Financial Times*, available at: http://www.thefinertimes.com/Middle-Ages/government-in-the-middle-ages.html (accessed July 7, 2019)).

5 Michael, Franz, *China through the Ages* (Westview Press, Boulder, 1986), Chapter 6.

6 Ibid., Chapter 4, "The Age of Reason".

7 Ibid., Chapter 6, "The Unified Empire".

These revolutionary governance changes were subsequently consolidated under the (notably less harsh and less ruthless) Han Dynasty (202 BC–220 AD).[8] The Han Dynasty established the long-term foundations of a Confucian-based society and empire by relying, above all, on Confucian scholars to serve the State within the system of bureaucratic government:

> The importance of the Han emperors' choice of Confucian scholars over all other schools for service to the state cannot be easily overstated. Confucian tenets postulated a moral universe whose precepts had to be followed by the emperor if he were to maintain the Mandate of Heaven; the scholars claimed the prerogative to interpret those tenets and thus exercise an authority independent of and even morally superior to that of the emperor. It was this dual system of authority by the emperor and the scholar-gentry that accounts for the durability of the Chinese imperial order of society and state.[9]

What is of importance, comparatively, is that in post-Roman Empire, Western Europe, a move towards reliance on centralized bureaucratic governance analogous to that established in China during the Qin Dynasty would not happen for another 1500 years, approximately, until the development of early Capitalist economies (fostered by the rise of the growing economic power of the Burghers) began to displace the highly fragmented, old feudal-agrarian political-economies.[10]

Unifying society

The First Emperor of China is remembered as:

> [A]n infamous tyrant and oppressor, a destroyer of old cultural values who burned the books, killed the scholars, and afflicted the people with forced labour for his massive public works.[11]

But Qin Shi Huang is also remembered as a great unifier who changed China politically, socially, economically, and intellectually in ways that have laid

8 "Han Dynasty – Chinese History", *Encyclopaedia Britannica*, available at: https://www.britannica.com/topic/Han-dynasty (accessed July 7, 2019).

9 Michael, *China through the Ages*, 73–74. These foundational Confucian (and related) concepts were a product of the experience of Confucius (inter alia) living during the chaotic Warring States period (475BC–221 BC). That is, they were a reaction to and driven by a deep, intellectual desire to solve societal conflict (ibid., Chapter 5, "Intellectual Revolution: A Hundred Schools of Thought"). Subsequently, these concepts laid the foundations for a succession of regularly long-lived dynasties. They proved remarkably successful in lowering conflict levels (compared to Feudal Europe), but they may also have lowered conflict-driven, innovative developments in statecraft, science and technology, et cetera (again compared to Europe after the end of the Middle Ages).

10 Ibid., 42.

11 Ibid., 60.

foundations which have endured to the present time. Weights and measures were standardized, roads were built, coinage was systematized at the same time as the old inter-Kingdom customs barriers were abolished, and the remaining feudal estates were broken up with land distributed amongst the peasants. Most important of all, the system of writing, using characters, was standardized using the Qin mode of writing these characters.[12]

The new Chinese Empire was thus established by deploying a uniform system of writing which could be applied across the entire Empire. This was particularly significant in China because the system for writing, using separate characters to record all aspects of life (including people, things, concepts, and actions) stood largely apart from the differing, spoken languages. Unlike the writing systems which ultimately developed in the ancient Middle East and then in Europe, this Chinese system of writing was, comparatively, weakly linked to the spoken word. That is, this was not an alphabet-based writing system where the spoken word is converted to writing by using code symbols to represent spoken sounds.[13]

In effect, to become literate in China required the learning of a second, *written* language involving a measurably more arduous learning process than learning to write one's own spoken word using an alphabet-based writing system. The great advantage which this strikingly different writing system offers is that it can potentially be read by everyone in the Empire regardless of whatever spoken language they happen to use. This was a commanding political (and socio-economic) benefit which arose from the Qin standardization of the written language. It is a benefit which China enjoys to this day.[14]

Ultimately, the intense loathing of the Emperor by the scholar class and the remaining nobility undermined the stability of the new Empire. The Qin Empire finally collapsed because of the mounting popular peasant outrage over the cruelty of the new, legalist regulatory system and the intolerable taxes imposed to fund the Qin Emperor's massive public works programme (including the Great Wall of China).[15]

Foundations consolidated

The replacement Han Dynasty (206 BC–221 AD) took over the new bureaucratic governance system of the Qin, but many of the harsh aspects of Qin governance were modified – or repealed. Most significantly, the Confucian (secular) ethical system, as it applied at both "macro" (governance) and "micro" (social-family)

12 Ibid., 61–62.

13 Grandemange, Adrien, *A Simple Explanation of Chinese Characters*, available at: http://blog.tutorming.com/mandarin-chinese-learning-tips/how-do-chinese-characters-work (accessed July, 2019). See also Michael, ibid.

14 For a contrary view, that Chinese written language system has been pivotal in containing innovation and development in China over many centuries, see Jenner, W. J. F., *The Tyranny of History: The Roots of China's Crisis* (Penguin-History, London, 1994).

15 Michael, *China through the Ages*, 66–67.

levels, was increasingly introduced, which, in turn, provided the Han Empire with a consolidating factor conspicuously absent during the Qin era: deep, influential, and highly durable, ***unifying*** ideological foundations. The concept of a *Scholar-Gentry* Bureaucratic Government (chosen by examination – in principle, from all levels within society) managing China, for the Emperor and his vast number of largely agrarian subjects, emerged.[16]

The Confucian ideological scheme had originally evolved over 200 years earlier, during the early Warring States period (403–221 BC) as the Zhou Dynasty began its long decline. This system (which was to prove more durable than any other political-social-economic method of State organization, anywhere) stipulated a moral system to which the Emperor had to adhere if he were to retain the Mandate of Heaven. Moreover, it preset a remarkable hierarchy of social classifications, in descending order of merit: scholars, peasants, craftsmen, merchants, and soldiers.[17]

Imperial durability

Professor Xu Chenggang explains that the Chinese Imperial system, which prevailed for well over 2,000 years, from 220 BC (Qin Dynasty) to 1912 (Qing Dynasty), lasted far longer than any other Imperial system.[18] He goes on to argue that the basic institutional structure outlined above, with its central reliance on bureaucratic governance, provided the foundations for this unprecedented durability.[19] There is also an important *path dependency* impact – this same system has had a lasting influence on today's China.[20]

The average life of Chinese Imperial Dynasties was a remarkable 300 years.[21] Unlike in Europe, emperors in China typically died, often of advanced age, in bed rather than more suddenly and violently.[22]

Over 2,000 years ago China, during the Qin Dynasty, set down the foundations of a new, advanced governance system designed to manage a very large-scale, stabilized, agriculture-based empire. This was fundamentally a continental empire. War and conquest were features of this empire but not on the scale which

16 "Han Dynasty – Chinese History", *Encyclopaedia Britannica*, available at: https://www.britannica.com/topic/Han-dynasty (accessed July 7, 2019).

17 Michael, *China through the Ages*, 71. What is most striking is the way that this hierarchy did not give warriors a pre-eminent ranking as found in Ancient Greek and Roman civilizations, for example.

18 Xu, Chenggang, "The Fundamental Institutions of China's Reforms and Development" (2011) 49 *Journal of Economic Literature,* 1076.

19 Ibid.

20 Ibid.

21 Lau, Laurence J. "Comments on Chenggang Xu, 'The Institutional Foundations of China's Reforms and Development'", available at: http://www.igef.cuhk.edu.hk/igef_media/people/lawrencelau/presentations/english/100127-1.pdf (accessed July 1, 2019).

22 Xu, Chenggang, "The Origins and Evolution of China's Institutions: A Comparative Institutional Analysis", *Presentation at Faculty of Law, Hong Kong University,* April 19, 2017.

typified the Roman Empire. Imperial domination of the agricultural economy kept the peasant farmers subjugated – but agriculture was not fundamentally slave-dependent as was the case in the Roman Empire. The macro or state-craft Confucian ideology in fact ranked the peasant farmers comparatively highly.[23]

Moreover, Imperial China never had need to develop any sort of highly institutionalized, bloody, "bread and circuses" communal activities[24] such as were a feature in Imperial Rome, incorporating regular, deadly gladiatorial contests:

> Roman Gladiators fought before the public in organized games held in large purpose built arenas throughout the Roman Empire for about 500 years. Fights were usually to the death. The majority of fighters were slaves, former slaves or condemned prisoners. Gladiator spectacles were one of the most watched forms of popular entertainment in the Roman world.[25]

Professor Michael stresses how the Confucian social order of the Chinese civilization-state has long underpinned the political-economies of so many (often long-lived) successive dynasties:

> The most remarkable aspect of Chinese imperial history has been the contrast between the ever-recurring hiatus in the political process with the rise and fall of dynasties on the one hand and the steadily evolving social order on the other. On this social continuity a unified political structure was always rebuilt. This converse interrelationship in imperial time between a constant society and an ever-reestablished dynastic state emanated from the acceptance of Confucianism as the social and political foundation for the Chinese polity.[26]

The West and China

Feudal Europe

The European Feudal System of governance emerged and endured in much the same form across Europe following the final collapse of the (Western) Roman

23 Michael, *China through the Ages*, Chapter 7, "The Empire Consolidated".

24 The Roman satirist, Juvenal, wrote, around 120 AD, in *Satire 10* of how "bread and circuses" had become the only remaining care of the Roman populace. See "Satire X – Juvenal – Ancient Rome – Classical Literature", *Ancient Literature*, available at: https://www.ancient-literature.com/rome_juvenal_satire_x.html (accessed July 20, 2019).

25 Cartwright, Mark, "Roman Gladiator", *Ancient History Encyclopedia*, May 3, 2018, available at: https://www.ancient.eu/gladiator/ (accessed July 20, 2019).

26 Michael, *China through the Ages*, 241. In 1986, Michael also argued, acutely in my view, that this extraordinary social ordering "[W]ill survive the onslaught of Mao and Communism to provide a strong humanist foundation for whatever Chinese order – under whatever name – may emerge from the debacle of Maoist Chinese Communism". Ibid., 240.

Empire around 476 AD until the Renaissance began, in Italy, in the fourteenth century.[27]

Feudalism in Europe was fully established by the ninth century. Briefly, it was a method of structuring European societies based on intricate relationship principles where the nobility (the Barons) held (often vast areas of) land from a Feudal Lord (the King, normally) in exchange for provision of service (often military), labour, and, in time, certain forms of feudal taxation. Others, of lower standing, held from the Barons, again, mainly in return for provision of certain services. At the bottom, the "food chain" was the vast majority of the population – the farmer peasants (who often worked the land in a state of bondage and enjoyed very few freedoms) and, during the earlier feudal period, especially, a significant number of slave workers.[28]

Feudal Europe was, compared to China, highly fragmented. Conflict and wars were common. Such conflicts often involved the use of cavalry, that is, horseback-mounted military groups. To sustain the many such feudal armies required substantial grazing lands for the horses. A notable feature of this conspicuously decentralized agrarian political–economic system was the lack of any sort of organized, bureaucratic system of governance and the comparatively limited productivity of the relevant agricultural economies.[29]

The Age of Discovery

Amongst other things, the Renaissance, beginning from the fourteenth century, generated a massive uplift in the study and understanding of state-craft – the means by which societies can be better organized and sustained – and better protected. As the understanding of effective state-craft developed, the emerging stronger States were able to expand and hold territory. In a sense, Europe was rediscovering the essence of the operational success of the once vast Roman Imperial System after spending close to a 1,000 years disconnected from this (in effect, European) fundamental macro-political understanding.

Substantial increases in the comprehension of the technology of long-distance sea voyaging followed and the "Age of (European) Discovery" (often energized by both economic and Christian-religious ambitions) commenced in the early

27 Newman, Simon, "Government in the Middle Ages", *The Finer Times – Financial Times*, available at: http://www.thefinertimes.com/Middle-Ages/government-in-the-middle-ages.html (accessed July 7, 2019).

28 Ibid.

29 "Medieval Life; Feudalism", *Lumen World History*, available at: https://courses.lumenlearning.com/boundless-worldhistory/chapter/medieval-life/ (accessed July 7, 2019). Measured according to Chinese experience, Europe endured a recurring series of intense "Warring States" periods during the almost 1,500 years from the Fall of the Roman Empire until the end of World War II.

fifteenth century led by the Portuguese and then followed, over time, by others, including the Dutch, the English, the French, the Germans, and the Spanish.[30]

The opium trade

The history of the modern era, from a Chinese standpoint, starts with opium trading that led to the First Opium War (1839–1842). The historian Julia Lovell notes that this is seen as the "traumatic inauguration of the country's modern history".[31]

Opium, a drug derived from the latex of the opium poppy, did not actually become a valued item of high-volume international trade until the late eighteenth century when the export of the drug to China for "recreational" purposes began in earnest. Prior to that, and for much of its history, opium was primarily used for medicinal purposes where it served above all as a painkiller. One of the earliest records of opium's medicinal role dates back to 1500 BC, when its uses were noted by the Ancient Egyptians in the *Ebers Papyrus*.[32]

In the case of Britain, trade with China was, for a long period, almost exclusively handled by the East India Company (EIC),[33] which was highly influential and had very close ties to the British Government. Exports of tea, silk, and porcelain, which were greatly sought-after in the domestic UK market, generated large trade surpluses for China. In contrast, China was largely self-sufficient and uninterested in British products.[34]

The British (and other) opium traders had largely been able to ignore (Qing Dynasty) attempts to stop the trade. Finally, in 1839, the Chinese Emperor took much stronger action than hitherto, when he appointed Lin Zexu, an official with a powerful and deserved reputation for incorruptibility, as Special Imperial Commissioner to Canton to suppress the opium trade. Lin swiftly confiscated

30 "What Was the Age of Exploration or the Age of Discovery?" *World Atlas*, available at: https://www.worldatlas.com/articles/what-was-the-age-of-exploration-or-the-age-of-discovery.html (accessed July 7, 2019). See also Michael, *China through the Ages*, 149–151.

31 Lovell, Julia, *The Opium Wars: Drugs, Dreams, and the Making of Modern China* (Picador, London, 2011), Introduction.

32 Brownstein, M. J. "A Brief History of Opiates, Opioid Peptides, and Opioid Receptors" (1993) 90 *Proceedings of National Academy of Science USA*, 5391.

33 The EIC was also known as the East India Trading Company. It was founded in 1600 by Royal Charter granted by Queen Elizabeth I and was initially given a monopoly over all of Britain's trade in the East. "East" meant (or came to mean) all of Asia plus south-east Asia. It played a vital role in the expansion of the British Empire and was a dominant player in world trade until it was dissolved by an Act of Parliament in 1874.

34 Tsang, Steve, *A Modern History of Hong Kong* (Hong Kong University Press, Hong Kong, 2004). In response to Lord Macartney's first embassy (from the UK) to China (1792–1794), the Qing Dynasty Emperor, Qianlong, claimed "our Celestial Empire possesses all things in prolific abundance" and therefore has "no need to import the manufactures of outside barbarians in exchange of our own produce".

and destroyed 20,283 chests of British opium valued at around £2 million.[35] This event prompted the British Government to send an expeditionary force to China in retaliation, triggering the start of the First Opium War that ultimately resulted in a Chinese defeat[36] and the ceding of Hong Kong Island to the British under the Treaty of Nanking in 1842 (the British had taken actual possession of Hong Kong Island in 1841).

The opium trade would continue to flourish in China for years to come and it was not until 1906 that China mustered the will to end its "opium addiction" once and for all with the Emperor issuing an edict that all opium importing, growing, and retailing must end in ten years.[37] China was able to obtain the support of the US in its efforts and this culminated in a bargain with Great Britain in 1907 in which both nations agreed to diminish opium export and cultivation over a ten-year period.[38] This method proved to be successful and by 1917, China was practically rid of opium.[39]

Much of Hong Kong's history is intrinsically linked to and in some instances even considered by scholars to be a "by-product" of the opium trade that flourished in Asia during the nineteenth century. This drug's relationship with Hong Kong is best summarized by historian Christopher Munn who wrote that: "the colony was founded because of opium; its principal merchants grew rich on opium; and its government subsisted on the high land rent and other revenue made possible by the opium trade".[40]

35 Ibid. Before the British traders surrendered their opium stocks to Commissioner Lin, they were reassured by the then Chief Superintendent of Trade, Captain Charles Elliot, that the British Government would compensate them for their losses. This meant that the opium stocks which Lin confiscated were technically property of the British Government and their subsequent destruction a direct blow to the British imperial treasury (ibid.).

36 Lin Zexu was born in 1785 in Fujian Province. He rose rapidly through the ranks of the senior bureaucracy. China's defeat in the First Opium War resulted in Beijing using Lin as a scapegoat for this defeat. He was punished by being sent to a remote posting in Xinjiang. His career never really recovered. He died in 1850. See Chang, Hsin Pao, *Commissioner Lin and the Opium War* (Harvard University Press, Cambridge, 1963).

37 La Motte, Ellen N., *The Opium Monopoly* (MacMillan, New York, 1920), Chapter 15.

38 Ibid.

39 Ibid. However, the closing of the China market did not spell the end of Hong Kong–based dealings in opium. Demand for opium continued to be met in other markets, including within the established Crown Colony of Hong Kong. It was not until after the World War II – and at the strong insistence of their American allies – that the British Commander-in-Chief, who ran the interim administration of post-war Hong Kong, issued a proclamation, in September 1945, which declared a total prohibition on the sale and distribution of opium in the colony. See Booth, M., *Opium: A History* (Simon & Schuster, London, 1996).

40 Munn, Christopher, "The Hong Kong Opium Revenue 1845–1885" in (Brook & Wakabayashi (eds.)) *Opium Regimes: China, Britain and Japan, 1839–1952* (University of California Press, Oakland, 2000), 107. Opium also contributed directly to the social development of the colony. The Belilios Public School (previously the Central School for Girls) was established in 1890 and was mainly funded by a donation of $25,000 from Emmanuel Raphael Belilios, a remarkably successful Hong Kong opium trader and philanthropist. Mr. Belilios also made donations to help set up the Alice Memorial Hospital, scholarships to help

Munn's first point, above, is easy to understand as the cession of Hong Kong to the British was a result of the First Opium War. The second point alludes to Hong Kong's importance as a "central warehouse" for opium export to China and to Chinese overseas communities[41] (it was estimated that in the late 1840s, three-quarters of the total opium crop produced in India passed through Hong Kong[42]).

The battles fought by Qing Dynasty China against the European imperial powers were mostly one-sided. Chinese defences, weaponry, organization, and training of troops could not match European, still less British, capabilities. Contemporary accounts noted the heavy losses suffered by the Chinese – "murder", "bodies of the slain ... found literally three and four deep", and the sea "blackened with corpses".[43] Defeat marked the start of China's "Century of Humiliation". The Treaty of Nanking signed in 1842 was the result of "gunboat diplomacy". Heavy reparations in silver had to be paid, five ports were forced open for trade, tariffs were abolished, and westerners were exempted from Chinese law in the treaty ports.[44]

To demand better trading terms, still, Britain and France waged and won the Second Opium War against China (1856–1860). This was when the magnificent Old Summer Palace in Beijing was pillaged and burnt – leaving yet another deep wound in the Chinese psyche. As well as paying heavy war reparations in silver, China was forced to grant more trading rights to the Western powers, to legalize the opium trade, and to cede the Kowloon Peninsula to Britain.

Predatory foreign powers continued to establish colonial outposts in China by coercion in the second half of the nineteenth century. By this time, militarily modernized, imperial Japan was aggressively seeking new possessions in East Asia. Japan was, in due course, to bring more horrific misery to China than any other single imperial power. In 1895, Japan crushed China in the First Sino–Japanese War and then, in due course, took possession of both Korea (previously a Chinese dependency) and Taiwan.[45] Soon after, the British, in 1898, extracted a 99-year lease of the New Territories from the floundering Qing government, radically expanding the size of colony of Hong Kong. There was an international assumption that the Chinese Empire was at the point of collapse after defeat by Japan: it was time to secure a share of the disintegrating state – to join in the "cutting of the melon".[46]

---

needy students pursue an education in universities, and a probation home to help Chinese girls who had been driven into crime and prostitution by poverty.

41 Important overseas markets for Hong Kong's prepared opium included the Chinese migrant-mining communities in California and Australia.

42 Munn, "Hong Kong Opium Revenue".

43 Lovell, Julia, *The Opium Wars*, Chapter 1.

44 Ibid.

45 Michael, *China through the Ages,* 179.

46 Ibid.

The period after 1842 – during which various treaties and conventions that ceded land to the Western powers and gave foreigners extraterritorial privileges – is regarded by the Chinese people (and the CPC today) as an era when China degenerated from being an independent country into a semi-colony.[47]

The Treaty of Versailles

The Qing Dynasty fell in 1912. China embraced republicanism. During World War I, China sent over 140,000 non-combatant labourers to the front lines to dig trenches, as well as to work for the allies on the railways and in ports and arms factories. They provided support to soldiers fighting on the front lines and even helped on submarines. Many of the labourers died or were injured in air raids and bombardments.[48]

China hoped that their positive contribution during the war would be recognized at the Paris Peace Conference by the victorious powers in 1919. The young and fragile Chinese republic wanted more than anything else to take back the German colony at Jiaozhou Bay, created in 1898, which included the settlement at Qingdao, in Shandong Province – since Germany lost the war. (Shandong Province had also become a German sphere of influence.) Instead, Japan was given possession of this territory in Shandong and the British took over Germany's other colonies in China under the Treaty of Versailles. The Western powers were concerned that if they returned the German colony in Shandong to China, it could bring a whole host of existing, imperial territorial claims into question. They were far more concerned about their interests than about being fair to China. And Japan, which had worked to exclude any Chinese combat role in World War I, was determined to expand its empire within China. The Chinese delegates in Paris were so angry that they refused to sign the treaty.[49]

China felt cheated, betrayed, and bullied by the key Western powers (Britain, France, and the US). What happened in Paris triggered the May Fourth Movement in China – students and intellectuals were bitterly disappointed and called for national renewal so that China would not be humiliated again. The Chinese believed they must find their own way and solutions to strengthen and transform the nation – a sense of nationalism swelled.[50]

47 Mishra, Pankaj, *From the Ruins of Empire: The Revolt against the West and the Remaking of Asia* (Picador, London, 2013).

48 Boissoneault, Lorraine, "The Surprisingly Important Role China Played in WWI", *Smithsonian Institute*, available at: https://www.smithsonianmag.com/history/surprisingly-important-role-china-played-world-war-i-180964532/ (accessed July 7, 2019).

49 Ibid.

50 Ibid.

The origins of the People's Republic of China

The betrayal at Versailles over Qingdao and related territory in Shandong Province was to have a range of far-reaching consequences well beyond the May Fourth Movement itself (which galvanized political activity across China). The leading Chinese intellectual, Liang Qichao, was part of the Chinese delegation at Versailles. He had visited the US for the first time in 1903 looking for revelations on how China could modernize and break free from the condition to which it had degenerated under the Qing Dynasty. What he found was not inspiration but a forewarning of the dangers of capitalist democracy: vast inequalities of wealth, squalid poverty, and widespread political corruption. "No more am I dizzy with vain imaginings", he wrote.[51] His work had an important influence on Mao Zedong, the future leader of the CPC and, in due course, of China.[52]

By 1919, Mao had moved from his home province of Hunan to the Chinese capital Beijing. His long-time radical-reformist mentor, Yang Changji, who had taught Mao in Hunan, moved to Peking University in 1918. Yang secured a position at Peking University for Mao as the assistant to the university librarian, Li Dazhao, an early Chinese Communist.[53] Yang could see past Mao's rural Hunan accent and ways and knew that he was highly intelligent and motivated. Mao learned rapidly and effectively about Marxism, Leninism, and communism. He became convinced of the clear need to adapt this thinking to address China's immensely complex and quite desperate circumstances.[54]

Mao attended, as one of 13 delegates, the first session of the National Congress of the Communist Party of China held in Shanghai in 1921. The CPC survived and ultimately succeeded, politically, whilst enduring many challenges, setbacks, and conflicts over the following three decades. The Second Sino–Japanese War, which ran from 1937 to 1945, was immensely bitter and horrific. The CPC fought this war more often in conjunction with the KMT than not, but it was a conspicuously watchful alliance. The Chinese Civil War between the CPC and the KMT broke out in 1946, after the complete defeat of Japan. The KMT was beaten and retreated to Taiwan by 1949. Mao Zedong declared the formation of the People's Republic of China in Beijing on October 1, 1949.[55]

The first three decades of the PRC, where Maoism prevailed, proved to be tumultuous and often massively harrowing and mortally threatening. Two events, led by Mao above all, crippled China economically and politically: The Great

51 Mishra, *From the Ruins of Empire.*

52 Ibid.

53 Liu, Liyan, "The Man Who Molded Mao" (2006) 32 *Modern China*, 483.

54 Ibid. See also Xu, Penghang, "The Birth of the May Fourth Movement Spirit", *Peking University,* May 4, 2019, available at: http://newsen.pku.edu.cn/news_events/news/focus/8408.htm (accessed July 8, 2019).

55 "The Evolution of China's Communist Party, 90 Years in the Making", *China Briefing*, July 1, 2011, available at: https://www.china-briefing.com/news/the-evolution-of-chinas-communist-party-90-years-in-the-making/ (accessed July 8, 2019). See also Michael, *China through the Ages,* Chapter 15, "The Nationalists".

Leap Forward (1958–1962), which resulted in a massive famine, and The Great Proletarian Cultural Revolution (1966–1976). Mao died at the age of 82 in September 1976. Maoism, as it has existed until then, rapidly receded following his death.[56]

The denial, at Versailles in 1919, of the return of Qingdao and related territory in Shandong is often referred to as the "Shandong Incident". The lesson which China took from the Shandong Incident was that American and Western European governments could never, ultimately, be trusted. It has been cogently argued that this incident crucially impelled China's turn towards communism and, ultimately, the creation of the PRC.[57]

The reawakening of China

Between 1978 (the beginning of the *Open Door* policy following the death of Mao Zedong in 1976) and 2018, total Gross Domestic Product (GDP) in China rose around 45-fold from US$218 billion to over US$10 trillion (measured in US dollars using 2010 prices).[58] *The Economist* noted in 2016 that the PRC had expanded its middle class by a total of more than 220 million in the period between 2000 and 2016.[59] *The Economist* also reported that the PRC lifted almost 700 million people out of extreme poverty between 1981 and 2010. In fact, China alone was responsible for 75% of total world poverty reduction over this period.[60] The middle class has continued to expand and is likely to double within 20 years or less to around 600 million[61] Over the next two decades, the

56 "The Evolution of China's Communist Party, 90 Years in the Making", ibid.

57 See, for example, the arguments developed by Professor Bruce Elleman set out in Boissoneault, Lorraine, "The Surprisingly Important Role China Played in WWI", *Smithsonian Institute*, available at: https://www.smithsonianmag.com/history/surprisingly-important-role-china-played-world-war-i-180964532/ (accessed July 7, 2019). See also Elleman, Bruce, *Wilson and China: A Revised History of the Shandong Question* (Routledge, Abingdon, 2015).

58 Garnaut, Ross, Song, Ligang, and Cai, Fang (eds.), *China's 40 Years of Reform and Development* (ANU Press, Canberra, 2018), Chapter 1, "Introduction".

59 See "China's Middle Class" *The Economist*, July 9, 2016, available at: http://www.economist.com/news/leaders/21701760-communist-party-tied-its-fortunes-mass-affluence-may-now-threaten-its-survival-225m?cid1=cust/ednew/n/bl/n/2016077n/owned/n/n/nwl/n/n/AP/n (accessed July 11, 2019).

60 See "Towards the End of Poverty", *The Economist*, June 1, 2013, available at: http://www.economist.com/news/leaders/21578665-nearly-1-billion-people-have-been-taken-out-extreme-poverty-20-years-world-should-aim (accessed July 11, 2019). The World Bank puts the figure lifted out of poverty in China at over 800 million, see "China Overview", *The World Bank*, April 6, 2016, available at: http://www.worldbank.org/en/country/china/overview (accessed July 11, 2019). See also Garnaut et al., *China's 40 Years of Reform*.

61 Professor Kerry Brown argues that the Chinese Middle Class is already the source of the greatest collective power in China (rather than the CPC) and that it is set to double within the next ten years or so. See Brown, Kerry, "Xi Is Not the Boss in US-China Struggle. Neither's Trump. Here's Who Is", *South China Morning Post*, June 29, 2019.

Chinese middle class looks set to grow to be more than double the size of the US middle class.[62]

According to a 2013 Pew Survey of Global Attitudes, 85% of Chinese were "very satisfied" with their country's direction compared to 31% of US citizens.[63] That level of satisfaction has edged lower in China since (in keeping with a further worldwide downward trend), but it still remains comparatively high.[64]

Professor Weiler sets out three types of governance legitimacy, which can be summarized as follows: process or input (democratic) legitimacy; performance or output legitimacy; and messianic or vision legitimacy.[65] Applying these broad legitimacy measures, the PRC today remains poorly rated in terms of process legitimacy. In terms of performance legitimacy, however, it is impossible not to concede that the PRC rating is exceptional. China also, today, has settled on a systematically articulated long-term vision – or "Chinese Dream".

Given the steadily rising living standards of so many and the extraordinary reduction in abject poverty levels, it is not surprising that China is a state which enjoys comparatively high, continuing levels of general, unassuming confidence and optimism.[66] China has managed to rebuild itself relying fundamentally on its most abundant resource, its own population. It has traded and educated itself to be where it is placed in the world order today. China has taken the best advantage of the Western developed world trading system, it is true (unfairly argue the US and other Western nations). But every other large impoverished nation has had the same opportunities – in a number of cases blessed with natural resources China can scarcely dream of. Only China has managed this astonishing level of real growth for the benefit of hundreds of millions of people.

China's opening up began over 40 years ago. As it gathered pace, China faced a huge range of problems, including severe challenges related to housing, education, medical services, environmental damage, governance transparency, corruption,

62 Martin, Emmie, "Nearly 70% of Americans Consider Themselves Middle-class – Here's How Many Actually Are" *CNBC*, September 26, 2018, available at: https://www.cnbc.com/2018/09/26/how-many-americans-qualify-as-middle-class.html (accessed July 11, 2019). The writer quotes from a Pew Research Centre survey from 2016 which says just over 50% of Americans are middle class, down from 71% in 1971.

63 See "What's Gone Wrong with Democracy", *The Economist,* March 1, 2014, available at: http://www.economist.com/news/essays/21596796-democracy-was-most-successful-political-idea-20th-century-why-has-it-run-trouble-and-what-can-be-do (accessed July 11, 2019).

64 See *2017 Edeleman Trust Barometer Reveals Global Implosion of Trust,* January 16, 2017, available at: https://www.edelman.com/research/2017-trust-barometer-global-results (accessed October 1, 2019); and Chen, Weihua, "Chinese Trust Government More Than Americans Do", *China Daily – USA,* October 27, 2017, available at: http://www.chinadaily.com.cn/opinion/2017-10/27/content_33762163.htm (accessed October 1, 2019).

65 Weiler, Joseph H. H., "Europe in Crisis – On Political Messianism, Legitimacy and the Rule of Law (2012) *Singapore Journal of Legal Studies,* 248.

66 One American commentator based in Hong Kong put it this way, using a space travel term: China's economy has now achieved *escape velocity.*

the legal system, public finance, and excessive debt levels.[67] Extraordinary progress has been made in addressing such problems, but both old and new challenges in the areas listed persist within an economically transformed China. They are accompanied today by rising public expectations and deep concerns about a vast ageing population.[68]

China's OPS also continues to use systematically repressive measures to manage actual and potential dissent within the Mainland PRC, today enhanced by the latest forms of surveillance. Prominent examples include the harsh controls and punishments applied to Fa Lun Gong practitioners since 1999[69] and to many Chinese human rights lawyers since 2015[70] and the severe, new comprehensive measures taken to control the Muslim, Uighur population, especially, in Xinjiang in China.[71] In the latter case, China argues its new system is designed, above all, to combat Islamic extremism and terrorism based on providing education and skills training.[72]

The notable military development of the PRC has properly been a topic of serious discussion. The territorial, defence-boosting reclamations in the South China Sea have generated critical analysis in the West and regionally.[73] Controversial as this build-up of military power may be to the US and a range of other powers, compared to other major powers, not least the US, non-military means clearly dominate the blueprint for the rebuilding of modern China. The Chinese build-up in the South China Sea is essentially defensive and meant to strengthen China's position to claim access to certain undersea and seabed resources in the area.[74] Meanwhile, China has a single overseas base (in Djibouti) compared to (and after cut-backs) almost 800 US military bases across 70 countries, which

67 *China's Economic Dilemmas in the 1990s: The Problems of Reforms, Modernization and Interdependence* (Study Papers – Joint Economic Committee Congress of the United States, Washington, 1991).

68 "China Power Project: Does China Have an Ageing Problem?" *Center for Strategic and International Studies*, August 11, 2017, available at: https://chinapower.csis.org/aging-problem/ (accessed July 12, 2019).

69 Cook, Sarah, "In July 1999, the CCP Created Exactly What It Had Feared", *The Diplomat*, July 19, 2019, available at: https://thediplomat.com/2019/07/in-july-1999-the-ccp-created-exactly-what-it-had-feared/ (accessed July 22, 2019).

70 See, for example, Lau, Doriane, "1413 Days and Counting: Li Wenzu's Fight for Her Husband's Freedom", *The Diplomat*, July 9, 2019, https://thediplomat.com/2019/07/1413-days-and-counting-li-wenzus-fight-for-her-husbands-freedom/ (accessed July 12, 2019).

71 Noack, Rick, "In a First, 22 Nations Condemned China's Repression of Uighur Muslims. Without the U.S.", *Washington Post*, July 11, 2019.

72 Ibid. See also Cui, Jia and Zhao, Xinying, "Education Helping Fight Terror", *China Daily*, August 17, 2019, available at: http://global.chinadaily.com.cn/a/201908/17/WS5d57330fa310cf3e35566449.html (accessed August 18, 2019).

73 See, for example, Farley, Robert, "Would China's South China Sea Bases be Wiped Out in a War?" *The National Interest*, May 9, 2019, available at: https://nationalinterest.org/blog/buzz/would-chinas-south-china-sea-bases-be-wiped-out-war-56577 (accessed July 12, 2019).

74 Ibid.

cost at least US$100 billion per year to maintain.[75] According to one estimate, the US maintains close to 200,000 military personnel (within an overall force of 1.3 million) offshore.[76] The US has recently announced the building of yet another all-new naval base (aimed at containing China) this time at Darwin, in Australia, at a cost of over US$200 million.[77] Total US military spending in 2018 was estimated to be US$649 billion, which is 36% of all military spending worldwide.[78] China's military spending in the same year was US$250 billion.[79] Britain, France, and Russia maintain around 30 offshore bases, combined.[80]

As Professor Nye points out:

> Soft power … when coupled with hard power … is a force multiplier. That combination, though hardly new (the Roman Empire rested on both the strength of Rome's Legions and the attraction of Rome's civilization) has been particularly central to US leadership. Power depends on whose army wins, but it also depends on whose story wins.[81]

US world leadership experience (built, inter alia, on the *Monroe Doctrine* and concepts such as *Manifest Destiny*) luminously demonstrates that any major rising power will seek to protect itself militarily, above all within its own region.[82] The humiliating (regularly terrifying) incursion and colonizing experiences of

75 Vine, David, "Where in the World Is the US Military?" *Politico Magazine*, July/August 2015, available at: https://www.politico.com/magazine/story/2015/06/us-military-bases-around-the-world-119321 (accessed July 12, 2019).

76 Bialik, Kristen, "U.S. Active-Duty Military Presence Overseas Is at Its Smallest in Decades", *Pew Research Centre*, August 22, 2019, available at: https://www.pewresearch.org/fact-tank/2017/08/22/u-s-active-duty-military-presence-overseas-is-at-its-smallest-in-decades/ (accessed July 13, 2019).

77 Maynard, Roger, "US Plans New Naval Base in Australia to Thwart Chinese", *The Times*, July 30, 2019, available at: https://www.thetimes.co.uk/article/us-plans-new-naval-base-in-australia-to-thwart-chinese-tcphn5t5t (accessed August 8, 2019).

78 McCarthy, Neil, "The Biggest Military Budgets as a Share of GDP in 2018", *Forbes*, June 27, 2018, available at: https://www.forbes.com/sites/niallmccarthy/2019/04/29/the-biggest-military-budgets-as-a-share-of-gdp-in-2018-infographic/#3902f3bb7508 (accessed July 13, 2019).

79 Ibid. Raw per capita military spending for America is around US$2,000 per person and for China it is around US$18 per person: it is over 100 times higher in the US.

80 Vine, "Where in the World".

81 Nye, Joseph S., Jr., "How Sharp Power Threatens Soft Power", *Foreign Affairs,* January 24, 2018, available at: https://www.foreignaffairs.com/articles/china/2018-01-24/how-sharp-power-threatens-soft-power (accessed July 12, 2019).

82 "President James Monroe presented the Monroe Doctrine in 1823.… This would become a pivotal moment in U.S. foreign policy. The document presented the United States as a force to be reckoned with [one which] would not hesitate going to war with any nation that did not respect the demands of the United States. Since the United States closed off the western hemisphere from all other nations they would not have to worry about other nations trying to colonize and could instead focus on manifest destiny and continue expanding the nation to the Pacific". See "Monroe Doctrine 1823", *Michigan State University – US Foreign*

China since the nineteenth century not surprisingly inform China's contemporary military focus.

China's new leader since 2013, President Xi Jinping, has introduced a potency to the leadership not seen since Deng Xiaoping was in charge. Xi Jinping combines an immense sense of messianic purpose with deep political experience and an uncompromising determination to tackle what he considers to be China's paramount concerns. Xi Jinping controversially secured constitutional confirmation in 2018 that he will not be confined to two terms as China's dominant leader.[83] His regime has been widely criticized with one trenchant critic arguing in depth why the PRC is now the "The Perfect Dictatorship".[84] Professor Andrew Nathan, a leading US–China-scholar, has articulated a less boldly stated critical review of the Xi era.[85] An Asian-based, international commentator has argued that Xi Jinping is exceptionally honest and competent using performance and governance measures.[86]

Awkwardly, this is a *perfect dictatorship* which has superintended more poverty relief and massive social uplift than any regime in history: democratic or authoritarian. The editors of a recent 700-page study of post-1978 China, published by the Australian National University Press in Canberra, put it this way:

> China's reform and opening up is in the process of delivering to 1.4 billion Chinese people the fruits of the most consequential socioeconomic change and institutional innovation in human history.[87]

The Sino–US relationship

The American perception of China has gone through an intriguing transition over the last century. Once, compassion was dominant. A high point of American empathy can be seen in the work of the 1938, Nobel Prize–winning, bilingual

---

Relations to 1914, available at: http://projects.leadr.msu.edu/usforeignrelations/exhibits/show/manifest-destiny/monroe-doctrine-1823 (accessed July 12, 2019).

83 Gan, Nectar, "Xi Jinping Cleared to Stay on as China's President with Just 2 Dissenters among 2,964 Votes", *South China Morning Post*, March 11, 2018, available at: https://www.scmp.com/news/china/policies-politics/article/2136719/xi-jinping-cleared-stay-president-chinas-political (accessed July 12, 2019).

84 Ringen, Stein, *The Perfect Dictatorship: China in the 21st Century* (Hong Kong University Press, Hong Kong, 2016). Using similarly stringent measuring points (as those applied by Professor Ringen) one could, after reviewing the figures set out above for American military spending worldwide, posit that the US may have created the most far-reaching martial empire since Roman times.

85 Nathan, Andrew J., "China: Back to the Future", *New York Review of Books*, May 10, 2018, available at: https://www.nybooks.com/articles/2018/05/10/china-back-to-the-future/ (accessed July 13, 2019).

86 Mahbubani, Kishore, *Has the West Lost It?* (Penguin-Economics, London, 2019), 30.

87 Garnaut et al., *China's 40 Years of Reform*, Chapter 1.

novelist, Pearl S. Buck. She wrote *The Good Earth* some 90 years ago, in 1929, when living in Nanjing.[88] The daughter of American Christian missionaries, she spent the period from 1892 (from five months old) until 1934 living in China. Her Chinese name was *Sai Zhenzhu. The Good Earth*, set before World War I, was published in 1931 and won the Pulitzer Prize in 1932. The 1937 Hollywood film of the same name, based on the book, was nominated for five Academy Awards in 1938 and won two. The book compellingly narrates the drama of Chinese village life with deep understanding (throughout her life, the author was an avid reader of Charles Dickens – arguably the best storyteller in English in book form).[89]

The Good Earth is widely regarded as having shaped a popular, cordial understanding of China as a vast, poor, peasant-based country possessed of a remarkable history. It influenced US concerns about Imperial Japan prior to those concerns being completely galvanized by the stunning Japanese bombing of Pearl Harbour in December 1941.

Today, stark hostility towards China is prominent in the US. What began as a US-Sino Trade War in early 2018 is now labelled by some observers as a new kind of Cold War.[90] American views have significantly moulded the discernment of China around the world over the last 100 years. They continue to do so.

It is a fact that China, within its enduring history, did not develop a system of governance where the governed played any sort of democratic role in selecting those who would govern. Such a system did evolve in a partial but significant way in Ancient Greece around 200 years before China's unifying Qin Dynasty was established in 221 BC. That experience in Greece has, over many centuries, fundamentally shaped the development of Western views (especially during the Enlightenment) on the best form of political governance.[91] China meanwhile has retained a top-down authoritarian governance system to this day, in keeping with its millennial, traditional understanding of how best to govern.[92] That governance system has performed exceptionally well, as noted above, over the last 40 years by delivering an unparalleled improvement in the livelihood of hundreds of millions of Chinese citizens, notwithstanding any ***democratic deficit***.

88 Buck, Pearl S. *The Good Earth* (John Day, New York, 1931).

89 "Pearl S. Buck – Author", *Biography*, April 2, 2014, available at: https://www.biography.com/writer/pearl-s-buck (accessed July 12, 2019). Pearl Buck died, aged 80, in 1973. Her love for China and its people was intense. She was condemned during the Cultural Revolution as an ***American Cultural Imperialist*** and forbidden to visit China. Later, after her death, her former residence at Nanjing University was converted into the *Sai Zhenzhu Memorial House*.

90 "China vs. America: A New Kind of Cold War", *The Economist*, May 16, 2019, available at: https://www.economist.com/leaders/2019/05/16/a-new-kind-of-cold-war (accessed July 12, 2019).

91 See, for example, Gay, Peter, "The Enlightenment in the History of Political Theory" (1954) *Political Science Quarterly*, 374.

92 Xu, Chenggang, "The Origins and Evolution of China's Institutions: A Comparative Institutional Analysis", *Presentation at Faculty of Law, Hong Kong University*, April 19, 2017.

As the American perspective on China has moved from bewilderment to antipathy, the American account of what has happened constantly stresses that the US and its allies are engaged in a recommenced battle to protect democratic values from a fresh authoritarian challenge, spearheaded by China. In fact, this outward justification is energized, above all, by the deeper challenge to US global political supremacy now unfolding.[93]

It is useful to consider the last change of superpower ascendancy over 100 years ago. In 1820, the UK economy was three times the size of the US economy. By 1870, in GDP terms, the UK and the US were close to level-pegging. By 1913, just before World War I, the US economy was 2.3 times larger than that of the UK. In 1820, both China and India had economies which were far larger than those of Britain and America. These, however, were static economies compared to both the UK and the US. Moreover, they were based on pre-modern economic systems which had to support vastly greater populations. In terms of global ascendancy, the UK was, thus, the dominant world "superpower" for most of the nineteenth century. By the time of World War I, that position had clearly been lost to the US.[94]

This transition from one dominant world power to the next proceeded with minimal resentment. Although the superpower "torch" was moving out of the British Empire family, the new dominant power was closely related in terms of ethnicity, language, and deeply shared traditions. Moreover, the UK soon found itself in need of vigorous US assistance to secure the defeat of Germany in World War I. Finally, the UK was able to rely on its own mature understanding of the changes underway and thus avoid too much counter-productive, national swaggering.

It is now around 100 years since that fundamental international transition. During this period, the US has played a major military role in stopping the German–Central Powers assault on Europe in World War I. In World War II, the US role was still more crucial in helping to defeat the unspeakable rise of Nazism (the greatest burden in this vast battle fell on the USSR[95]) and in destroying the barely less horrific Japanese onslaught across East Asia, South East Asia, and the Pacific (including Australia).

By the end of World War II, the US was outstandingly dominant, despite the cost of fighting the war. This US supremacy ushered in an era within the

93 Biswas, Bidashi and Goel, Anish, "What Comes after US Hegemony?" *The Diplomat*, December 19, 2018, available at: https://thediplomat.com/2018/12/what-comes-after-us-hegemony/ (accessed July 12, 2019).

94 "United States vs. Great Britain: Income and Population since 1500", *Visualizing Economics*, December 23, 2007, available at: http://visualizingeconomics.com/blog/2007/12/23/united-states-vs-great-britain-income-and-population-growth-since-1500 (accessed July 12, 2019).

95 Pennington, Reina, "Was the Russian Military a Steamroller? From World War II to Today" *War on the Rocks*, July 6, 2016, available at: https://warontherocks.com/2016/07/was-the-russian-military-a-steamroller-from-world-war-ii-to-today/ (accessed August 18, 2019).

Western Hemisphere, especially, of continued peace, subject to American oversight. It also facilitated foundation building for the new global trading system which assisted many nations – the US most of all.[96] China, in particular, has, over the last 40 years, taken exceptional advantage of this US superintended regime.[97]

This US ascendancy was built on immense power, which included the capacity, regularly used, to shape transnational outcomes to a remarkable extent. This era has regularly been referred to the *Pax Americana* drawing on terminology extending back the *Pax Romana* of the early centuries of the Roman Empire (after 27 AD). In like manner, it was said, the clear dominance of American military, economic, and political power provided the means for the US to oversee an era of extended peace, particularly after World War II.[98]

More recently, certain leading US commentators have critically analyzed what they call China's *sharp power*. This sharp power is juxtaposed with two other long, commonly used, international political terms, *soft power* and *hard power*. Christopher Walker and Jessica Ludwig argue that sharp power "is not principally about attraction or even persuasion; instead, it centres on distraction and manipulation".[99] Soft power is a term coined by Joseph Nye in 1990, which he has more recently defined in the following way: "[S]oft power is the ability to affect others by attraction and persuasion rather than through the hard power of coercion and payment".[100]

In fact, the US has itself deployed *all three powers*, soft, sharp, and hard, for many decades. One public policy analyst in the US, George Scialabba, argued, in 1985, that Third World regimes following policies considered unacceptable to the US were "subjected to American hostility, subversion or even invasion". Scialabba continued that "[R]hetoric aside, promoting democracy, self-determination and human rights has little to do with American foreign policy".[101] More recently, one reviewer of two books examining the remarkable careers of

96 Biswas and Goel, "What Comes after US Hegemony?"

97 Levy, Philip, "Was Letting China into the WTO a Mistake?" *Foreign Affairs*, April 2, 2018, available at: https://www.foreignaffairs.com/articles/china/2018-04-02/was-letting-china-wto-mistake (accessed July 12, 2019).

98 Mackintosh, Stuart P. M., "America First and the End of Pax Americana", *Europe Now Daily*, November 8, 2018, available at: https://www.europenowjournal.org/2018/11/07/america-first-and-the-end-of-pax-americana/ (accessed July 12, 2019).

99 Walker, Christopher and Ludwig, Jessica, "The Meaning of Sharp Power: How Authoritarian States Project Influence", *Foreign Affairs*, November 16, 2017, available at: https://www.foreignaffairs.com/articles/china/2017-11-16/meaning-sharp-power (accessed July 12, 2019). See also Copper, John, "The New Concept of Sharp Power in International Politics: A Critique", *IPP Review*, February 15, 2018, available at: https://ippreview.com/index.php/Blog/single/id/652.html (accessed July 13, 2019).

100 Nye, Joseph S., Jr., "How Sharp Power Threatens Soft Power", *Foreign Policy*, January 24, 2018, available at: https://www.foreignaffairs.com/articles/china/2018-01-24/how-sharp-power-threatens-soft-power (accessed July 12, 2019). See also Nye, Joseph S., Jr., *Soft Power: The Means to Success in World Politics* (Public Affairs, New York, 2004).

101 Scialabba, George, *Low Dishonest Decades: Essay & Reviews 1980–2015* (Pressed Wafer, Brooklyn, 2016), 110.

the brothers, John Foster Dulles (US Secretary of State, 1953–1959) and Allen Dulles (CIA Director, 1953–1961), credits them with creating a legacy, for the US, of perpetual war. The CIA, it is argued, was finally converted, under Allen Dulles, from being an intelligence clearing house to being a "perpetual covert war machine".[102]

In another essay, in 1983, entitled "Indian Country", Scialabba argued how one binding US national myth (chiefly crafted by Hollywood) was centrally important. This pivotal aspect of American folklore related to the extraordinary feat of coast-to-coast nation-building which underpinned the creation of the US as we know it today. During the Vietnam War, as Scialabba notes, American soldiers, drawing on this Wild West imagery, called those parts of South Vietnam controlled by their adversaries "Indian country".[103] Another essayist, Pankaj Mishra, recently observed that "Welcome to Injun country" was a bonding term still widely used by US service personnel deployed in war zones.[104] The case being made is that the exceptional ***national*** experience of "Winning the West" – as the modern US was being forged in the nineteenth century – has served as an enduring motif within the template for making and deploying US ***international*** policy ever since. A recent estimate by another commentator in Australia, Joseph Camilleri, is that the US has, over this post-war period, been involved in more than 50 attempted regime changes and military interventions outside of the US.[105]

In 2018, the former US President, Jimmy Carter, noted that the US had only been at peace for 16 years of over 240 years as a nation. America was, he said, "the most warlike nation in the history of the world". The US had spent almost US$6 trillion waging wars in the Middle East and Afghanistan and Pakistan since 2001. Over roughly the same period, China had built close to 30,000 km of high-speed rail services, President Carter noted.[106]

For around three decades after the commencement of China's "open door" policy in 1978, the US generally welcomed the rise of China. Immense business opportunities were recognized and trade boomed. At the same time, there was

102 Sanchez, Dan, "The Dulles Brothers and Their Legacy of Perpetual War", *Medium,* March 3, 2016, available at: https://medium.com/dan-sanchez/the-dulles-brothers-and-their-legacy-of-perpetual-war-94191c41a653 (accessed July 26, 2019).

103 Scialabba, *Low Dishonest Decades*, 43.

104 Mishra, Pankaj, "Why Do White People Like What I Write? A Book Review of Coates, Ta-Nehisi, *They Were Eight Years in Power*", *London Review of Books,* February 22, 2018, available at: https://www.lrb.co.uk/v40/n04/pankaj-mishra/why-do-white-people-like-what-i-write (accessed July 12, 2019).

105 Camilleri, Joseph A. "Many Are Thinking: We Can Surely Do Better as a Nation", *John Menadue – Pearls and Irritations*, February 16, 2018, available at: https://johnmenadue.com/joseph-a-camilleri-many-are-thinking-we-can-surely-do-better-as-a-nation/ (accessed July 12, 2019).

106 Wilkins, Brett, "Jimmy Carter Lectures Trump: US 'Most Warlike Nation in History of the World'", *TELSUR – English,* April 18, 2019, available at: https://www.telesurenglish.net/opinion/Jimmy-Carter-Lectures-Trump-US-Is-Most-Warlike-Nation-in-History-of-the-World-20190418-0020.html (accessed July 13, 2019).

rapidly increasing academic, intellectual, and general interest in China. The spoken and unspoken expectation, especially viewed from the US, was that a modernizing China would follow a path of economic and political *convergence* over time (discussed in Chapter 10). This is not, though, how matters have unfolded: China has not adhered to this Washington-shaped, macro political–economic script. The US mood has gone from being sorry for China, then helpful to China, to being increasingly hostile to China. Before we consider the acrimonious consequences of this growing animosity, it is good to consider what within the US worldview may have animated this comparatively sharp change of outlook.

How the US has addressed perceived threats to its self-asserted (and largely effective) global hegemony during the twentieth century follows a clear pattern. Defeated serious competitors (Japan and Germany) are now firm allies. Japan and South Korea remain quasi-tributary states harbouring very large US military outposts.[107] Given the number of US bases in Germany, it might also be so described. The USSR is no more and Russia, whilst still powerful in certain ways, no longer presents any sort of dominant existential threat. The rest of the leading economies in the world (outside of China) are allies or at least largely share certain primary political values – with common membership in the OECD and overlapping membership in NATO in many cases. India, for all its potential – and its recent economic growth – remains mainly a huge Third World country with a similar population to China but a GDP less than 25% of China's GDP.[108] The remaining nations around the world present no significant challenge to US global supremacy in view of their small size, terrible poverty, or habitual local conflict. Often a combination of these factors grimly applies.

This leaves China. China's economy is now around 45 times the size it was 40 years ago. In raw US dollar GDP terms, it is already around 60% of the size of the US economy and more than double the size of the Japanese economy.[109] In the history of US foreign policy experience, China is in a class by itself.

Moreover, as immense as China's difficulties are, they remain less intractable than the range of acute challenges facing many advanced Liberal-Democracies, and especially the US. Increased societal polarization (sometimes characterized as *identity-politics*) is now an embedded part of the political landscape. Just what are

107 In the pre-modern era, a Tributary State would offer material tributes or a mark of submission to a particular more powerful State with which it was durably engaged. See "Tributary State", *Definitions*, available at: https://www.definitions.net/definition/tributary+state (accessed September 15, 2019). There is resonance between this meaning and the special relationship which the US maintains with those States hosting significantly large US military bases.

108 In 2018, the nominal GDP size of China was around five times greater than that of India. Measured by Purchasing Power Parity (PPP), China's economy was still 2.5 times larger than that of India. See "List of Countries by Projected GDP – International Monetary Fund World Economic Outlook – 2018", *Statistics Times*, May 6, 2018, available at: http://statisticstimes.com/economy/countries-by-projected-gdp.php (accessed March 24, 2019).

109 Garnaut et al., *China's 40 Years of Reform*.

the core values of the US is matter of far greater debate, partly as a consequence of worthy projects to seek a more fair society. Today *several Americas* seem to coexist uneasily within the USA.[110]

One result of this souring of agreement on what should lie at the pivot of the collective US identity was the bitter contest evident during the Presidential Election in 2016, which saw Donald Trump emerge as a divisive, for many, victor.[111] In 2018, Thomas Friedman argued that President Trump was the "biggest threat to the integrity of [US] democracy today".[112] Madeleine Albright, meanwhile, described President Trump as "the most anti-democratic leader that I have studied in American history".[113] Another American columnist, David Leonhardt, argued that Donald Trump was "the most dangerous, unfit American President of our lifetimes".[114] A book by former FBI Director, James Comey, argued that President Trump was someone "who is untethered to the truth".[115]

This is the thorny context within which China has gone from being seen, above all, as a huge, prima facie hard-working, even likeable, offshore neighbour to being a vast and rapidly growing nemesis. The change of perception is most evident in the US, where official, semi-official, academic, and media questioning of China have all been briskly accelerating. The wave of predominantly anxious commentary has raised many questions: to what extent is China growing at US expense; how far is China unfairly standing on the shoulders of the US-Western intellectual property advances and the US-Western shaped and policed world trading system; and how swiftly is China growing into a new existential threat to the US (and the West).[116]

Some of this rush of re-examine is relatively sober, analytical, and informing even if the discussion is regularly shaped by the conclusion. The materials on offer range through to fairly wild-eyed fear-mongering at the other extreme. A *Sinophobia* narrative has now been advanced across the developed West (and beyond),

110 Babones, Salvatore, *The New Authoritarianism* (Polity Press, Cambridge, 2018).

111 Ibid.

112 Friedman, Thomas L., "Biggest Threat to US Democracy in Plain Sight", *New York Times News Service,* February 20, 2018, available at: http://gulfnews.com/opinion/thinkers/biggest-threat-to-us-democracy-in-plain-sight-1.2176739 (accessed July 13, 2019).

113 Albright, Madeleine, *Fascism: A Warning* (Harper Collins, New York, 2018).

114 Leonhardt, Davis, "The Tragedy of James Comey", *New York Times,* April 8, 2018, available at: https://www.nytimes.com/2018/04/08/opinion/james-comey.html (accessed July 13, 2019).

115 Comey, James, *A Higher Loyalty: Truth, Lies and Leadership* (Flat Iron Books, New York, 2018).

116 Chandler, Clay and Barret, Eamon, "The US-China Cold War Has Begun", *Fortune,* October 6, 2018, available at: https://fortune.com/2018/10/06/the-us-china-cold-war-has-begun/ (accessed July 13, 2019). The authors write that "Vice President Pence's speech to the Hudson Institute Thursday has been widely portrayed in the global press as an official declaration that the world's two largest economies are engaged in a 'New Cold War'. It is hard to read it any other way".

not least in Australia, where one academic has published a book arguing that Australia is already on the way to becoming a puppet-state of China.[117]

Germany and Japan showed the depraved madness of adopting a militarized route to national growth. China's rapid modern rise has shunned aggressive, international military posturing as a fundamental component in its planning. Confucian state-craft has for more than 2,000 years regarded the military as a necessary aspect of large-scale governance – but one which must be controlled.[118] The experience of China over the last 200 years has underlined the need for powerful military defences, of course. The build-up of military power by the PRC has been controversial, especially across the South China Sea – but, as noted above, non-military means dominate the blueprint for the rebuilding of modern China.

There is one further aspect associated with the growing Sino-antipathy phenomenon which should be mentioned. In 2012, as the London Olympics progressed, an article entitled "Sinophobia, the Last Acceptable Racism", by Ross Clark, was published in *The Spectator*, a UK weekly. Clark argued that the success of Chinese swimmers, in particular, was annoying to their Western rivals, and their unfounded, critical responses reflected an irrational suspicion of China.[119] It would be inaccurate to say that the relatively recent growth of the anti-China narrative in the West, led by the US, derives from the sort of Western racial superiority norms dominant 100 years ago. It remains a fact, however, that China has created a remarkable civilization which is both the world largest and its most enduring – and it is not Caucasian. This difference was highlighted in 2019 by Professor Kiron Skinner, Director of Policy Planning in the US State Department, when she said that, "It's the first time that we will have a great-power competitor [China] that is not Caucasian".[120] Concurrently, there is evidence of an amplified focus in the US on charging Chinese-Americans with industrial espionage and other charges, many of which are later dropped due to lack of evidence.[121]

An example of the rising US-Sino tension was evident in the arrest by Canada in December 2018, at the request of the US, of the chief financial officer of

117 Hamilton, Clive, *Silent Invasion: China's Influence in Australia* (Hardie Grant, Melbourne, 2018).

118 Michael, *China through the Ages*, Chapter 7, "The Empire Consolidated".

119 Clark, Ross, "Sinophobia, The Last Acceptable Racism", *The Spectator*, August 12, 2012, available at: https://blogs.spectator.co.uk/2012/08/sinophobia-the-last-acceptable-racism/ (accessed July 13, 2019).

120 Musgrave, Paul, "The Slip That Revealed the Real Trump Doctrine", *Foreign Policy*, May 2, 2018, available at: https://foreignpolicy.com/2019/05/02/the-slip-that-revealed-the-real-trump-doctrine/ (accessed July 13, 2019). Musgrave argues that this talk of clashing civilizations revealed "the racist, and dangerous, lens of the new U.S. statecraft". Professor Skinner may have overlooked the fact that the US had been challenged before by a non-Caucasian great power which led to a most deadly war with Japan from 1941 to 1945.

121 Magnier, Mark, "Fearing a New 'Red Scare' Atmosphere, Activists and Lawmakers Fight Targeting of Chinese-Americans", *South China Morning Post*, August 27, 2019, available at: https://www.scmp.com/news/china/diplomacy/article/3024441/fearing-new-red-scare-atmosphere-activists-and-lawmakers-fight (accessed August 27, 2019).

a prominent Chinese transnational corporation (Huawei). Some commentators described this episode as a form of legalized hostage-taking aimed at strengthening American bargaining power in the US–China Trade War. Professor Jeffrey Sachs of Columbia University argued that:

> Quite transparently, the US action ... really seems to be part of ... [a] broader attempt to undermine [China's] economy by imposing tariffs, closing Western markets to Chinese high-technology exports and blocking Chinese purchases of US and European technology companies. One can say, without exaggeration, that this is part of an economic war on China – and a reckless one at that.[122]

The subsequent detention in China (on claimed national security grounds) of two Canadians appears to be a response-in-kind.[123] Confirming, to a degree, this rather medieval approach to international negotiating, the American President said that he would intervene in the arrest of Huawei's chief financial officer if it helped secure a trade deal with China.[124]

Implicit in the grand narrative of the European Enlightenment, shaped as it was by transforming Christianity, was the conviction that (Caucasian-crafted) rationally based, liberal principles offer a foundational best option for the exercise and control of political power. It follows from this worldview that these principles have universal application and their universal standing is best confirmed by their increased application.[125] This perspective still shapes how the West – and especially the US – apprehends China.[126]

Liberal elites in the US are, in fact, feeling two levels of primary anxiety: externally there is the rise of China; internally, President Trump is in the White House. However, the Trump-elite and the liberal elite both share measurable common ground when it comes to alarm over China. Both groups appear convinced by the new account of China as being a central trading partner, but also, more than

122 Sachs, Jeffrey D., "The U.S. Not China Is the Real Threat to International Rule of Law", *The Globe and Mail,* 10 December, 2018, available at: https://www.theglobeandmail.com/opinion/article-the-us-not-china-is-the-real-threat-to-international-rule-of-law/ (accessed July 14, 2019). See also Black, Christopher, "Canada Takes a Hostage: Free Meng Wanzhou", *New Eastern Outlook*, December 8, 2018, available at: https://journal-neo.org/2018/12/08/canada-takes-a-hostage-free-meng-wanzhou/ (accessed July 14, 2019).

123 Vanderkuppe, Nathan, "Two Canadians Detained in China for Four Months Prevented from Going Outside, Official Says", *The Globe and Mail,* April 10, 2019, available at: https://www.theglobeandmail.com/world/article-two-canadians-detained-in-china-are-prevented-from-seeing-the-sun-or/ (accessed July 14, 2019).

124 Sink, Justin, "Trump Says He's Intervene in Huawei Case to Get China Deal", *Bloomberg,* December 12, 2018, available at: https://www.bloomberg.com/news/articles/2018-12-12/trump-says-he-d-intervene-in-huawei-cfo-s-case-for-trade-deal (accessed July 14, 2019).

125 Gray, John, *Enlightenment's Wake* (Routledge Classics, Abingdon, 2007).

126 Gray argues that the *Enlightenment project* has the status of a civil religion in the US. Ibid., 215.

ever, a threat to US global hegemony, with liberal elites exhibiting more hostility than President Trump.[127]

Professor Graham Allison has drawn a parallel between the US-Sino disputation and the *Thucydides Trap*. He argues, based on his reading of the history of Ancient Greece, that the dominant city-state-based power, Sparta, was drawn into a terrible destructive war with rising Athens because Sparta feared the challenge to its hegemony posed by Athens.[128] Professor Waldron, an American historian specializing in China, has challenged this Allison analysis in terms of both its reading of history and the applicability of this analysis to the Sino–American case. In fact, Professor Waldron implicitly aligns the current rise of modern China with that of Nazi Germany in the 1930s. He does this smoothly – but dubiously. Professor Waldron provides a closely argued case which supports, on balance, the Sino-phobia narrative.[129]

Notwithstanding the combined insularity of the Ming and Qing Dynasties (1368–1912), China has historically been comparatively open to the ideas of others. The fact that uniquely amongst the world's major civilizations (and especially compared to Western Civilization), China has relied on essentially secular ethical and governance systems for over 2,000 years helps explain this.[130] Moreover, China, historically, throughout the Imperial Era, did not rely on or feel a messianic need to convert widespread-others to the *Chinese-way* in order – in significant part – to validate the inherent superior, universal wisdom embodied in that Chinese worldview.

Regardless of how the Allison–Waldron debate should be resolved, there is a clear lesson to be drawn from the discussion: the US needs to find a durable way to engage with and allow the rise of China for the mutual benefit of both nations – and the world.[131] The demonstrated ability of the PRC, over the last 40 years,

127 Copper, John, "Trump vs. the Democrats on China", *IPP Review*, June 13, 2019, available at: https://ippreview.com/index.php/Blog/single/id/993.html (accessed July 13, 2019). In a new book, Professor Copper makes the case that, within the US policy-making elite, Trump best understands how the US and China can build a new, long-term constructive relationship under challenging circumstances. Copper, John Franklin, *Donald J. Trump and China* (Hamilton Books, Lanham, 2019).

128 Allison, Graham, "The Thucydides' Trap", *Foreign Policy*, June 9, 2017, available at: http://foreignpolicy.com/2017/06/09/the-thucydides-trap/ (accessed July 13, 2019).

129 Waldron, Arthur, "There Is No Thucydides' Trap", *The Straits Times*, June 18, 2017, available at: http://www.straitstimes.com/opinion/there-is-no-thucydides-trap (accessed July 13, 2019).

130 Michael, *China through the Ages*, Chapter 5, "Intellectual Revolution".

131 Neil Bush, son of the late President George H. W. Bush (who was Head of the US Liaison Office in Beijing (prior to the US granting diplomatic recognition to China in 1979) from 1974 to 1975) and founder and Chairman of the *George H. W. Bush Foundation for US-China Relations* argues strongly in favour of this basic view. See Bush, Neil, "The US-China Relationship Is Mutually Beneficial, so Drop the Paranoia and Adopt the George H. W. Bush style", *South China Morning Post*, July 11, 2019, available at: https://www.scmp.com/comment/opinion/article/3018019/us-china-relationship-mutually-beneficial-so-drop-paranoia-and (accessed July 14, 2019).

to meet and overcome so many varied, sometimes desperate, ordeals strongly suggests that, despite its immense array of problems, China looks well positioned to maintain this rise.[132]

China today has a very strong, centralized leadership structure in place. Its economic and social resource bases are far stronger than they were and they are continuing to grow. Notwithstanding the strictures of the single-party political system, overall societal morale remains robustly high and supportive of the current political system based, above all, on its unmatched performance legitimacy. In the US, meanwhile, for complex reasons, a number of which have been outlined above, endemic polarization means that collective morale is comparatively less full-bodied and coherent.

It is fair to expect that the Sino-phobia narrative may gather pace and run for a long time yet in the US and the West. The US, above all other major states, remains most wedded to the universalist political insights and liberal-template wisdom of the Enlightenment. The harm which can follow here arises from the way that this broad Enlightenment thinking can close out or discredit other ways of looking at the world.[133] This frame of reference underpins the analysis which argues that, as China plainly cannot be controlled like Japan or Germany, for example, it needs to be strategically contained.

Both China and the US face immense stress in the coming decades as they each come to terms with the other. This unique trial, which is of singular importance for the entire world, will be most testing for America: its 100-year dominant superpower status cannot continue unmodified. There is a plain lesson for the US in that historical shift from UK to US global hegemony over 100 years ago. Such a transition cannot be managed entirely without friction. But it can be accomplished with either greater or less ease – with major reciprocal benefits when the impulse towards anxious or swaggering resentment is well controlled.[134]

132 Jolly, Richard, "Review of Kishore Mahbubani's 'Has the West Lost It?" *Institute of Development Studies*, June 19, 2018, available at: https://www.ids.ac.uk/opinions/richard-jolly-reviews-kishore-mahbubanis-has-the-west-lost-it/ (accessed August 7, 2019).

133 Gray, *Enlightenment's Wake.*

134 We may need to be patient. In mid-2019, the former US Ambassador to the UN (2017–2018) Nikki Haley set out a strident case for increasing the US confrontational approach saying that, "China wishes to usurp our country's leadership role, certainly in Asia and evidently in the rest of the world", see Haley, Nikki, "How to Confront an Advancing Threat from China: Getting Tough on Trade Is Just the First Step", *Foreign Affairs*, July 18, 2019, available at: https://www.foreignaffairs.com/articles/china/2019-07-18/how-confront-advancing-threat-china (accessed July 20, 2019). Former US President Jimmy Carter argues that the core of the problem lies not with China but with the US which he described, in 2019, as, *the most warlike nation in history of the world*; see Wilkins, "Jimmy Carter Lectures Trump". Recent evidence indicates that even the closest allies of Washington may need to be watchful with respect to self-serving US artifice. See Tisdall, Simon, "How Trump's Arch-Hawk Lured Britain into a Dangerous Trap to Punish Iran", *The Guardian,* July 20, 2019, available at: https://www.theguardian.com/world/2019/jul/20/britain-lured-into-deadly-trap-on-iran-by-trump-hawk-john-bolton (accessed July 22, 2019).

Hong Kong and China

Previous chapters have examined a range of key interactions between Hong Kong and China. These include the relationship between BHK and Beijing (Chapter 4) and between the HKSAR and Beijing, (Chapters 6 and 7). Those discussions demonstrate that Hong Kong's relationship with China has always been fundamental to Hong Kong's existence and welfare. The discussions also show how this relationship has, at times, been comparatively stable, but even then it has been an ongoing process of engagement; it has never been a static or steady-state association. At times it has been shaped by vast changes in political–economic circumstances.

A central purpose of this section is to review the current state of this vital relationship and consider some key parameters likely to shape the relationship over the coming decades. Broadly speaking, the HKSAR is now, over 20 years after 1997, displaying deep, historically sourced anxieties in part because the basic parameters are looking more sharply clear. (This discussion also supports the closing analysis in Chapter 10.)

Anxieties

Crucial instances of political stress testing dating back almost 100 years have been reviewed in Chapter 7. The most recent example of high-level stress testing discussed in that chapter occurred in 2019 when massive protest marches occurred, accompanied later and separately by violent protests which regularly descended into rioting. The trigger for these protest marches and the rioting was the proposal to amend the FOO to allow for the judicial supervised extradition of certain persons sheltering in the HKSAR but accused of serious crimes around the world – including across Greater China. This proposal came to be widely referred to as the *Extradition Bill.* The level of insistent political violence generated is the worst seen in Hong Kong in over 50 years. There is a risk that it may become embedded within the political fabric of the HKSAR for some considerable time.

What factors have driven this grim development? One primary source traces directly back to the Maoist era in PRC history. Hong Kong has seen significant immigration from the Mainland dating back to soon after BHK was established. Since 1949, there have been several waves of mass migration from the Mainland. First, many on the losing (KMT) side in the Civil War came, followed by those who were dispossessed or who were left desperately impoverished after 1949. Next, the terrible famine unleashed by Mao Zedong's catastrophic Great Leap Forward (1958–1962) drove very high levels of emigration by those just seeking to escape alive from China. Then Mao launched the Cultural Revolution (1966–1976) which created still more mass flight from chaos and deadly internal conflicts.

These shocking, earth-shaking events in China occurred some two generations ago. But the memories are terrible. Those who experienced these events have passed on recollections to younger generations. A significant minority in Hong Kong appears to hold a foundational view that the CPC is essentially malevolent.

This dominantly depressing reading of the PRC underpins and feeds into wider currents of concern within a sizeable minority of younger Hong Kong generations. The comprehensive teaching of Chinese general and political history was never a BHK priority for a range of reasons. Most Hong Kong students grew up without the benefit of such learning – unlike in Macau where the focus was almost the reverse of that in BHK.[135] This minimalist teaching approach continues.[136] It is combined, unfortunately, with certain tilted narratives on a range of controversial issues, including the OCM and the Basic Law which are designed to cast Beijing decision-making in a negative light.[137]

This wider context within which this anxious view of Beijing exists is the robust liberal, civil rights legacy of over 150 years of British rule in Hong Kong. Christine Loh puts it this way:

> While Hong Kong was returned to Chinese sovereignty in 1997, the political "core values" of its people are "Western" and "liberal". After all, Hong Kong was a British colony for a very long time, and its legal and administrative systems are rooted in the liberal tradition even though the vast majority of Hong Kong people are ethnically Chinese.
>
> Hong Kong people looked to the West for ideas, education and trade. Western market liberalism was on the rise at one time, and its attraction was capitalism and personal freedom under a well-developed system of the rule of law. That was seen to be the ideal way of organising society and for personal advancement. [138]

Realities

Some of the clearest *realpolitik*[139] views on where the HKSAR now stands within China have been offered by informed regional observers of Hong Kong. Bilahari Kausikan, a plain-speaking, former Secretary of the Ministry of Foreign Affairs in

135 See Lo, Sonny Shiu Hing, "Opinion – Why Is Macau Far More Stable than Hong Kong?" *Macau Business*, September 11, 2019, available at: https://www.macaubusiness.com/opinion-why-is-macau-far-more-stable-than-hong-kong/ (accessed September 12, 2019).

136 Ibid.

137 Ho, Lok-sang, "Professional Teachers' Union Should Improve Delivery of Liberal Studies" *China Daily,* July 16, 2019, available at: https://www.chinadailyhk.com/articles/117/209/182/1563191525819.html?newsId=88966 (accessed July 16, 2019).

138 Loh, Christine, "A Grand Dialogue Might Heal Divided Hong Kong – If We Dare Hold One", *South China Morning Post*, July 8, 2019, available at: https://www.scmp.com/comment/opinion/article/3017425/can-grand-dialogue-help-people-reflect-and-heal-divided-hong-kong (accessed July 16, 2019).

139 "Practical politics decided more by urgent needs of the country, political party etc., than by morals or principles", *Cambridge English Dictionary*, available at: https://dictionary.cambridge.org/dictionary/english/realpolitik (accessed July 17, 2019).

Singapore, argues that the harsh truth for Hong Kong is that the Extradition Bill protests will achieve nothing:

> As I write this, demonstrations in Hong Kong continue, although the extradition bill that sparked them has been shelved. This is the latest phase of protests that began in 2014 with the Occupy Central or "umbrella movement".
>
> The proximate causes may be different, but they all arise from the disquiet of many Hong Kong people with Beijing's sway. I do not know when the demonstrations will end. But I am quite certain about what they will achieve: absolutely nothing!
>
> ...
>
> Ever since the end of the Qing dynasty in the late 19th century, the legitimacy of Chinese governments – imperial, republican or communist – has rested on the ability to defend China's sovereignty and its borders. I don't think Beijing is eager to exercise direct control over Hong Kong. But the unity of China is not a matter on which any Chinese government will ever compromise.
>
> The Hong Kong people, and the West generally, may have thought that the emphasis of the "one country, two systems" slogan lay on the second phrase. But for Beijing it was clearly always on one country. I shall not speculate about whether there was any real coincidence between what Britain's leaders privately believed in 1997 and what they now say they believed.
>
> Beijing was willing to tolerate two systems provided it did not undermine one country. But this is precisely what the demonstrators, particularly those who have resorted to violence in defiance of the law, are now doing.[140]

He later observes that:

> For 155 years from 1842 to the handover in 1997, London ruled Hong Kong as a colony, not a democracy; the people of Hong Kong were subjects, not citizens. It was only on the very deathbed of colonial rule that Britain found religion and raised political expectations that no Hong Kong government can fulfil.
>
> The people of Hong Kong are now citizens – of China. The rights they enjoyed as a British colony were not very different from what they were granted under one country, two systems and substantially more than those enjoyed by other citizens of China. It will not get any better.[141]

140 Kausikan, Bilihari, "Harsh Truths for Hong Kong: Extradition Bill Protests Will Not Achieve Anything", *South China Morning Post,* July 10, 2019, available at: https://www.scmp.com/week-asia/opinion/article/3018003/harsh-truths-hong-kong-protests-will-not-achieve-anything (accessed July 17, 2019).

141 Ibid.

Recently declassified UK diplomatic files reveal that, prior to 1997, the former Prime Minister of Singapore, Lee Kuan Yew, characterized Governor Patten's 1995 political reforms in Hong Kong as ill-timed, futile, and in breach of the spirit of UK agreements and understandings with China. In 1992, at Hong Kong University, Lee said, in Patten's presence, that Beijing could view the campaign by Patten to introduce major political reforms in 1995 as an Anglo-American conspiracy to influence the democratization movement in China, with Hong Kong used as a pawn.[142]

Another commentator based in Singapore, Michael Petraeus, makes a number of resonating points. He argues that Hong Kong relies almost completely for its remarkable significance on the fact that it is next to (now part of) China: *the world has come to Hong Kong not because of Hong Kong but because of China.*[143] In his view, the economic slippage of the HKSAR is already apparent and it is increasing. Hong Kong's utility to China is steadily ebbing as cities like Shanghai and Singapore stand more ready than ever to take up opportunities arising from the serious stability uncertainties now being visited on Hong Kong from within.[144] Singapore's role in providing the location for regional headquarters appears to be growing at the expense of Hong Kong.[145]

Petraeus notes, acutely, that:

> The paradoxical reality is, however, that as long as Beijing is resisting [the political upheaval and violence] in the HKSAR, it means it sees value in Hong Kong worth fighting for. But when it concedes a defeat – which is cheered as a win by its opponents – it is an ominous sign for the city's future.[146]

Alex Lo expands on this point by arguing that such a turning point would indicate that Beijing would then have concluded that Hong Kong cannot be trusted to perform a greater role in China's development.[147] Professor Prasad is based at Cornell University and is a member of the US think tank, the Brookings Institution.

142 Cheung, Gary, "Singapore Leader Lee Kuan Yew Blasted Britain's Handling of Hong Kong's Early 1990s Electoral Reform, Declassified Cables Show", *South China Morning Post*, July 18, 2019, available at: https://www.scmp.com/news/hong-kong/politics/article/3019039/singapore-leader-lee-kuan-yew-blasted-britains-handling (accessed July 18, 2019).

143 Petraeus, Michael, "Hong Kong's Suicide: The Beginning of the End", *Critical Spectator*, July 10, 2019, available at: https://criticalspectator.com/china/hong-kongs-suicide (accessed July 17, 2019).

144 Ibid.

145 "Singapore Wins Regional Financial Hub Race by Default", *Asia Sentinel*, June 18, 2019, available at: https://www.asiasentinel.com/econ-business/singapore-wins-regional-financial-hub-race-by-default/ (accessed July 19, 2019).

146 Petraeus, "Hong Kong's Suicide". Ibid.

147 Lo, Alex, "Hong Kong Youngsters Are Mortgaging Their Future", *South China Morning Post*, July 15, 2019, available at: https://www.scmp.com/comment/opinion/article/3018686/theres-no-escaping-harsh-truth-youngsters (accessed July 17, 2019).

He argues that China no longer needs Hong Kong. The exceptional economic growth across the Mainland means, he says, that the economic consequences of seeing yet more slippage in Hong Kong's role and prosperity are comparatively modest.[148] Moreover, Hong Kong people are anxious about the fact that the HKSAR looks set to become less and less important within China.[149]

There are, though, strong arguments made in favour of Hong Kong retaining its special role within China, despite both the massive growth, relative to the HKSAR, of the Mainland economy and the steady rise in concerns about basic social stability within the HKSAR.[150] These strengths include the following: Hong Kong's proximity to the Mainland and the unparalleled economic and wider links laid down over decades; its "Luxembourg" role within the PRC (highly effective and separated financial, taxation, and currency systems); its proven Rule of Law regime; and its manifestly strong professional service sector. Neither Singapore nor Shanghai can currently match all of these, it is said. The HKSAR thus (for now) retains a distinct advantage. The argument is also made that the mass political protests are meant to defend the Rule of Law in Hong Kong.[151] This latter argument, in my view, cannot stand up. The pivotal problem is that so many of these demonstrations have been followed, as day is by night, with inexcusable political violence and rioting, which are fundamentally destabilizing for any Rule of Law regime.[152]

The historical circumstances leading to the referendum on independence for Catalonia from Spain in 2017 are measurably different to those underpinning political turmoil in the HKSAR. Yet there are lessons which can be drawn. The referendum was declared to be unconstitutional by Spain's highest court.[153] A number of political leaders in Catalonia who drove the independence project then faced very serious charges of rebellion, disobedience, and misuse of public funds.[154] More importantly, mass protesting using an array of tactics has led to

148 Prasad, Eswar S., "Why China No Longer Needs Hong Kong", *New York Times*, July 3, 2019, available at: https://www.nytimes.com/2019/07/03/opinion/hong-kong-protest.html (accessed July 17, 2019).

149 Loh, "A Grand Dialogue".

150 Huang, Tienlei, "Why China Still Needs Hong Kong", *Peterson Institute for International Economic*, July 15, 2019, available at: https://www.piie.com/blogs/china-economic-watch/why-china-still-needs-hong-kong (accessed July 18, 2019).

151 Ibid.

152 Chung, Kimmy, Su, Xini, Lum, Alvin, and Carvalho, Raquel, "Police Ban Marches as Hong Kong Readies for 11th Weekend of Mass Anti-Government Protests", *South China Morning Post*, August 15, 2019, available at: https://www.scmp.com/news/hong-kong/politics/article/3023006/police-ban-marches-hong-kong-readies-11th-weekend-mass-anti (accessed August 18, 2019).

153 "Catalonia: Spain's Top Court Rules Referendum Illegal as Catalan Leaders Double Down", *ABC News*, October 18, 2017, available at: https://www.abc.net.au/news/2017-10-18/catalonia:-spains-top-court-rules-referendum-illegal/9060092 (accessed July 18, 2019).

154 "Who Are the 12 Catalan Leaders Facing Years in Prison?" *Al Jazeera*, February 12, 2019, available at: https://www.aljazeera.com/news/2019/02/12-catalan-leaders-facing-years-prison-190206105939774.html (accessed July 18, 2019).

a destabilizing of the social order since 2017, especially in Barcelona, the capital of Catalonia, once Spain's most prosperous city.[155] By late 2017, around 3,000 companies (including two leading banks) had relocated their headquarters from Barcelona.[156] Moreover, in the period since social stability began to be shaken, crimes rates in Barcelona have measurably risen.[157] By mid-2019, the number of companies which had relocated headquarters away from Catalonia was over 5,200.[158] It does not follow that this is fate which now awaits the HKSAR but what has happened to Barcelona provides a lucid warning.

Remedies

As the political turmoil and extended violence have unfolded, a number of commentators have urged calm and suggested possible processes to diffuse the intense levels of political polarization. These mechanisms have broadly argued for a carefully developed institutionalized mechanism for ongoing dialogue, influenced by related processes used offshore including in South Africa and Singapore,[159] or a major, judicially led, independent enquiry.[160]

155 Aguado, Jesus, "Exclusive: Banco Sabadell Mulls Moving Top Management from Catalonia", *Reuters,* December 18, 2017, available at: https://www.reuters.com/article/us-spain-politics-catalonia-banks-exclus/exclusive-banco-sabadell-mulls-moving-top-management-from-catalonia-idUSKBN1CM33Q (accessed July 18, 2019). Catalonia, containing around 16% of Spain's population, has typically accounted for 20% of Spain's GDP.

156 "Adéu to Catalonia: Companies in the Region Vote with Their Feet against Political Uncertainty: Over 3,000 Firms Have Moved Legal Headquarters to Elsewhere in Spain; 1,000 Have Shifted Their Fiscal Base", *The Economist*, December 14, 2017, available at: https://www.economist.com/business/2017/12/14/companies-in-the-region-vote-with-their-feet-against-political-uncertainty (accessed July 18, 2019).

157 Caranco, Rebeca, "Barcelona Becomes Spain's Leader in Rising Crime Rates" *El Pais,* February 19, 2019, available at: https://elpais.com/elpais/2019/02/18/inenglish/1550485905_119074.html (accessed July 18, 2019).

158 Tahir, Javier, "The "Process" Has Pushed 5,244 Companies Out of Catalonia, *ABC Economy,* June 18,2019, available at: https://www.abc.es/economia/abci-proces-empujado-salir-cataluna-5244-empresas-201906172045_noticia.html (accessed July 19, 2019).

159 See Loh, Christine, "Hong Kongers Want and Deserve a Fair Society", *The Economist,* August 20, 2019, available at: https://www.economist.com/open-future/2019/08/20/hong-kongers-want-and-deserve-a-fair-society (accessed August 23, 2019); and Lo, Alex, "Time Ripe for Leadership and Reconciliation", *South China Morning Post,* July 17, 2019, available at: https://www.scmp.com/comment/opinion/article/3019017/time-ripe-leadership-and-reconciliation (accessed July 18, 2019).

160 See Li, Andrew, "A Commission of Inquiry into Police Conduct Can Help Hong Kong's Healing Process – An Amnesty for Protesters Cannot", *South China Morning Post,* July 9, 2019, available at: https://www.scmp.com/comment/opinion/article/3017672/commission-inquiry-police-conduct-can-help-hong-kongs-healing (accessed July 18, 2019); and "Anthony Cheung Urges Inquiry before a Turn for the Worse", *The Standard,* July 15, 2019, available at: http://www.thestandard.com.hk/breaking-news.php?id=131323&sid=4 (accessed July 18, 2019).

Two key demands of the protesters, both the broad movement and the militant wing, are that an independent Commission of Enquiry into police behaviour be established and that all arrested protesters be released unconditionally – asking, in effect, for an amnesty for such protesters.[161] The former Chief Justice of the CFA, Andrew Li, supports establishing a Commission of Enquiry, headed by a senior judge, but he is not in favour of any amnesty – he believes rioters should be sentenced according to law, bearing in mind the need to deter others.[162]

The discussion about any form of amnesty or unconditional release of protesters charged is sometimes misinformed. An amnesty was granted by the Governor to a range of police officers in the 1970s during the BHK era after the ICAC was established. At that time, however, as discussed in Chapter 4, the British AL system of governance gave far greater freedom of action to the Governor than any Chief Executive of the HKSAR can enjoy. For most of the BHK era, the Government had nominal total control over the government and over (the appointed) membership of LegCo. Moreover, there were very few limiting restrictions on the Governor's powers in the Letters Patent or the Royal Instructions.

Matters are fundamentally different under the Basic Law. Article 63 provides that the Department of Justice shall control criminal prosecutions free from any interference: this includes free from any interference by the Chief Executive. Indeed, the Chief Executive is responsible under Article 48 for the implementation of the Basic Law, which includes ensuring that Article 63 is properly observed. Those who have urged the Chief Executive to declare some sort of amnesty for criminally charged protesters are, thus, pima facie, urging her to act contrary to the Basic Law. Grenville Cross, a former Director of Public Prosecutions in the HKSAR, argues that to pay heed to such improper exhortations could make the Chief Executive complicit in an attempt to pervert the course of justice and possibly subject her to a charge of misconduct in public office.[163]

The proposals for a judicially led Commission of Enquiry raise different difficult questions. Apart from gaining acceptance as being "independent", there is the fact that any such initiative would need, at least, the tacit agreement of Beijing. Next, there is the pivotal matter of the *terms of reference*; what should any such commission investigate? In neither of the two proposals (from Andrew Li and Anthony Leung) noted above are any detailed terms of reference provided. Based on the reports of the two proposals, the primary emphasis appears to be on enquiring into police behaviour, especially during the violent political turmoil

161 "'All Five Demands Must Be Fulfilled': Thousands of Hong Kong Anti-Extradition Law Protesters Rally in Sha Tin", *Hong Kong Free Press*, July 14, 2019, available at: https://www.hongkongfp.com/2019/07/14/five-demands-must-fulfilled-thousands-hong-kong-anti-extradition-law-protesters-rally-sha-tin/ (accessed July 18, 2019).

162 Li, "A Commission of inquiry".

163 Cross, Grenville, "If Hong Kong's Extradition Bill Protesters Want to Defend the Rule of Law, They Must Also Be Prepared to Face It", *South China Morning Post*, June 26, 2019, available at: https://www.scmp.com/comment/opinion/article/3015981/if-hong-kongs-extradition-bill-protesters-want-defend-rule-law-they (accessed July 18, 2019).

which has erupted. Such a focus is too narrow and is bound to be seen by police as tilted against them.

In fact, the Independent Police Complaints Council (IPCC) began its own enquiry into the conduct of Police in dealing with the 2019 political turmoil and rioting in mid-2019. The Head of the IPCC said, although he was not against establishing a general Commission of Enquiry, any such commission should *not* look at any individual officer's culpability. That task, it was argued, should be left to the IPCC, otherwise relevant officers could be "disciplined twice", which would be improper.[164]

A forthright alternative suggestion for a Public Enquiry has been advanced by Professor Ho Lok Sang. He argues strongly for a wide-ranging enquiry. He takes the view, noted above, that any enquiry merely looking into possible misuse of force by the Police is plainly too narrow. Ho argues that a full enquiry should look at the responsibility of all the different actors involved, including all political parties, legislators, lawyers (including the Hong Kong Bar Association and the Hong Kong Law Society), the Police, the clergy, teachers, social workers, and various NGOs. Above all, the role of foreign interests and possible foreign support for rioters should be investigated. Finally, the commission should look at the proposed Extradition Bill to see how well it complied with appropriate international guidelines and also investigate to what extent the bill was misrepresented as to its content.[165] A former Deputy Commissioner of the ICAC, Tony Kwok favours the setting up, by LegCo, of a Select Committee, drawing on current members of LegCo from across the political spectrum to undertake a comprehensive enquiry. Kwok does set out comprehensive terms of reference for this proposal, which include the legitimacy of introducing the Extradition Bill, the credibility of the Mainland legal system, the misunderstandings about the Extradition Bill due to inadequate official explanations or a successful campaign of misinformation, and who may have organized (and financed) any such misinformation campaign. He argues that a range of persons be asked to testify before such a committee including the police, student leaders, and the leadership of the Civil Human Rights Front (the organizer of the mass marches).[166]

The difficulty here, however, is that any broad terms of reference covering most if not all standpoints could be far too demanding for even the most accomplished judge (or panel of judges) to address. To attend to the very great array

164 Lum, Alvin, "Commission of Inquiry is Possible but Let's Not Look into Individual Police Officers' Conduct: IPCC Chief Anthony Neoh", *South China Morning Post*, August 20, 2019, available at: https://www.scmp.com/news/hong-kong/politics/article/3023480/commission-inquiry-possible-lets-not-look-individual-police (accessed August 20, 2019).

165 Ho, Lok-sang, "HK Needs Inquiry into Recent Political Unrest", *China Daily*, July 22, 2019, available at: https://www.chinadailyhk.com/articles/88/228/113/1563809463344.html (accessed July 23, 2019).

166 Kwok, Tony, "A Select Committee Should Be Set Up to Investigate Riots", *China Daily*, July 8, 2019, available at: https://www.chinadailyhk.com/articles/64/153/61/1562588205336.html?newsId=88236 (accessed July 18, 2019).

of issues might require hundreds of witnesses to give evidence, with many parties seeking representation and cross-examination rights. Any such commission might require years to report (and would inevitably become a "dripping roast" for lawyers). A distinguished, former CFA judge, Henry Litton, argued that no judge in his right mind would accept an appointment to a commission with such wide terms of reference.[167]

A Commission of Enquiry is appealing on the face of it given its potential to provide an institutional circuit-breaking mechanism to allow all to step away from violent street-politics. But it does not look practicable in either narrowly or widely based versions. Certainly, any enquiry could only commence if one were to be established after the HKSAR had returned to a condition of sustained political stability. There was a judicially headed Public Enquiry after the Star Ferry Riots in 1966 – which riots lasted around four days (see Chapter 7). Following the far more serious 1967 riots (also see Chapter 7), there was an official report – not a Public Enquiry – written by senior officials and sent to London, once again after stability had returned.[168] Other Public Enquiries since 1997 have involved investigations of specific or short-lived episodes with relatively clear parameters. [169]

To rebuild stability and the Rule of Law and to address deep concerns made evident in 2019 will, inter alia, require much frank, open, and tolerant discussion conducted using existing platforms or assemblies and possibly new forums.[170] The HKSAR will need to tackle with yet more vigour its most profound socio-economic problems. None of this is easy. None of this can be done within any sort of short time frame.

Closing observations

As explained in Chapter 7, the politically very successful campaign against the proposed Extradition Bill in 2019 relied heavily on amplifying extant, deep general fears and more specifically on over-wrought images of predatory criminal prosecution behaviour being visited on the HKSAR by Beijing. This alarmist campaign was propagated drawing on the fertile zone of continuing, post-1949 anxiety outlined above. The hundreds of thousands drawn onto the streets of

167 Lum, Alvin, "Hong Kong Protesters Want to Protect Freedoms? Work on Defending 'One Country, Two Systems' First, Retired Judge Henry Litton Says", *South China Morning Post*, August 20,2019, available at: https://www.scmp.com/news/hong-kong/politics/article/3023630/hong-kong-protesters-want-protect-freedoms-work-defending (accessed August 21, 2019).

168 Ip, Regina, "Hong Kong Needs Real Economic and Social Reform Right Now, Not an Independent Inquiry into the Turmoil", *South China Morning Post*, August 11, 2019, available at: https://www.scmp.com/comment/opinion/article/3022104/hong-kong-needs-real-economic-and-social-reform-right-now-not (accessed August 18, 2019).

169 Ibid.

170 A number of commentators have supported creating an institutional body or bodies focussed on building understanding and reconciliation. See, for example, Loh, "A Grand Dialogue".

Hong Kong to march against the Extradition Bill were expressing genuinely felt alarm and hostility – that they or family members might someday be extradited. These amendments are needed, as explained in Chapter 7, above all to remedy the use of the HKSAR as a refuge for serious criminals from around the world and from Greater China. The amendments were also deeply controversial. Those who marched against them did so sincerely when taking such remarkable mass action, but their motivation was influenced by populist, hostile mass campaigning.[171]

Thus, those in the huge major protest marches came to feel that:

> Even with all the operational safeguards written in, if the Mainland wants to extradite someone, people in Hong Kong fear the local system won't be able to resist the pressure; and once taken to the Mainland they don't believe there would be a fair trial.[172]

Given Hong Kong's deserved reputation for maintaining the highest-quality, independent judiciary in East Asia, these views appear misguided.[173] If opinions are, collectively, very strongly held, however, the desire to look further for evidence and factual information has trouble gaining traction. When these opinions are heavily shaped by social media sources, the problem, as one commentator explained, is that accuracy and truth are of secondary importance to speed and clarity when advancing political views online. [174]

The 2019 experience of highly organized[175] mass political violence has also led to an unsatisfactory pattern of apologist demands from many in the broad PD camp to excuse or exonerate those committing violent acts (seen by millions on television in the HKSAR and around the world) including, in one case, a protester biting the end off a police officer's finger. The reasons given for making these demands were a combination of the need to heal deep rifts within society and

171 On the negative impact of populist politicking (on left and right), see Remeikis, Amy, "Alastair Campbell on the 'Populist Virus' and Why Bill Shorten Lost, *The Guardian*, July 13, 2019, available at: https://www.theguardian.com/politics/2019/jul/14/alastair-campbell-on-the-populist-virus-and-why-bill-shorten-lost (accessed July 17, 2019). See also Cohen, Dan, "Behind a Made-for-TV Hong Kong Protest Narrative, Washington Is Backing Nativism and Mob Violence", *The Grayzone*, August 17, 2019, available at: https://thegrayzone.com/2019/08/17/hong-kong-protest-washington-nativism-violence/ (accessed September 1, 2019).

172 Loh, "A Grand Dialogue".

173 Cross, Grenville, "Hong Kong's Rule of Law Is Alive and Well", *Hong Kong Free Press*, October 28, 2017, available at: https://www.hongkongfp.com/2017/10/28/grenville-cross-sc-hong-kongs-rule-law-alive-well/ (accessed July 17, 2019).

174 "Hearts and Minds – All Warfare Is Based on Deception", *At the Feet of Socrates*, July 30, 2019, available at: https://atthefeetofsocrates.blogspot.com/2019/07/hearts-minds.html (accessed August 5, 2019).

175 Lo, Clifford, "Police Looking for More than 700 'Core' Extradition Bill Protestors Involved in Recent Clashes in Hong Kong", *South China Morning Post*, July 20, 2019, available at: https://www.scmp.com/news/hong-kong/politics/article/3019445/police-looking-more-700-core-extradition-bill-protesters (accessed July 22, 2019).

to contend that the perpetrators essentially lacked personal agency: the HKSAR Government or the Police or other factors somehow forced them to take violent, destructive action.[176] Some appear to argue that this is not real violence but some sort of *alternative violence* because it is pursued in a good cause.[177] Others maintain that the violent protesters are a small minority – a splinter group.[178] Or the violent protests are mentioned – with zero reflection on their dire impact on the Rule of Law in the HKSAR.[179] When there has been PD condemnation of the unprecedented level of political violence, it has been selective.[180]

President Xi Jinping spoke in Hong Kong on the twentieth anniversary of July 1, 1997. He singled out Hong Kong for particular praise in that carefully prepared speech.[181] But he also stressed that there was a redline (covering any sort of advocacy of Hong Kong independence or any threats to national security)

176 Alex Lo argues that a range of key PD politicians are "apologists for the most destructive and criminal behaviour". He notes how those involved in political violence say the police made them do it; the Chief Executive made them do it; Beijing made them do it. Responsibility lies with anybody but themselves. See Lo Alex, "Police Should Go Home and Let Young Riot", *South China Morning Post,* July 16, 2019, available at: https://www.scmp.com/comment/opinion/article/3018841/police-should-go-home-and-let-young-riot (accessed July 17, 2019). See also Cross, Grenville, "Hong Kong Watch: Biased from the Outset and More Blinkered Now", *China Daily,* July 16, 2019, available at: https://www.chinadailyasia.com/articles/212/154/134/1563278372595.html?newsId=89098 (accessed July 17, 2019).

177 Lhatoo, Yonden, "Violence" What Violence? It's All Peace and Love on the Hong Kong Protest Front", *South China Morning Post,* July 13, 2019, available at: https://www.scmp.com/news/hong-kong/law-and-crime/article/3018481/violence-what-violence-its-all-peace-and-love-hong (accessed July 17, 2019).

178 Chugani, Michael, "Hong Kong People Deserve the Nobel Peace Prize for Their Dignified Protests against China's Iron Grip" *South China Morning Post,* July 11, 2019, available at: https://www.scmp.com/comment/opinion/article/3017988/hong-kong-people-deserve-nobel-peace-prize-their-dignified-protests (accessed July 17, 2019).

179 See, for example, "People vs. Power: The Rule of Law in Hong Kong", *The Economist,* July 13, 2019, available at: http://gonzaloraffoinfonews.blogspot.com/2019/06/people-vs-power-rule-of-law-in-hong.html (accessed July 17, 2019); and Yu, Verna, "'Don't Mess with Us': The Spirit of Rebellion Spreads in Hong Kong", *The Guardian,* July 13, 2019, available at: https://www.theguardian.com/world/2019/jul/13/dont-mess-with-us-the-spirit-of-rebellion-spreads-in-hong-kong (accessed July 17, 2019).

180 Rarely were anti-government rioters rebuked by PDs, but the Police were admonished continuously together with those who violently attacked protesters returning to Yuen Long, in the New Territories, after a march – followed by another anti-government riot – on July 21, 2019, See Lam, Jeffie, Mok, Danny, and Lum, Alvin, "At Least 45 Injured as Rod-Wielding Mob Dressed in White Rampages through Yuen Long MTR Station Beating Screaming Protestors", *South China Morning Post,* July 22, 2019, available at: https://www.scmp.com/news/hong-kong/law-and-crime/article/3019524/least-10-injured-baton-wielding-mob-suspected-triad (accessed July 22, 2019).

181 Fu, Hualing, "What Does Xi Jinping Intend for Hong Kong: A China File Conversation", June 30, 2017, *China File,* June 30, 2017, available at: http://www.chinafile.com/conversation/what-does-xi-jinping-intend-hong-kong (accessed July 22, 2019).

which should not be crossed.[182] One deeply concerning aspect of the 2019 anti-government protests has been the way that the primary cause given for the violent protests and riots shifted, for the most aggressive protesters, from being about the Extradition Bill to emphasizing separatism as a pivotal aim.[183] Political slogans widely daubed during certain highly charged and violent protests used catchphrases stressing themes such as *Reclaim (or Liberate) Hong Kong with a Revolution of Our Times.*

The discovery of Hong Kong's largest, clandestine bomb-making facility in July, 2019 located within a warehouse used by a Hong Kong independence advocacy group (which denied knowledge of the bomb-making preparations) increased the cause for concern. Apart from prepared petrol bombs, around two kg of the very dangerous explosive triacetone triperoxide (TATP) was found.[184]

By mid-2019, Hong Kong was no longer the same city it had durably been for many decades until early 2019. Over that long time span, Hong Kong has coped with and recovered strikingly well from many taxing politically experiences. The successive political violence and riots in 2019 turned Hong Kong into a more dangerous and less stable city. The lasting impact of this grim legacy will only become well-defined over time. However, certain aspects of that impact are becoming more clear already. These are discussed in the final chapter.

182 Ibid.

183 See, for example, Lo Alex, "How to Promote Terrorist Wannabes", *South China Morning Post,* July 21, 2019, available at: https://www.scmp.com/comment/opinion/article/3019492/how-promote-terrorist-wannabes (accessed July 22, 2019); and Cross, Grenville, "One Country, Two Systems Worth Defending", *China Daily,* July 18, 2019, available at: https://www.chinadailyhk.com/articles/248/95/238/1563449621934.html (accessed July 22, 2019). Bernard Chan, Convenor of the HKSAR Executive Council (or Cabinet), said that the Government could never satisfy the demands of the core anti-government protestors as "they don't want Hong Kong to be part of China", see Bradsher, Keith, "Hong Kong's Approach to Protestors: No More Concessions", *New York Times,* July 19, 2019, available at: https://www.nytimes.com/2019/07/19/world/asia/hong-kong-protests-carrie-lam.html (accessed July 22, 2019).

184 Lo, Clifford, "Three Arrested as Police Bust Hong Kong's 'Largest Ever' Bomb Plot on Eve of Major Anti-Government Protest", *South China Morning Post,* July 21, 2019, available at: https://www.scmp.com/news/hong-kong/law-and-crime/article/3019429/bomb-disposal-squad-called-after-explosive-substance (accessed July 22, 2019).

10 Conclusion

The British legacy

The terms *imperialism* and *colonialism* are sometimes used interchangeably in the literature but a regular distinction is often drawn. Imperialism is said to carry the essential idea of State A enjoying a level of dominance over State B (and possibly other states). Colonialism indicates the practical implementation of imperialism, typically involving the migration of governance personnel, managers, and possibly workers from State A to State B to take economic advantage of State B and to develop State B in the image of State A to some degree.[1]

During the height of the British Empire, the UK engaged in both imperialism and colonialism on an immense scale. Moreover, it created an empire which was, in large part, not contiguous with the UK. It was said that *the sun never set on the British Empire.*[2] In 1815, the British (and allies) finally triumphed in the Napoleonic Wars against France. Within another 100 years, the British Empire had expanded to cover almost 25% of the land mass on earth and, at 412 million people, almost a quarter of the world's population. In terms of territory, it was the largest empire in history.[3]

Many other empires have existed. The Chinese Empire was a continental empire with an imperial reach which eventually, under the Qing Dynasty (1644–1912), covered a massive core area and certain contiguous states. (The PRC today occupies most of the same imperial Chinese territory as occupied by the Qing Dynasty.[4]) The Roman Empire was far more a maritime empire but one

1 "Colonialism vs. Imperialism", *International Relations,* November 21, 2016, available at: http://internationalrelations.org/colonialism-vs-imperialism/ (accessed July 25, 2019).

2 Misachi, John, "What Does the Sun Never Sets on the British Empire Mean?", *World Atlas,* May 20, 2018, available at: https://www.worldatlas.com/articles/what-does-the-sun-never-sets-on-the-british-empire-mean.html (accessed July 25, 2019).

3 Ibid.

4 The PRC today incorporates Tibet and Xinjiang plus Hong Kong and Macau (as Special Administrative Regions). A claim is made over Taiwan (a "renegade Province"), but it remains outside of the PRC. Mongolia is now acknowledged by Beijing to be outside the PRC. For an interesting review of this history of acquired areas within Qing Dynasty China (and the PRC), see Chappell, Jon, "China Imperial Past and Present", *The Asian Dialogue,* September 28, 2015, available at: https://theasiadialogue.com/2015/09/28/chinas-imperial-past-and-present/ (accessed July 30, 2019).

centred on the Mediterranean Sea. The Russian Empire and the Mongol Empire provide additional examples of continental-based empire building.

The Age of Imperialism, however, is most associated with European empire building which encompassed massive colonial developments, after new breakthroughs in maritime technology and ship-building ushered in the Age of Discovery.[5] Later, Japan aggressively joined in this enterprise.[6] Today, although the US likes to argue that it is not an imperial power,[7] this claim does not stand up to serious examination – see detailed discussion in Chapter 9 explaining the unparalleled US military and economic-imperial reach. By these measures, the former USSR was also an imperial power both in the continental sense and based on its powerful offshore influence over *tributary states*, such as Cuba.[8]

The Belgians, British, Danes, Dutch, French, Germans, Portuguese, Spanish, amongst others, all engaged in significant offshore imperialism and colonization. The British proved to be better at global empire building and colonization than any other imperial power. Not only was the British Empire the largest empire the world has seen but it was the most durable of its type. The British Empire was assembled by force, especially by naval power, and maintained through the exercise of hard, sharp, and soft power across its many components.

Significant lessons arising from the American War of Independence, which led to the striking loss of colonial possessions in North America, were learned by the British. Within the diminished – but soon re-expanding – British global domain, a form of cooperative colonialism displaced the earlier more exploitive version.[9] The British developed improved modes of governance and administration, which relied on professionally trained, colonial officials, who typically found a lifelong career overseeing and running the vast empire.[10]

These systems, which embodied a particular, applied version of Diceyan Constitutionalism, provided the crucial building-blocks (software and hardware using current terminology) for the vast British colonial project. What the British brought to the project of imperial colonization was a measurably more developed,

5 "What Was the Age of Exploration or the Age of Discovery?" *World Atlas*, available at: https://www.worldatlas.com/articles/what-was-the-age-of-exploration-or-the-age-of-discovery.html (accessed July 7, 2019).

6 "Japanese Imperialism", *Indiana University*, available at: http://www.indiana.edu/~hisdcl/G369_2002/japanese_imperialism.htm (accessed July 25, 2019).

7 Haley, Nikki, "How to Confront an Advancing Threat from China: Getting Tough on Trade Is Just the First Step", *Foreign Affairs*, July 18, 2019, available at: https://www.foreignaffairs.com/articles/china/2019-07-18/how-confront-advancing-threat-china (accessed July 20, 2019).

8 Ader, Emile B., "Soviet Imperialism or Communist Ideology – The Real Threat" (1963) 38 *Social Science*, 75.

9 Cullen, Richard and Tso, Kevin "Using Opium as a Public Revenue Source – Not as Easy as It Looks: The British Hong Kong Experience" (2012) *British Tax Review*, 226.

10 Tso Kevin K. S., "Fundamental Political and Constitutional Norms: Hong Kong and Macau Compared" (2012) 13 *Australian Journal of Asian Law*, available at: https://papers.ssrn.com/sol3/papers.cfm?abstract_id=2159544 (accessed March 20, 2019).

long-term strategic perspective. They took lessons from colonial failures as well as successes.

This colonial governance framework, it transpired, worked better than anyone likely at first expected when matched with a significantly self-organizing, hard-working Chinese population situated within a smaller-scale jurisdiction such as Hong Kong (and Singapore). The British in Hong Kong found themselves governing a society which drew on centuries of deep mutual understanding which underpinned the conspicuously self-reliant, core aspects of Chinese Familialism (see Chapter 2).

The way in which this pivotal interaction worked, more often than not in a beneficial way during the BHK era (within the context a British-shaped, legalized, authoritarian system), has been discussed in detail in Chapters 4 and 5. The most respected legacy arising from that era is the Rule of Law regime (with its clean governance hallmarks) which put down such very strong roots in Hong Kong. A crucial foundation for this remarkable achievement is that, ever since 1842, Hong Kong has equipped itself well to apply sufficient funding to build and maintain this enviable Rule of Law scheme.

The worst legacy of the BHK era was for a long time justifiably seen as a fine benefit conferred on Hong Kong by wise, pragmatic policy-making: the 75% of Hong Kong given over to country parks green belts and countryside areas.[11] No other city of Hong Kong's size has such vast green areas adjacent to dense residential areas. Today, however, this parkland proximity comes at a very great cost. The most pressing social problem in the HKSAR is providing decent housing for all of its 7.5 million (and increasing) population. Yet any attempt to access even well under 5% of country parks to address the housing crisis is met by unremitting protests from those (typically already well housed) who regard the green zones as a semi-sacred bequest, which must never be compromised.[12]

The contemporary context

Without question, the most significant contextual factor affecting both the latter years of BHK and the entire HKSAR period has been the reawakening of China. As explained in Chapter 9, between 1978 and 2018, total GDP in China rose around 45-fold from US$218 billion to over US$10 trillion (measured in US dollars using 2010 prices). The PRC has now lifted some 850 million people out of extreme

11 "Country Parks and Conservation", *HKSAR Government – The Facts*, April, 2019, available at: https://www.gov.hk/en/about/abouthk/factsheets/docs/country_parks.pdf (accessed August 17, 2019).

12 Wang, Xiangwei, "Carrie Lam Can Defuse the Hong Kong Protests by Taking on the Property Tycoons", *South China Morning Post*, August 17, 2019, available at: https://www.scmp.com/week-asia/opinion/article/3023162/carrie-lam-can-defuse-hong-kong-protests-taking-property-tycoons (accessed August 17, 2019).

poverty since 1981 according to the World Bank.[13] China alone was responsible for 75% of total world poverty reduction over the period from 1981 to 2010. In less than 20 years, it is expected that China's middle class may grow to be more than double the size of the US middle class. This astounding growth, the fastest sustained expansion by a major economy in history, has generated many positive consequences worldwide. China has, for example, been the single largest contributor to world economic growth for more than a decade, since 2008.[14]

This rapid rise has also generated certain challenges which are of central importance when it comes to analyzing the position of Hong Kong in China today. These can be divided into two broad categories: how the Hong Kong–Beijing relationship has been recast profoundly by this rise; and how the Sino-US relationship has, at the same time, been adversely re-formed.

During the final period of British rule, Hong Kong, in 1993, had an economy that in GDP terms was about 27% of the size of the Mainland economy. China's population at that time was close to 200 times the size of the Hong Kong population (and still is). Mainland China had an economy that was, in basic GDP terms, less than four times the size of the BHK economy and this was *after* about 15 years of rapid catch-up development within China, post-1978. Today, the HKSAR economy is less than 3% of the size of the Mainland economy and, with each passing year, it is shrinking in relative significance. China has gone from being less than "four Hong Kongs" in 1993 to being around 40 Hong Kongs today – on its way to becoming well over "100 Hong Kongs" by 2049, when the PRC will be 100 years old.

Prior to and after the handover in 1997, *convergence theory* was influential.[15] According to this view, China, in order to maintain the very strong growth achieved in the first 15 years after opening-up, would surely have to move towards a localized but still recognizable form of Western liberal, free-market governance, where the government would be measurably downsized and be far more hands-off. A capitalist private sector (significantly transnational with US corporations dominant) would become the primary driving force within the Chinese economy.[16] Apart from the fall of the Berlin Wall and Fukuyama's crystalizing *End of*

13 "China Overview", *The World Bank*, April 8, 2019, available at: https://www.worldbank.org/en/country/china/overview (accessed July 27, 2019).

14 Ibid.

15 As Chandran Nair says, "Ever since Thomas Friedman published *The World Is Flat* it has become fashionable to see convergence everywhere", see Nair, Chandran, "Forget 'Convergence' – This Is the Age of Divergence", *Huff Post*, August 17, 2016, available at: https://www.huffpost.com/entry/convergence-age-divergence_b_7998274?guccounter=1&guce_referrer=aHR0cHM6Ly93d3cuZ29vZ2xlLmNvbS5oay8&guce_referrer_sig=AQAAACECSE2y0yQLj-XPn_TodYJLztcTG3ai6e59iwa8HOfuZ46OTGoY0ExflTGDl7PTcDF_EUb1roYcU-8gun6N4jWZnwaHVLcE2v_ebjoptO0Y2CK-OEo4U3JFgijQEzlY0Nj0Jtdz4Gw7Bca-VtO1rXu7h4kOSI87IfNMb6l_59wNC (accessed August 1, 2019).

16 Rudd, Kevin, "The United States and China – A Relationship Adrift", *Asia Society Policy Institute*, September 19, 2018, available at: https://asiasociety.org/policy-institute/united-states-and-china-relationship-adrift (accessed July 30, 2019).

History narrative,[17] those Hong Kong comparative economic performance figures appeared to clinch the validity of this perspective. As the handover of BHK to China approached in 1997, this surely put Hong Kong in a strong position. Within China, its economic importance meant that it would be able to punch above its weight and influence not just successful economic opening-up but also help shape liberalizing political change within the PRC.

This view has proved to be wrong. The PRC has achieved a continued, unprecedented transformation without need of this envisaged politically liberalizing influence.[18] China, it transpires, has been able to rebuild itself by primarily drawing on its extraordinary, enduring social ontology and its exceptional, deeply grounded political-institutional history (see Chapter 9).

The comparative economic strength of the HKSAR within China has diminished greatly over the last two decades. Michael Petraeus is right when he says that: "the world has [always] come to Hong Kong not because of Hong Kong but because of China".[19]Professor Prasad may be overstating matters when he says that, already, China no longer needs Hong Kong.[20] But it is the case that China needs Hong Kong measurably less today than Hong Kong needs China. The HKSAR continues to enjoy extraordinary Mainland-based opportunities. But its diminishing relevance within China is unambiguously clear.

Next, we need to reflect briefly on some relevant prior history and the Sino-American New Cold War as it has come to be labelled, with emphasis, both in the UK and the US.[21]

Fortunes were made in the US through participation in the opium trade with China in the nineteenth century, though not on the same scale as in the UK. The attitude of the US to China following the overthrow of the Qing Dynasty and the establishment of the Republic of China in 1912 was, in the main, supportive.

17 Fukuyama, Francis, *The End of History and the Last Man* (Avon Books, New York, 1992).

18 Nair, Chandran, "China's Rise Is Not a Gift of the West: This Argument from Many China Watchers Has a Colonial Stench to It", *Berggruen Institute – World Post Archive*, July 30, 2019, available at: https://www.berggruen.org/the-worldpost/articles/chinas-rise-is-not-a-gift-of-the-west/ (accessed August 1, 2019).

19 Petraeus, Michael, "Hong Kong's Suicide: The Beginning of the End", *Critical Spectator*, July 10, 2019, available at: https://criticalspectator.com/china/hong-kongs-suicide (accessed July 17, 2019).

20 Prasad, Eswar S. "Why China No Longer Needs Hong Kong", *New York Times*, July 3, 2019, available at: https://www.nytimes.com/2019/07/03/opinion/hong-kong-protest.html (accessed July 17, 2019).

21 The former Prime Minister of Australia, Kevin Rudd, who is also a recognized international public policy commentator argued, in 2018, that, although the US and China were by then engaged in a trade war, an economic war, and a technology war, a New Cold War had not yet commenced (Rudd, "The United States and China"). For the contrary view, see Edel, Charles and Brands, Hal, "The Real Origins of the U.S.-China Cold War", *Foreign Policy*, June 2, 2019, available at: https://foreignpolicy.com/2019/06/02/the-real-origins-of-the-u-s-china-cold-war-big-think-communism/ (accessed July 28, 2019); and "A New Kind of Cold War: China v America", *The Economist*, May 16, 2019, available at: https://www.economist.com/leaders/2019/05/16/a-new-kind-of-cold-war (accessed July 30, 2019).

There were major potential business opportunities and the broad idea of this huge country, with its extraordinary history, modernizing at last was attractive. After the US-supported KMT lost the Chinese Civil War in 1949, the US adopted a hostile stance towards the new PRC, which endured from 1949 during the staunchly (at times rabidly) anti-communist, Cold War period until 1972, when President Nixon became the first US President to visit the PRC. The year before, in 1971, the UN General Assembly had voted to admit the PRC to the UN as the sole representative of China and as one of the five permanent (veto-wielding) members of the UN Security Council (contrary to US wishes). The KMT, Republic of China (on Taiwan) was expelled from these UN positions at the same time.[22] In 1979, President Jimmy Carter finally extended US diplomatic recognition to the PRC (at the expense of Taiwan, once more).[23]

This recognition was timely coming, as it did, shortly after the commencement of China's open-door economic policy in 1978, under Deng Xiaoping, following the death of Mao Zedong in 1976. For around three decades after the commencement of this policy, the US generally welcomed the rise of China. Immense business opportunities were recognized and trade boomed. At the same time, there was rapidly increasing academic, intellectual, and general interest in China. As discussed above, the spoken and unspoken expectation, especially viewed from the US, was that a modernizing China would follow a path of economic and political convergence over time. After the collapse of the Soviet Union in 1991 – and the formal end of the Cold War – Francis Fukuyama's *End of History* theorizing seemed to confirm that this must be so. China joined the World Trade Organization (WTO) in 2001, with US support.[24] The primary end-point for this convergence would surely be a version of the US model of liberal-democratic individualism wedded to dominant, private capitalism.[25] In fact, strong arguments have been made that an Age of Divergence steadily displaced any of the wishes for convergence (based on technology, free markets, and democracy) as a consequence of tensions generated by excessive Western consumption ideals, evangelical Western universalism, and oversold technology remedies.[26]

22 "Oct. 25, 1971: People's Republic of China In, Taiwan Out, at U.N.", *New York Times – Learning Blog*, available at: https://learning.blogs.nytimes.com/2011/10/25/oct-25-1971-peoples-republic-of-china-in-taiwan-out-at-un/ (accessed July 28, 2019).

23 Glass, Andrew, "US Recognizes Communist China, December 15, 1978", *Politico,* December 15, 2018, available at: https://www.politico.com/story/2018/12/15/us-recognizes-communist-china-dec-15-1978-1060168 (accessed July 30, 2019).

24 Mahbubani, Kishore, *Has the West Lost It?* (Penguin, London, 2019), 22.

25 Fukuyama, *End of History* (book). See also Nathan, Andrew, "China's Rise and International Regimes: Does China Intend to Join or Overthrow Existing Norms and Institutions?" *Critical Issues Confronting China Seminar Series – Harvard University*, December 10, 2014, available at: http://projects.iq.harvard.edu/files/asia-center/files/nathan_12-10-2014.pdf (accessed July 13, 2019).

26 Nair, "Forget 'Convergence'".

By 2008, the Global Financial Crisis (GFC), which had been incubated in the US, was bedevilling economies around the world.[27] China coped better than all other very large economies as it had the capacity to adopt an expansionary fiscal policy and did so. This helped ease the worst impact of the GFC worldwide and especially in some strong China-trading jurisdictions like Australia.[28] It was at this time that US hostility towards China began to lift significantly.[29] The US felt that China began (under President Hu Jintao) to take advantage of the US-created distress America faced with the onset of the GFC, by becoming more self-assertive in its foreign policy.[30] In fact, the extraordinary growth in the Chinese economy signalled geopolitical change was not only happening but was bound to happen.[31] China also drew an important long-term lesson from the GFC: the deep systemic flaws in the US-shaped, Western macro-financial regime allowed serious financial abuses which free-market regulation had failed to curb.[32] Apart from the pivotal geoeconomic shift underway, there were, thus, strong indications that China should become more self-reliant with respect to macro-economic policy setting and look less to the West for guidance.

In 2013, Xi Jinping became China's President. China's self-assertiveness has risen measurably since. In 2016, Donald Trump won the US Presidential Election. Since 2017, US hostility towards China has steadily intensified. As discussed in Chapter 9 – and above – the Sino-US Trade War, which the US initiated in 2017, has now been widely recast as a New Cold War. China has gone, within a decade, from being seen as a huge, briskly advancing offshore neighbour promising immense business potential to being a vast and rapidly growing arch-rival. China is now openly and repeatedly portrayed as the most significant threat faced by the US (and the West).[33] In the meantime, former US President Jimmy Carter

27 "The Global Financial Crisis", *Reserve Bank of Australia*, available at: https://www.rba.gov.au/education/resources/explainers/the-global-financial-crisis.html (accessed July 28, 2019).

28 Ibid.

29 Edel, Charles and Brands, Hal, "The Real Origins of the U.S.-China Cold War", *Foreign Policy*, June 2, 2019, available at: https://foreignpolicy.com/2019/06/02/the-real-origins-of-the-u-s-china-cold-war-big-think-communism/ (accessed July 28, 2019).

30 Ibid.

31 Rudd, "The United States and China".

32 See Sun Shilian and Zhang, Jianming, "Ripple Effect: The Profound Impact of the Global Financial Crisis", *Central Banking*, April 12, 2018, available at: https://www.centralbanking.com/central-banks/economics/3456071/ripple-effect-the-profound-impact-of-the-global-financial-crisis (accessed July 28, 2019).

33 Chandler, Clay and Barret, Eamon, "The US-China Cold War Has Begun", *Fortune*, October 6, 2018, available at: https://fortune.com/2018/10/06/the-us-china-cold-war-has-begun/ (accessed July 13, 2019). The authors write that "Vice President Pence's speech to the Hudson Institute on Thursday has been widely portrayed in the global press as an official declaration that the world's two largest economies are engaged in a 'New Cold War'. It is hard to read it any other way".

reminded us in 2018 that the US is "the most warlike nation in the history of the world".[34]

We need to remember, though, that this is a dissimilar Cold War to that which prevailed between the USSR and the US. A conspicuous difference is the durable and essentially positive Sino-American macro-economic dimension. Geopolitically, relations have been, over many decades, far more stable than those between the US and the USSR for the 40-plus years after the end of World War II. Open military conflicts between the US and the PRC have been the exception rather than the rule: the Korean War (1950–1953) where both Chinese and American troops were directly opposed and the US-Vietnam War (1955–1975) where China provided significant logistical support for Vietnam. Today, the US and China are, respectively, the two most powerful economies in the world (in that order, still) and those economies are still deeply and constructively intertwined at very many levels, notwithstanding recent unwinding. The benefits flowing to China from this engagement have been very great, but the gains for the US have also been hugely positive.[35]

Nevertheless, the reality which China now finds itself confronting is exceptional. A once immensely dominant and still immensely wealthy and inordinately well-armed US has increasingly positioned itself as an indignant superpower that is struggling to find a mature way to accommodate the difficult new world order emerging around it.[36] This task may be much harder for the US due to the divisive emergence within the body-politic of forceful examples of *neo-tribalism* over recent years. One commentator speaks of the "raging tribalism ... which threatens to dominate western politics for years – perhaps decades".[37] Kishore Mahbubani, meanwhile, speaks of the West, "flailing about, attacking Iraq, bombing Syria, sanctioning Russia and baiting China".[38]

34 Wilkins, Brett, "Jimmy Carter Lectures Trump: US 'Most Warlike Nation in History of the World'", *TELSUR – English,* April 18, 2019, available at: https://www.telesurenglish.net/opinion/Jimmy-Carter-Lectures-Trump-US-Is-Most-Warlike-Nation-in-History-of-the-World-20190418-0020.html (accessed July 13, 2019).

35 Rudd, "The United States and China".

36 See Zakaria, Fareed, "The Self-Destruction of American Power", *Foreign Affairs,* July/August 2019, available at: https://www.foreignaffairs.com/articles/2019-06-11/self-destruction-american-power (accessed August 2, 2019); and Campbell, Kurt M. and Sullivan, Jake, "Competition without Catastrophe: How America Can Both Challenge and Coexist with China", *Foreign Affairs,* August 1, 2019, available at: https://www.foreignaffairs.com/articles/china/competition-with-china-without-catastrophe (accessed August 2, 2019).

37 Keane, Bernard, "Australia Is Caught in the Blast Zone of Rampant Nationalism", *Crikey,* August 6, 2019, available at: https://www.crikey.com.au/2019/08/06/australia-toxic-nationalism/?utm_campaign=CrikeyWorm&utm_medium=email&utm_source=newsletter (accessed August 7, 2019).

38 Mahbubani, *Has the West Lost It?*, Chapter 1.

Hong Kong today

When Richard Hughes first argued in 1968 that "Hong Kong is China", he was making a powerful cultural-political point.[39] That Hong Kong is now an inalienable part of China is a political-legal fact. In 2019, Professor Lawrence Lau aptly observed that "Hong Kong will always be part of China".[40] Soon after, President Trump confirmed that Hong Kong is a part of China.[41]

It remains the case, however, that a generally well-educated and articulate, agenda-setting significant minority within the HKSAR retains a long-term, deeply watchful, often acutely hostile view of the CPC, Beijing, and China and this regularly spills over into expressions of antipathy towards Mainland Chinese.[42] One seasoned commentator sees, in Hong Kong, a "bone-deep Sino-phobia" which importantly sways the broad pro-democracy movement. This well-placed anti-Communist alliance (with concentrated influence across the education, media, and legal sectors) has helped disenchant and radicalize many younger Hong Kong residents, according to this view.[43] Many members of this group are also church members, both Catholic and Protestant.[44]

39 Hughes, Richard, *Borrowed Place, Borrowed Time: Hong Kong and Its Many Faces* (2nd ed.) (Andre Deutsch, London, 1976).

40 Lau, Lawrence J., "Neither Violence Nor Beijing Can Fix Hong Kong's Housing Shortage and Lack of a Social Safety Net", *South China Morning Post,* July 30, 2019, available at: https://www.scmp.com/comment/opinion/article/3020441/neither-violence-nor-beijing-can-fix-hong-kongs-housing-shortage (accessed July 30, 2019).

41 "Trump Calls Hong Kong Protests 'Riots', Says Internal Matter for China", *Straits Times,* August 2, 2019, available at: https://www.straitstimes.com/world/united-states/trump-says-he-wont-give-advice-to-china-on-hong-kong-protests (accessed August 2, 2019).

42 See, for example, Fong, Leslie, "Why Macau Has Been Spared the Political Turmoil Now Gripping Hong Kong", *South China Morning Post,* July 27, 2019, available at: https://www.scmp.com/week-asia/opinion/article/3020177/why-macau-has-been-spared-political-turmoil-now-gripping-hong (accessed July 30, 2019); Lhatoo, Yonden, "Add Oil, Hong Kong, as Our Beloved City Burns with Hate", *South China Morning Post,* July 27, 2019, available at: https://www.scmp.com/news/hong-kong/politics/article/3020347/add-oil-hong-kong-our-beloved-city-burns-ugly-hate (accessed August 1, 2019); and Gracie, Carrie, "Beijing's Struggle to Win Hong Kong's Young Hearts", *BBC News,* June 29, 2017, available at: https://www.bbc.com/news/world-asia-china-40439845 (accessed August 1, 2019);

43 Hon, Thomas, "Hong Kong Politics: A Never-Ending Farce", *Counterpunch,* January 15, 2018, available at: https://www.counterpunch.org/2018/01/15/hong-kong-politics-a-never-ending-farce/ (accessed August 1, 2019).

44 Many of these churches have suffered sometimes inordinately at the hands of the CPC during the Maoist era and also since. They understand, too, about the harassment and persecution of Christian entities in East European communist countries after World War II. These feelings have seen one Catholic leader in Hong Kong express grave reservations about Pope Francis engaging constructively with Beijing. See "Zen Presents Letter to Pope Warning Him on China", *UCA News,* December 28, 2018, available at: https://www.ucanews.com/news/zen-presents-letter-to-pope-warning-him-on-china/83839 (accessed August 7, 2019).

The most radical minority within the younger militant activists appears to desire the complete collapse of the PRC. It is they who led the calls for independence from the PRC, to *Reclaim Hong Kong with a Revolution of Our Times.*[45] According to one leading PD LegCo member, many young people in Hong Kong take the view that *China is authoritarian, vulgar, brutal, materialistic and uncivilized.*[46]

The wave of violent protesting which commenced in mid-2019 in Hong Kong after the introduction of the Extradition Bill has been discussed above. As explained in Chapter 7, the Extradition Bill provided the foundations for (rather being the fundamental cause of) the following mass protests and rioting. The proposed amendments, as modified, provided substantial safeguards. However, the topic became the subject of immensely heated debate. The claimed dangers to Hong Kong residents (and visitors to Hong Kong) were successfully inflated and then reported and marketed across all media sectors. The idea that almost anyone in Hong Kong might be lifted across the border to face the Mainland criminal justice system gained conspicuous traction (within the poorly grounded but quite broad perception of an unrelentingly fearsome China outlined below).

One commentator (noting the Sun Tze maxim – *all warfare is based on deception*) explained some of the deep persuasive power of what unfolded in this way:

> Realizing the power of social media makes every activist a propagandist and commentator. Harnessing all options, unconstrained by the rules of traditional news outlets, they've delivered their version of events with speed and clarity. Accuracy and truth are secondary to this process but that is not the point.[47]

In June 2019, two remarkable major protest marches in quick succession, involving hundreds of thousands of protesters, followed on from the very wide general and media-based campaign against the Extradition Bill. The continuous, radical political violence and rioting took off soon afterwards.

45 Taylor, Jerome and Yu, Elaine, "Hong Kong Anti-Police Violence Protesters Driven from Beijing's Top Office with Tear Gas", *Hong Kong Free Press,* July 28, 2019, available at: https://www.hongkongfp.com/2019/07/28/hong-kong-anti-police-violence-protesters-driven-beijings-top-office-tear-gas/ (accessed August 1, 2019). The abuse of their street-power against those who are defenceless and demands for exemptions from the general Rule of Law are further aspects the militant protesting with its constant overtones of violence. See Li, Audrey Jiajia, "Hong Kong Protesters Must Not Become the Monsters They Are Fighting and Lose Moral Legitimacy", *South China Morning Post,* August 1, 2019, available at: https://www.scmp.com/comment/opinion/article/3020794/hong-kong-protesters-must-not-become-monsters-they-are-fighting-and (accessed August 2, 2019).

46 Cheung, Fernando, "Protestors Are Fighting for an Open Society", *The Economist,* August 20, 2019, available at: https://www.economist.com/open-future/2019/08/20/protesters-are-fighting-for-an-open-society (accessed August 22, 2019).

47 "Hearts and Minds – All Warfare Is Based on Deception", *At the Feet of Socrates,* July 30, 2019, available at: https://atthefeetofsocrates.blogspot.com/2019/07/hearts-minds.html (accessed August 5, 2019).

The reply of the HKSAR Government to the escalating crisis was flexible at the margins (regarding details of the Extradition Bill), but the Government remained deeply fixed on securing passage of the legislation. This commanding stiffness added further significant fuel to the political confrontation and to the media campaigns being waged with rising intensity against the Extradition Bill (see Chapter 7). The Government found it increasingly difficult to respond effectively and a very heavy burden fell on the Police as they fought to control the widespread political lawlessness.[48]

Five demands which had to be met for the violent demonstrating to be called off were presented: a complete withdrawal of the Extradition Bill, the withdrawal of the "riot" characterization of the June 12 protests, the unconditional release of all arrested protesters, the formation of an independent commission of inquiry into police behaviour, and universal suffrage.[49]

In mid-2019, the leader of the now banned Hong Kong National Party (discussed in Chapter 7) was arrested with others in possession of explosives and certain weapons.[50] A further cache of offensive weapons (together with over US$60,000 in cash) was located soon after, while activist, online harassment, and fraud directed at police officers and relatives increased as the protests continued.[51] It is over five decades since Hong Kong last saw such open and widespread lawlessness. There are serious questions as to what extent foreign involvement may have helped energize the organized riots[52] and how they have been funded given, for example, the extensive use of expensive protective

48 See Wu, Willa, "Ex-Prosecutor Commends Police Courage, Restraint", *China Daily*, August 7, 2019, available at: http://www.chinadaily.com.cn/a/201908/07/WS5d4ae542a310cf3e35564767.html (accessed August 22, 2019); and Cohen, Colin, "Reasons to Still Believe in Our City", *Newsletter – Boase Cohen & Collins*, August 20, 2019.

49 Cheng, Kris, "All Five Demands Must Be Fulfilled: Thousands of Hong Kong Anti-Extradition Law Protesters Rally in Sha Tin", *Hong Kong Free Press*, July 14, 2019, available at: https://www.hongkongfp.com/2019/07/14/five-demands-must-fulfilled-thousands-hong-kong-anti-extradition-law-protesters-rally-sha-tin/ (accessed August 8, 2019).

50 Mok, Danny, "Andy Chan, Founder of Hong Kong National Party, among Eight Arrested in Raid while Family of Three Detained over Smoke Bombs in Separate Operation", *South China Morning Post*, August 2, 2019, available at: https://www.scmp.com/news/hong-kong/politics/article/3021065/andy-chan-founder-banned-hong-kong-national-party-among (accessed August 2, 2019).

51 "Two Arrested for Inciting Violence Online, One Held for Fraud Using Police Data", *The Standard*, August 2, 2019, available at: http://www.thestandard.com.hk/breaking-news.php?id=132392&sid=2 (accessed August 2, 2019).

52 Cheung, Tony, "Former Hong Kong Leader Tung Chee-hwa Accuses the United States and Taiwan of Orchestrating 'Well-Organised' Recent Protests", *South China Morning Post*, July 31, 2019, available at: https://www.scmp.com/news/hong-kong/politics/article/3020829/former-hong-kong-leader-tung-chee-hwa-accuses-united-states (accessed August 2, 2019). See also Goodrum, Ian, "US Fooling No One with Its Claims of Innocence in HK", *China Daily*, August 25, 2019, available at: http://www.chinadaily.com.cn/a/201908/26/WS5d6338cfa310cf3e35567d1b.html (accessed August 26, 2019). Goodrum argues that Hong Kong, with its manifest US economic connections and wealth inequalities, is particularly open to having local negative sentiments amplified to help build a crisis.

equipment by thousands of radical protestors.[53] According to one recent estimate noted earlier, the US has, over the post-war period, been involved in more than 50 attempted regime changes and military interventions outside of the US.[54] Moving beyond broad statistics and proving foreign involvement is daunting, however.

How has it come to this? As discussed in Chapter 9, those who experienced terrible events in China after 1949 (for example, the Great Leap Forward and the Cultural Revolution) before escaping to BHK have passed on vividly dark recollections to younger generations. It is the CPC which was responsible then as it is today, as the sole governing party in China. This depressing portrayal of the PRC underpins and feeds into intense local concerns, not least related to housing, education, and career prospects, within a sizeable minority of younger Hong Kong residents.[55] In fact, these are globally experienced problems across the First World, especially. As shown in Chapter 5, more lower-income HKSAR residents, young and old, are measurably better off than their counterparts in Australia or New Zealand, for example, in terms of basic housing provision, education options, and safer streets – combined with zero or low tax rates. However, most political opposition is local (to vary a phrase) rather than comparative, not least in Hong Kong. There is an intense belief amongst a sizeable number, amplified by sharing, that living in the HKSAR is a grim experience.[56]

The majority of Hong Kong students grew up without the benefit of any measured and detailed learning about modern China. One commentator has argued that after the bloody ending of the mass protest in Tiananmen Square on June 4, 1989,

53 The international media have devoted a striking amount of time to coverage of the 2019 protests in the HKSAR, yet there appears to have been no serious investigative reporting of how the protests and rioting have been funded. One estimate of the cost of supporting the OCM, which ran for around three months in 2014 is over US$25 million. See Moak, Ken, "Why China Claims US, UK behind HK Protests" *Asia Times*, August 1, 2019, available at: https://www.asiatimes.com/2019/08/opinion/why-china-claims-us-uk-behind-hk-protests/ (accessed August 2, 2019).

54 Camilleri, Joseph A. "Many Are Thinking: We Can Surely Do Better as a Nation", *John Menadue – Pearls and Irritations*, February 16, 2018, available at: https://johnmenadue.com/joseph-a-camilleri-many-are-thinking-we-can-surely-do-better-as-a-nation/ (accessed July 12, 2019).

55 Curiously, the leader of the main protest organizer, the Civil Human Rights Front, said that the unrest did *not* stem from social problems. See Wan, Cindy, "Beijing Is Wrong Say Democrats", *The Standard*, July 30, 2019, available at: http://www.thestandard.com.hk/section-news.php?id=210151&sid=50041560 (accessed August 3, 2019).

56 Lee, Jeong-ho, "Hong Kong Can Solve Socio-Economic Problems, Like Singapore Did: Ex-Diplomat Kishore Mahbubani", *South China Morning Post*, September 4, 2019, available at: https://www.scmp.com/week-asia/politics/article/3025662/hong-kongs-socio-economic-problems-can-be-solved-just-look (accessed September 7, 2019).

a small number of Hong Kong Chinese, rightly horrified by the events of June 4, were readily recruited, thereafter, into a loose alliance to work against Beijing.[57]

As discussed in Chapter 6, the Basic Law contains strong suggestions that a system of full democracy is possible. But there is no promise that this is to be achieved within any stated time frame. Article 45 (Chief Executive) and Article 68 (LegCo) each speak of universal suffrage being an ultimate aim to be achieved in accordance with the principle of gradual and orderly progress – implicitly, after the year 2007.[58] For many in the PD camp, the failure of Beijing to live up to what they argue is the promise in the Basic Law of full democracy for the HKSAR is proof of comprehensive bad faith.[59] In fact, significant partial reforms of the composition of LegCo and its electoral system were agreed to in 2010, when the Democratic Party took a firm position but also demonstrated a significant facility for political negotiation. All other attempts at political reform have come to nothing, however.

China's exceptional rise and the continued successful operation of the OPS have each amplified national security concerns, especially as US hostility to China has accelerated. In these circumstances, it is unsurprising that Beijing, although not completely opposed to political reform in the HKSAR, is now more determined that this must unfold *in accordance with the principle of gradual and orderly progress*, as stated in the Basic Law.[60]

Yet stipulation politics have continued to dominate the political reform discussion in Hong Kong over the last decade, with RPDs having the pivotal role in agenda setting: willingness to negotiate or to compromise is seen as unacceptable political weakness.[61] As explained in Chapter 7, the opportunity to take a significant step forward to introduce universal suffrage for the 2017 Chief Executive Election was voted down in LegCo in 2015 by the PDs (after the OCM protests folded in late 2014). The compromise required was to agree (under protest) to the acceptance of a vetting process designed to ensure the fundamental loyalty to Beijing of all candidates allowed to stand. The ultimatum politics evident during the 2019 mass protest marches have been even more extreme.[62] These demands have also arisen from a movement which has a plainly violent, minority wing but which, even more than the OCM, lacks any sort of clear, coherent leadership.

57 Moak, Ken, "Why China Claims US, UK behind HK Protests" *Asia Times*, August 1, 2019, available at: https://www.asiatimes.com/2019/08/opinion/why-china-claims-us-uk-behind-hk-protests/ (accessed August 2, 2019).

58 Both Articles 45 and 68, respectively, refer to Annex 1 and Annex 2 of the Basic Law. Each of these identifies the year 2007, after which reform may be envisaged, but in terms of "if there is a need".

59 See the well-articulated overview of this position in Chan, Cora, "Demise of "One Country – Two Systems"?" *Verfassungblog*, June 28, 2019, available at: https://verfassungsblog.de/demise-of-one-country-two-systems/ (accessed August 3, 2019).

60 As this term is understood by Beijing.

61 Cheung, "Protestors Are Fighting".

62 Lo, Alex, "Protest Demands Are Impossible to Meet", *South China Morning Post*, August 2, 2019, available at: https://www.scmp.com/comment/opinion/article/3021262/protest-demands-are-impossible-meet (accessed August 3, 2019).

Although some feel that leaders are dispensable in modern social movements, this view is mistaken. As Michael Edesess cogently explains:

> A strong moral leader will have the authority to negotiate with the government, whereas a leaderless movement refusing to cede an inch risks sending each protester on the road to pointless martyrdom.[63]

For Beijing, this recurrent, all-or-nothing position-taking indicates bad faith on the part of the PDs, now made worse by the association of some PDs with violently extreme activists.[64] Accusations have been made by the pro-Beijing media in Hong Kong that the PDs and radical activists are forming a "pro-violence" faction.[65] Indeed, Beijing's worst fears have been confirmed. Those most given to repetitive rioting who form the vanguard of the militant activists openly call, with violence, for a revolution in the HKSAR to achieve some form of separation from the PRC. They have moved beyond campaigning for universal suffrage and true democracy as a paramount goal.[66] Organized violent activism, designed to secure regional secession, is not just a serious crime in China but also in the UK and Spain, where official responses have been severe and lethal at times.

It is hard not to conclude that for a significant minority in Hong Kong, there is a bedrock belief that the CPC is fundamentally bad – for some, simply evil. The project, conceived and organized by the CPC, which has achieved the greatest poverty relief ever seen anywhere, by orders of magnitude, over the last 40 years does not seem to count within a political reckoning which remains rooted in the worst memories of post-1949 China. The characterization of China's achievements since 1978 as some sort of *Frankenstein nightmare* by Professor Janos Kornai in 2019 is amazingly inappropriate.[67] The additional American-led argument that somehow China's self-made rise is actually a "gift of the West" is also

63 Edesess, Michael, "If Hong Kong Protesters Have a Dream, They Need Their Own Martin Luther King to Realise It", *South China Morning Post,* July 31, 2019, available at: https://www.scmp.com/comment/opinion/article/3020505/if-hong-kong-protesters-have-dream-they-need-their-own-martin (accessed August 3, 2019).

64 This PD-radical solidarity has included the defence of violence as a legitimate political tactic. See Cross, Grenville, "No Concessions to Extremists, Foreign Agencies or the Misguided in Hong Kong" *CGTN,* July 31, 2019, available at: https://news.cgtn.com/news/2019-07-31/No-concessions-to-extremists-foreign-agencies-or-the-misguided-in-HK-IKX4nG74J2/index.html (accessed August 3, 2019).

65 See Lo, Sonny Shiu Hing, "Beijing's National Security Policy on Hong Kong", *Macau Business,* August 1, 2019, available at: https://www.macaubusiness.com/opinion-beijings-national-security-policy-on-hong-kong/ (accessed August 2, 2019)

66 While mainstream PDs claim that all the protesting has a primary focus on securing universal suffrage, the militant wing, using political violence repeatedly, seeks to differ: they want independence for Hong Kong, above all. See Wan, "Beijing Is Wrong"; and Taylor and Yu, "Hong Kong Anti-Police Violence".

67 Nair, "China's Rise".

vainly wrong.[68] Whatever the failings of the CPC, this has been an extraordinary triumph unmatched in human history.

Meanwhile, there are signs amongst both onshore and offshore Mainland Chinese of growing impatience with the tendency of Hong Kong residents to stress all the downsides they see arising from being part of China coupled with a failure to weigh their good fortune in the balance, which fortune is a direct product of the highly beneficial, to the HKSAR, economic relationship with China. They consider that the HKSAR enjoys special treatment, but the city demonstrates serial ingratitude and constantly makes trouble for China.[69]

At one level, it is curious that the young in Hong Kong are significantly less happy than their counterparts in Singapore.[70] The curiosity here arises from the fact that political, media, and social controls in Singapore are plainly more stringent than in Hong Kong. Western human rights norms are made heavily subject to the public interest as set down by the government in Singapore: a shrewdly developed form of soft authoritarianism applies.[71] The young in Singapore are thus enjoying greater happiness not as a result of greater human rights freedoms than enjoyed in the HKSAR, on the contrary. The basis of their better living experience is, above all, the safety and stability which are hallmarks of the Singapore governance regime. As noted in Chapter 5, Singapore does very well according to international Rule of Law measures and conspicuously well in terms of low-corruption assessments. It is also a highly efficient and successful city-state – building on that robust, low-crime, Rule of Law regime.[72]

In the case of almost all of the US measures taken to counter or contain the rise of China, over recent years, Washington has cited US national security concerns as being pivotal. The logic of running a single-party State guarantees an intensified emphasis on national security. The continuing US antipathy towards China amplifies this focus in Beijing. It is within this context that repeated visits

68 Ibid. If there were any dominant substance in such an argument, then it follows that the rise of the US to world superpower status, starting from the late nineteenth century, was not down to American entrepreneurship but was a "gift of the UK".

69 Kan, Karoline, "Mainland Chinese Lack Sympathy for Hong Kong Protestors", *Nikkei Asian Review,* July 30, 2019, available at: https://asia.nikkei.com/Opinion/Mainland-Chinese-lack-sympathy-for-Hong-Kong-protesters (accessed August 1, 2019).

70 Leung, Kanis, "Younger People in Hong Kong Less Happy than Peers in Singapore Even before Extradition Bill Crisis, Survey Shows", *South China Morning Post,* July 31, 2019, available at: https://www.scmp.com/news/hong-kong/politics/article/3020705/younger-people-hong-kong-less-happy-peers-singapore-even (accessed August 1, 2019).

71 Numbers of Western commentators, especially, have labelled Singapore as being a "soft authoritarian" State. For a thoughtful overview of this debate, see Huang, Kun, "Is Singapore an Authoritarian Government", *Quora,* October 7, 2017, available at: https://www.quora.com/Is-Singapore-an-authoritarian-government (accessed March 17, 2019).

72 Mahbubani, Kishmore, "Why Singapore Is the World's Most Successful Society", *HuffPost,* December 6, 2017, available at: https://www.huffpost.com/entry/singapore-world-successful-society_b_7934988 (accessed August 1, 2019).

from Hong Kong to the US by a wide range of leading PD figures seeking US backing and assistance for their causes – and to counter Beijing – play out.[73]

One former PD LegCo member, now a non-portfolio member of the HKSAR Cabinet (Exco) argued, in mid-2019, that:

> We need to gain the trust and confidence of Beijing so they can allow us the freedom of political reform. They don't want to see Hong Kong as a base of subversion. And I'm sorry, we are doing exactly that.[74]

The Extradition Bill marches in 2019 repeatedly turned into violent anti-Government and anti-Beijing political protests, involving large-scale rioting and unprecedented attacks on the Police, all of which badly undermined Hong Kong's highly valued Rule of Law regime.[75] What happened showed how a prized achievement secured over many decades could be put at grave risk within a matter of months.[76]

The serious political-legal problems facing Hong Kong are increasingly accompanied by worrying political-economic challenges. The alternative locations for doing business within the Mainland, especially Shanghai and Shenzhen, are steadily becoming more competitive in terms of providing logistic, business, and professional services.[77] A new Beijing policy has already signalled how Shenzhen can take over significant aspects of Hong Kong's role within China, stressing the scope for both economic and administrative reforms to secure this outcome.[78]

73 See, for example, Cheung, Tony, "Beijing Slams Hong Kong Tycoon Jimmy Lai and US Officials over Washington Meetings on Extradition Bill, Using Words 'National Scum and Hong Kong Sinners'", *South China Morning Post,* July 9, 2019, available at: https://www.scmp.com/news/hong-kong/politics/article/3017868/beijing-foreign-office-slams-hong-kong-tycoon-jimmy-lai-and (accessed July 28, 2019).

74 "Political Reform Needs Beijing's Trust Says Ronny Tong", *The Standard,* June 12, 2019, available at: http://www.thestandard.com.hk/breaking-news.php?id=129550&sid=4 (accessed July 28, 2019).

75 President Trump confirmed that Hong Kong "had riots for a long period of time". He added that the problem was a matter between Hong Kong and Beijing because "Hong Kong is a part of China". See "Trump Calls Hong Kong Protests 'Riots', Says Internal Matter for China", *Straits Times,* August 2, 2019, available at: https://www.straitstimes.com/world/united-states/trump-says-he-wont-give-advice-to-china-on-hong-kong-protests (accessed August 2, 2019).

76 Lhatoo, Yonden, "It's Not Only Law and Order, Hong Kong's Protest Crisis Is Taking a Tragic Toll on Basic Humanity and Decency", *South China Morning Post,* August 3, 2019, available at: https://www.scmp.com/news/hong-kong/politics/article/3021315/its-not-only-law-and-order-hong-kongs-protest-crisis-taking (accessed August 4, 2019).

77 Lee, Amanda, "Hong Kong Protests Could Threaten City's Status as an International Shipping Hub, Analysts Say", *South China Morning Post,* August 16, 2019, available at: https://www.scmp.com/economy/china-economy/article/3022986/hong-kong-protests-could-threaten-citys-status-international (accessed August 16, 2019).

78 Ma, Josephine, Wong, Catherine, and Xie, Echo, "Why China Is Looking to Shenzhen – Not Hong Kong – to Reinvent the Future", *South China Morning Post,* July 31, 2019, available at: https://www.scmp.com/news/china/politics/article/3020710/why-china-looking-shenzhen-and-not-hong-kong-reinvent-its (accessed August 3, 2019). See also Hinata,

These increasing PRC "success stories" have diminished Hong Kong's ranking within China. This, arguably, has amplified Hong Kong's "identity crisis", intensifying hostility to the Mainland within certain sections of society.[79]

Some highlight how Hong Kong's robust Rule of Law regime, not least in the area of Commercial Law, gives the HKSAR a very special advantage which cannot be matched on the Mainland. It would be a mistake, however, to assume that the key elements of such a Commercial Law regime – independent, highly professional courts, and a well-trained legal profession – cannot be replicated within one or more particular, chosen jurisdictions in China over the next one to two decades.[80] Singapore has demonstrated how this can be resiliently managed, with the State retaining close control over how the Public Law system operates. Jianlin Chen argues that by carving out politically sensitive cases from the jurisdiction of the courts, the judiciary in Singapore is allowed to focus on everyday justice and the pursuit of professionalization without the disturbance of politics.[81]

It must be recognized the sort of independent Commercial Law regime envisaged *within* the PRC will not be established swiftly. China's OPS is an exceptional state where "the political sphere is directly dominated by the Party and a legal sphere operates in the long shadow of the Party".[82] The problem is to move from allowing "private law breathing room to facilitate market transactions" to manifest a commitment to a highly professionalized Rule of Law regime to govern Commercial Law within a chosen jurisdiction within China.[83] The growing levels of legal professionalization in China are clear, however, and, although the Private Law legal system remains "necessarily shallow in its roots and fragile in its existence, the soil for its growth is there".[84] For the reasons already outlined, the political and economic incentives to build an independent Commercial Law regime – over the next 10–20 years – within a particular jurisdiction within the

Yusuke, "China Works to Turn Shenzhen into the New Hong Kong", *Nikkei Asian Review*, August 19, 2019, available at: https://asia.nikkei.com/Spotlight/Hong-Kong-protests/China-works-to-turn-Shenzhen-into-the-new-Hong-Kong (accessed August 19, 2019).

79 Fu, Yu, "The Hong Kong Demonstrations and Identity Crisis", *IPP Review*, August 26, 2019, available at: https://ippreview.com/index.php/Blog/single/id/1063.html (accessed September 1, 2019).

80 *The Economist* acknowledges the shrinking significance of the HKSAR within the overall Chinese economy but still stresses Hong Kong's "huge importance" to China in terms of banking and related services and its Rule of Law strengths (see "Chinese Troops Must Stay Off the Streets of Hong Kong", *The Economist*, August 8, 2019). This analysis is too static. It fails to see the possibility of substantial legal sector developments in Commercial Law in the PRC over the next two decades. Another measure of the constrained perspective is the way this editorial warns darkly about the use of any Mainland forces in the HKSAR to help cope with the continuous rioting and yet fails to denounce the rioting itself.

81 See Chen, Weitseng and Fu, Hualing, "Authoritarian Legality, the Rule of Law and Democracy" (on file with the author).

82 Fu, Hualing, "Duality and China's Struggle for Legal Autonomy" (2019) 1 *China Perspectives,* 3.

83 Ibid.

84 Ibid.

PRC have intensified measurably in 2019. There are good reasons to expect that Shenzhen may be particularly well placed to take up this opportunity. It is adjacent to Hong Kong and already directly connected by high-speed rail with convenient, co-located border-crossing facilities (see Chapter 6). There are already an increasingly large number of highly skilled, Commercial Law professionals practising in the HKSAR who have dual Mainland and Hong Kong qualifications. Shenzhen could thus draw on this pool of relevant legal talent and those recruited would retain an option to live in Hong Kong whilst working across the border.

Another factor or some significance is that the Hong Kong Dollar is a freely tradable currency, whereas the Chinese Yuan is not. How long, however, will this distinction continue to advantage the HKSAR? Even given the restraints imposed by the Sino-US Trade War, the change to full convertibility of the Yuan is still regarded as a question of when, not if, with 2030 now proposed as a delayed but feasible target year.[85]

A debate template which treats rights-as-trumps significantly shapes discussion within the public space in the HKSAR. The need for this focus is robustly justified as a key bulwark against the intrusion of over-mighty Beijing.[86] Unfortunately, when most fervently felt, this belief system also underpins general uncompromising attitudes which leave little room for active negotiation. Moreover, it adds contextual support for violent, at times fanatical, anti-government activism.

The potentially adverse social-economic impact on the HKSAR is plainly evident.[87] But for those convinced by their militant virtue, this is either not seen or is not a matter to be concerned about as a greater good is sought.[88] It seems that some militant protestors believe, remarkably, that Hong Kong retains a capacity to trigger a collapse of the Chinese economy. Because this would punish a China which is scorned, this is a desired outcome.[89] All of these ill-advised viewpoints

85 Yiu, Enoch, "Trump's Policies Make a Fully Convertible Yuan by 2020 Impossible, Say Financial Experts", *South China Morning Post*, January 11, 2018, available at: https://www.scmp.com/business/banking-finance/article/2127771/trumps-policies-make-fully-convertible-yuan-2020-impossible (accessed August 20, 2019).

86 Chan, "Demise of One Country Two Systems".

87 Russolillo, Steve and Chiu, Joanne, "Protests Take a Toll on Hong Kong's Economy", *Wall Street Journal*, July 31 2019.

88 Risks identified as flowing from the many weeks of violent political upheaval include significantly slowed growth across many sectors (equivalent to the impact of the SARS epidemic); rising bankruptcies; credit-rating downgrades; and forfeiture of Hong Kong's leading position as an international finance centre. See Young, Raymond, "Small Steps by the Government Could Defuse Hong Kong's Biggest Crisis", *South China Morning Post*, August 10, 2019, available at: https://www.scmp.com/comment/opinion/article/3022270/small-steps-government-could-defuse-hong-kongs-biggest-crisis (accessed August 10, 2019).

89 Vincent, Danny, "Hong Kong Protests: What Do Young People Want?" *BBC News*, August 22, 2019, available at: https://www.bbc.com/news/newsbeat-49371809 (accessed August 22, 2019.

amplify the risk of Hong Kong's steady economic decline within China.[90] By mid-August 2019, there was a measurable threat of a recession in Hong Kong driven, in part, by the previous two to three months of political rioting. The stock market was down by 25%, tourist arrivals down by 30%, and hotel prices reduced by 50%: the threats to a range of businesses – and to employment – were severe.[91] The HKSAR Government announced a series of ***mini-budget*** measures to counter the impact of the downturn.[92]

The Chinese future

The analysis in Chapter 9 makes clear how China's current success stands on the shoulders of and draws on well over 2,000 years of unequalled civilizational history. The accompanying discussions of the British legacy, the strained Sino-American relationship, and where Hong Kong currently finds itself each provides important context for reviewing the future political constitutional options which face the HKSAR. Before commencing that assessment, however, it is important to look broadly at how China itself may be set to adapt over coming decades in terms of its fundamental political operation.

One needs to make certain grounded assumptions in undertaking this analysis. First, for reasons given above, it is clear that Hong Kong is now, in fact and constitutionally, an inalienable part of China. Next, the CPC has been the valid single governing party of the PRC since 1949 and, although one cannot say that this will remain so forever, the most sound working assumption to adopt is that the CPC will retain an enduring, dominant governing role within China. Considered research by a principal American long-term observer of China supports this assumption.[93] Recent analysis also argues that China is better placed than the US

90 Chan, Bernard, "Allowing the Unrest to Hurt Hong Kong's Image as a Safe City Will Hurt All of Us", *South China Morning Post,* August 2, 2019, available at: https://www.scmp.com/comment/opinion/article/3020827/allowing-unrest-hurt-hong-kongs-image-safe-city-will-hurt-all-us (accessed August 2, 2019).

91 Leung, Kanis, Yeo, Rachel, Tsang, Denise, Lee, Danny, and Chan, Athena, "Hong Kong's Core Industries Hammered by Anti-Government Protest Crisis with Deep Drops in Retail, Tourism and Stock Market", *South China Morning Post*, August 22, 2019, available at: https://www.scmp.com/news/hong-kong/hong-kong-economy/article/3023985/hong-kongs-core-industries-hammered-anti (accessed August 23, 2019).

92 Wong, Olga and Cheung, Tony, "1.43 Million Taxpayers, Low-Income Households Set to Benefit as Hong Kong Government Unveils 'Mini Budget' Amid Gloomy Economic Outlook", *South China Morning Post*, August 15, 2019, available at: https://www.scmp.com/news/hong-kong/politics/article/3022938/hong-kong-government-set-announce-mini-budget-measures-ease (accessed August 15, 2019).

93 See Mearsheimer, John, *Harper Lecture: Can China Rise Peacefully?* December 18, 2013, available at: https://www.youtube.com/watch?v=0DMn4PmiDeQ (accessed September 2, 2019). Professor Mearsheimer is candid about his personal desire to see the US remain, in the twenty-first century, the dominant hegemonic power it became in the twentieth century. However, he is equally candid in assuming that China's exceptional economic rise will likely continue, which means that, given a population four times larger than that of the US, it will

to endure a long trade war.[94] Another respected commentator says, unambiguously, that China will grow to become the world's largest economy.[95] Moreover, apart from all the political institutional and operational measures taken to secure the continuation of the OPS in China, still more important in terms of sustaining the Party in its primary political role is the incomparable, poverty-reducing, performance legitimacy achieved (under CPC leadership). This is the foremost outcome of the new *social contract* forged between the CPC and the Chinese people to which the CPC has adhered.[96] Internationally, what is striking is that China's emergence as a great power has not, as in so many cases in the past, relied on a concomitant geopolitical impulse to disrupt the world order. China wants its weight to be felt – but within the existing world order.[97]

What, however, may flow from the firmly predicted continuing growth in China, with its huge 1.4 billion population and unique history? We saw in Chapter 2 how Rawls furnishes us not only with a conception of a workable relationship between liberty and economic welfare in liberal-democratic society but also with a workable approach to the evaluation of undemocratic and non-liberal policies adopted in societies at a lower level of advancement (in the Rawlsian sense) compared to developed liberal democracies. Such policies can be justified if they are to everybody's advantage, which is mainly a question of economic welfare, and if they prepare the way for the development of a society, which is more just and fair. There is a prima facie argument that China's OPS satisfies the first part of this Rawls-based assessment of basic legitimacy. Economic development in the PRC over the last 40 years has stressed the provision of certain primary goods (such as enhanced life expectancy, access to education, and work opportunities and basic liberties) to the widest spectrum of the population. This, though, leaves the question open as to what sort of more just and fair future one should expect to see built on these foundations.

As explained above, it is foreseeable that China's middle class may grow to be double that of the US, within another 20 years. It is reasonable to predict that this will be a society where the population anticipates distinctly enhanced governance transparency and accountability, conspicuously lower corruption levels, and measurably improved justice and fairness. But what benchmarks should we

---

develop into the world's largest economy over coming decades. Mearsheimer also notes that the resulting challenge for the US would not be any less, even if China were to adopt some form of liberal democracy (which is not something he expects to happen).

94 Wu, Wendy, "US Firms that Leave China on Donald Trump's 'Order' Will Only Hurt Themselves, Experts Say", *South China Morning Post*, September 1, 2019, available at: https://www.scmp.com/news/china/diplomacy/article/3025213/us-firms-leave-china-donald-trumps-order-will-only-hurt?utm_medium=email&utm_source=mailchimp&utm_campaign=enlz-scmp_today&utm_content=20190902&MCUID=1ff1e043d2&MCCampaignID=0e5fbd783b&MCAccountID=3775521f5f542047246d9c827&tc=33 (accessed September 2, 2019).

95 Mahbuban, *Has the West Lost It?*, 90.

96 Ibid., 14.

97 Lee, "Hong Kong Can Solve".

anticipate might be applied looking forward, in China, to test such progress? Rawls would point to justice as fairness, based on the Western political philosophy paradigm which, in an economically well-developed society, should prioritize basic liberties over the pursuit of economic welfare.

When Rawls published his seminal *A Theory of Justice*, in 1971, the world was a place where Western views and thinking remained as globally dominant (not least in politics, philosophy, economics, and science) as they had been for the previous 200 years. Although all those deep influences, which trace back to the Enlightenment, continue to shape life globally, today's world is no longer the same. The rise of China – and India – and the comparative decline of the US and Europe are now geopolitical facts on the ground and these trends are set to continue.[98]

Kishore Mahbubani says that such shifts in economic dominance are of crucial importance for the world and particularly for Asia. Moreover, especially in East Asia, the test of societal accomplishment is, above all, grounded in measures of widely shared economic success.[99] Singapore, Mahbubani argues (using this yardstick), has created the world's most successful society.[100] There is resonance here with Joseph Weiler's analysis of performance legitimacy discussed in Chapter 2.

Mahbubani's arguments highlighting Singapore's remarkable enduring success as a society are important in this discussion about China. Singapore remains what is regularly termed a soft authoritarian state (see above). The basis of the better living experience in Singapore includes the safety and stability which are hallmarks of the Singapore governance regime coupled with low-corruption levels and high efficiency which spreads economic and social benefits widely across the entire population. Western human rights norms are made subject to the public interest, as detailed by the Singapore Government and understood by the

98 By 2050, one study by PriceWaterhouseCoopers argues that China and India will account for well over one third of the world economy while the US and Europe will account for under 25%. See Jolly, Richard, "Review of Kishore Mahbubani's 'Has the West Lost It?'", *Institute of Development Studies*, June 19, 2018, available at: https://www.ids.ac.uk/opinions/richard-jolly-reviews-kishore-mahbubanis-has-the-west-lost-it/ (accessed August 7, 2019).

99 Jolly, ibid. There is a *utilitarian* aspect to making successful, broad economic outcomes a paramount assessment concern. Utilitarian concepts, with their individualist underpinning, are tempered in East Asia, however, by the impact of social ontologies which stress the importance of "molecular" living (through the family).

100 Mahbubani, Kishmore, "Why Singapore Is the World's Most Successful Society", *HuffPost*, December 6, 2017, available at: https://www.huffpost.com/entry/singapore-world-successful-society_b_7934988 (accessed August 1, 2019). There are, however, some internal political stresses in Singapore; see Bowie, Nile, "Singapore's Lee Family Feud Gets Political", *Asia Times*, August 12, 2019, available at: https://www.asiatimes.com/2019/08/article/singapores-lee-family-feud-gets-political/ (accessed August 13, 2019).

majority of the population.[101] Personal autonomy is important, but it does not trump all else as a measure of societal well-being.

Does Singapore today present, writ small, China's political-economic destiny in 30 years? We cannot know this for sure but, broadly speaking, the idea of China growing and adapting to become "200 Singapores" is more a probable prospect, looking forward to the 100th anniversary of the PRC in 2049, than any sort of significant convergence with the mainstream, Enlightenment-grounded, Western liberal-democratic model. This is the China which Hong Kong may credibly anticipate being a part of, over decades to come. A China that, if all goes as well as it might, will retain a strong paternalistic State subject to the robust sort of legalized governance accountability and transparency regimes one finds embedded in Singapore. Following this prototype, such a regime would also tolerate religious and other societal freedoms and work to fix manifest inequalities of wealth. Based on the Singapore model, this process of development may, in due course, include democratic elections – paired with a widely supported, dominant single party. Finally, Chapter 4 explains how crucial adequate financing is to secure a widely effective Rule of Law regime. China's remarkable economic growth at least means it has a growing capacity to satisfy this requirement.

Some may argue that the example of Taiwan, with its fully-fledged multiparty democracy, offers a more persuasive alternative model for the PRC to follow in the medium-long term. If my argument about the primacy of performance legitimacy (drawing on Mahbubani and Weiler) is correct, however, Taiwan now presents, comparatively, a multi-decade record of too much economically distorting, political contestation and not enough consistent performance legitimacy. Moreover, Professor Xu has argued (see Chapter 9) that China's historical institutional structure, with its central reliance on bureaucratic governance, provided the foundations for the unprecedented durability of the Chinese imperial system. According to this argument, this same system has had a lasting influence on modern China. When this *path dependency* factor is taken into account, the Singapore model offers the more congruent and sustainable prototype, alternative political framework, compared to Taiwan.

There is one other Taiwan aspect that should be addressed. Taiwan is regarded, by Beijing, as "renegade province" which remains part of China. Some (including the KMT) in Taiwan accept that there is just "One China" but take a different view of what that term means. Others like the Democratic People's Party (DPP) implicitly or explicitly seek to establish Taiwan as a fully independent nation.[102]

101 Sim, Dewey, "Are Singaporeans Gloating at the Unrest Gripping Hong Kong?" *South China Morning Post*, August 10, 2019, available at: https://www.scmp.com/week-asia/politics/article/3022253/are-singaporeans-gloating-chaos-caused-hong-kong-protests (accessed August 10, 2019).

102 All these matters are discussed in a helpful background paper prepared by the US Council on Foreign Relations, see Albert, Eleanor, "China–Taiwan Relations", *Council on Foreign Relations*, July 2019, available at: https://www.cfr.org/backgrounder/china-taiwan-relations (accessed August 8, 2019).

The *modus vivendi* which has allowed the Mainland and Taiwan to engage economically on a very large scale has been subject to stress periods (most of all when the DPP is in power in Taiwan), but it has endured for the benefit of both jurisdictions for many decades.[103] OCTS has long been proffered by Beijing to Taiwan as a basis for resolution of the cross-strait standoff which has lasted since 1949. Both the KMT and especially the DPP have rejected these overtures.[104]

Time, however, is on Beijing's side. There are cogent arguments, based on history and political-economic developments to date, that Taiwan will, in some manner, eventually be reunited with the Mainland. To begin with, there is little realistic chance of Taiwan ever being widely recognized around the world as an independent nation without the agreement of the PRC, which remains unthinkable. Next, current levels of integration are strikingly advanced. To take just one key example, well over 1 million Taiwanese already work and live on the Mainland and the number continues to grow.[105] The Taiwan–Beijing relationship remains strained, but this is a very mature – and largely stable – form of a strained relationship, where substantial mutual benefits are manifest.[106]

As noted in Chapter 5, the Joint Declaration speaks of the Basic Policies for the HKSAR listed therein remaining unchanged for 50 years (in Clause 1(12)). The Joint Declaration does not, however, mandate that any change must take place in 2047. Although there is resonance with Clause 1(12) of the Joint Declaration in Article 5 of the Basic Law of the HKSAR, there is no Basic Law "sunset provision". The Basic Law is drafted to operate indefinitely notwithstanding regular statements to the contrary in the international media.[107] The Basic Law can be amended, however, as is discussed below. And, although this is not likely, it can be repealed by the SCNPC after July 1, 2047.[108]

The Basic Law is the operational cornerstone of OCTS. If OCTS is working well for the HKSAR – *and for Beijing* – then we can predict that it retains strong prospects of continuing to be applied in the long term. If the experience is that it

103 Heng, Michael, "The Two Sides of the Taiwan Strait: A Contrarian View", *IPP Review*, August 2, 2019, available at: https://ippreview.com/index.php/Blog/single/id/1044.html (accessed August 8, 2019).

104 Albert, "China–Taiwan Relations".

105 Heng, "The Two Sides of the Taiwan Strait". See also Tai, Michael, "Two Reasons Taiwan Must Come to Terms with China", *South China Morning Post*, December 3, 2018, available at: https://www.scmp.com/comment/insight-opinion/united-states/article/2175825/two-reasons-taiwan-must-come-terms-china (accessed August 8, 2019).

106 War between the PRC and Taiwan remains a possibility; this has, however, essentially been avoided for 70 years despite several periods of high tension.

107 See, for example, Cheung, Helier and Hughes, Robert, "Why Are There Protests in Hong Kong? All the Context You Need", *BBC News*, July 25, 2019, available at: https://www.bbc.com/news/world-asia-china-48607723 (accessed August 2, 2019), where the authors say that in 28 years' time the Basic Law expires, which is wrong.

108 After July 1, 2047, a repeal of the Basic Law would not directly contravene either Article 5 or Clause 12(1) of the Joint Declaration. Special circumstances would have to apply for a complete repeal to make sense (for example, the passage of a new PRC Constitution).

is not working well for *both* Hong Kong and Beijing, then its long-term durability in its current form is called into question. It remains more likely than not that a version of OCTS – and the Basic Law – may be retained after 2047. But it is also more probable that both will be changed substantially in 2047 (if not before) after what has unfolded in 2019 in the HKSAR, not least to cover operational areas such as those noted below related to LegCo, the media, education, and Article 23.

For the HKSAR – and OCTS – 2019 has been a turning point year. Hong Kong has experienced levels of continuous violent political pressure not seen for over 50 years. The massive peaceful protests which ushered in this period of politics by confrontational intimidation were originally centred on the argued, amplified risks to Hong Kong people arising from the Extradition Bill. The clearest majority marching did so to make their case and not to create an insurgency against the local government still less against Beijing. The focus of the groups which, in due course, took over from (some say hijacked) the peaceful mass protests has been quite different, however. One commentator argues that four main, violent activist groups emerged as the militant protesting grew: thrill seekers, anarchists, separatists, and terrorists, with the latter two being the most dangerous.[109] The separatists grew in importance and influence with their clear message to *Reclaim (or Liberate) Hong Kong with a Revolution of Our Times.* The campaign to separate the HKSAR from China included another clear refrain, *Hong Kong is not China* combined with the destruction of copies of the Basic Law and attacks on symbols of China in Hong Kong, including the national flag. The terrorist group included those who actively sought to elevate the level of violence, inter alia, by bomb-making, including the potential use of TATP, the explosive responsible for 52 deaths in the London bombings of 2005 and 130 deaths in the Paris bombings in 2015.[110] Eventually, the five demands headlined after the protesting gathered pace in June were heard less, replaced by the separatist slogans noted above, stressing the liberation of the HKSAR.[111]

Unfortunately, too many within the PD camp either sought to excuse or explain the violence as being, incongruously, primarily the fault of the HKSAR

109 Cross, Grenville, "If Reason Prevails, Hong Kong Still Has a Future", *China Daily – Hong Kong*, August 8, 2019. See also Vanderklippe, Nathan, "How Hong Kong's Protestors Have 'Already Reached a Point of No Return'", *The Globe and Mail*, August 11, 2019, available at: https://www.theglobeandmail.com/world/article-how-hong-kongs-protesters-have-already-reached-a-point-of-no-return/ (accessed August 12, 2019).

110 Ibid.

111 "New Phase as Protesters and Police Clash across Hong Kong in Guerilla-Style Battles", *South China Morning Post*, August 10, 2019, available at: https://www.scmp.com/news/hong-kong/politics/article/3022290/new-phase-protesters-and-police-clash-across-north-hong?utm_medium=email&utm_source=mailchimp&utm_campaign=enlz-scmp_today&utm_content=20190811&MCUID=1ff1e043d2&MCCampaignID=20ac9c318d&MCAccountID=3775521f5f542047246d9c827&tc=3 (accessed August 11, 2019).

Government.[112] These "devil-makes-them-do-it" arguments implicitly claim that the violent protestors lack the basic personal agency (or responsibility) to tell right from wrong. It is a challenge to sustain the Rule of Law when such a principle is maintained (not least by prominent lawyers).[113] Some PD members tried to urge more restraint by radical and violent protestors while others reduced their public appearances possibly concerned not to be associated with the increasing extent and levels of violent protesting and intimidation.[114] It is difficult to find anyone from within the PD mainstream who stood up to say, openly and clearly, that the violent protesting was simply wrong and contrary to the most basic principles of the Rule of Law.

Among the large numbers engaged in confrontational and violent protesting, many still argued that, as the HKSAR Government did not otherwise listen to them, they had no choice but to resort to violent protesting.[115] Differences emerged within the militant protesting ranks but less radical elements felt they must continue to show solidarity with the most radical and violent protestors.[116] According to one review, the peaceful marchers and the well-equipped confrontational group (engaged in rioting) were co-dependent. One activist, who admitted to violent protesting, reasoned that the two groups comprised a joint force.[117]

Certainly, both the HKSAR Government and Beijing took the same unbending view towards the serial political rioting: the Extradition Bill had been declared "dead"; there would be no further concessions or compromises whilst the violence

112 This is an example of acute determinism which leads to arguments denying free will and excusing inexcusable behaviour. To what extent certain media coverage may embolden radical protestors or even grant implicit permission for violent activism is matter worthy of further analysis. One new study has investigated the influence of the media on far-right, aggressive activism. See Morton Rick, "Murdoch Media Fuels Far-Right Recruitment", *The Saturday Paper,* August 10, 2019, available at: https://www.thesaturdaypaper.com.au/news/politics/2019/08/10/murdoch-media-fuels-far-right-recruitment/15653592008581 (accessed August 12, 2019).

113 Cross, "If Reason Prevails".

114 Chan, Athena and Tsang, Emily, "Pan-Democrat Lawmakers Call on Protesters to Calm Down to Avoid 'Falling into Government's Trap', while Hong Kong Feminist Activist Incurs Wrath of Demonstrators over Tin Shui Wai Arrests", *South China Morning Post,* August 7, 2019, available at: https://www.scmp.com/news/hong-kong/politics/article/3021713/pan-democrat-lawmakers-call-protesters-calm-down-avoid (accessed August 9, 2019).

115 Cheung, Gary and Lum, Alvin, "Two Months On, What Do Hong Kong Protestors Really Want", *South China Morning Post,* August 9, 2019, available at: https://www.scmp.com/news/hong-kong/politics/article/3022057/two-months-and-nearly-2000-rounds-tear-gas-later-what-do (accessed August 9, 2019). This is another deployment of severe determinism to justify lawless behaviour.

116 Ibid.

117 Zaharia, Marius, Tam, Felix, and Jim, Clare, "Frontline Protesters Make Case for Violence in Hong Kong Protests", *Reuters World News,* August 22, 2019, available at: https://www.reuters.com/article/us-hongkong-protests-violence-analysis/frontline-view-making-the-case-for-violence-in-hong-kong-protests-idUSKCN1VB2LV (accessed August 23, 2019).

continued; and above all, the violence, which had become a serious threat to the well-being and economy of the HKSAR and to the sovereignty of China within Hong Kong, had to cease.[118] The possibility of a full enquiry of some sort (presumably with wide terms of reference – see Chapter 9) was left open – after the cessation of all violence.[119]

Meanwhile, the recognition by Beijing of how seriously they regarded what was happening in Hong Kong was made clear by repeated references to threats perceived not just to the HKSAR but to the OCTS regime and to national sovereignty and national security through the creation of a budding East European style *colour revolution*.[120] All talk of the specific deployment of any Mainland forces in Hong Kong was avoided, but clear general warnings of intervention by Beijing if the crisis worsened were repeatedly voiced.[121]

Some argue that Beijing's obduracy over political reform in the HKSAR combined with ongoing poor decision-making and lack of responsiveness by the HKSAR Government (combined with partial immobilization) explain most of how Hong Kong came to find itself in the midst of this crisis. It must be said that Hong Kong, itself, is primarily responsible for getting itself into this awful predicament and the Government is not blameless. There is, however, a more elemental reason why primary responsibility lies in Hong Kong. For many years, as explained in Chapter 6, the PDs were able to use filibustering and related techniques to reduce the operating efficiency of LegCo greatly. Much needed amendments to LegCo procedures in December 2017 reduced the scope for this obstructive approach markedly. But in 2019, with the Extradition Bill, the PDs demonstrated an ability not just to slow down LegCo procedures but a capacity, given the right political opportunity (and significant, persuaded public support), ultimately, to close down the operation of LegCo entirely (see Chapter 9) for a period. They were able to thwart the normal daily operation of one of the key constitutional institutions of government in the HKSAR. It is true that the government took an unyielding approach prior to the extraordinary shutdown of LegCo, which invited increased confrontational politics. However, the ferocity of the PD opposition to the Extradition Bill in LegCo followed by their utilization of the subsequent political opportunities were the primary sources from which the crisis developed.

So where does this leave Hong Kong looking forward. It was inevitable that the HKSAR would become drawn into and affected by the US-Sino Trade War.

118 A formal announcement was eventually made that the Extradition Bill was to be withdrawn.

119 Zaharia et al., "Frontline Protestors". See also Chung, Kimmy and Cheung, Tony, "Hong Kong Protests Have 'Obvious Characteristics of Colour Revolution', Top Beijing Official Warns Amid 'Worst Crisis since 1997 Handover'", *South China Morning Post*, August 8, 2019, available at: https://www.scmp.com/news/hong-kong/politics/article/3021877/protests-colour-revolution-threatening-hong-kong-abyss-top (accessed August 9, 2019).

120 See Chung and Cheung, ibid.

121 "Zhang Warns Beijing 'Would Intervene' as Crisis Worsens", *The Standard*, August 8, 2019.

But the eager relationship building between leading PDs and leading politicians in Washington – and US Consulate staff in Hong Kong meeting leading anti-government activists – has aggravated the negative aspects, for Beijing, of Hong Kong's role within this geopolitical contest.[122] Those politicians, media operatives, and others in Hong Kong who are actively hostile to Beijing and also to the local government are openly calling for support from outside to counter Beijing in substantial ways at time when geopolitical stress is rising.[123] As it happens, it is far from clear that it is the US which is best placed to secure the greatest advantage from this economic conflict [124]

Hong Kong is truly remarkable. It is inconceivable that opposition politicians or activists from Singapore, for example, could undertake such journeys and engagements repeatedly without being sanctioned. But in the HKSAR, despite all the PD-claimed reductions in rights, it is expected that such persons from Hong Kong must be allowed to act in ways contrary to the expressed interests of Beijing, return to the HKSAR, and repeat such exercises without intervention.[125] And they are allowed to do so.[126] Moreover, the conspicuous freedom to protest in public outlined in Chapter 7 continued to be applied in the HKSAR as far as was possible throughout the period of systematic political rioting which began in mid-2019. Then there is the fact that violent protesters have been allowed to take maximum measures to disguise their identity and they have become expert at covering or destroying CCTV cameras (and even traffic lights) and using

122 "US Calls China 'Thuggish' after HK Complaint", *RTHK*, August 9, 2019, available at: https://news.rthk.hk/rthk/en/component/k2/1473553-20190809.htm (accessed August 9, 2019).

123 Wong, Joshua and Chow, Alex, "The People of Hong Kong Will Not Be Cowed by China", *New York Times*, August 31, 2019, available at: https://www.nytimes.com/2019/08/31/opinion/hong-kong-protest-joshua-wong.html?action=click&module=Opinion&pgtype=Homepage (accessed September 1, 2019). Interestingly, after being arrested on serious charges in Hong Kong on August 30, 2019, Mr. Wong was advised he was still free to travel to the Washington to advocate adverse US economic intervention in the HKSAR. See "Hong Kong Pro-Democracy Activists Charged over Siege of Police Headquarters in June", *Hong Kong Free Press*, August 30, 2019, available at: https://www.hongkongfp.com/2019/08/30/hong-kong-pro-democracy-activists-charged-siege-police-headquarters-june/ (accessed September 1, 2019).

124 Wang, Xiangwei, "Trump's Face Changing Used to Rattle China, but Time Is Now on Beijing's Side", *South China Morning Post*, August 31, 2019, available at: https://www.scmp.com/week-asia/opinion/article/3025145/trumps-face-changing-used-rattle-china-time-now-beijings-side (accessed September 1, 2019).

125 See, for example, Nip, Amy, "Protest Group Calls for Foreign Assistance", *The Standard*, August 8, 2019, available at: http://www.thestandard.com.hk/section-news.php?id=210466&story_id=50041917&d_str=20190808&sid=11 (accessed August 9, 2019).

126 Ng, Kang-chung, "Hong Kong Opposition Lawmakers Promise Not to 'Bad-Mouth' City during Meeting with US Officials, but Will Give Honest Appraisal of Extradition Bill Unrest", *South China Morning Post*, August 13, 2019, available at: https://www.scmp.com/news/hong-kong/politics/article/3022489/hong-kong-opposition-lawmakers-promise-not-bad-mouth-city (accessed August 15, 2019).

intimidating collective laser lights,[127] often with impunity. Another comparative measure of freedom in the HKSAR is that while in Australia prisoners are typically not allowed to use the Internet or post on social media,[128] those imprisoned for crimes related to the OCM and the Mong Kok Riot in 2016 were able to maintain public communications via the Internet.[129]

All of this using and exploiting freedoms to the utmost for general activism and remonstrating (and while sustaining repetitive violent protesting) is a part of the mixture of factors undergirding the transition of the HKSAR into its worst crisis since 1997. There is almost certainly going to be a reaction, in time, to this profoundly disruptive political experience.

At this point, it is apt to recall that the British encountered repeated political crises in Hong Kong during their 155-year tenure (see Chapter 4). Commentators today regularly observe how the British managed to cope, adapt, and carry on very well after dealing with these crises. The British, however, possessed two key advantages denied to both the HKSAR and Beijing. First, they essentially enjoyed political-executive carte blanche, which they deployed recurrently, with discretion. There was no set of powerful constitutional rules as laid out in a Basic Law that constrained decision-making. Next, there was not the remotest need to abide by the principle of "Hong Kong people ruling Hong Kong" as embodied in OCTS and the Basic Law.[130] The British were able to remove and replace Governors and senior civil servants at will. And they did so repeatedly to help address crises and to upgrade needed special skills, for example.[131] Beijing, on the other hand, has to abide by all these constraining Basic Law stipulations. It has to work, with the HKSAR Government, within this conspicuously more restrictive constitutional framework.

Singapore is an independent city-state nation, of course. But it is still also reasonable to observe, for the sake of argument, that Singapore would make an ideal

127 Protest organizers have tried to play down this usage and even ridicule complaints from the Police. See Un, Phoenix, "Light Relief When Eyes Not Targeted", *The Standard*, August 8, 2019, available at: http://www.thestandard.com.hk/section-news.php?id=210460&sid=2 (accessed August 9, 2019). It is guaranteed, however, that if the Police used such instruments against protestors, there would be cries of foul play.

128 "Cardinal George Pell: Purported Letter from Prison Sparks Investigation", *The Guardian*, August 10, 2019, available at: https://www.theguardian.com/australia-news/2019/aug/10/cardinal-george-pell-purported-letter-from-prison-sparks-investigation (accessed August 11, 2019).

129 Lam, Jeffie, "Hong Kong's Pro-Independence Activist Edward Leung Appeals to Youth to Shun Hatred while Protesting over Extradition Bill in Note from Prison", *South China Morning Post*, July 29, 2019, available at: https://www.scmp.com/news/hong-kong/politics/article/3020526/hong-kongs-pro-independence-activist-edward-leung-appeals (accessed August 11, 2019).

130 "Hong Kong People Ruling Hong Kong – Introducing Hong Kong", *Hong Kong Economic and Trade Office*, August 6, 2019, available at: https://www.hketolondon.gov.hk/intro/hksar.htm (accessed August 10, 2019).

131 Goodstadt, Leo, *Uneasy Partners* (Hong Kong University Press, Hong Kong, 2005).

Special Administrative Region within the PRC: it is so successful, so well run, and so well controlled. There is a persuasive guide, here, for how Beijing might wish to see Hong Kong's political-legal framework further developed.[132] One key to its stability is the way that Singapore relies on a far more comprehensive set of firm legal controls to monitor and regulate political expression in the broadest sense. Most recently, Singapore passed a law in 2019 to augment the regulation of Internet-based communications and to control online "fake news" quite tightly.[133] These rules for maintaining stability as a paramount concern have also been widely internalized by Singaporeans.[134]

Hong Kong is not Singapore and it will always be different in fundamental ways. But this does not mean that the system of legal restraints in the HKSAR cannot be adapted and tightened with a view to taking out stronger insurance against destabilizing rebellions[135] or insurgencies[136] in the future. It is also worth remembering that strict public media (and education) controls were one of the measures used repeatedly by government during the BHK era to deal with perceived threats to political stability and social order.[137] Any move towards tighter legal controls on wilfully disruptive political activism in the HKSAR could, thus, also draw lessons from the British experience.

The British also passed the Emergency Regulations Ordinance (ERO) in 1922 in response to major industrial turmoil at that time. The British used the ERO in 1922 and again in 1967 to help quell deadly political riots at that time (see

132 As discussed above, a number of Hong Kong residents have shown interest in relocating to Singapore with its soft authoritarian, Rule of Law stability, to escape the instability and increasing lawlessness in the HKSAR. See also Sim, "Are Singaporeans Gloating".

133 See Jaipragas, Bhavan, "Singapore Introduces Anti-Fake News Law to Counter Falsehoods Aimed at 'Exploiting' the City's 'Fault Lines'", *South China Morning Post,* April 1, 2019, available at: https://www.scmp.com/week-asia/politics/article/3004196/singapore-introduces-anti-fake-news-law-counter-falsehoods-aimed (accessed June 7, 2019); and Staff and Agencies, "Singapore Fake News Law a 'Disaster' for Freedom of Speech, Says Rights Group", *The Guardian,* May 9, 2019, available at: https://www.theguardian.com/world/2019/may/09/singapore-fake-news-law-a-disaster-for-freedom-of-speech-says-rights-group (accessed June 7, 2019)

134 Sim, "Are Singaporeans Gloating". In this same article, one Hong Kong resident protested that Singaporeans kept labelling certain Hong Kong protestors as violent rioters and also said that Hong Kong people should accept that Hong Kong is part of China. Unfortunately, the Singaporean assessments are essentially accurate.

135 A rebellion is how one Hong Kong commentator described what unfolded in the HKSAR in 2019, see Chugani, Michael, "Can Carrie Lam, or Anyone, Defuse the Hong Kong Rebellion before the National Day Fireworks on October 1?" *South China Morning Post,* August 8, 2019, available at: https://www.scmp.com/comment/opinion/article/3021754/can-carrie-lam-or-anyone-defuse-hong-kong-rebellion-national-day (accessed August 10, 2019).

136 An insurgency was how one other Hong Kong commentator described what unfolded in the HKSAR in 2019, see Cross, "If Reason Prevails".

137 Loh, Christine, *Underground Front – The Chinese Communist Party in Hong Kong* (2nd ed.) (Hong Kong University Press, Hong Kong, 2018).

Chapter 7).[138] The ERO remains operative in the HKSAR and the Government did not rule out its possible use in 2019, in a selective way.[139] Concerns were expressed about the compatibility of ERO regulations with the rights guarantees in the Basic Law (which did not apply in 1922 or 1967).[140] This issue could, however, be resolved by an Interpretation under Article 158 of the Basic Law or by an Advisory Interpretation (see Chapter 6) supporting the use of the ERO if the particular circumstances were seen to require this. This would be a radical step but one allowed by Basic Law.

Before we look at the what and how of any such possible legally based framework adaptations, a pertinent question to ask is what may stand in the way of the HKSAR being persuaded to build a dominant consensus, from within, which reimagines Hong Kong as a constructive, long-term leading centre providing advanced business, professional, and technical services, inter alia, for all of China (and especially for the Greater Bay Area (GBA)[141])? After more than 20 years of post-reunification experience and taking into account what has unfolded in 2019, several key areas of concern can be identified: the failure to meet recurrent, powerful demands for *true democracy*[142]; the operation of LegCo; the role of the media (mainstream and social media); education; and the lack, thus far, of any new laws to implement Article 23 of the Basic Law. Social media (see Chapter 8) appear to have been foundational in stimulating anti-government sentiment in 2019 and also in aiding the organization of continuously disruptive and violent protesting.[143]

138 Cheung, Gary and Lum, Alvin, "Is Hong Kong on the Brink of Declaring Emergency Rule to Deal with Anti-Government Protesters?" *South China Morning Post*, August 30, 2019, available at: https://www.scmp.com/news/hong-kong/politics/article/3024980/hong-kong-brink-declaring-emergency-rule-deal-anti (accessed September 5, 2019).

139 Ibid.

140 Ibid.

141 The Greater Bay Area refers to Beijing's far-reaching scheme to link the adjoining Pearl River Delta cities of Dongguan, Foshan, Guangzhou, Hong Kong, Huizhou, Jiangmen, Macau, Shenzhen, Zhaoqing, Zhuhai, and Zhongshan within a long-term plan to secure major economic and technological benefits. See for a critical review, Preen, Mark, "What Is the Greater Bay Area Plan?" *China Briefing*, February 21, 2019, available at: https://www.china-briefing.com/news/the-greater-bay-area-plan-china/ (accessed August 11, 2019).

142 The OCM considered the system of universal suffrage to elect the Chief Executive of the HKSAR offered by Beijing in 2014 to be a form of "sham democracy", as a Pro-Beijing dominated, Nominating Committee would vet candidates. True democracy did require universal suffrage but also full freedom to allow candidates from across the political spectrum to run – including candidates nominated by a civil (voter) nomination system – see Chapter 7. See also "Hong Kong's Umbrella Revolution – the Guardian Briefing", *The Guardian*, September 30, 2014, available at: https://www.theguardian.com/world/2014/sep/30/-sp-hong-kong-umbrella-revolution-pro-democracy-protests (accessed August 11, 2019).

143 Liu, Luis, "Social Media Are Polarizing Our Society and Instigating More Radicals", *China Daily*, August 25, 2019, available at: http://www.chinadaily.com.cn/hkedition/2019-08/26/content_37505438.htm (accessed August 26, 2019).

The tutelage contestation related to China within secondary education in the HKSAR has been noted above. Resolving how to implement reform here is a long-term project with no ready answers in sight, so strongly opposed are the points of view within the teaching profession. Moreover, this challenge does not readily lend itself to legalized primary solutions.

The matter of political reform in the HKSAR has been discussed at length in Chapter 6. We know where the serious points of difference lie and we know the reasons supporting the positions taken. After 2019, it is fair to say that there is little chance of any progress being re-commenced on the political reform project in Hong Kong until well-based political stability is restored.[144] Many argue that without serious, true democratic, political reform, there can be no stability.[145] However, the experience in BHK, especially post World War II, shows that complete democracy is not a necessary condition to establish an excellent Rule of Law regime, long-term stability, and an extraordinary growth in prosperity.

After the OCM and related experiences of 2014–2015, the matter of enacting new laws to apply in Hong Kong in accordance with Article 23 of the Basic Law became a matter of much increased importance for Beijing.[146] The recurrent, violent political protests in 2019 and the unfolding Sino-American New Cold War have amplified these concerns.

Article 23 provides that:

> The HKSAR shall enact laws on its own to prohibit any act of treason, secession, sedition, subversion against the Central People's Government, or theft of state secrets, to prohibit foreign political organizations or bodies from conducting political activities in the Region, and to prohibit political organizations or bodies of the Region from establishing ties with foreign political organizations or bodies.

Article 23 has been the subject of controversial debate within Hong Kong since before 1997.[147] The attempt to introduce new Article 23 laws in 2003 failed,

144 Ting, Victor, "Secretary for Constitutional and Mainland Affairs Patrick Nip Rejects Calls for Political and Electoral Reforms, Saying 'Emotions Are High and Mutual Mistrust Runs Deep'", *South China Morning Post,* August 10, 2019, available at: https://www.scmp.com/news/hong-kong/politics/article/3022283/secretary-constitutional-and-mainland-affairs-patrick-nip (accessed August 11, 2019).

145 See, for example, Tisdall, Simon, "The Fight for Democracy in Hong Kong Is the Defining Struggle of Our Age", *The Guardian,* July 2, 2019, available at: https://www.theguardian.com/commentisfree/2019/jul/02/hong-kong-democracy-china (accessed August 11, 2019).

146 Ng, Kang-chung, "Fear and Loathing: Which Way Forward for Article 23 National Security Law in Face of Stiff Opposition in Hong Kong?" *South China Morning Post,* November 22, 2017, available at: https://www.scmp.com/news/hong-kong/politics/article/2121035/fear-and-loathing-which-way-forward-article-23-national (accessed August 11, 2019).

147 See Fu, Petersen and Young (eds.), *National Security and Fundamental Freedoms: Hong Kong's Article 23 under Scrutiny* (Hong Kong University Press, Hong Kong, 2005).

after the first massive peaceful public march in that year (see Chapter 7). Any new Article 23 laws, going forward, are likely to be measurably more stringent than those proposed in 2003. Briefly, one can foresee laws which firmly prohibit the advocacy of secession, in any form, of the HKSAR from the PRC or any seditious advocacy plainly designed to subvert the operation of either the HKSAR Government or Central People's Government in Beijing. Where any such advocacy is organized and accompanied by violence, increasingly severe sanctions may be applied. Such laws can be expected to cover primary advocacy and the use of both public and social media to support, for example, secession.[148]

The Special Branch of the Hong Kong Police Force (which effectively dates back to 1930 and the creation of the first Anti-Communist Squad) was disbanded prior to the handover, in 1995, in accordance with a policy decision of the BHK Government in the late 1980s. At its height, Special Branch had around 1,000 employees.[149] The experiences of 2019 suggest that apart from any general strengthening, the HKSAR Police may now need to rebuild a well-resourced version of the previous Special Branch to bolster its existing (post-1995) covert surveillance capacity.[150]

The PD group has demonstrated in 2019 that even when it lacks the votes to reject new legislation, where the political circumstances are sufficiently controversial, it may be able to render LegCo unworkable by calling on very strong public support through mass rallies (followed up, in 2019, by highly intimidating, street-based political protesting and rioting). It is hard to envisage how any new full-bodied Article 23 laws can be passed by LegCo.

Hong Kong is currently facing a period of very difficult adjustment, however. It would be hasty to conclude that the LegCo "logjam factor" means Article 23 laws cannot be passed in Hong Kong either until that factor is fixed or until after 2047 (when as explained earlier, the OCTS *guarantee* – but not necessarily OCTS itself – expires). Article 159 allows for amendment of the Basic Law. It has not so far been used, though some PDs advocated its use during the co-location dispute (see Chapter 6). Article 159 provides that:

> The power of amendment of this Law shall be vested in the National People's Congress.
>
> The power to propose bills for amendments to this Law shall be vested in the Standing Committee of the National People's Congress, the State Council and the Hong Kong Special Administrative Region. Amendment bills from the Hong Kong Special Administrative Region shall be submitted

148 Related legislation is needed, also emulating wide adoption in the EU, prohibiting militant protestors, especially from taking comprehensive measures to conceal their identity (using masks and the like). Clearer laws on making or collecting weapons (and their nature) may also be needed.

149 Fu, H. L. and Cullen, Richard, "Political Policing in Hong Kong" (2003) *Hong Kong Law Journal*, 199.

150 Cross, "If Reason Prevails".

> to the National People's Congress by the delegation of the Region to the National People's Congress after obtaining the consent of two-thirds of the deputies of the Region to the National People's Congress, two-thirds of all the members of the Legislative Council of the Region and the Chief Executive of the Region.
>
> Before a bill for amendment of this Law is put on the agenda of the National People's Congress, the Committee for the Basic Law of the Hong Kong Special Administrative Region shall study it and submit its views.
>
> No amendment of this Law shall contravene the established basic policies of the People's Republic of China regarding Hong Kong.

The Committee of the Basic Law is a Committee formed under the SCNPC.[151] Ultimately, initiation (and passage by the NPC) of any amendment of the Basic Law under Article 159 lies within the power of the SCNPC.

Article 18 of the Basic Law provides that:

> The laws in force in the Hong Kong Special Administrative Region shall be this Law, the laws previously in force in Hong Kong as provided for in Article 8 of this Law, and the laws enacted by the legislature of the Region.
>
> National Laws shall not be applied in the Hong Kong Special Administrative Region except for those listed in Annex III to this Law. The laws listed therein shall be applied locally by way of promulgation or legislation by the Region.
>
> The Standing Committee of the National People's Congress may add to or delete from the list of laws in Annex III after consulting the Committee for the Basic Law of the Hong Kong Special Administrative Region and the government of the Region. Laws listed in Annex III shall be confined to those relating to defence and foreign affairs as well as other matters outside of the limits of autonomy of the Region as specified by this Law.
>
> In the event that the Standing Committee of the National People's Congress decides to declare a state of war or, by reason of turmoil within the Hong Kong Special Administrative Region which endangers national unity or security and is beyond the control of the government of the Region, decides that the Region is in a state of emergency, the Central People's Government may issue an order applying the relevant national laws in the Region.

It is no longer implausible, post-2019, to imagine that the SCNPC itself could initiate the introduction of a set of Article 23 laws into the HKSAR, if it concluded (a) that these laws were badly needed; and (b) there was little or no likelihood

151 "The Nomination of the Hong Kong Members of the Committee for the Basic Law of the Hong Kong Special Administrative Region", *Press Release, HKSAR Government*, November 21, 2018, available at: https://www.info.gov.hk/gia/general/201811/21/P2018112100442.htm (accessed August 11, 2019).

that such laws could ever be passed by LegCo in a timely way without further, attendant serious political disruption.

The Beijing-perceived need for such laws is well explained by Fu Hualing in a recent book chapter. The basis of this need briefly has two dimensions: to maintain territorial integrity (to prevent any form of secession) and to prevent subversion, by whatever means, of the PRC governance system (and the governance of the HKSAR).[152] Clear, wrongful behaviour within these stipulated categories transgresses the redline laid down by President Xi Jinping in Hong Kong on July 1, 2017 (see Chapter 9). Professor Fu also adds a timely reminder that:

> If the Hong Kong Government has no will or capacity to address these national security concerns, the mainland will take over the matter and exert direct, hands-on control in Hong Kong. The options remain wide open: cross-border law enforcement as occurred in the case of the booksellers remains on the table as an extra-legal hard power solution; China could mobilise its blunt power to impose a national security law on Hong Kong; and in the worst case scenario, China may apply its own criminal law in Hong Kong extraterritorially on the grounds of the criminal impact of acts in the mainland. Which option Hong Kong may have to face depends on how effective Hong Kong is in its dialogue with autocrats in Beijing.[153]

These acute comments were made prior to the 2019 Protests and Riots, which have amplified their cogency. Article 18 (above) deals with the matter of when (Mainland) territorially confined national laws may be applied in the HKSAR. There is, however, a sturdy argument that the Basic Law has left a loophole which does allow the application of Mainland laws in the HKSAR outside of Article 18, where national laws have, within their text, clear extraterritorial reach. PRC Criminal Law uses a double nexus test (nationality-based and crime-based) to achieve application extraterritorially around the world to all places where it does not apply directly – which includes the HKSAR.[154]

But let me return to a consideration of applying new Article 23 laws, drafted in Beijing, in Hong Kong by relying on the mechanisms provided within the Basic Law. The process for achieving this could involve:

- An amendment to Article 23 to say that, *Laws shall be enacted to prohibit (etc.)* replacing *The HKSAR shall enact laws on its own to prohibit (etc.)*;

152 Fu, Hualing, "China's Imperatives for National Security Legislation", in (Chan and de Londras (eds.)) *China's National Security: Endangering Hong Kong's Rule of Law?* (Hart Publishing, Oxford, 2020) (forthcoming – copy on file with the author).

153 Ibid.

154 See Cullen, Richard and Fu, H. L., "Some Limitations in the Basic Law Exposed" (1999) 22 *China Perspectives*, 54.

- An amendment to Article 18 adding *national security* to the listed areas, in paragraph 3 – so that it would read (in part) *Laws listed in Annex III shall be confined to those relating to national security, defence and foreign affairs.*

Article 18 would then allow national security laws drafted in Beijing to be added to Annex III of the Basic Law. Those laws could validly be applied within the HKSAR, in accordance with Article 18, by promulgation – they would not have to be passed or ratified by LegCo.

This is certainly a radical option, but it is one which is constitutionally feasible under the Basic Law. It is a plan which, if adopted, might well cause very significant political disruption, with further protestor violence, in the HKSAR. But at the end of the day, Hong Kong would have a new set of rigorous Article 23 laws in place. The upside of such a far-reaching change is that the risks, from Beijing's point of view, of proceeding with further political reform in the HKSAR would be measurably reduced. The need for some method to link Article 23 enactments with political reform has been argued by one commentator.[155] Even using the Article 159 method outlined above, the SCNPC could adopt a watchful, step-by-step approach, covering only one or two priority national security concerns, initially.[156]

Another even more radical way to apply new Article 23 laws in the HKSAR would be for the SCNPC to declare a State of Emergency in the HKSAR and apply National Laws directly in accordance with Article 18. Beijing refrained from declaring any emergency as the violent political turmoil grew in Hong Kong in 2019, although the grounds for it doing so (and the SCNPC makes this decision unilaterally under Article 18) arguably existed.

The operation of Article 158, which provides for interpretation of the Basic Law, has been reviewed in detail in Chapter 6. It is fair to expect that Article 158 may be used over the coming one to two years as Beijing firms up its responses to what happened in the HKSAR in 2019. The usage pattern, which is discussed in detail in Chapter 6, shows that Article 158 has been deployed, above all, to respond in a focussed way to particular problems, which regularly involve controversial political issues. From the Beijing perspective, there are many problems arising from the events of 2019 to be addressed. It is conceivable that, if Article 159 were to be used, as outlined above for the first time, this might be accompanied by some level of related Article 158 Interpretation, for example, to confirm that any proposed amendment was consistent with *the established basic policies of the People's Republic of China regarding Hong Kong*. Article 158 could also

155 See, for example, Cheung, Tony, "Article 23 National Security Law in Hong Kong Could Help Win More Democracy, Government Adviser Ronny Tong Says", *South China Morning Post*, May 1, 2019, available at: https://www.scmp.com/news/hong-kong/politics/article/2144199/article-23-national-security-law-hong-kong-could-help-win (accessed August 11, 2019).

156 Ibid.

be used to explain the relationship between any new Article 23 laws (dealing with National Security concerns) and the individual rights guaranteed through Chapter III of the Basic Law.

Finally, we need to bear in mind the point made in Chapter 6: the Basic Law is a special constitutional law that was created for the HKSAR under the PRC Constitution of 1982. The potential conflict between the differing grundnorms underlying these two constitutional instruments has, to date, not been discussed in depth, but this matter is set to assume increasing importance. The Basic Law draws its ultimate authority from what is the paramount Constitution within this constitutional order.

Geography is destiny[157]

Macau was a colonial outpost for far longer than Hong Kong. Though it is much smaller and has its own history and social ontology, it has coped distinctly well within its own, very similar, OCTS regime over the last 20 years. This success is not seamless, but Macau has almost wholly avoided the endemic political confrontations which so regularly mark the experience of the HKSAR since 1997. The economies of both Hong Kong and Macau depend fundamentally on engaging, to great advantage, with Mainland China: ultimately it is China which bankrolls their very high living standards. Macau, however, is not beset by strong minority perceptions which, despite this highly beneficial, dependent relationship, still see the CPC-controlled Mainland as being predominantly a threat. Nor, in Macua, is there any significant minority disdain for Mainland Chinese and for China itself.[158]

Hong Kong has a very different history. The AL system, developed and adapted over the British era from 1842–1997, supported the extraordinary, overall success story of BHK (Chapters 4 and 5). On these Diceyan foundations, Hong Kong built, over time, durable First World prosperity coupled with stability and a first-rate Rule of Law system. Shortly prior to 1997, limited democratic elements were added and these were enhanced with effect from 2012 (Chapter 6). The transition from BHK to the HKSAR in 1997 provided a "through train" for Hong Kong's exceptional AL system. Recurrent stress testing of this system has demonstrated its long-term resilience (Chapter 7). While this AL system has habitually underpinned stability and prosperity in Hong Kong, it cannot guarantee these outcomes. New, unsettling episodes in Hong Kong's political-legal history have unfolded in 2019.

157 Fong, "Why Macua Has Been Spared".

158 For a succinct discussion of the range of reasons Macau never incubated the potential for persistent querulous politics of the sort which have thrived in Hong Kong; see Lo, "Opinion – Why Is Macau Far More Stable Than Hong Kong?" Lo argues that after political riots in 1966 in Macau, the Portuguese Colony moved fairly swiftly to introduce social and political reforms which strengthened the understanding of China and a sense of Chinese identity across the broad population. Nothing of this sort happened in BHK.

A number of Hong Kong residents share an Anglo-American-influenced collective belief in the paramount value of democracy and individual rights. This collective elemental understanding, which is a legacy of the BHK era, is strongly embraced by the comprehensive PD group and it remains embedded within the general social ontology of the HKSAR. This PD assemblage is highly sceptical of the good faith of the CPC and is regularly convinced of prevalent bad faith. Mutual feelings of deep watchfulness have developed. Amongst younger, radical activists, the antagonism directed towards China is strikingly higher.[159] The events of 2019 have confirmed that the presence of this key section within the broad Hong Kong political profile has allowed Hong Kong to incubate a potential for rebellion or insurrection. The lack of progress with expected political reforms after 1997 has amplified these rising political tensions. Finally, social media, poorly anchored by any serious concern about proved facts, have acted as constant, powerful polarizing agents far more focussed on disruption and even destruction than anything else.[160] This is not a new problem. There is quotation dating back over 100 years, commonly attributed to Mark Twain, which confirms this: *A lie can travel halfway around the world before the truth can get its boots on.*[161]

The expectations of political reform are not unreasonable, but it is plain that Beijing retains the final power to guide and approve the extent and pace of those reforms. For those seeking true democracy in the HKSAR, this is not as it should be. Indeed, they say that this controlling power has been used to thwart what is *promised* in the Basic Law. For Beijing, the lack of preferred new Article 23 laws in the HKSAR is acting, not least as the New Cold War begins, as a further impediment to introducing enhanced political reform in Hong Kong.

The broad PD group (despite plain divisions within[162]) has demonstrated a telling capacity to make the HKSAR manifestly difficult to govern at times.[163] It

159 China (not just the CPC) is seen to be, *authoritarian, vulgar, brutal, materialistic and uncivilized.* See Cheung, "Protestors Are Fighting".

160 Lo, Alex, "Our Social Media Warriors Are Reaching a Dead End", *South China Morning Post*, September 11, 2019, available at: https://www.scmp.com/comment/opinion/article/3026771/our-social-media-warriors-are-reaching-dead-end (accessed September 12, 2019).

161 "A Lie Can Travel Halfway around the World while the Truth Is Putting On Its Shoes", *Quote Investigator*, available at: https://quoteinvestigator.com/2014/07/13/truth/ (accessed September 15, 2019). While the quotation is real, someone other than Mark Twain was the likely author.

162 The entire PD group houses many different viewpoints from radical to moderate. But, consistently, the radicals disproportionately set the agenda for political activism. Within the moderate wing, there is a continuing apprehension about upsetting the unity (and the radical wing) of the overall group. See Bradsher, Keith, "Beijing's Hong Kong Strategy: More Arrests, No Concessions", *New York Times*, August 30, 2019, available at: https://www.nytimes.com/2019/08/30/world/asia/hong-kong-protests-beijing.html (accessed August 31, 2019).

163 This entrenched political habit of default opposition predates 1997, though it has intensified over the last two decades. See Cartland, Rachel, "Opposition Went Astray En Route

has used various stalling countermeasures to apply pressure (severely in 2019), inter alia, to try and secure agreement for expected political reforms. There is something of a political stalemate. The PDs retain this powerful negative competence and Beijing retains an even more powerful rejection capacity. One consequence of this enduring experience of politics by confrontation is almost certainly a narrowing of the Beijing-perceived space for liberalizing experimentation with modified governance systems inside the OPS.

One thing does seem clear. First, the best future for the HKSAR within China rests on safeguarding the operation of OCTS – and the Basic Law – over the long term. Next, to secure this outcome, the HKSAR requires substantially enhanced means to protect national security. These must be measured enhancements, but they are plainly needed. Local, regional, and international geopolitical factors now all underscore this basic political equation with some intensity.

In 2019, the HKSAR found itself stalled at a fork in the road. In one direction lie the conspicuous opportunities for the HKSAR to develop its role, within the GBA, as China's premier World City.[164] To do this, Hong Kong needs to form a wide, collective, measurably more robust understanding of and commitment to certain *One Country* norms embodied in OCTS, especially those related to national security and territorial integrity.

It also has to build a sturdy, widely agreed capacity to "row together" as it seeks to build its own success within a successful China. It does not look easy for Hong Kong to come to a comprehensive agreement, internally, to do this. It is not impossible, however, and the durable attractions are conspicuous.[165] These crucially include a strengthening of OCTS so that it continues to apply beyond 2047 – along with the Basic Law.

The pushback factors are intense, however, and those who support them feel that resistance (even militant and violent resistance) is just and proper.[166] Many bridges have been burnt. One legendary, nineteenth-century revolutionary,

---

to Democracy", *China Daily*, September 5, 2019, available at: https://www.chinadailyasia.com/articles/2/49/240/1567613750365.html?newsId=94175 (accessed September 5, 2019). Predictably, perhaps, having made governance as difficult as possible, those who obstruct then highlight claimed evidence of failure to govern properly.

164 In 2001, the HKSAR Government "branded" Hong Kong as Asia's World City; see "Asia's World City", *Information – HKSAR Government*, available at: https://www.info.gov.hk/info/sar5/easia.htm (accessed August 12, 2019).

165 It may be possible to build support for a broad political centre movement focussed on leading the HKSAR out of its political crisis. See Loh, Christine, "Hong Kongers Want and Deserve a Fair Society", *The Economist*, August 20, 2019, available at: https://www.economist.com/open-future/2019/08/20/hong-kongers-want-and-deserve-a-fair-society (accessed August 23, 2019).

166 Lian, Yi-heng, "Hong Kong, Carrie Lam Didn't Do It for You", *New York Times*, September 4, 2019, available at: https://www.nytimes.com/2019/09/04/opinion/hong-kong-carrie-lam-withdrawal.html?action=click&module=Opinion&pgtype=Homepage (accessed September 5, 2019).

Simón Bolívar, observed, after the triumph of a long, bitter rebellion in South America, that: *We have gained independence but lost everything else.* Another observation was that: *Anarchy is the worst enemy of freedom.*[167]

China may be able to help. Certain possible procedures outlined above would impose greater legalized controls on organized, militant, and violent anti-government and independence activism. These are quite drastic measures, which are not risk-free, but they could help to rebuild durable stability. If such measures were combined, inter alia, with serious, fresh political reform initiatives and ongoing, major livelihood improvements within the HKSAR, this would strengthen Hong Kong's capacity to view its role within China with growing levels of positive anticipation and, above all, a sense of shared destiny.[168]

Beijing has made clear that political reform remains open for discussion, but it must proceed based around the controlled but significant reforms offered in 2014 (see Chapter 6).[169] One can envisage how this stipulation could be met and at the same time, the process for further reform could be opened up, for example, by a negotiated agreement to create an institutionalized HKSAR–Beijing ongoing review of first-level reforms, which could lay foundations for later reforms.

The other fork in the road may lead the HKSAR, over the next several decades, to make a transition, possibly amidst further intervals of intense political disputation with violence, to being a second-tier city within the PRC. Compared to where it is today, it could become something of a backwater, although still a city with an extraordinary history.[170]

One commentator foresees that Hong Kong is on the way to becoming a relegated sub-city of Shenzhen (the now larger city directly across the border from

167 "Hemos ganado la independencia a costa de todo lo demás" – *We Have Gained Independence but Lost Everything Else.* "Anarquía es el peor enemigo de la libertad" – *Anarchy Is the Worst Enemy of Freedom.* See García, Luis Navarro, "La Independencia de Hispanoamerica, Un Proceso Singular" (2010) *Temas Americanistas*, 8.

168 Sheng, Andrew and Geng, Xiao, "Elites, Inequality Are HK's Real Problem", *China Daily*, September 5, 2019, available at: https://www.chinadailyhk.com/articles/144/19/175/1567655091408.html?newsId=94233 (accessed September 5, 2019).

169 Pepper, Suzanne, "Elements of a Solution Appear in Hong Kong, but No Sign of a Breakthrough in Beijing", *Hong Kong Free Press*, September 7, 2019) available at: https://www.hongkongfp.com/2019/09/07/elements-solution-appear-hong-kong-no-sign-breakthrough-beijing/ (accessed September 8, 2019).

170 A decline, to less than 10%, in the number of Hong Kong residents aged between 18 and 29 who see themselves as primarily "Chinese" points to how Hong Kong may be nurturing this self-diminishing, isolationist outcome. See "Almost Nobody in Hong Kong under 30 Identifies as 'Chinese'", *The Economist*, August 26, 2019, available at: https://www.economist.com/graphic-detail/2019/08/26/almost-nobody-in-hong-kong-under-30-identifies-as-chinese (accessed August 27, 2019).

Hong Kong), within the GBA, by 2047.[171] Another, noting the rise of Shenzhen, observed that:

> In view of Hong Kong's declining economic importance to China and its tendency to become a source of conflict, perhaps Hong Kong should be more worried about abandonment by China than intervention.[172]

Hong Kong has overwhelmingly and with all its extraordinary achievements been created by the people of Hong Kong, within a remarkable British-supplied foundational framework. The future fate of Hong Kong also, overwhelmingly, lies in the hands of Hong Kong people.

As Andrew Sheng and Xiao Geng explain, acutely reinforcing comments above:

> Hong Kong's people must make a vital calculation. As the most international part of China, Hong Kong has a major role to play in shaping China's ongoing global integration and encouraging openness. If it abdicates this role, China's central government will forge ahead anyway, leaving Hong Kong behind.[173]

171 Lo, Alex, "Hong Kong, Fast Forward to 2047", *South China Morning Post*, August 12, 2019, available at: https://www.scmp.com/comment/opinion/article/3022458/hong-kong-fast-forward-2047 (accessed August 13, 2019). See also for a similarly bleak prediction, Ho, Lok-sang, "The Crux of Hong Kong's Problems", *China Daily*, August 12, 2019.

172 Ip, Regina, "Hong Kong's Reputation Is Being Damaged", *The Economist*, August 20, 2019, available at: https://www.economist.com/open-future/2019/08/20/hong-kongs-reputation-is-being-damaged (accessed August 22, 2019).

173 Sheng, Andrew and Geng, Xiao, "Self Harm in Hong Kong", *Project Syndicate*, July 29, 2019, available at: https://www.project-syndicate.org/commentary/hong-kong-protest-movement-hurting-city-future-by-andrew-sheng-and-xiao-geng-2019-07 (accessed August 2, 2019).

Appendix: key definitions

Authoritarian is a term which can be significantly subdivided. It is, thus, common to speak of "soft authoritarianism" and "hard authoritarianism", autocracies, and oligarchies, for example.[1]

In this book, by *Authoritarian*, I mean:

> A governance regime where the ruling authority enjoys ostensible plenary power combined with indefinite political tenure.

By (modern) *Constitutionalism*, I mean:

> The principle that the authority of government derives from and is limited by a body of fundamental law.[2]

By *Authoritarian Legality*, I mean:

> Authoritarian Government which is operationally committed to a degree of Constitutionalism.

A simple and relevant example may help to add clarity. British rule in Hong Kong largely conformed to the definition of AL set out immediately above.[3] The gov-

1 The literature on the typology of authoritarianism is extensive. Examples are given in Chapter 1.

2 Derived from Fehrenbacher, Don E., *Constitutions and Constitutionalism in the Slaveholding South* (University of Georgia Press, Atlanta, 1989). The "modern" annotation signifies that the "constitutional" enduring normative ordering of systems of government (compared to dominant, pure brute force ordering) long predates the development of modern Constitutionalism (as defined above) in the UK (late seventeenth century) and then in the US (late eighteenth century), above all. Thus, it is fair to describe the Imperial Chinese dynastic system dating from over 2,000 years ago as being constitutionally ordered – though the complex, enduring normative framework was neither fundamentally legal nor still less a form of fundamental law. See, further, Walker, David M., *The Oxford Companion to Law* (Clarendon Press, Oxford, 1980), "'Constitution' (3): The Fundamental Political and Legal Structure of Government of a Distinct Political Community".

3 Unlike the Governors of Hong Kong, who were simply appointed to their position in each case, the Chief Executive (Governor equivalent) of the HKSAR is chosen via an election every

ernance system which applied in the UK in 1842 at the time of the establishment of BHK was certainly not democratic in the modern sense – the total number of enfranchised (male only) voters was around 7% of the total adult population of the UK.[4] Nevertheless, governments did *not* enjoy indefinite political tenure – government changed hands, from one political party to another, as the result of regular elections.[5] Thus, although the UK at that time notably restricted the vote to male citizens of certain means, this was not a system of government based on AL (as defined above).

Another term employed in this paper is "Social Ontology". This is not a term in everyday use. And it is not a term with an entirely fixed meaning. It has, nevertheless, been put to work for over 100 years with possibly the first recorded usage being in 1910, by the German Philosopher, Edmund Husserl.[6]

I have adopted the following working definition of Social Ontology:

> [Social Ontology means] the study of the social realm, where the latter is taken as comprising those phenomena whose coming into being and/or continuing existence depends necessarily on human beings and their interactions. The concern … is with the following two projects in particular: 1) Social scientific ontology: the study of what is, or what exists, in the social realm, including the nature of specific social existents of interest; and 2) Social philosophical ontology: the study of how social phenomena exist, their modes of existence, connections between social existents, common properties, and so on. It is an explication or understanding of the basal "what there is" to social existence.[7]

five years. These are "small circle" elections, however, where it is not conceivable that anyone not sanctioned as acceptable to Beijing could be selected.

4 "Lowering the Voting Age to 16: Timeline", *UK Citizenship Foundation*, obtained from: http://www.citizenshipfoundation.org.uk/main/page.php?82 (hard copy retained by author).

5 "Victorian Britain", *BBC British History*, obtained from: http://www.bbc.co.uk/history/british/timeline/victorianbritain_timeline_noflash.shtml (hard copy retained by author).

6 "The Origin of Social Ontology", *University of Vienna*, obtained from: http://social.univie.ac.at/varia/ (hard copy retained by author).

7 This definition is derived mainly from Lawson, Tony, "A Conception of Social Ontology" in (Pratten, Stephen (ed.)) *Social Ontology and Modern Economics* (Routledge, Bingdon, 2014) obtained from: http://www.csog.econ.cam.ac.uk/documents/AConceptionofSocialOntology.pdf (hard copy retained by author). The definition also draws on Schatzki, Theodore, "Social Ontology, Philosophically" obtained from: http://www.sbs.ox.ac.uk/sites/default/files/Research_Areas/Science_And_Technology/Docs/Schatzki.pdf (hard copy retained by author). Schatzki puts it this way: "By 'social ontology' I mean ideas about, including the self-conscious study of, the nature, character, or basic features, structures, or elements-constituents of social life. A social ontology, accordingly, is a statement or understanding of the nature, character, or basic features, structures, or constituents of this. It is an explication or understanding of the basal "what there is" to social existence."

Index

For Product Safety Concerns and Information please contact our EU
representative GPSR@taylorandfrancis.com
Taylor & Francis Verlag GmbH, Kaufingerstraße 24, 80331 München, Germany

www.ingramcontent.com/pod-product-compliance
Ingram Content Group UK Ltd.
Pitfield, Milton Keynes, MK11 3LW, UK
UKHW010959180926
475701UK00004B/468

* 9 7 8 1 0 3 2 1 7 4 4 0 2 *